Foxfire 7

Foxfire 7

edited with an introduction by
PAUL F. GILLESPIE

Anchor Press/Doubleday
Garden City, New York
1982

Paul Gillespie is Vice President of the Foxfire Fund, Inc. and now teaches classes in photography and *Foxfire* magazine production at Rabun County High School in northeast Georgia. He was a student of Eliot Wigginton during the very early days of *Foxfire*'s existence and upon graduation from college, returned to the mountains to begin work with Foxfire's expanded educational programs. During 1981, he assumed the teaching and administrative duties of Eliot Wigginton, who was away on leave of absence to pursue the writing of educational texts.

Foxfire 7, like its predecessors, contains articles first published in *Foxfire* magazine. Subscriptions to the magazine are $8.00 per year and may be obtained by writing to The Foxfire Fund, Inc., Rabun Gap, Georgia 30568. The Anchor Press edition is the first publication of *Foxfire 7* in book form. It is published simultaneously in hard and paper covers.

ISBN: 0-385-15243-4 Hardbound
ISBN: 0-385-15244-2 Paperbound
Library of Congress Catalog Card Number 80-2962
Copyright © 1973, 1980, 1982 by The Foxfire Fund, Inc.
All Rights Reserved
Printed in the United States of America

First Edition

CONTENTS

INTRODUCTION   9

HISTORICAL OVERVIEW   13

RELIGIOUS DENOMINATIONS   28

Baptists BEN COOK, SOUTHERN BAPTIST; BLY OWENS,
SOUTHERN BAPTIST; JOE BISHOP, SOUTHERN BAPTIST;
HOWARD SOUTHARDS, INDEPENDENT BAPTIST;
HOWARD PARHAM, PRIMITIVE BAPTIST; LYSTRA
PRIMITIVE BAPTIST CHURCH; CLYDE NATIONS, JR., TED
LANEY AND CLYDE NATIONS, SR., FREE WILL BAPTISTS;
SELMA MOSELY, BLACK BAPTIST; BEULAH PERRY,
BLACK BAPTIST.   28

Catholics LINA DAVIS, ROMAN CATHOLIC.   104

Church of Christ WAYNE RAWLINGS, CHURCH OF CHRIST.   110

Episcopalians RUFUS MORGAN, EPISCOPALIAN.   118

Jehovah's Witnesses ERNEST CLARK, RUTH STOCKTON AND
REPPIE JONES, JEHOVAH'S WITNESSES.   139

Methodists E. L. ADAMS, METHODIST; JULIE MCCLURE,
METHODIST; CONLEY HENRY, METHODIST;
LEONARD VISSAGE, METHODIST; E. C. PRESLEY,
METHODIST.   170

Pentecostals RAY DRYMAN, CHURCH OF GOD; TOLIVER VINSON,
CHURCH OF GOD; GRANNY REED, CHURCH OF
GOD; JAKE QUILLIAMS, CHURCH OF GOD;
CHARLES LEE, FIRE BAPTIZED HOLINESS CHURCH.   198

Presbyterians L. B. GIBBS, PRESBYTERIAN; CLYDE HICKS,
PRESBYTERIAN; SID MCCARTY, PRESBYTERIAN.   233

THE CAMP MEETING   265

    Loudsville Methodist Campground   267

    Cullasaja Assembly of God Campmeeting and
    Campground   274

THE TRADITION OF SHAPED-NOTE MUSIC   280

    Singers of Shaped-Note Music christian harmony,
                                   richard moss christian
                                   harmony, quay
                                   smathers.   293

    "I Love to Sing . . ."   299

    Gospel Shaped Note Music jim raby, henry fountain,
                                     aunt addie norton, lonnie
                                   smith, horace page, hyman
                                   brown, esco pitts, ernest
                                   watts, ferd watts and
                                   wilbur maney.   304

BAPTISM   347

FOOT WASHING   351

THE PEOPLE WHO TAKE UP SERPENTS   370

    A Church of God   372

    Dinner on the Grounds   421

    Sunday Night   423

APPENDIX   429

NOTES   484

GLOSSARY   488

EDITORIAL CONTRIBUTORS   491

INDEX   497

This book is especially dedicated
to Grandpa Ray Dryman and Preacher Ben Cook
who encouraged us with their friendship,
patience, and Christian love.

INTRODUCTION

During the spring of 1975, and shortly before my graduation from the University of Virginia, I came home to Rabun Gap to visit my family and to think about the future. Graduate school, some travel, a job in Atlanta—these were all viable options, but at this point I was still very much undecided. I hoped that the tranquility and serenity that so often accompanies this particular season in these parts would help me better sort out what was going on inside.

One incredibly warm, breezy, and vibrant afternoon I stopped by the *Foxfire* office which, at that time was at the Rabun Gap-Nacoochee School. It was much like I had remembered it almost four years before. Collected artifacts of many shapes and sizes still hung, rested, and were propped everywhere. In shelves, on cabinets and tables, they stood as vivid reminders of an era gone by. There were berry buckets and spinning wheels and homemade fiddles. In one corner was a miniature moonshine still fashioned by Buck Carver and in another was some large and striking folk art designed and carved by C. P. Ligon.

Of course, there were students everywhere (I later found out that I had dropped in during the *Foxfire* journalism class). I could overhear several of them making new discoveries in the photography dark room. Others were opening mail and dealing with correspondence and circulation. One group had just brought back an interview with Kenny Runion, a local craftsman and story teller, and were eagerly listening to this tape; and as always there were those faithfully putting in their time on the transcribers, painstakingly writing out each and every word of a two-hour interview.

Among all of this activity, adult staff members Suzy Angier, Margie Bennett, and Eliot Wigginton were busily running to and fro—offering encouragement, advice, planning strategy, but for the most part letting the students follow their instincts, make their own decisions and bear up under the ensuing responsibility. *Foxfire*, the program designed to provide alternative and experiential educational approaches to learning, was, it seemed, still working well.

As I surveyed all of this activity and organized confusion, I remembered my days as a *Foxfire* student. And they were not those dreary and overly sentimental class reunion type of remembrances, but more that as a high school student I had done something real and workable, positive and productive. I remembered the many hours that I had spent at Aunt Arie Carpenter's, the eighty-seven-year-old lady who lived by herself in a log home, and how her quiet and gentle, but powerful philosophy and outlook on life had a profound effect on my development. I remembered the time Mike Cook (who is now in charge of television and video production for *Foxfire*) and I went up to Harley Thomas' and recorded on paper and film his demonstration of the intricate dovetail notch that was once used in the mountains as a way of constructing the walls for a log cabin; or Jake Waldrop, who took us on a hike through the mountains in search of ginseng and showed us how to make a turkey call from a bone in the wing of that animal. I can also remember the introductions and articles that Wig made us write and rewrite about those experiences, and how I was glad he did when I got to college.

As I looked around that small but busy office and work area, I felt good and I knew this experiential philosophy was contining to go forward in the right directions. In that office that same afternoon, Wig and I had a chance to discuss and reflect and talk about the future of the organization. Wig indicated that he would like to see planned and well thought out expansion of the program into other areas with the addition of new staff members as well. Royalties coming in from the *Foxfire* books were providing additional income to hire more people. I felt like the *Foxfire* organization was still something I wanted to be a part of; and after some discussion, I left that afternoon with a job I felt good about, and six years later as I sit here and struggle with these words, my enthusiasm for the ideals, expectations, and goals of the *Foxfire* organization remains high.

One of my first responsibilities was to work with a group of students who had been involved for a year in the *Foxfire* process of writing, editing, and producing small articles for the magazine and who wanted to take this involvement one step further by working on something more complex and lengthy. Keith Head, who at that time was from Scaly Mountain, was one of those students who thought he was ready to tackle a more difficult project. We both did not know what his project would be until he showed me a tape transcription of an interview he had with his great-grandfather, Grandpa Ray Dryman, who was one of the oldest members of the Pentecostal Church of God in this area. He discussed at great length his involvement with the church and his personal religious experiences. It was in great detail that "Grandpa Ray" talked of the handling of fire, speaking in "tongues," and other occurrences in his church. Keith and I strongly felt great interest in this interview, and we agreed that as his project he could again talk to his grandfather and others in our area who demonstrated strong religious faith and gather more information for a better in depth study to document "religion" in this part of the Appalachians.

Keith's study took on new importance and the material collected soon took up a whole filing cabinet drawer. The more we found out, the more we realized that the subject of "religion" was broad, controversial, and personal. To be as fair and objective as possible, many old church preachers and other church people were visited and recorded.

Somewhere along the way, Keith and I came to the realization that we would not be finishing up this project during that school year. I was developing and teaching other courses and projects, and the scope of this subject made us realize that we still had a long way to go. Keith was hired to work the summer and after another year in college he came back in 1977 for yet another summer of research, interviewing, and editing. Another student, Wendy Guyaux, who was headed to the University of Georgia in the fall, joined Keith in these undertakings. Together they visited more preachers and church members from almost every denomination in our area and traveled many miles to singings, baptisms, camp meetings, foot washings, and revivals.

By 1978, after these sporadic but intense work efforts on this project, we felt most of the research was completed. We were still uncertain as to the final form and format our work would take. There was a strong feeling among our students and staff that due to the importance of religion to the people of our region and the fact that it provides the basis for many of their beliefs, attitudes, and activities, that the material should be compiled and offered as one of the *Foxfire* book series. Doubleday, Inc., accepted the idea, and, thus, *Foxfire 7* was officially slated for final workup and delivery. This title was chosen because *Foxfire 5* had just been released and *Foxfire 6* was near completion and ready to go.

By this time, of course, Wendy and Keith were heavily involved with college studies and work, but other students helped in numerous ways. Certain groups of *Foxfire* students were largely responsible for putting together other chapters that appear in this book, particularly the ones about shaped-note singing and snake handling; Carol Rogers (who took the cover photograph for the hardback version of *Foxfire 6*) spent the most of one summer printing photographs and conducting some final and essential interviews, including those with Richard Moss and Quay Smathers, both Christian Harmony singers; and Rosanne Chastain and Tammy Ledford, two of my photography students, were responsible for the cover photograph that appears on the hardback version of this publication.

It was also during this time that other help was given. Keith and Wendy had strongly felt all along that due to the complex and sometimes controversial nature of the subject matter, some scholarly writing by a qualified individual would strengthen the validity of their documentation and set the work in proper context. Thus, when Dr. Bill J. Leonard, Assistant Professor of Church History at the Southern Baptist Theological Seminary, Louisville, Kentucky, offered his services, we accepted. Dr. Leonard wrote a general religious and historical overview and a pertinent history of each of the denominations we covered, the latter appearing as appendixes. In addition, Dr. Edith Card, professor of music at Clemson University, Clemson, South Carolina, who had previously worked with *Foxfire's* music and folklore teacher, George Reynolds, and his students, wrote the much-needed technical and explanatory preface that appears at the beginning of the chapter on shaped-note singing. Local resident and student teacher Susan Davis also added her editing and advisory skills in the final stages and helped us to finish up.

This student-conceived-and-produced project presents a subject that at times has been extremely controversial. The word "religion" triggers a different response in each of us. We have tried to be careful to not make judgments concerning what is repeated herein. Religion is personal and each of us chooses to deal or not to deal with it in our own way. We found interesting the diverseness of beliefs even among the members of a single church. Moreover, the various churches of a single denomination were not always in agreement about every doctrine and ordinance.

This book has been stimulating but difficult at times to compile. This is the first *Foxfire* book dealing with a single subject, but one that affects so many people in the mountains. Attempts were made to cover all major denominations (these denominations are presented alphabetically herein); however, since this book is a study focusing on the documentation of religious beliefs exerting the most influence in our particular area of Appalachia, some may have been omitted. To these, we offer our apologies; and to those who were gracious enough to allow us to come into their homes and hearts, we express our gratitude.

Simply, this book is about those who appear within, giving personal accounts of the faith that means so much to them. As you read the material, remain mindful of the power of the religion of the people in this area. They are not adverse to share.

PAUL F. GILLESPIE

HISTORICAL OVERVIEW

By Bill J. Leonard

In the sultry heat of a July evening a throng of worshippers moves toward the open-ended tabernacle from which the sounds of organ music—vibrato blaring—fill the summer air. They enter the building to sit on rough, straight-back pews on which are strewn the worn gospel hymnbooks. The air is heavy with the smell of the sawdust which covers the floor. There is singing, then prayers, accompanied by an occasional "Yes, Lord" and "Thank you, Jesus," spoken spontaneously from members of the congregation. The preacher, selected moments before at the inspiration of the camp director, enters the pulpit and the sermon begins. The words come pouring from his mouth, warming the already heated night: "Saved . . . Lost . . . Heaven . . . Hell . . . blood bought . . . Bible-believing . . . crucifixion, resurrection . . . second coming . . ." And the sins—sins of sex and alcohol, lying and cheating, disobeying parents, dancing, movies, skipping church, refusing to believe the Bible, rejecting the Holy Spirit. And then the answer: JESUS!! Trust Him, love Him, serve Him, accept Him, believe on Him, fear Him, follow Him.

Finally comes the call: "Come and receive the good news." "Stand and sing, sing, and sing some more."

> Just as I am without one plea
> But that Thy Blood was shed for me
> and that Thou bidst me come to Thee
> O Lamb of God, I come. . . .

They come—first one and then another. Some in stoic silence, some with quiet abandon, some in torrents of tears. And with their coming all heaven breaks loose. Shouts of "Glory," "Praise the Lord," "Hallelujah," "Glory to God," as salvation and revival come to a people.

The crowd responds, the preacher responds, the organ responds. Then, all are seated once again. For another preacher has been chosen, another sermon is ready to be proclaimed. Plenty of time for one more service, one more call to repentance, that is, if Jesus tarries. . . .

The camp meeting, anchored firmly in the American past, continues as a reality in West Virginia, Georgia, the Carolinas, and throughout the Bible Belt of the American heartland. It expresses one important emphasis of American religion: the abiding concern for heart religion and conversionistic faith.

The sign outside reads, "Old Regular Baptists," and inside the one room, clapboard structure a foot washing is going on. Men sit on one side, women on the other. Members bind aprons around their middles, take battered dish pans and tattered towels, to kneel before fellow Christians in a ritual as old as the Christian church.

The preacher sounds out the scripture text in a kind of singsong, chant-like cadence:

> "The Bible says . . . that the Lord Jesus . . . on the night of his arrest . . . laid aside his garments . . . and taking a towel . . . washed his disciples' feet . . . OOOOOOO, them feet-washin' Baptists, they'll be here till the Lord comes again."[1]

After the washing comes the supper. "Do this in memory of me." Again women serve women, men serve men. A bit of homemade, unleavened bread, a taste of unfermented grape juice, sealed with a handshake or a gentle embrace. No one takes the bread and the cup who has not washed feet. And so it goes in the mountains of eastern Kentucky, western Carolina, and northern Georgia, where a people preserve their heritage and reenact it in the present.

There is a small church in West Virginia where a meeting is going on three to four nights a week, four to six hours a night. The setting is the Pentecostal/Holiness tradition, complete with shouting, speaking in tongues, singing, and loud preaching, most of it carried out to the beat of a bass guitar, drums, and the omnipresent electric organ. It is a lively affair, but on certain nights it gets even livelier. For on the floor near the pulpit there is a box, approximately three feet long, covered with a screen and padlocked tightly at the top. Eleanor Dickinson, in a popular study called *Revivalism!*, describes its purpose: "At some time during the service, usually while music and dancing is going on, a preacher will unlock the box, reach in and pick up one or more snakes. Anyone in the congregation may come forward and reach for a snake if he or she feels moved to do so."[2]

Elzie Preast, the late lay pastor of the church, reasoned, "But it [the Bible] does say 'They shall take up serpents,' and Jesus is the one that's doing the talking. Said, 'They shall take them up.' Well,

I've got to do it, or somebody's got to do it, or else Jesus is a liar. If we don't do it, Jesus can raise up a people that will do it."[3]

These are but a few of the images which the words, "mountain religion," bring to mind. Camp meetings, foot washings, snake handling, holy rollers, tongues speaking, tent revivals, loud preaching, and emotional exuberance are thought by many to characterize the Christianity of the southern highlands. While these qualities of religious experience are found throughout the region, caricatures and stereotypes all too easily become inseparable from reality. This volume seeks to preserve something of the reality of Appalachian Christianity as found in the memories of those who experienced that religion for themselves.

No one who knows the *Foxfire* series needs to be told of the value of oral history in preserving the heritage of a people. From the first, these books have sought to encourage the young to hear and retell the stories of the old, to record the recollections of generations whose secrets are almost forgotten, and to describe those profoundly simple skills which others have forgotten, take for granted, or ignore. From furniture-building to home remedies, from recipes to folklore, *Foxfire* has helped to recount the history of a people in one corner of the American nation.

In these efforts, the religious traditions of Appalachia cannot be overlooked. Although occasional articles or limited editions of the *Foxfire* magazine have given some attention to mountain religion, the editors believe that a complete volume of the *Foxfire* books should be devoted to this topic. Clearly, this is due to the fact that religion has made such a significant impact on Appalachian life. In the harsh frontier surroundings religion provided a way of coping with the hurts, pains, and disappointments of a sometimes hostile environment. In the shared events of birth and rebirth, happiness and common humanity, it was a source of celebration. Through religion a people developed symbols to express life's highest values, reinterpreting traditional Christian observances and creating new ones.

The religion described in this collection of reminiscences is the product of a variety of influences, biblical and doctrinal, social and economic, national and regional. The materials illustrate something of the nature of American Christianity as experienced in one geographical region of the Republic.

The American Christianity:
Many Churches Under God

First, American Christianity was characterized by both pluralism and uniformity, qualities clearly evident in the interviews provided here. With the advent of religious liberty (a freedom not present in most of the early colonies), no one denomination or sect could demand the allegiance of the entire population. No state could use the civil power to coerce attendance at religious services or to secure financial support for any religious group. This meant that standard-brand denominations, independent-autonomous-noncooperating churches, sects, or cults could flourish in the mountains (or elsewhere) under the reasonably protective arm of the first amendment to the Constitution. Pluralism, then, is that term used to describe an American religious community made up of multiple groups, each more or less equal under the law.

Few religious bodies experienced harassment from the state. Snake handlers and Jehovah's Witnesses may have had their share of legal problems, but most churches were free to practice their faith without government intervention. Thus a multitude of churches, denominations, and sects appeared in the nation and in the Appalachians.

As these interviews indicate, freedom of religion led to great diversity in doctrine and practice. Baptism might be by immersion (dipping the whole body in as much water as possible) or by sprinkling (touching the head or forehead with a minimal amount of water), administered to infants, children, or adults in fonts, creeks, rivers, or fiberglass "baptistries" inside the church house with a mural of the Jordan River painted in the background. Salvation might be immediate and dramatic or quiet and gradual. It might be received once and for all, or repeatedly lost and found. For some, only an elect minority can be saved, while other churches insist that salvation comes to all who freely respond to God through repentance of sin and faith in Jesus Christ.

Pluralism helped to create competition between those churches seeking converts from among the same constituents. A group which claimed to be the "true" church often felt compelled to prove that it was "truer" than other groups making the same claim. Baptists debated Methodists and Presbyterians over baptism, while Methodists and Presbyterians argued over perseverance of the saints. Such competition is illustrated in the comments of the frontier Methodist who remarked, "We had a revival meetin' last week and no one was saved. The Baptists down the road had a meeting the same week and, thank God, they didn't save anybody either."

These conflicts over doctrine and practice do not obscure the uniformity which is also characteristic of both American and southern religion. In America until the late nineteenth century, and in the South until more recently, Protestantism was the dominant religion. There was denominational diversity, but within certain basic Protestant boundaries.

Although many groups sought to trace their origins to Jesus, the New Testament church or even John the Baptist, all shared doctrine drawn from the Protestant Reformation and the work of Martin Luther, John Calvin, and the radical Anabaptists. Even the influx of Catholic and Jewish immigrants, which by the early 1900s had created new forces of religious influence in America, had little immediate impact on the Protestant establishment of the South. The authority of the scripture, the centrality of the sermon, the need for justification by faith alone, the necessity of individual morality, and the presence of a strong inner piety were indicative of the importance of the Reformation on common theological views of the American Protestant majority.

Second, the Christianity of Appalachia has been greatly influenced by the revivalism which characterizes much of the religious life of America. From the Great Awakenings, which swept the colonies in the 1740s, to the frontier revivals of the early 1800s to the evangelistic crusades of the twentieth century, revivalism brought both style and substance to American religion. Indeed, revivals established a basic form for worship and evangelism in the churches of the mountains.

Revivals are those outpourings of religious enthusiasm which occur periodically in the church. Revivalism has been defined as "the Protestant ritual (first spontaneous but, since 1830, routinized) in which charismatic evangelists convey 'the Word' of God to large masses of people who, under this influence, experience what Protestants call conversion, salvation, regeneration, or spiritual rebirth."[4] They seek to bring conversion to those outside the church and renewal to those already converted. Revivals might begin spontaneously in the ordinary life of the church or grow out of carefully organized camp meetings and protracted gatherings. Through revivals, pluralistic churches secured converts to Christianity in general and their denomination in particular. Much of the religious life of America has been influenced by revivalistic method and theology, particularly in those groups—Baptist, Methodist, Presbyterian, Holiness—so prevalent in the southern highlands.

Revival preaching—loud, dramatic, earnest, lengthy, and spontaneous—set the pattern for preaching in most mountain churches.

The traveling evangelist, who got results and drew great crowds with his (and only occasionally her) charismatic personality, became a model which local pastors often had to imitate if they wished to retain the respect and attention of their congregations. Sermons were taken from scripture but moved hurriedly to contemporary hurts, fears, and sins. Conversion was the prime aim of most sermons, as preachers promised the rewards of heaven and threatened the fires of hell to those who did not repent.

Revivals also established a style of worship based on the controlled spontaneity of a new type of Protestant liturgy. Hymns were personal and vigorous, with religious words set to catchy and popular melodies. Leaders, soloists, or choruses often sang the verses while the congregation joined in on the refrain. Hymns taught Bible stories, doctrines, and ethics. Some aided the growth of denominational identity and competition in the frontier.

The Methodists sang:

> We've searched the law of heaven,
> Throughout the sacred code;
> Of Baptism there by dipping
> We've never found a word.
>
> To plunge is inconsistent
> compared to holy rite;
> an instance of such business
> we've never found as yet.

The Baptists, not to be outdone, responded:

> Not at the Jordan River,
> but in that flowing stream
> stood John the Baptist preacher
> when he baptized Him
> John was a Baptist preacher
> when he baptized the Lamb.
> So Jesus was a Baptist
> And thus the Baptists came.[5]

With the preaching and the singing came the congregational involvement: shouts of amen, hallelujah, sometimes glossolalia (speaking in tongues), and other expressions of emotional enthusiasm. Converts related the specifics of their salvation experience, while penitents confessed their sins. "Altar calls" or "invitations" challenged the sinner to come to the anxious bench to be "prayed through to victory." Southern churches incorporated these revival practices in many of their weekly services until the revivalistic style became the basic form of worship in many congregations.

The revivalistic approach to preaching, singing, and salvation helped to establish a style of evangelism which came to characterize Appalachian religion. Conversion became more immediate and was seen as an intimate, personal experience, often quite dramatic in nature. It was the response of the heart to the call of God in Christ, and it affected all facets of human nature. Sinners were saved "from the top of their heads to the tips of their toes," and if it really "took" they were made new creations in every aspect of life.

A third characteristic of American religion evident in these interviews is the concern among many groups to recreate the New Testament church in the present day. Many churches, denominations, and sects came to believe that they had reconstituted, restored, or rediscovered the true practices and doctrines of the primitive Christian community.[6]

The new American land, so long undiscovered by European Christians, seemed the place which providence had prepared for the restoration of New Testament Christianity. Here, unpolluted by the trappings of popery, the worldliness, and the immorality of Europe, the church could blossom again. This was the "New Israel," the City set upon a Hill to provide light to all the nations. Optimism about America's place in the reestablishment of biblical Christianity likewise influenced the relationship of religion and nationalism in Appalachia and throughout the country.

American religion, pluralistic, Protestant, revivalistic, competitive, and restorationist, provided trends and tendencies which shaped significantly the Christianity of Appalachia. These interviews reflect some of those trends as they were uniquely developed in the southern highlands.

SOUTHERN CHRISTIANITY: THE RELIGION OF A CULTURE

The religion of Appalachia was also greatly influenced by the Christianity of the American South. This Bible Belt religion permeated the social and cultural life of the region, defining more sharply the nature of Christianity in America. While there were many denominations in the South, southern religion was shaped by what might be called the Baptist/Methodist religious establishment.

The Baptists were everywhere, in all kinds of churches with diverse doctrines and varying practices. Southern, Independent, Missionary, Regular, Separate, and Two-Seed-in-the-Spirit-Predestinarian Baptists (to name only a few) might vie for the souls of the southerners, but all were Baptists, and the Baptists had southern religion sewed up (or washed up as their opponents might suggest).

Add to that the Methodists, with their ubiquitous circuit riders, and the religion of southern Appalachia was almost complete, except for an occasional Presbyterian or Disciple of Christ. When the Pentecostals arrived they found a welcome reception among some mountain folk but also some strong opposition when their enthusiasm for tongues and healing created disturbances outside the religious boundaries set by other southern Protestants. In earlier days, the Catholics and Episcopalians did not often fare much better if they challenged the more revivalistic establishment.

Southern religion also reflects intensity in its concern for faith, morality, and evangelism. Southern Christians often seem to believe more, and believe more intensely, than many groups outside the South. Southerners generally reflect more conservative theology, with a commitment to the "unchanging" truths of the faith. The religious establishment in the South often places its greatest stress on the need for personal salvation, the unflinching allegiance to certain crucial doctrines, and the importance of a rigorous personal morality.

All persons need salvation and the whole society, indeed, the whole world, must hear the "old, old story of Jesus and his love." Evangelism and missions thus occupy a major place in southern religious activities. Through door-to-door witnessing, radio evangelism, or missionaries sent abroad, the southern churches give evidence of their concern for personal evangelism. The need to "snatch souls from the burning," bring all the world to faith in Christ, and take the gospel to all nations has long been an imperative for southern evangelicals.

The proof of genuine conversion is found in a distinctive Christian lifestyle and, thus, personal morality is another strong concern of southern churches. Separation from the world and uniqueness in morals, dress, and attitude are important evidences of Christian discipleship. Campaigns for moral reform and civic decency have frequently united southern Protestants beyond doctrinal differences. Crusades against gambling, tobacco, alcohol, and prostitution have produced some of the strongest ecumenical activities of southern churches.

Not all groups, however, can agree on what constitutes Christian morality. Differences over the use of makeup and jewelry by women, movies, dancing, television, and music are common among southern churches and denominations.

Another important force within southern religion is fundamentalism. While that particular theological orientation is certainly not limited to the South, it has been a major influence upon the doctrines and practices of the southern churches. Fundamentalism is not unique to one denomination, but appears to varying degrees in many southern religious groups. It represents that effort to establish a set of unchanging propositions or doctrines which are absolutely "fundamental" to Christian faith.

Fundamentalism, as a movement in America, has often been associated with that period of the 1920s when questions of biblical authority, theory of evolution, and science threw the churches into an uproar, culminating in the infamous Scopes' Monkey Trial held in Dayton, Tennessee, in the summer of 1925. Those events have served more to caricature the fundamentalism which existed both before and after the controversies of the twenties.

Fundamentalists in the South represent no clearly organized movement, and many of their number would disagree vehemently over which set of doctrines is most fundamental. The force of fundamentalism may have less to do with specific doctrines than with the way in which fundamentalists approach religious truth.

First, fundamentalists often have difficulty separating the reality of genuine religious experience from the need to believe certain basic propositions about the gospel. They are convinced that one cannot be called Christian who does not affirm the truth of a wide variety of necessary articles of the faith.

Second, fundamentalists usually insist that any deviation from essential doctrines represents a compromise of the truth. There is one truth, one way, and compromise is a sign of weakness in the faith and a betrayal of the gospel. There are no shades of wrong or right, no half-truth concerning God. Doubts about one proposition will surely weaken the structure of all doctrines.

Third, once the basic propositions are affirmed the individual has the answers, or at least the formula, for dealing with whatever circumstances life may bring. The fundamental foundation of the faith thus provides a secure base upon which the believer may stand in confronting the struggles of life. One may not know all the truth, but the principles by which truth can be known have been discovered and accepted.

Fourth, although there are many different doctrines accepted by a variety of fundamentalist Christians, the common dogma, essential to all others, is found in the fundamentalist interpretation of biblical authority. Whether the doctrine is baptismal immersion (independent Baptist), baptism "for the remission of sins" (Church of Christ), speaking in an unknown tongue (Pentecostals), or taking up serpents (snake handlers), if the scripture is not trustworthy on one doctrine, how can it be trustworthy on any? Most modern fundamentalists would insist that scripture holds within it no contradictions, errors, or "mistakes" and is the infallible, inerrant word of God. Modern versions of the Bible may contain errors, copying mistakes, or mistranslations; no such problems exist in the original, but no longer extant, manuscripts of the scripture. The concern for doctrinal purity in translations of scripture has placed many fundamentalists, especially in Appalachia, on the side of the King James Version and against the use of any one of many modern translations from the *Revised Standard Version* (a particular anathema) to the paraphrased *Living Bible* (somewhat more acceptable among certain groups). The KJV, published in England in 1611, is thought to represent the best text for the church and is often considered as inspired as the original Hebrew and Greek texts. As one classic line has it, "If the King James Version was good enough for the Apostle Paul, it's good enough for me."

In addition to biblical inerrancy, fundamentalists will likely affirm the following essential doctrines: the reality of the Genesis accounts of creation; Adam and Eve as the genuine "parents of the race"; the virgin birth of Christ; the substitutionary or sacrificial atonement of Christ; the bodily resurrection of Christ; the literal second coming of Christ; the reality of Christ's miracles as described in the gospels.

Finally, fundamentalists often display a tendency to speak infallibly on matters of faith and morals. This has frequently led preachers, revivalists, and church members to consign to hell those who did not accept "the plain truth" of one group's particular ideas.

Fundamentalism is alive and well in twentieth-century Appalachia. It shapes churches, sometimes splits them, and keeps them arguing with friends.

Fundamentalism informs but does not completely dominate another significant facet of southern religious life: the need for personal religious experience. This process begins with conversion, but it is more than that, since continued encounter with God is absolutely necessary for vital Christian witness throughout the life of the individual. In the revivalistic churches of the South, conversion—intimate experience with God through Christ—is the rite of passage into both the kingdom of God and community of the church. No one who has failed to experience Christ personally can be fully accepted into Christian society. Thus, conversion carries with it both eternal and temporal ramifications. The imperative for conversion of every person is the central theme of much of the preaching in southern and Appalachian churches. For the evangelical preacher there are two types of people, the saved and the lost, those on their way to heaven or hell, with no middle ground in between. As Billy Sunday insisted:

> You are going to live in heaven or you are going to live forever in hell. There's no other place—just the two. It is for you to decide. It's up to you and you must decide now.[7]

The preachers, therefore, are called primarily to awaken the lost to their need of salvation. Sermons focus on the state of the individual before God, the evil of the human heart, the promises of heaven and the threat of hell. More "modern" evangelists often emphasize the joys of the Christian life, the rewards of the saved, and the triumph of heaven, much to the chagrin of the "old-fashioned" preachers, who continue to paint vivid pictures of the torment of a literal, burning, fiery hell, "where the worm dieth not and the fire is not quenched." (Mark 9:44)

The way of salvation varies in southern churches. In some, it is a process of nurture, growth, and confirmation. In others, it is a dramatic event characterized by emotional upheaval as the sinner turns from sin and the world to the forgiveness and love of Christ. The process of this life-changing experience may be brief or lengthy, depending on the preacher, the church, or the individual. It includes a recognition of sinfulness, a deep sorrow for sin, a turning from sin to the mercy of God (repentance), an acceptance of Jesus Christ as the sacrifice whereby sins are forgiven with a direct invitation to Christ to "come into" the human heart and take control of the life. In many southern churches it is essential that the converted know the exact time—day, hour, moment—when salvation occurred. Failure to know such a time may mean that the experience was invalid and the process must be repeated.

Following conversion, the newly converted individual must continue to grow in grace and know successive experiences with God. In some individuals, this may result in a second decisive experience: the baptism of the Holy Ghost, whereby the Christian is sanctified for holiness of life. In this event, particularly important in the Pentecostal/Holiness tradition, the believer is empowered by the Spirit to live the life of Christ daily. Many believe that the sign of this "second baptism" is the gift of unknown tongues. This experience is discussed further in the section on Pentecostalism.

Another pivotal religious experience, frequently described in these interviews, is the "call to preach." This is a moment of crisis in which particular (primarily male) believers are singled out for "the greatest of all callings," the proclamation of the gospel. For many, this occurrence is more powerful than conversion. Sometimes the call comes by means of an audible voice, accompanied by a bright light or a dramatic vision. In many cases, the person fights against the call as the last possible vocation into which he (sometimes she) should go. In fact, in many churches, the harder the preacher fights the call the more authentic is the experience.

Personal religious experience is a non-negotiable requirement in most evangelistic southern churches. As the accounts provided here indicate, the experiences, while varied, have many common elements. Visions, voices, dreams, and emotional upheavals are not uncommon. In these occurrences, the principles of scripture are internalized: The individual passes from light to darkness and acknowledges the reality of inner religious truth.

The type of religion reflected in these interviews is unique, less because its qualities are evident only in the South, than because its influence uniquely permeates the culture of the southern Bible Belt. In many sections of the South, religion serves as a dynamic force for social control and influence. To be southern is to be religious, Christian, Protestant, Baptist, or Methodist. The religion reflected in this book is southern. But it is also Appalachian and that involves other qualities and characteristics.

APPALACHIAN CHRISTIANITY: PLURALISM IN THE MOUNTAINS

Although greatly influenced by religious trends in America and in the South, Appalachian religion also developed its own unique qualities. First, the relative isolation of the region helped insulate the churches from many forces of social and theological change. The religion established by the early settlers was probably preserved longer in the remote mountain areas than in the more accessible urban centers of the nation. Isolation often retarded cooperation between churches and limited the exchange of divergent ideas. Isolation contributed to the conservatism of the churches and the tendency to view local religious traditions as closest to those of the New Testament. It also helped succeeding generations to have a secure religious heritage and an identity as Christian believers.

Second, the geographical isolation, theological conservatism, and rugged individualism of mountain life helped create a spirit of independence in the churches. Independent churches with no connections outside the local body were often the norm in Appalachian religious life.

Many churches were founded by traveling evangelists and then guided by lay preachers who lived in the community. This was particularly true of Baptist and Holiness churches where local autonomy and congregational government meant that congregations could be founded independent of boards, presbyteries, or bishops. Even those mountain churches with some denominational affiliation frequently reflect a greater concern for autonomy than for strict adherence to the procedures and recommendations of the parent body.

The subjective nature of faith, the independent spirit, and the local church structure also provide a context in which church disputes and divisions are common. Much of the diversity of mountain religion is related to the many church "splits," which occur and from which new congregations are founded. Appalachian churches often illustrate the old adage that Christian denominations "multiply by dividing."

A third influence upon the religion of Appalachia is found in the folk ways of the mountains. Mountain traditions, music, stories, and lifestyle were important factors in shaping the religious experience of the region. Those biblical images compatible with the hardships and benefits of mountain life were particularly evident in the preaching and worship of the churches. Folk singing with a guitar rather than the organ worked its way into Appalachian hymnody. Deliverance from the drudgery of hard work, escape from poverty, and the assurance of a better world to come are common themes in the sermons of many preachers. The people of the mountains interpret Christian faith in ways compatible with their own experience and struggles.

As Appalachian religion developed its own unique expressions, it also created new symbols and reinterpreted existing ones. The churches established new traditions and invested local customs with religious significance. The walking of the aisle or altar call came to symbolize conversion in the life of an individual. The conversion experience itself was often referred to as "walking the aisle," "coming forward," or "coming down to the front" (of the church).

The fellowship meal, the personal testimony, the right hand of Christian brotherhood, the experience of speaking in tongues, and other common events held symbolic as well as concrete meaning in different churches and communities. These symbols spoke beyond words to give identity and security to congregations and denominations.

The interviews provided here illustrate the way in which religion and lifestyle interact in the southern highlands of America. They represent an effort to preserve what might be called "peoples his-

tory," the perception of religion and its place in society as understood by the people who practice it daily. This is not religion as
articulated in precise theological formulas and dogmas. It is the
description of faith as lived out by the practitioners in what some
might describe as the "grass roots" of the church.

This is history as oral tradition and popular recollection, discovered as a people describe those beliefs, symbols, and observances
which offer them a sense of value, meaning, and a place in the
society of Appalachia. The memories of baptism, sermons, conversions, and revival meetings speak volumes about the way in which
religion is perceived by the people who have chosen it.

Appalachian Christianity has also had its own particular stereotypes, which, in the popular mind, identify all religion in the region.
Ignorant preachers, holy rollers, snake handlers, radio evangelists,
and barefoot believers worshipping in log churches are among those
images which often caricature the religion of the southern highlands.
True, there are certain forms which fit the stereotypes and these
interviews reflect some of those popular experiences. But the interviews also reveal that there are many other expressions of religion
which go beyond the caricatures. Not all the preachers, for example,
are uneducated. Nor does the lack of formal education imply the
absence of learning among many mountain clergy who are self-
taught in matters of scripture, history, and theology. The obsession
of mountain churches for individual conversion and a rigorous personal ethic does not necessarily indicate a lack of commitment to
social action or political involvement. Holy roller is no longer (if
it ever was) an appropriate designation for the people of the Pente-
costal/Holiness tradition. Neither is snake handling the extensive
practice which modern media coverage might suggest.

Furthermore, not all the people of Appalachia express their faith
through some form of organized religion. Many have little interest
in any form of religion at all. While Christianity has a strong influence
on mountain society, many persons appear to get along quite well
without benefit of clergy. These obvious unbelievers need not expect
to practice their unbelief in peace. As the known and hardened
sinners of the community, they are often the object of pastors, laity,
and traveling evangelists, who seek to move them from the broad
way of destruction to the narrow way of eternal life. The stereotypes
and their contradictions frequently exist side by side in the mountains.

Finally, the religion which developed in Appalachia is in transition.
As a more mobile, more secular generation moves in and out of

the mountains, the changes created affect all facets of life, including religion.

Those who remember need to tell their story while they are able. The children of this new era may well have forgotten, repudiated, or reinterpreted the practices and traditions of the past. They need to be reminded of those events which shaped the faith of their forebears. Students of American religion may find these accounts helpful in preserving another facet of history and religion of Appalachia. As "outsiders" with new religious traditions move into the region, they need to become aware of the heritage of religion which has preceded them, whether they accept it or not.

For American religious pluralism no longer applies exclusively to the Judeo-Christian religious establishment. Indeed, it may be that in contemporary Appalachia, "Hare Krishna" will one day sound across hills and hollers where only hallelujahs have been heard before.

RELIGIOUS DENOMINATIONS

Baptists

Baptist, Baptist, Baptist,
Baptist till I die
I'd rather be a Baptist
and eat that Baptist pie!

Nationally, there are at least fifty different religious groups who call themselves Baptists. This collectively large denomination therefore is extremely diverse and, except for a few important and central beliefs, can rarely agree on religious doctrine. One main reason for this diversity is the Baptists' strong belief in autonomy, especially at the local church level. Even in the more structured subgroups of Baptists, much emphasis is placed on allowing each individual church to choose much of its policy and to chart much of its own direction. This sometimes sets the stage for disagreement among members of a particular church and it is not uncommon for other churches or types of Baptists to be conceived from these disagreements.

As a group, the Baptists are a strong force in the mountains. In addition, large subgroups, such as the Southern Baptists are also greatly appealing and attract many followers on their own. These interviews represent Baptist diversity and strength, and included are those who present the views of Southern, Independent, Free Will, Primitive, and Black Baptists. As you read this section, be mindful of common threads of Baptist theological belief, but look for specific differences that make the types of Baptists so unique.

PAUL F. GILLESPIE

BEN COOK, Southern Baptist

The old horseback-riding circuit preachers of yesteryear have their own special place in both religious history and folklore. To me, they have already etched themselves into legend along with other grand and glorious once-upon-a-time characters such that settled these mountains and made them their home. And

PLATE 1   Reverend Ben Cook.

I'm sure that the old circuit riders were a special group of men in terms of boldness and dedication—to arise from bed early on a January Saturday or Sunday morning and greet the dawn along with a howling north wind and journey ten to fifteen or more miles over treacherous, icy, rock-strewn mountain trails to conduct services. And I'm positive that it would take a more brave soul than myself to conduct an evening service that same Saturday or Sunday in still a different location and then journey home on foot or horseback through the inky blackness of virtual wilderness forests and thickets.

One of the preachers who remembered riding these circuits was Reverend Ben Cook, a Southern Baptist preacher from the mountains of Jackson County, North Carolina. The son of a preacher, Mr. Floyd Cook, and one of nine children, Ben was born in the Caney Fork section of that same county. In fact, until his death in February 1979, Reverend Cook had lived in that part of western North Carolina for all but three of his eighty-three years. Reverend Cook was a preacher for the better part of five decades and pastored in over twenty churches. During these years, he conducted many revivals and other special services and, even in his retirement, he accepted speaking engagements and preached when he was called on. Reverend and Mrs. Cook raised a large family of seven who gave them fifteen grandchildren and fourteen great-grandchildren.

During the few years we were fortunate enough to know Ben, he helped us immensely with our study of mountain religion. He provided us with entertaining, moving, and informative material, and also helped us to arrange an interview with another retired Baptist minister. It was from him and his congregation that we obtained permission to document a foot-washing service at his church.

Every time Paul Gillespie, our advisor, and Wendy Guyaux (a fellow student who has worked with me on this project) and I had the opportunity to visit, Ben was always more than willing to sit and talk with us, show us something of importance and just plain help us any way he could. Personally, I hope that this story, told in his own words, can capture, in some way, a part of the spirit of this great man of God.

KEITH HEAD

I was about, I guess, sixteen years old [when I became a Christian]. You know, back then they believed in waiting 'til they got up [in age]. My father was a minister and he and old Frank Arrington was in a revival meeting at John's Creek. It was a school building back then and I went there—me and my brother and Ham Mash— we were all converted at the same time. I was about sixteen years old and I got under conviction. I wanted to be saved but I wanted it to be done in secret [to] see if I could live right. Then I'd tell it. I found out you can't do it that way. [I] prayed all week and was under conviction. I got to feeling good but I wasn't satisfied. I went there to the altar at John's Creek, an old school building, and down under a seat—they had those old time seats there in the school building—I don't know what happened but there was a light that shone, brighter than the sun. It shone from the top of my head all over me and everything was just as white as snow. The congregation looked like angels, and the people that I hated, why, they were the first ones that I put my arm around. The people that I'd called hypocrites back when I was a sinner were the first that I got a'hold to and I loved them. I shouted all over the church— I don't know what happened. It took a long time before I realized what *had* happened. Before I got home the devil tried to make me doubt it and he tried to make me believe that it was just excitement, but I prayed and the Lord gave me a sign that I was saved. My brother was saved, too, in the same meeting, and we joined the Balsam Grove Baptist Church and were both baptized together. Ham Mash professed religion that night and Lem Parker, an old man, was saved the same night. We were all baptized out there in the creek.

I never did doubt my salvation. I was down under a bench when I was saved. I had to give up everything, I had to forget everything, I had to die to everything. When I was born of the Holy Spirit of God, it shone all over me and through me. It made me love everyone. That's my beginning.

How did you feel led to be a preacher?

My father was a minister. I felt impressed to preach; I was burdened to preach. [My father] took sick, took pneumonia fever. I went and prayed and asked the Lord that if I was called to preach, I wanted to be certain because it was a great burden to start out in the world. I'd heard so many hard things said about preachers. I dreaded the thought of preaching. I asked the Lord that if I was called to preach to let my father tell me before he died. Just before he died the pneumonia fever broke, his heart got weak, and he called me into his room. He said, "Do you know you're called to preach?"

And I denied it and said, "No, I didn't know it."

He said, "You are," and then he died in a little bit.

For a year I tried to keep from preaching. I just didn't want to preach. I was out in the mountain, fox hunting with a bunch of people, and I was so burdened. They went up on the mountain and I said, "I'll stay here with the horses and if I get better—I told them I had a headache—I'll come up there and hear the race. So that night—I don't know whether I was asleep or awake—I saw the angels and Jesus Christ. He said, "You were called to preach and you won't do it." And He said, "It's too late. It's over." I believe I'd've died that night if I hadn't agreed to preach. I told the Lord that night that if I lived to the next Sunday, I'd preach. The next Sunday I preached in a little church, Cathan's Chapel, my first sermon. I don't know how long I preached. The Spirit of the Lord just absolutely took over. I believe you've got to be led by the Spirit of God to preach a gospel sermon that will have an effect on people. The Spirit of God has to carry the message to the hearts of people.

My mother pulled me off the pulpit shouting when I preached my first sermon. I guess it was as good a sermon as I ever preached in my life. I'd conducted funerals [before]. My father was the only preacher that lived up there on the head of Caney Fork. He pastored [several] churches up there. There wasn't anybody that could conduct funerals. I'd conducted funerals and I'd been a deacon a long time in the church before I was called to preach. I could lead prayer, that wasn't any trouble to do that. When I got ready to preach, I just got up and read some scripture and took a text, and then I don't know what else happened. The spirit of the Lord just took over.

I prayed. I read and prayed. Now I think that a man ought to prepare himself and to do everything he can to prepare, and then to trust the Lord like he didn't know anything. Because if God doesn't give you a message, it won't amount to anything. I used to wonder why we didn't get dying grace now. Everyone would like to have it. You'd like to have it, but you don't need it. God told Paul, "My grace is sufficient." You need living grace now. And when you get sick, you need grace for sickness. Then when you come to death, you need dying grace. Now the preacher can read, pray, and do everything else. He won't get preaching grace until the very moment he gets in that pulpit. When he gets in there and it comes time for him to have that grace, it comes. I get scared to death lots of times. I've had to preach to large churches and great congregations of people. The thing about it—you've got to turn yourself loose to the Lord. There are lots of people that try to do it themselves. You can't preach yourself. The Holy Spirit will lead if you let it.

Is preaching something you have to be "called" by the Lord to do?

Certainly. I don't believe anybody could preach unless they were called. That's the Divine Call. I went to the preacher's schools; I went to Raleigh, and I went one year to college up here at Cullowhee. Then I tried to get all the books so that I could prepare myself to preach and I've had good success. Yes, that's a Divine Call. The only way a preacher could succeed is to be called by the Lord. I believe in heartfelt religion. I think that there's too many, probably, that are trying to preach that are not called to preach.

What was it like when you first started out?

I went on horseback. There weren't any automobiles back when I first started. I rode across the mountains into Canada [North Carolina], right over there close to where that Bly Owens [another mountain preacher] lived. That was before he ever preached. I'd go there and preach at Saul's Creek in the morning on Saturday. We had Saturday meetings back then. I'd preach there and then I'd go on to Wolf Creek ten miles away and preach in the evening. Then the next morning, I'd get up there and preach at eleven o'clock and then come back to Saul's Creek to preach [in the evening]. Then I'd go home. That was more than twenty miles. Back then I went and [sometimes] it had rained all day or snowed all day. It looked like it would kill you to cross that mountain and go and preach. That's when I began preaching. You never did get sick from that.

I'd ride across the mountain to Caney Fork [also]. Then I began pastoring churches [regularly]. I pastored Tuckaseegee and Yellow Mountain and Cedar. Then I came down to Lovedale and was pastor there for twelve years. Then I was elected to Balsam Church up here next to the Haywood [County] line. I preached there twenty-one years and built that church down there; it was called Pleasant Balsam. We built that back during the Depression. Then I went from there down to Richland, near Waynesville, North Carolina, and pastored there for five or six years. I've pastored about twenty-one churches in my fifty-four years [of preaching]. I've baptized about thirty-five hundred people in my life. I can't tell you how many I've married.

When I started out, I had good success with churches and revival meetings. I think I've been an evangelistic preacher all the time I've run revival meetings and got acquainted with the churches. [When] I pastored up at Tuckaseegee, we had a great meeting up there. We had a revival meeting that went on a month. When we started there hadn't been a meeting there in years with any success. Me and Lawrence Crawford preached together. Lawrence was a one-armed preacher; he's been dead for several years. We started a meeting there and he stayed one week and went home. He said it wasn't doing any good. The second week a little child died and I attended the funeral. Then the Wesleyan Methodists had a woman minister over there and she died. Then a Parker woman, Matt Parker's sister, died. [There were] three deaths there in three days and *that* started a revival meeting. Sometimes the Lord has to preach in other ways. He's got to prepare [people] to hear. He said that "all things work together for good to them that love the Lord." Sometimes it takes death to open the door for the gospel.

We went from house to house and there were thirty-eight baptized in that revival meeting. When I baptized there, there was so much ice floating—it was in the wintertime—that I'd have to wait for the big sheets of ice to get over to keep from hurting [the people being baptized]. They said I'd freeze to death, but I baptized thirty-eight and I came out and wasn't too cold. You know, I've never heard of anybody taking a cold being baptized. There's something about it. Of course, it's the Lord.

I remember back when I was a young preacher and running a revival meeting, every church up in there would come. They'd every one come to the revival meeting. They would just run a house over. The yard would be full of people. You know, people had *time* to read the Bible. They didn't have all these amusements we have today. The only thing they had was the Bible. They believed in the Bible and they had time to get acquainted with each other. We're living in such a fast age of the world [now] that it seems like people don't have time to get acquainted with each other. Back when my father was a minister, when somebody came that he knew—maybe he was hoeing corn—he'd just stop and sit down and talk three or four hours or half a day and they'd eat dinner. The corn was in weeds, but he'd just talk all day with people. They had plenty of time to get acquainted. They loved each other better.

I remember when my father was sick. He had Bright's disease and they had to go to Waynesville, North Carolina, and get a doctor and bring him across the mountain. He'd swell so big and they had to come here and draw the water out of him. He looked like he was going to die. [The neighbors] that summer made us the best crop that we ever had. They came in here and planted the corn, helped hoe it and gather it. That was love.

They'd have workings and they'd clean off land, great fields of land. They'd pile [brush] and burn it. They'd have what you call corn shuckings and come in and shuck out a man's corn. Then they would come on and have bean stringings and all like that. [The people] were all together—united together. And at the first meeting that I ran at Balsam Grove when I was a young preacher, we had two services—one of a morning and one of an evening. [The people] quit doing anything [for two weeks]. They just cooked and ate. That's all they would do until that meeting was over with. The women had their place where they had prayer meeting and I had about eight or ten men up on a hill. They were people that couldn't get right with the church and I took them up on the mountain. I remember there were six or seven that professed religion there on that hill and they shouted all over top of that hill. It was a rough hill and I can show you it today. We didn't do anything until that service was over. You know, if people could use two weeks [like that] in the year—God lets you have the rest of the time except two weeks—drop everything and serve the Lord. What would you think that would do for the churches?

When they ran this [revival] meeting down here at Lovedale, we started by having singing. We'd ask people and I got them to come from Knoxville, Tennessee and all around. We had loudspeakers on the church out there at Lovedale, and on Sunday morning we'd play some of those old hymns over the loudspeakers and they could hear it all over the country. We'd play these old hymns like "Amazing Grace" and that'd draw people out. We got about two hundred and fifty over there in Sunday school; didn't take too long. I'd go every Sunday morning and preach and sing for thirty minutes, and I'd advertise revival meeting over the radio; announced it. Then we'd get singers from everywhere. We'd make them a collection. That singing helped to get a congregation of people. Then revival started and I don't know what happened.

It was the greatest thing. I preached out there a month and two nights and I'd say that we averaged fifteen hundred people every night. They were blocked all around that church and they were even down into the highway. They came from four or five counties here, and it was the biggest meeting I guess that's ever been held in Jackson County. Me and Bill Crawford baptized ninety-one there in the river at one time. The Spirit of God just lit up that whole hilltop there. While I was preaching on the inside, Hornbuckle, an Indian down there at Cherokee, was outside preaching. They had lots of conversions on the outside of the church and up in the cemetery. The Spirit of God came down. Lost people'd just come to the altar. That's the mountain peak, I feel like, in my life because I reached the high up there.

There's a time when people really want a revival. You know, there's a time, He said, to do all things. You can't have a revival meeting unless the church wants it. I've thought of it in that way. Let the church get ready for [a] revival meeting. I think you ought to plan ahead and pray. I believe in starting a revival meeting with a prayer meeting—having a prayer meeting for about a week before you begin a revival.

One time I was up on Caney Fork—just a country preacher up there—and they voted over there at the First Baptist Church in Hazelwood, North Carolina, for me to hold a revival meeting.

The preacher came over and said, "The church, Sunday night, voted for you to conduct a revival meeting down here at the First Baptist Church in Hazelwood."

I said, "I'm just a little country boy. I feel like that's too great a burden for me." I said, "You go home and I'll pray until tomorrow evening." I said, "If the Lord gives me a burden, I'll be there. If He doesn't give me a burden, I'll not be there."

I prayed until the next evening. I got a burden and I went over there. I believe it was fifty-some odd were baptized because of that meeting there in Hazelwood. I went back a year or two later and baptized forty-eight. I baptized over one hundred people into that church there in two revival meetings. I suppose that most of their old members [were the ones] I baptized there.

PLATE 2

PLATE 3   Baptizing conducted by Reverend Ben Cook.

I ran a meeting [in Macon County]—a revival over near Rainbow Springs where the old sawmill was. I've also preached down there when they were off for noon dinner. I'd preach there at the mill—me and Joe Bishop. We'd go on the mountain and pray. That was a shouting meeting. The superintendent of that job was the singing leader. Lord, he'd shout!

One fellow there made fun of the people. They had a bad mountain to go down with their lumber. They'd stop their train there and they'd have prayer before they'd turn over the mountain because it was dangerous and steep. And this brakeman made fun of them having prayer. He got under conviction there in that revival meeting and he couldn't be saved, but one day they stopped their engine to pray before they turned over the mountain and he got religion there. He was called to preach after that. He had to go right where he'd made fun of those fellows praying. That was the most religious company I've ever seen—Ritter Lumber Company. They really did support that revival. I could go out for dinner with people and they had a place for me to stay every night. The company arranged that. That was during the Depression. When the revival was over with they gave me a hundred dollars in an envelope and that sounded like a whole lot of money back in those days!

When I first started out like that, I went into a community and I stayed there until the revival meeting was over with. I didn't go back home. It seemed like that if you got out away from that church so far, you'd get out of the spirit and it was better to stay among the people and work with them.

What took place when somebody came to get saved?

They'd get down on their knees and come weeping. I believe that you've got to have a broken heart and a contrite spirit. The gospel and the Holy Spirit convicts a man of sin and when he's convicted—I've seen them come falling into the altar, crying for the mercy of God. Let them stay there until they get right with God. And when they get right with God, they'll endure the end.

One night we had a meeting that had been going nine weeks and there were about fifteen or twenty on the altar and no one had been saved. A little boy, seven or eight years old, had been coming to the altar every night; no one would invite him, but he'd come. Everyone thought he was too little to be saved, to be accountable. I didn't pay any attention to him and I'd always go to the mountain top and pray before I would come to preach on Sunday night. I was up there praying and all I could see was that little boy on that altar. And something said to me, "Have you ever instructed him?"

I said, "No, I haven't and no one else has either."

So I went back that night and old Uncle Abe Norman was the preacher. It was his grandson. I was praying and all I could see was this little boy. I said, "I don't know, he might be closer to death than any of these men here." You know, they all came up and got around that little boy and he was saved. Then there was ten or fifteen saved just about as fast as they could come up, after he was saved. I baptized that little boy down there in the river and that following week he was killed over there on the highway with a car. That taught me that God knows His business. I baptized him down there in the river and that following week he was killed and I attended his funeral over there. That little boy had that whole thing tied up there. God knows. That little boy was closer to death and closer to hell than those old men were. Things like that have helped me along life's way. You know, the Spirit will lead you if you let it. When it tells you to do a thing, it's right. I don't care— you don't need to argue with it.

How do you feel about snake handling?

I was pastor of a church up there at Yellow Mountain when there was a preacher up there that believed in the handling of snakes. I knew about that. He tried to make a big show of it, you know, but I don't believe in tempting God. I think that those things are danger- ous. I don't think Paul knew that that serpent was in there when he picked up [wood] to build that fire, but when it got warm, it thawed up and bit him. They thought he'd die but he didn't. He shook it off. Now this preacher up here on the Cullowhee Mountain— I was pastor up there at Yellow Mountain not too far from where he was—told them to bring a snake on Sunday night and he would handle it. There were two guys there and I don't think that they had the right kind of spirit. They caught a rattlesnake and deviled it all week just to make it ill. It would strike at everything, you know. They took it in and took it out and it bit [the preacher]. He threw it down on the floor and they told him to pick it up and it bit him again. I do know that they used all the medicine that they could find on that fellow and it liked to have killed him.

Do you believe in shouting?

I believe in shouting. I think pride has just almost killed the Spirit of God [and people don't shout much any more]. My mother shouted as long as she lived. When Jesus Christ comes back to earth again,

He's coming with a great shout. Isn't He? David said, "Let them shout from the tops of the mountains." I think we've got something to shout about if we're born of the Holy Spirit of God. To be delivered from the power of sin and death is something to shout over.

These old pioneer mothers, back forty or fifty years ago, were always shouting in church. In the revival meetings there were some of the old mothers that could do things the preacher couldn't do. When some of those old Christian mothers began to shout, it convicted sinners. I think that shouting is just a gift of God and I think it's a part of the service of God. I love to see the day when they glorify God.

Do you have an altar in your church?

I believe in an altar. We've got one over here. When we built New Hope Church, we put that in the cornerstone over there, that the old-time altar be retained in that church as long as time lasts. I think an altar is for the Christian. You take those prophets back there, the first thing they did, and when Noah got out of the ark, the first thing he did was build an altar. And when Abraham started the journey, he built an altar. We have one and we come to that altar—the Christian people do every [Sunday] morning before the preaching starts.

The altar's not for sinners; it's for Christians. The mercy seat is for sinners. It's in the same place and sinners come there to the mercy seat. The Christians pray with them until they get right.

Did you ever have any foot washings?

Yes. We still have them over here [at New Hope] yet. When this church was established twenty-one years ago, it went to get in the [Baptist] Association. We had some modern preachers that objected to a foot-washing church being taken into the Association. We had a council [meeting] and I went in there with all the preachers of this county that was in the Tuckaseegee Association. I said, "These old pioneer preachers practiced foot washing and Jesus Christ practiced it. If you're telling me that I can't be a Baptist and can't follow the teachings of the Lord Jesus Christ and do the things He did, I don't want to be in the Association. We'll go out before the Association and I'll read the thirteenth chapter of John and if they're not going to observe that and not going to let that be Bible, let's just tear it out. We'll put it before the whole Association and see what they think about it." They agreed to [let us] have foot washings and be in the Association.

We put the ladies on one side of the church and the men on the other side. The men wash the men's feet and the women wash the women's feet. That's about the best service you've ever been in. We have communion at the same time. We do it whenever there's a fifth Sunday in the month.

Do you believe in Divine healing?

I don't think anybody doesn't believe in Divine healing. I think Jesus Christ has just as much power today as He had when He was here on earth. I don't think that that's ever been done away with. I believe that people are being healed today.

I'll tell you one experience I had and the reason why I believe in Divine healing. I was up at Cathan's Chapel, the church where I first started preaching. I was at a revival meeting. We were having a good meeting there and I was the only preacher. In the evening I took sick—my bowels were running off and [I was] vomiting—just as sick as a man could be. Time began to run out before the service and there wasn't anybody to preach. I went across the little creek there—I can go yet today to the very place I went to—and I said, "Lord, I believe You're in this revival meeting. People's being saved. I don't have any medicine and if you want me to preach, heal me now." The Lord healed me that minute. That's been fifty-three years ago and that's just as right to me today as it was then. I could go to that place today and show you the spot of earth where that happened. Now that happened to me and that's been a great grace for me. Lots of times when doubts and things come, I could go back to that spot of earth where that took place. I believe in Divine healing.

How could you recognize a Christian?

You could tell them because of the way they talked and the way they lived. You could discern between the righteous people and the wicked people. They had the old-time altar in the home. They brought the children up to love and fear God. The seed has to be planted in the heart of the child. You can take a child and you can make anything out of him if you start in time. I believe that most of these criminals that come out—I think it's neglect of the parents back there in the home.

There's never been a time as hard to live the Christian life as there is now. There's so many things to get the attention of people and draw them away. Back in the olden days, back in my mother's and father's day, we didn't have any newspapers. All we knew was

Jackson County and what was said. Where I lived up there, it took you a whole day to come to Sylva in an ox wagon. There was a tanner down there and in the summertime we'd peel tan bark and drag it off the mountain and load it on a wagon and bring it down here to Sylva and buy things we needed. In the fall of the year, we had hogs and things like that to kill and we'd bring them down here and get what we had to, salt and stuff we didn't make on the farm. We just about had to eat what we made and make what we eat back then. You [can] hardly imagine how it was then—maybe come to Sylva once or twice a year. I heard my grandfather talk about going to Walhalla, South Carolina, and getting things that they had to have in wagons. Back in these mountains, they'd raise cattle, sheep, and hogs and they could take stuff like that down in there and swap it.

How do you feel about church today?

A lot of church today is form. Back in the days of Jesus, those Pharisees had control of the Temple and Jesus didn't have anything to do with the Temple. He couldn't; He was born in the manger and wrapped in swaddling cloth. That showed that pride could never enter into the Kingdom of God. Now you've got to get down to the manger if you're ever [to be] born into the Kingdom of God. That's how Jesus came into the world. He said, "Pride is an abomination in the sight of God." I think that's what's wrong with the churches today. They're not reaching the lost world. It's been several years since I've seen an old man saved. Today you've also got to get young people to join the church.

I think, however, that the church is the greatest institution on earth. To be a true Christian we have to put Christ first in our life. If it wasn't for the church today, this world wouldn't last an hour.

PLATE 4   Reverend Bly Owens.

BLY OWENS, Southern Baptist

We set off to find Reverend Bly Owens on a cold, snow-blustery day in early March. It seems like yesterday. Ben Cook and Joe Bishop had both mentioned Reverend Owens to us, and we knew we had to meet this man of whom they had spoken so kindly. After traveling what seemed like forever, mostly on a winding dirt road, Paul and I deduced more than once we were hopelessly lost. Time and time again, we pulled out our crude map and directions and, in anticipation, we kept saying, "just a little further."

After traveling some twenty miles from the paved highway, we rounded a curve and came to the end of the road. We later learned we were in an area that is known as Wolf Mountain and there we found a small weather-worn frame house and the Reverend Bly Owens. Our time in travel was well spent.

As we pulled into the driveway a tall, commanding man surrounded by a flock of grandchildren came out to greet us. He had been making ax handles from hickory wood, but was more than glad to talk to us about religion and his "blessed Savior." Throughout our interview this warm, kind-spoken man would become deeply touched, pause, muse, sometimes lighting his pipe, and transport us back through time as he related his life and evangelical experiences.

After our first visit, we went to see Reverend Owens several more times. Once, Wendy and I found him shaking a swarm of bees into one of his many hives and expressing his utmost concern that neither she nor I get stung. On numerous occasions he would attend to the whims of his grandchildren and communicate with them without directing his attention away from us. We always left Bly's house believing that this profound man never knew what a stranger was, and as one of the oldest preachers in Jackson County, we are proud to have him as a part of our religious study.

KEITH HEAD

Man has tried everything he could to please the Lord but [man is] not doing what the Lord required of the human family. They've tried all kinds of old music and everything to worship the Lord and the Lord is displeased with it. We've gone down the last twenty years. If time were to last and we'd go twenty years longer it would be hard to pick up any spirit at any church. The Lord required this—and I've been a Bible reader about fifty years, I guess fifty-five years—the Lord required a living sacrifice. Not an old guitar or a dead audible, but a living sacrifice, whole and acceptable, which is your reasonable service. Well, that's hard to get out of the people today—to give their bodies as living sacrifices. That's what the Lord commanded the human race from the foundation—to give their bodies as living sacrifices. The Lord didn't require something of me and you that we couldn't do.

The Lord has not left the people, the people have left the Lord to a great extent. Well, in my day—if you go back sixty-five or seventy years ago (I'll soon be eighty-four years old)—there is just as much difference in the service of the Lord back then and now as there is in a sunshiny day and a dark night. Now that's true. Well, they've got fashions and they've got forms. If you'll show me—yonder lays two old King James Version X Bibles—if you'll show me a proper word in there I'll acknowledge to you. It's all plain and common—recorded from Genesis to Revelations.

The Lord said in the sixteenth chapter of Revelations that he would send hail upon the earth—every stone about the weight of a talent. Instead of repenting, they blasphemed the name of God and repented not to give Him glory; that's God's Word. Well, he poured out His vile upon the sun and the sun scorched men with heat and they repent not to give Him glory. Last summer we were down on Savannah between Dillsboro and Franklin [North Carolina]. Made two crops up there at the mouth of Betty's Creek. There was some of the hottest sunshine, it was like fire heat. Just like building a big fire you know. Well, then He said—the Lord spoke of the last war. There will be wars and rumors of war and earthquakes and famine in different places. We've had wars, we've had earthquakes. America never has had a famine, but it looks like it's liable to come.

It looks like we're living in the days of tribulation today. He said it would grow worse and worse until the end. Now that's the Bible; that's God's Word. Then you'll find it in all of these gospels. Now the first two thousand years from the creation God looked down and saw man's heart [and it was] evil continually. There wasn't but one righteous person and that was old Noah. He said, "Noah, knoweth thou thy grace in the eyes of God?" Noah walked with God. He said, "Noah, go build an ark. I'm going to destroy both man and beast whom I have created, off of the face of the earth." It wasn't anything his sons had done or wasn't anything his daughter-in-law had done, wasn't anything his wife had done. They were spared through Noah's righteousness. Noah went and warned the people that the flood was coming. They made light of him. Lot of people made light of the gospel but when the waters began to climb to the highest peaks, they pushed the children up. They said, "Old Noah told the truth." It stood many feet above the highest peak.

Well, at the end of the next two thousand years, God saw that He had to have a sacrifice whereby man could be saved. A person wouldn't go to heaven, they couldn't be raised from the dead. The grave held the body. When He found the sacrifice, it was His only begotten son. It was the third part of the Godhead which was in the Trinity. They crucified Him and He rose and went back and sent the Holy Ghost. He said to His disciples, "It is good that I go away. If I go not away the Comforter will not come which will teach you the ways of all truth and all righteousness and bring all things unto your remembrance, whatsoever I have told you."

And now we are coming upon the last two thousand years. [There will be] fires and vapors before the great and terrible day of the Lord; that you'll find in Malachi. That's the last book of the old Bible. An airplane going over—a smoker you know. You've seen them going over and leaving a very long string of smoke. [The first time I saw one] I thought it was burning up and I came to the house and got my Bible and ran a reference on smoke. I found [that we would] have a sign in the sun and in the moon—there would be fire and vapors of smoke before the great and terrible day of the Lord. That's the Bible; that's the Lord's Word. We are getting right down and we are liable to see that any time. Our Bible's about fulfilled.

I was walking the railroad when the Lord saved me. I could go [there] today. I was walking the railroad when Christ came down on the cross right in the prettiest light in front of me. It was a mile to the church. The first thing I knew I was in the churchyard. I can go back to that just as plain as it was when it happened. I've witnessed a lot right down through life. I've witnessed leadership of the Spirit down through life.

Now listen fellows, I'm a Quaker in a way. I believe in waitin' 'til the Spirit moves. That was a Quaker. He believed in moving when the Spirit moves. I certainly believe that. I've run a revival in this room and baptized three grown people and they're living today. I don't believe in over-persuading people. I believe in giving them their choice. So there isn't but one thing under the sun that'll ever cause a wicked person to repent; that is the Word preached in power and purity. Go to that heart and you won't get away from it. I was a mean boy back yonder, twenty-eight years old when I got right. I was twenty-eight the fourth day of June and joined the church and was baptized in the first days of October. If I live 'til the fourth of this next June I'll be eighty-four. I've been down the road a long time. There were things in the beginning years that the devil would throw in my way. I can smile at Satan's rage today and move on. It won't hinder me, no sir.

Why did you decide to become a preacher?

Lord have mercy; I didn't decide nothing. I'd rather had my head cut off than to turn out to preach. But one night on that bed right there, I felt my calling. Well, I had blood poison shoot up from my wisdom tooth and run down here and it got to my collar bone. My brother-in-law went after old big Doc Nichols. He came to me and said, "Bly, if it would have been thirty minutes later, there wouldn't have been a doctor in the world that could have saved you." But before he got there, it was just as plain to me as—well, it was a calling. God had laid His hand on me and said, "Bly, go into the world and warn people of the great wrath of God."

I said, "Lord, I'll take your Word and I'll go and stand by as long as life lasts by your help."

I can't get away from that today and if I would have said, "No, Lord, I can't go," in two or three days I'd've been under the ground. And that's been years ago. Well, in three hours I was better and I was up in a few days.

The first message that the Lord gave me you'll find in Isaiah. Isaiah said, "Lord, send me." That was up in the field up yonder. I could show you in full where I went to pray. The Lord just opened that up to me. I went to Charley's Creek Church—the first message I ever preached in my life. God called me.

Do you remember any strong revivals?

When they'd run a meetin' somewhere, [it would run] ten days and [they'd] baptize forty-five and fifty grown people. I've seen 'em fall just like setting one of those ax handles up there and turning it over. [It would just] lay and lay. But I guess if it was to happen in the church today, half of the people who claim to be Christian people would run out of the house scared. I've seen that in my day.

Old Preacher Jordan ran a revival meeting over here in the edge of Transylvania [County, North Carolina] at what's called Macedonia. He wanted to have success. A big Spanish Oak stood right close at the end of the church and a thunder rain came up. Lightning struck that Spanish Oak tree and tore it all to pieces. The old preacher fell on his knees and asked the Lord to strike the people with the Spirit as lightning struck that tree. And they fell at the spring [near the church], they fell in the yard, and they fell in the church. One woman lay forty-eight hours before she came through. My brother went and seen them baptized. I've been there lots of times at Macedonia—a spirited church. It's way over a hundred and fifty years old.

I've been over many a person a praying when they hollered and screamed that the Lord had saved them. Numbers and numbers of them. Got a neighbor that lives on the hill right over there. He put his arms right around my neck, down like that and I raised him up. Him and his boy. Yes sir. A couch sat over there where that record player is. He was just tore all to pieces and praying and evidence had come to me that the Lord had saved him. I said, "Marvin, pray on and see where you are. Evidence has come that the Lord has saved you." He just finally calmed down and after a while, he got up. Well, I was having night meetings here—run about a week here and my wife's baby sister was here and my boy's wife. He came by the next evening and wanted to know where I was at. I was off and gone. He said, "Bly just told me last night when the Lord saved me." Says, "I want to tell him I want to come back tonight and join the church for baptism."

Would you tell us about some of the baptizings with which you were involved?

[A man] that lives up the road here had a girl grown and a grown boy. They got right. I baptized them in Wolf Creek Lake down here. I baptized three crowds in that lake. I moved up here on Tennessee Creek after that. I said I wasn't gonna baptize no more after that in that lake. That old mud. That mud was so deep—old stick mud would pull the socks off your feet! Yeah, I like to fell myself in there. I couldn't pull my feet up!

I went into a home over here and preached to those people. There were three in the family and not one of them belonged to the church. The woman was turned into eighty years old and the man into seventy-nine. My last message there, they all got right. I baptized five down there beyond that first bridge. Well, that summer I baptized sixteen in that holy water. Well, that man and that woman is laying on the hill up yonder. I don't know how many people are laying on that hill that I baptized.

We've got wise people in the world. We've got presidents and we've got the Senate and the Congress. There's never been a person yet that could figure out—that little girl that was here a minute ago—there's never been a person yet that could figure out the worth of that little soul. The Lord said the price of the soul of man was above rubies or the cattle of ten thousand hills. We get out here then, and maybe one soul gets saved and we say, "Well, we didn't do much good." But if you could gain the cattle of ten thousand hills in one hour, you'd think you were going to be a millionaire. But the price of the soul of man is above all that. That's the Bible. That's the Lord's Word.

PLATE 5   Reverend Joe Bishop.

JOE BISHOP, Southern Baptist

Reverend Joe Bishop and his wife, Pearl, live in a comfortable little house in a small clearing near a peaceful rolling creek in the sparsely populated community of Punkintown. Born in August 1897, one of eleven children in a farming family, Reverend Bishop is one of the oldest Baptist preachers we have interviewed. He has known and held revivals with other Baptist ministers, including Ben Cook and Bly Owens.

Joe Bishop has served in the Baptist ministry for many years and has pastored in eight churches. Another of the old circuit-riding preachers, Reverend Bishop has dedicated his life to his family, community, and the growth of different churches and the teachings of Christ. Due to the overwhelming support of his congregation, he still pastors a church in the Punkintown community where he has lived for the past thirty-five years.

KEITH HEAD

I was just a big sinner, drunkard, gambler—everything wicked. And after coming out of World War I I got under conviction going to preaching. Brother Haggard [A. A. Haggard] from Tennessee ran a tent revival in Gastonia and I was saved there. I went to the altar—I'd been praying before I went to the altar. I didn't stay at the altar very long until I was saved. Then the change came. I walked down the streets, the lights shined brighter, I was in a new world.

Paul said, "Behold, old things are passed away and all things have become new." I was living in a new world around me. Wasn't any trouble then for me to quit drinking and bootlegging or gambling or anything. It was gone. I never went back to it for fifty-six years now.

I knew it down in my heart [that I was called to preach]. Fact of the matter, I knew from the time I was a little boy that I'd preach sometime. Yes, I'd preach, have a baptizing, and baptize dogs! [It was] just a natural gift to me. Preachers are not trained into being ministers, although we need all the schooling we can get. God told the old prophet, "I called you in your mother's womb." There're born preachers with a gift, a talent. Then you go ahead and accept Christ and develop that talent. Begin to preach. A man's got a natural talent just like singing or anything else. Preaching is not a joke; it's real.

I walked these mountains, preach right on through the rain and snow. Never backed up for anything. We didn't get much pay; the people didn't have much. Back during the Depression, they could hardly pay a preacher. A lot of them quit, but I kept on going. I walked to Liberty Church over in Macon County, pastored there ten years and walked through these mountains. I walked to Mountain Grove Church, Ellijay Church.

I've had lots of revivals. That church at Rainbow Springs that Ben Cook told you about—we had a big revival out there. I had a revival over at Cowee Church in Macon County; it went on five weeks I believe. Old Brother Clay was pastor [of that church]. That was the first time I ever preached a revival in this area. I was going to school down at Sylva. I've had good revivals here at my church. [One time] we lined the converts up along the gravel road down there to give them the right hand of church fellowship; I always gave the converts a handshake [after they were baptized].

I baptized a fellow out here when the pond was frozen. I wasn't the pastor; Brother Hooper was, but he was late getting here and they sent out here [for me] and said that a fellow wanted me to baptize him. Somebody came out here and told me. I went out there and I said according to our belief—the church charter—you got to have seven members. They ran up there and got Mrs. Hyatt and a bunch of women and some of the men—picked some up. They didn't have the pond fixed, had to dam it up some. There was an old boy standing there and he helped me baptize the fellow. About the time we got through, the pastor and all them came. There was ice all around the edge of [the pond].

I baptized, I believe, forty-one on what they called a cold Saturday. I walked about a quarter to half a mile down the road in my sock feet after I came out of there; it was down around zero. I baptized over here at Mountain Grove, on the pond there at old man Adams' mills. It froze and the water poured over there and there were icicles hanging down there as big as your leg. I'd baptize at twenty below just as quick—no difference to me. He called me to do the job; I'll do the job and leave the rest up to Him. There's been lots of people baptized in cold weather and ice broken out. Of course now, in general, people hold their revival meetings in the summertime. But I never did go for that too much; I believe just anytime God leads men to get the people together, let them preach.

Do you believe in shouting?

People shout at the Baptist Church. They had a lot of shouting up here, used to; not as much as they used to. You shout when the Spirit moves you! Jesus was going into Jerusalem riding on a donkey. The disciples were with Him and they spread their garments down on the way; they were shouting praise to God. The Pharisees went up to Him and said, "speak to your disciples that they make their noise"—in other words, emotion. And He said if they didn't cry, these very stones would cry. So that meant something was going on. If a fellow doesn't believe in shouting, he better stay out of heaven! There will be lots of it up there.

Have you ever seen any Divine healing?

Yes, I've had several [experiences with Divine healing]. Well, right down here—you go down and ask the Chairman of the Board of Deacons or any of these fellows here—there was a girl down there and the doctor gave her up; they said she couldn't live and they called me up from the road—I was going down to the store. I knelt there [with her] and prayed; I got up and said, "That girl will get well." Later, a man came up to my house and I said, "What in the world has happened?"

He said, "A miracle's happened. That girl is just perfectly well now." She's living in Shelby now—raised a big family.

I prayed with a woman over here at Wautauga; she had locked bowels—no doctor up there. I just had took Wautauga [begun to preach there] and I was walking down through there and her little girl called me. I didn't know the people. I was practically a stranger myself over there. I went in there and had prayer with her. I prayed for God to let her live. I went down there and got old Brother

Corder and we took her to the hospital. They operated on her and the doctor told her husband, "She's going to have a hard time to live. Gangrene's set in."

She holiered out there and told them, "I'll live." As quick as she got through a prayer, I knew. Yes, I believe in Divine healing. She got well and raised two kids.

I had two operations in the last month and a half. I came out of the hospital and came on home. I've had lots [of Divine healing]. I believe in that. But I don't believe in foolishness now. Yes sir, with the help of doctors, I believe in getting down there with God and praying your way through.

How do you feel about snake handling?

I think it's just pure foolishness because of the power in a poisonous snake. It'll kill you if you don't get something done about it. God never puts you in a position where He would impose on you affliction of that kind. It's going against the law of nature, the natural things. If I cut my finger off, it's going to hurt and it's going to bleed. And if you get in there and let a snake bite you—I know one fellow was talking about it and I said, "If God tells me to handle a snake, I ain't going to do it."

When you sum up salvation of religion and God's plan, it takes good, common bay horse sense all the way through. Religion is so strange; everybody's got religion. They've got some kind of religion, something they bow to—they pray to the moon or the cows or something. Salvation in the New Testament is just good, common bay horse sense. That's all you can make out of it—God saves a man by faith in the Lord Jesus Christ. We don't always do that, of course.

How do you feel about stringed music in the church?

Some of the old people didn't believe in that. I put it this way to one old lady: "The Lord made all the music because it's good and the Devil stole part of it!" I was at a revival and a bunch of fellows came in a quartet and they had a guitar with their music. There was an old woman there and she was kind of boss there; she built the church there with her own money—a fine building. They never would contrary her because she was a good woman; a good Christian. She said, "You can't bring that in here. You'll have to leave that out." Well, that left out their singing; they came to sing.

I said, "Why?"

She said, "I don't believe in string music."

I said, "Move the piano then. Get it out of here."

She said, "What?"

I said, "Yes m'am, the piano's string music."

She said, "Well, I love you, Joe. I'll take your word for it. Come on in."

And that settled the question. She'd always ruled that out, see.

I had a tuning fork. Hit that thing on the wall somewhere and take off with it! But young singers growing up now can't do that. They don't know enough about music.

How do you feel about speaking in tongues?

Well, I think that tongue's a language. It's mentioned there in Acts. I think if God had given it to anybody, He'd given it to me as much as I've prayed and worked. I'm not going to argue with them about their belief in that. Evidently God gave it to those people there at Pentecost. They were there from every nation under heaven and they heard them speak in their own tongue. God gave it to them there. It's possible He could give it to a person today.

Have you ever had any visions?

All the time; God said where there's no vision, the people perish. The church and each member of it needs a vision. Each Christian needs to have a vision; a vision of the lost world. I had a vision or a dream one night in the hospital; all the next day it seemed like I was in another world. I saw the Judgment. Everything had kind of an orange color. All kinds of people were there. I saw my family there; others were trying to hide. It was a vision, I think, of the Final Judgment.

What has been your greatest joy as a minister?

Winning souls. Seeing people saved. Going to them personally, talking with them, praying with them; then watching them live it. I don't worry about the money. I'd stayed in the gambling business, the bootlegging business or something if I wanted money. I'm over eighty years old [now], and I'd walk one hundred miles if I knew I could win one soul. Yes, that's what I prayed for when I'd get sick a lot of times—God let me get well and win one more soul.

PLATE 6   Reverend Howard Southards.

HOWARD SOUTHARDS,
Independent Baptist

I have attended many church services down through the years and there are certain sermons that I have heard [that have] remained in my memory as being more powerful and dynamic than others. These include Reverend Clendennon's "Open Your Windows Eastward," Hal Lindsey's, "The 1980s— Countdown to Armegeddon," and another I heard several years ago at the Kettle Rock Baptist Church preached by Reverend Howard Southards and entitled "God's Fence Around Hell." In this message, the Independent Baptist minister spoke of the love of God and His many efforts to attempt to save all men.

To me, this one message typifies the sermons of Reverend Southards, which constantly stress God's love for and patience toward His people and the opportunities He gives sinners to repent. Although Reverend Southards is a pastor and leader, he sees his role as being a servant to his God and his congregation. He offers help and encouragement to those both in and out of his church and strives to live the Christian example. He refuses to compromise or give in on issues he sees as important to the development of Christianity and the church in today's world. Simply, it seems that Reverend Howard Southards is a part of that "fence around hell."

KEITH HEAD

I've always enjoyed sharing my experience with the Lord with other people. Approximately thirty-three years ago this month, I felt the call of God to be saved. I was fourteen years old. I had gone to church all of my life; my daddy and mother were Christians, they had raised me in church. I'd gone to Sunday school and church all of my life but not until that Saturday afternoon did I really feel the call of God to be saved. We used to have services on the first Saturday and Sunday in the month; that's the only time the preacher came around. He pastored three or four churches and he'd only come to our church once a month. So that Saturday afternoon—I remember the verse of scripture he preached from in St. Luke, chapter three, verse nine: "Now therefore the ax is laid to the root of the tree and every tree that bringeth not forth good fruit is hewn down and cast into the fire." And I could almost feel the flames of hell engulfing me. When that preacher got through preaching, he gave the invitation to be saved. We had what we called a mourner's bench in the church. Praise God! I made my way down to that mourner's bench. I didn't shake a preacher's hand to get saved. I didn't sign any card to get saved, but I fell on my knees there at that mourner's bench. A boy of fourteen years old. I'd never tasted a drop of whiskey, I'd never taken God's name in vain, I'd never said a curse word, but I realized that I was a sinner going to hell.

On that mourner's bench about three o'clock in the afternoon— I can remember just as well as if it were today—I cried out, "God, be merciful to me, a sinner. Don't let me go to hell. Save me!" I can't tell you what happened; I honestly don't know. All I know is something happened to me. I can't explain my physical birth, but I know I was physically born. I can't explain my spiritual birth, but I know that I was spiritually born that day. That Saturday afternoon about three o'clock, I was born into the family of God. And that same Saturday, God wrote my name in the Book of Life just as sure as this world. By my faith, I've seen my name in the Book of Life. Now maybe other people haven't had that experience, but I've seen my name there and I know that I'm saved. There's a lot of things I don't know but one fact I know for sure—beyond a shadow of a doubt—there's not enough devils in hell to make me believe that I'm not saved. I *know* I am! Beyond anything else in this world, I *know* that I'm saved because that Saturday afternoon something different happened to me. I was saved; born again of the Spirit of God. And I praise God for it. Amen!

[When I was called to preach,] I felt that the Lord was dealing with me in a special way—not that I felt I was a better Christian than anyone else; I didn't feel that I was closer to the Lord than anyone else. But I will tell you this: Before my calling happened, I had gone back to the altar and asked God to baptize me with the Holy Ghost. Now this is another thing that [some] Baptist folks will laugh at you about, but it is definitely taught in the Word of the God. I had gone back to the altar and asked God to baptize me with the Holy Spirit so that I could be a witness for Him. I was ashamed to mention the name of Jesus to people and if I felt somebody was lost and needed witnessing to, I'd back away; I couldn't do it. I just didn't have the power of God in my life. Well, I got the feeling of the Holy Spirit of God. And then I felt like the Lord wanted me to preach His Word. Like any human being, I began to back away because I felt I was incapable of doing it; I just couldn't do it. But the Holy Spirit kept dealing with me and I kept saying, "God, there are other people that have more education than I have."

But God kept saying, "Son, I'm counting on you. I want you to go."

I kept saying, "Lord, I can't leave my family. I just can't do it. I just can't do it. I just can't accept the responsibility. I'm just not capable. I wasn't born to do that."

But God kept saying, "Son, I want you to preach."

For three and a half years I carried that burden of this thing, knowing that I should be preaching but trying to get out of it. But all the time I knew that sooner or later I was going to have to preach because there is a calling for which there is no repentance. God knows what He's doing; He doesn't make a mistake. And for three years, I ran from this. I tried to get out of it.

I went to prayer meeting one Wednesday night and during that prayer service at our church, I was under such a burden that I can't even remember who the man was that preached—I can't even remember what he preached about. All I knew was that if I didn't get that burden off my heart, I was going to die. I almost had a nervous breakdown. I was working at the [Atlanta General Motors] plant [then]. So I came home from that prayer meeting—I'd gone by myself because my wife had stayed home with one of the kids who was sick—and I told my wife I was going to have to preach.

She said, "Well, if the Lord's calling you, you better preach."

I went to bed and I was just hoo-hooing; I was crying and I got out of the bed and got down on my knees and I prayed and asked God to take the burden. I said, "Lord, I'll preach if you want me

to." But somehow the burden was still there. I got back up and got into bed and went to sleep. I got up the next morning and went to work and along about nine o'clock that burden hit me so heavy, I thought I was going to die. And I just burst out crying up there in the plant where I worked among all those men.

This fellow [there] thought he'd done something to me and he asked me, "What's the matter?"

I said, "Well, I'm going to have to preach. God's calling me to preach."

He said, "Well, I knew you were going to have to. You're too good a fellow for the Lord not to use you in a special way."

I came back home that night. I got down on my knees and I said, "Lord, I know I can't do much and I know there's others that could do a better job, but if you want me to go, here I am. I'm willing to do the best I can." And that burden left me. I'm not the greatest preacher. I'm one of the sorriest that God's got, but He has used me. And I praise God for that. Ever since that day, ever since that burden lifted, I've tried to preach what God lay on my heart. The first message I preached was in John fourteen and six: Jesus said, "I am the Way, the Truth, and the Life." I never changed my message since then. He's still "the Way, the Truth, and the Life." I haven't another gospel to preach *but* Jesus. God has blessed me and God has used me. I know that I'm the least of God's preachers, but I praise God that He called me. Thank God, that He did. There's a great responsibility and there's a great burden. But there's a great blessing, too, in being a preacher of the gospel.

[I am with] the Independent Baptist Church and [it] is not affiliated with the Southern Baptist Convention at all. We're independent of the Southern Baptists and our fellowship headquarters are in Springfield, Missouri. There's over sixteen hundred churches in our independent fellowship, but every church in our fellowship is autonomous and each rules and regulates their own business. In other words, nobody tells us what to do, not even our fellowship headquarters. They don't dictate anything to us. We're autonomous in that we control our own business. We rule our own house, in other words.

We split from the Southern Baptists and the original split came somewhere along about 1950 when the Revised Standard Version of the Bible came out. The Revised Standard Version of the Bible came out [and this Bible] rearranged the scriptures where it doesn't even read like our King James Version. And we Independents will not accept any version of the Bible other than the King James Version. We stand upon the King James Version. We don't want any revised versions. We don't accept any of those. That was the main thing it [the split] came over.

The Revised Standard Version leaves things out that are important in the scripture. In the King James, for instance, in John, chapter fourteen—a familiar scripture—it says, "In my father's house there are many mansions," and in the Revised Standard, it says, "In my father's house are many rooms," and there is a vast difference. There is a difference between a room and a mansion—a vast difference. Then it [the Revised Standard Version] also denies the virgin birth; it says that Jesus was born of a young woman. And I'm not saying that she wasn't a young woman when Jesus was born. But there's a difference between a young woman and a virgin. The King James Version definitely declares that Jesus was born of a virgin. Had He not been, we wouldn't of had any gospel to preach. But He was virgin-born and they left that out. Therefore, these old-timers couldn't accept that and I don't either. I refuse to accept that Jesus was born of a young woman. He was definitely born of a virgin, because the Bible specifically says that He was.

That was the main issue on why the Independents split out from the Southern Baptists. There are several other [issues] that the Independents and Southern Baptists don't agree on. This cooperative program that the Southern Baptists have—[from that] they send part of their money to their theological seminaries [one of which is] up in Louisville, Kentucky. And in this seminary, they have infidels teaching. I cannot honestly send my money knowing good and well that young men are going up there [to learn] to preach and that these infidels are teaching them that the book of Genesis is a myth— that you can't believe the creation, and that in the book of Jonah, the miracle that happened to Jonah didn't really happen. These infidels are teaching these young preachers all of this and then they come back to these little churches like here in Macon County and they'll tell you there's errors in the Bible and that it's not the infallible Word of God and then they tear the churches all to pieces. I cannot support them by paying salaries [to those] up there that are teaching in those schools. I've got to answer to God for where I give my money and I'm not going to support such as that.

We send our money directly to our own missionaries. One of the missionaries that we support was over at the church the other day. He came back from Africa. We send money [from our church] directly to him. Not necessarily on a [regular] schedule—sometimes once a month or once every three months, or just whenever we feel like it. We send it directly to our missionary and he, in return, sends me a receipt that he received every penny of that money. I take that receipt and read it to my church in a business meeting. No one else gets their hands on that money but him. Every penny of it goes directly to the missionary. The Southern Baptists send part of their money to this cooperative program and with that money [they pay their missionaries] and then they have to pay all their people to operate that program.

I can't agree with [the Southern Baptists] on these things. That's why we're independent. We're completely disassembled from them. We're not affiliated with them at all.

In most Independent Baptist churches like my own, we definitely believe in shouting. As a matter of fact, we have shouting on Wednesday night over at our church. People shout on Wednesday night, just like they do on Sunday [morning] and Sunday night. But one [person] sent me word the other day that I was living on emotionalism. And I told him, "No, I wasn't living on emotionalism, I was living with it!" We believe in emotion—definitely believe in emotion. If the Holy Spirit doesn't touch a person until they can praise God once in a while, they're not close enough to God! They need to get a little closer! And we definitely believe in shouting; just as well get use to it, because we're going to shout when we get to heaven! So now's a good time to get tuned in! I'll tell you what we have done. We've formed a prayer chain over at our church. Everybody'd hold hands and just complete the circle of the church. And people get to praying and then get to shouting.

Basically the Independent Baptist Church believes in the old-time way; in other words, what the old-time Baptists use to be. As the song says, "We believe in the old-time preaching, praying, singing, and shouting." The modern Baptists have excluded all of that. And they have a little sermonette and little form of Godliness. [They've] left the Spirit of God out. Most of the Southern Baptist churches you go to and in some of the Independent, they'll hand you a little bulletin back at the door and they already have the program fixed out. They know a month in advance what's going to take place. But we don't do that; we just believe in letting the Holy Spirit of God lead us. Now we have a certain time to meet over there but what's going to take place after we get there, we have no idea. [We] just let the Holy Spirit lead us. [We] just worship God in spirit and in truth.

I know a lot of people believe in Divine healing. We Independent Baptists do, too. We believe in anointing people with oil. I have a bottle in my pulpit. I anoint people with oil and pray for them because it's in the Bible. But do you know some people look down their noses at me and say that I'm a fanatic? They say that I've flipped my lid . . . that I'm crazy, that I'm old-fashioned, I'm a fogy because I believe that. But I've seen people healed by the power of God because we obey what God's Word says to do. God heals because we do what He says do.

We had a lady that asked us to pray for her. [She] had cancer. She had been to the doctor over here in Sylva [North Carolina], and the doctor told her that she definitely had cancer. Another preacher, another man, and myself anointed her with oil and prayed for her on a Saturday night and God instantly healed her. She went back to the doctor on Tuesday; they x-rayed her and examined her and that doctor came out of that office shaking his head and said, "When you were over here the other day, you were eaten up with cancer. Now I can't find anything wrong with you but a little ulcer in your stomach." God instantly healed her.

I'm going to give you my own personal experience. I had a kidney stone. I spent five days in the hospital and they x-rayed me every day and knew just exactly where that thing was every day. The kidney stone moved from the top of my kidney down to the bottom of my kidney within those five days. I never passed the stone in those five days and my doctor told me that I could come home. He said, "Go home and get on the lawnmower; ride the lawnmower and mow the grass and this and that and maybe you'll pass it." This was on a Thursday. He told me to come back to his office on Monday to be x-rayed again. I came home, went to church on Sunday, and had my deacons anoint me. I had my oil over at the church and I had them anoint me and pray for me. And boys, just as sure as I'm sitting in this chair, God took that kidney stone out of me and I haven't got a scar. I went back to the doctor's office on Monday and was x-rayed. The doctor came down from operating at eleven o'clock and he looked at those x-rays and he said, "You take him back in there and x-ray him again."

Then he called me back into the office where he was developing the film and he said, "Well, it's gone."

And I said, "Sure it is. I know it is."

He said, "We can't find it on the x-ray."

And I said, "Sure it's gone."

Just as sure as I'm sitting in this chair, God took that stone out of me. We obeyed what God's Word said to do and they anointed me with oil and prayed for me. And if that verse of scripture isn't any good, then neither is John 3:16. But it's all the infallible, inspired Word of God and we believe it just exactly as it is. Don't try to leave it out or add to it or take from it—just accept it like it is and believe it like it is and preach it like it is.

I've [also] seen instances in my church. Now, I know someone would make fun of me if I tell them we anoint people when they have a sick headache. They'd make fun of me and say, "Well, a headache will go away anyhow." But I believe in talking to God about everything—about a headache, a cold or anything else. God's interested in the little things as well as the big things. So I've anointed people over there with a sick headache and immediately it would be gone! And I anointed a lady over there the other day that had the doctor tell her she had pleuresy. They had gone on vacation over in Gatlinburg [Tennessee], and had to come home; she got sick and had to come home. I anointed her and prayed for her and God immediately healed her. God does those things! He definitely does those things. But some people will laugh at you. They'll say "Ah, that's for the Pentecostal people," or "That's for somebody else." But praise God, it's for me just the same as anyone else. That's why some call me a fanatic and an old fogy and others call me trash. A fellow called me on the phone the other day because of what I've preached and he said I was going to hell and leading my whole church to hell. But I just stand for the Word of God. I'm just as sure saved as I'm sitting here in this chair. There is something about it that I know—I know! The devil can't make me doubt it. Praise God!

PLATE 7   Howard Parham.

HOWARD PARHAM, Primitive Baptist

Low in number in this area, the Primitive Baptists draw criticism from many groups, including other branches of the Baptist faith, because of their belief in predestination. As Mr. Parham says, "We believe that God's got it all planned and [everything's] already predestinated; we're just here to carry out what He has predestinated for us to do." The Primitive Baptists do not believe in missionaries, Sunday school, or the use of musical instruments in the church. Even though the Primitive Baptists are criticized, Mr. Parham remains steadfast in his faith: "The old Primitive Baptists, I'm not ashamed of them at all. I know they've dwindled down to nothing, but I'm still convinced they're more right than ever now."

This interview is presented in two parts. The first contains Mr. Parham's discussion of the Primitive Baptists and in the second he talks about the old Lystra Primitive Baptist Church which still stands today. The section about Lystra Church first appeared in Foxfire *magazine, Fall, 1976.*

KEITH HEAD

The two [religions] that came here to start with, I understand, was just the Catholic and the Primitive Baptist, and the rest of them just sprung off from them. I don't know when they first landed at Plymouth Rock up yonder, but it was way back there around 1600 and something, and that's been a long time ago. Of course, the Indians were already here and they had their belief.

The Primitive Baptist wasn't took up in this [part of the country] 'til 1902. [Until then] there were just Baptists [here]. In 1902 this association right here took up the Primitive Baptist—they put the "Primitive" to it to make it original. The others call theirselves just Baptists. What we call Missionary Baptists, sprung off from the Primitive Baptist. They sprung off on foreign mission, and the regular Primitive Baptists don't believe in foreign mission; we don't believe we can carry the gospel anywhere because it's all God's work. We believe that God's got it all [planned] and [everything's] already predestinated; we're just here to carry out what He has predestinated for us to do. We do have "called" preachers. He can call some in the foreign nations as good as He can here, because He said, "I have a people in all kindreds and tongues." But He don't predestinate us to work in foreign missions. Therefore, that's what the big difference is right there.

We don't believe you can have anything to do with your salvation and the Missionary Baptists believe they do. [We believe] He speaks and it's done, and He commands and it stands fact. If He tells one of His little ones to "come unto me," then they'll come; they can't resist. You can't resist the power of God. But the Missionary Baptists will tell you that you've got to do first, before God will do. 'Course, there's several different kinds of Baptists: Missionary Baptists and Free Will and all that; and, of course, they've got the Churches of God. But [all those beliefs are based] on the same principle. They believe in the "good do" system—*you've* got to do before God can do—and we just don't believe in it. We believe that all God's children will do good [or bad] because it's predestinated for them. That's the biggest split right there. Regular Baptists don't believe in predestination. [We believe everybody was predestined] before the *world* was even made.

The Presbyterians believe in predestination to a certain extent. We've got some people now that call themselves Primitive Baptists who believe that God predestinated all good things, and the bad things are left to the people, but we don't believe that way. We believe that God predestinated all things, good and bad. What we call "bad" is for God's good to serve His purpose, and it brings out the good. All that we call evil brings out the good.

He's got an elect family. That's another thing where [the Baptists] split. [Regular Baptists] don't believe that God's got just an elect family. They believe that just anybody [can be saved]. When He

said, "All come unto me," He was talking about all that He had
elected. He already had said that He had an elect family. So, there's
a lot of difference—just as much as night and day—in regular Primitive Baptists and regular Baptists.

There isn't nobody that can live above sin. [God] just comes in
momentarily and then He withdraws. You'll sin. When God withdraws His Spirit from you, you're in sin; you're already a sinner.
You don't have to go out here and do anything, 'cause you're a
sinner then. If [people] could [live above sin], there wouldn't have
been any need for Christ to come. That was His purpose of coming
on this earth. It was God's will for Him to come here and live above
sin. He's the only one that's ever done it.

I couldn't say that I've been born again. I have to go back to
where I say I hope I have, and that's as far as I can go. You've
just got to hope, and you don't know [whether you're saved or
not]. You see, in the eighth chapter of Romans, Paul was speaking
to the Romans and he said, "You're saved by hope." And, if you
see a thing, why should you hope for it? It was just like me coming
home tonight: I was hoping I'd have a good supper, but when I
got here and got the supper, then my hope ceased, because I'd
come into possession. That's the only way you'll ever know about
heaven . . . when you come into possession.

When I [began going to the Primitive Baptist Church,] I went
for years expecting to join there. That's one thing that they don't
do; they don't ask anybody to join the church—never. So, one August
meeting (they used to have August meeting over there and communion and foot washing), I went, but I decided I wouldn't join that
day, because a lot of [my people] would be there. I wanted to join
when there wasn't anybody there much, so if they turned me down,
it wouldn't be embarrassing to the old flesh. But I did. I had an
experience that day when they called for the opening of the doors
of the church.

You have to get up and tell your experience—what the Lord's
done for you—when you join. The biggest thing I had to get up
and tell about was how much I loved them all and how I loved
the church, and that I didn't feel fit to be with them, but I did
want a home with them. I got up, I walked down that aisle, and it
was just easy as everything—as the old saying goes, "as falling off
a log." I felt like I was just walking on air, and that was a great
experience. I'd always had the experience where I wanted to hug
every one of their necks, and I got to do it when I joined the church.
Then, the next Sunday was the baptizing, and I had a great experi-

ence there. When I walked into the water and was baptized, I felt like there was something that was washed away. No doubt at the time. But, I've doubted that a lot of times since. So, I live in doubt the biggest portion of my time. They are all that way, every Primitive Baptist that I know. A true Primitive Baptist doesn't know if he's saved.

I had another experience. When I was coming from church one time, I was coming down this road up here, and I could see every-thing—every blade of grass and everything. I was just lifted up, worshipping God, and nothing could bother me. I didn't need any-thing, 'cause I was taken out of this world. I believe that. But, I've often thought a lot of times since then, "What was that?" I believe I knew at the time; but, you see, that's it, you don't ever know. You'll never get [the Primitive Baptists] to tell you that they know they're saved or know they're a child of God. They'll say, "I hope I am."

We don't believe in Sunday school because we don't believe [just anybody] can teach God's Word unless it's God's will. He did tell His disciples to go teach, and those that He told to go teach we believe are the preachers. As far as picking up the Bible and teaching it [in Sunday school], we just don't believe in it. What we do believe in is the preacher getting up there and preaching. You take whenever a preacher gets up and preaches . . . if I haven't experienced some-thing he's talking about, it isn't worth anything to me—not a thing in the world. But, when he gets to preaching his experiences and my experience, and both of these are alike, then there is where your teaching comes in. He will bring across some points that you haven't thought of. The scripture says "teaching and preaching is to stir up your pure mind." You've already got that pure mind in there; it's just got to be stirred up, and that is one way God has got of doing it—through that man. The man had nothing to do with it because [the Bible] says, "Every good and perfect gift comes down from above."

We don't have any music, no piano, no nothing. We just sing. When you're blessed to sing and blessed to hear it, it's prettier than anything else in the world. There isn't any piano to drown it out, either. It's really pretty. I think I've heard as good of singing right over there at Lystra [Primitive Baptist Church] as I've ever heard in my life, I'm telling you, with no piano. They've just never believed in it. We believe in piano and music in homes. I like good string music—all of them do, but that's worldly stuff. When you go to worship God, they just don't believe in taking the worldly stuff and putting it in the church. All those old songs that we use were inspired by God just like the scriptures were. We believe that they aren't anything but sermons themselves. We feel that if God blessed us to sing, we've got the music. We don't need the piano there to drown out the music.

We don't have any special services as far as sunrise service, serenade, and all that. [We have church] once a month. That's the way all Primitive Baptist churches are. Once a month—maybe a Saturday and a Sunday. It used to always be eleven on Saturday and eleven on Sunday, but I've noticed some of these churches now, on account of people working in public work, have it at two-thirty in the afternoon on Saturday. Over at Lystra, it went on at eleven on Saturday and Sunday.

We don't believe in any such a word as revival. There isn't but one revival, and that's Jesus Christ, Himself. The Baptists say they have a revival to revive the people up. We don't believe that one person can revive another up; Jesus Christ does that alone. We do have "attracted" meetings we call it, and associations and things like that. That's to get together, all the churches. But as far as a revival, we never refer to it as that.

[At Lystra] we used to have associations and a union meeting. We'd have a union meeting in the spring, and then an association in the fall, and [each time] all the churches would meet together. We used to have our association the second weekend in October—Friday, Saturday, and Sunday.

Every time each church would have to make a report [as to whether] they were in peace [with one another]. If [the churches] weren't in peace, the association wouldn't recognize them. They'd have to get in peace among themselves. [For example,] sometimes the members would get out with each other or somebody might bring a charge against a member. They would deal with that until they got it settled and if he didn't straighten up his ways, then he would have to be turned out [of the church]. Even out here in natural life, two brothers might trade around somewhere and fall out with each other. If they did, they'd have to straighten that out and get back in fellowship with each other or whichever one that's in fault would be turned out—whichever one they determine is in fault, or both. They'd sure turn them out. The preacher hasn't got any say-so at all in the Primitive Baptist church, it's the deacons that rule the church. But whenever they turn anybody out of the church,

somebody's got to make a motion. Then they appoint a committee
to go out and see what the trouble is and see if they can't correct
it. If they can't, then they go ahead and turn them out.

[At association] they have their business part, then they'd go into
the preaching. They'd have visiting preachers. I've been up to North
Carolina a good many times on three-day meetings and heard twenty-
seven preachers. I'm hoping to hear ten or fifteen this weekend.
They start preaching around nine or ten o'clock, and go on 'til
about two or three, something like that, and maybe have a lunch
on the ground.

We communed quarterly [every three months], then we washed
feet once a year. [We had a communion table] for the deacons to
sit at to serve the wine and the bread. Just as soon as we'd get
through communion in August, we always go through the foot washing after the preaching. We'd turn two benches together and spread
towels over it for them to wash each others' feet. The women would
wash each others' feet and the men would wash each others' feet.
That's the purpose of the women [sitting on one side of the aisle]
and the men on [the other]. That's the way they always were.
Churches are still set up that way. There's a church right up here
above Athens [Georgia] called Mt. Zion, and I go there every second
Sunday. The men sit on [one] side and the women on [the other].
It's just a custom. It's not anything the regular Primitive Baptists
have got against women, 'cause they generally think well of the
women folks.

[According to John,] when the supper was ended, Christ girded
Himself with a towel and began to wash His disciples' feet. He
washed all His disciples' feet. Then He said, "You call me Lord
and Master, so am I. Ye should wash each others' feet hereafter."
[Washing feet] shows humbleness. Now I'll tell you, when I first
joined the Primitive Baptist church, I was a fairly young man, and
to let one of them old gray-haired men get down and wash my
feet . . . if that didn't make you feel little!

I'm telling you, it sure takes something out of you, but it's a
great communion to wash each others' feet. You know, there's a
Missionary Baptist church below Comer that pulled out and split
from our church. They washed feet there for years and years until
one of the women stole the other women's hose and that broke
up the foot washing. That's what they tell me. Now, I don't know,
I wasn't there.

There's been some changes [in the church]. It isn't like it was when I first joined. Paul set the church up to Timothy and them back yonder in Corinthians. When he was setting up the church, he told them that the woman was to be silent in the church, and not to speak 'til they got back home. [That] if they had anything to bring to the church, to tell their husband. That's the way it always was, but I've noticed now that women are taking more part in the church. So, it isn't exactly like it was. It's changed some.

We don't have offerings. When the meeting's over, if anybody wants to give the preacher [some money, they can]. We just give him something for his expenses. We'd try to pay him his way to here and back. As far as the offerings, there's never been an offering taken. There's never been a plate passed around in a Primitive Baptist church that I ever knew of—not a true Primitive Baptist church.

[Primitive Baptists dress up for church] now, but I remember a time that they'd come to Lystra in their overalls and brogan shoes. Of course, that's about all they had way back in the thirties, and they didn't think anything about it. Since I've been a member (I joined over there in '51) I've known them to come in overalls.

They're not against [going to ballgames and movies] or going to a dance or anything because that's worldly stuff. [It's acceptable] as long as you conduct yourself right. We've got it on the church record where they turned some out for not paying their debts, or being drunk or disorderly. Turn them out of the church. The biggest portion of Primitive Baptists believe in taking a drink. I've always had my preacher a drink when he comes, but that's as far as they want to go. If a man can't control it, that's it.

God can [heal people]. That's all the healing there is. You take these doctors and all. What skill they've got comes from God; it's just a blessing from God that they've got, and they can't heal anybody. It's a blessing that God gives. I've seen Oral Roberts do it on TV, but as [far as I'm concerned] it's just a show. I don't know what it is—I couldn't say. What I say doesn't make it so and it doesn't make it not so; it's either so or not so to start with. But, to me, it's just a show.

They don't believe in speaking in tongues—unknown tongues they call it. I know the scripture speaks of the unknown tongue and all that in certain places, but the unknown tongue is already spoken in the Primitive Baptist church. If you go and hear [the minister] preach and you haven't experienced what he's preaching about, that's unknown tongues to you to start with. That's where the unknown tongue comes from.

[Primitive Baptists don't believe in snake handling.] I know Paul did that. Paul was even bit by the worst snakes there were. But, you see, that was to be put on record to show God's power.

We got an old Lystra church book here—1803. It says on the first page that twelve people established it in 1803. Yes sir, that book's that old. I'm the only member there now—only member. It hasn't ever changed since I've known it, but the thing of it is, it's gone dead, I reckon. We would have been having some services there maybe once a year anyhow, if we could've had a way to do it, because it doesn't have any windows in it or anything. They've busted them all out. Back [in the old days] people didn't bother nothing like they do now. I just don't understand that. They're tearing [the church] up now. Why they want to do that, I don't know. You know what? Times have changed.

When I was a boy I worked in the field. When I came out from school, I went over yonder and cleaned off terraces or whatever there was to do 'til night. I didn't have time to run out. [When school was out] I knew to get home to work. You had to pick cotton in the fall, you had to chop cotton in the spring and things like that. Boys don't have anything to do now.

Sunday, a boy nineteen years old hung himself—a first cousin of mine hung himself in the bathroom. [Life] must be pretty boring to them for some reason. Of course, to my understanding, he was on some kind of pills and that might have been what caused it. I'll just tell you, people can get mighty messed up. I got married when I was nineteen, and I worked every day at home 'til I did get married. You didn't have any time to be getting out and getting hold of pills much; of course, you didn't have enough money to buy any with anyhow. I went off many a night with a nickel in my pocket and I'd buy a girl a pack of chewing gum and have a date, too. I wasn't embarrassed and the girl wasn't either, 'cause they didn't expect anything. I would have liked to have had some money, but I guess I'd been in some more devilment if I had money just like boys are today.

There was fifteen in our family. There were four of us boys and my dad would put in a couple of gallons of gas in the old A Model we had back then, and when you burnt that out, that was as far as you could go. That's all he ever put in the truck at one time. That was all he could afford! Gas was eighteen and twenty cents a gallon. It hasn't gone up now like other stuff has. Gas could go to a dollar a gallon and still be cheaper than a lot of things that's went up. But you see, [gas prices are] what people harp on most, 'cause they use more of it now than anything—especially young people, they can't be still.

The biggest sign [that the end is near] to me is how progress has been made in the last seventy-five years. Back before the 1900s, they were still knocking rocks together to strike matches and things. After World War II everything, approximately, is push-button. Back in the thirties, we didn't have an electric stove. We still had to cut wood for the heat and get by with that old fireplace. [Progress] is the biggest sign that things are getting near the end. It's rolling faster and faster—like a ball going down a hill; the further it goes, the faster it goes over, and by the time it hits the bottom it's really rolling—things are really going. If this world was to go on fifty more years [we'd] be killing each other like flies just like it was in the old days, because there would be so much here. Maybe we wouldn't be doing it on a purpose, but it would just [be happening]. So the end is coming on. In my day, just in my day, the world has changed.

According to the scripture, we're in the last evening now. That's the way I believe, and I've heard a lot of Primitive Baptists say it. We're in the evening of time. I do believe that. But I don't know how long that's going to go on, because, you see, with God there is no time. He says a thousand years is the same as one day, and one day is the same as a thousand years. There's no time with God. So, I don't know what the evening of time is now. According to history, the world's been standing about six thousand years that they've got record of. It was probably here longer than that. Definitely, every two thousand years Noah's Ark came and the second Christ came. Now the third is coming up, and something is definitely going to happen. According to the scripture, there's going to be a resurrection for all God's children. Whenever He speaks, they're all going to come forth from all parts of the earth—even the ones out of the sea. They'll come forth.

According to the scripture, there's going to be some children of God here on earth when [the end] comes, and they'll be caught up in the air. He's done elected so many people. Do we say God's [unjust to choose certain people]? God forbid. Didn't the potter have a right to take the same lump of clay and make one vessel to honor and one to dishonor? So much more has God got a right to do that. He's got a right to choose one and leave [the other]. There will be some that have to go through the sting of death. The scriptures say so. As far as me [knowing] when that is, He says, "Even the angels in Heaven won't know." So, as far as me predicting when it will be, I don't know; but I do believe we're in the evening of time now. It's the teaching of the Bible. The scripture is going to be fulfilled. I don't know how you all feel.

The old Primitive Baptists, I'm not ashamed of them at all. I know they've dwindled down to nothing, but I'm still convinced they're more right than ever now. A lot of people say they fall out with us because we think we're the only ones that are right. Why, if I didn't think I was right, I sure wouldn't be in it! I'd be somewhere else! Naturally, I think I'm right! There's just as much purpose in every denomination as there is in ours. There's a purpose in it. There's a purpose in all things for the children of God.

PLATE 8

Lystra Primitive Baptist Church

When I was younger, I had always heard about a church near where I live. It was supposed to be haunted and, supposedly, if you ran around it three times, a witch would chase you around it the fourth time. I kept hearing that, so I went there one time and was going to run around it, but I got scared, and up to now I have never run around it.

One weekend, years later, Wig and I went to Augusta [Georgia] on a Foxfire trip and we came back by my house for dinner. I had told Wig about this church and of some of the superstitions that surround it. He was interested, so I took him by there and he liked it. It was pretty run down and there were wasps' nests everywhere. Some of the gravestones were broken and pushed over, and the wrought iron that had been around some of the graves was stolen or torn down. Vandals had written all over the outside walls of the building. Inside, on a table, was a message that someone had written to the vandals telling how much the church had been loved once and asking them to stop. It was signed, "A person who loved this church."

We said that even though the church was run down, it would make a good article if I was willing to look into its history. He said he had never seen a church like this before where the benches faced the pulpit from three directions. He asked me if I would like to do an article on it and I agreed.

My parents helped me find the only living member of the church and that was Howard Parham. So Bob Sjostrom, one of my classmates, and I went

PLATE 9

*down for an interview. Since I had already been on a couple of interviews,
Wig let Bob and me do it by ourselves. When Mr. Parham heard we were
coming, he went to the church and painted over all the writing so we could
get a good picture. He carried us to the church, himself, and showed us around.
He also showed us all the records of the meetings, as well as the plate and
the deed to the church. I really respect Mr. Parham for going to that much
trouble just for us. He's really a nice man.*

*After we came back, I started printing my pictures and transcribing my
tape and finishing up the article. Now that I have learned about the church,
I am no longer scared of going to it. It's really a peaceful place. I wouldn't
even be scared there at night. Knowing about the church has drawn me a
lot closer to it and it means a lot more to me now than just a building that
is supposed to be haunted.*

MIKE DRAKE

HOWARD PARHAM: The church was first built over in Oglethorpe
County across the river. It was and still is a Primitive Baptist church.
The people moved over to this place and this building was built
in 1820. They built it close to a spring so they wouldn't have to
dig a well and close to water for a baptizing hole. My granddaddy
got baptized [in that hole] with ice on the banks. He wanted to be
baptized right then and didn't want to wait till the water got warm.

[After they moved] they changed the name from Skull Shoals to
Lystra. So this building is about a hundred and fifty years old. We

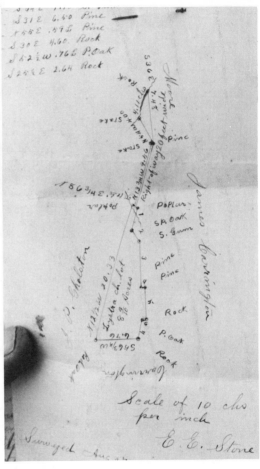

have a little better than nine acres here and I've got the deed to it. It just belongs to the church.

Twelve people over there established the church. They were the Carringtons, Adams, Meadows, and Davises. They elected Timothy Carrington the minister and John Meadows as one of the deacons. They were still fighting Indians when the church was established. At that time, there was no community and no roads.

The most members they ever had, according to my records, was fifty. They only have one member now and that's me. They had slave members there and a balcony set up for the slaves. They didn't

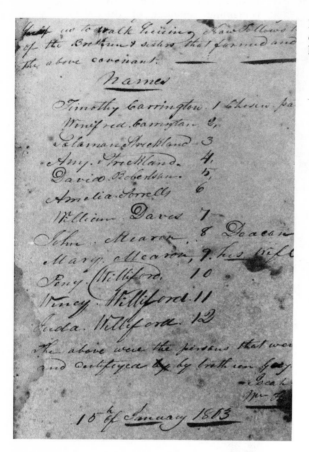

PLATE 12   A page from one of Mr. Parham's church books listing the original members.

PLATE 13   Handcarved decoration adjacent to the church in the cemetery.

sit down with the [white] people. Once they turned a slave out for beating his wife. The women sat on one side of the church and the men sat on the other. [They] always did that.

They had foot washings up until they quit having services. Every year in August they had communion and foot washings. We always called that Attracted Meeting. We had a three-day meeting in August and foot washings on one day. We would still do that if we still had meetings. Each of the brothers would wash the others' feet and the sisters would wash each others' feet. [They would] just pair off and that has been going on ever since the church has been there.

PLATE 14 Mike and Mr. Parham inspect graves in the Lystra cemetery.

PLATE 15 A small outhouse behind the church was provided for the women.

[People are still buried there] but they don't have the [funeral] services there at the church. They have services somewhere else and bring them in there and bury them. There has been two or three buried there in the last year. Some families take care of some of the old graves and the rest are just growing up.

PLATE 16   Tombstones in the Lystra cemetery.

ISAAC DAVID
GEORGIA
PVT GA TROOPS
REVOLUTIONARY WAR
1757   1840

PLATE 17

[The church] just isn't used for anything at all now. My wife and I go over there to see about it every week. That's about all there is. We're hoping to have meetings and services back there if people would ever leave it alone and quit tearing it up. [There's no need] to put the windows and things back in the way they get broken and torn up. I fix the church and put the windows back in it myself.

PLATE 18

CLYDE NATIONS, JR., TED LANEY, and
CLYDE NATIONS, SR., Free Will Baptists

One day last summer while en route to one of the many interviews for this publication, we came upon a unique and interesting old sign. Its form was that of an old gigantic and genuine sawmill blade and upon it in large white letters were the words, "Sawmill Hill Free Will Baptist Church." Our curiosity and interest in the doctrine of Free Will Baptists then started us on a search of the church's pastor and we made plans to come back into the area.

We learned that the Reverend Clyde Nations, Jr. was the preacher at the little church and that he also owned and worked at a little general store near it. When we approached Reverend Nations, he was naturally cautious but as soon as he found out that our intentions were sincere he readily agreed to share with us his philosophy and theology. Being busy, he asked us to come back in an hour. Upon our return we were pleased to learn that Reverend Nations had asked his father and Ted Laney, both Free Will Baptist preachers, to meet with us at the store. We were led to a small shed adjoining his store and as we pulled up some old Coke crates to sit on among tires and various and numerous boxes of supplies, we began an interview that proved to be one of the most informative and moving.

Our first meeting and interview as well as other visits led to a warm friendship and an invitation to a revival at the Sawmill Hill Free Will Baptist Church. Again, we were met with wonderful cooperation and cordiality as Reverend Nations allowed us to record the proceedings and introduced us to the congregation. From relationships like this one, we strongly feel that this particular publication takes on an ever greater importance and significance.

KEITH HEAD

How is the government of the Free Will Baptist Church set up?

REVEREND CLYDE NATIONS, JR.: We believe that the individual is a free moral agent. We believe that each church is a free body. My church is not responsible to [any other] church, neither is [any other] church responsible to my church. My church is not responsible to any organization, neither is any organization responsible to us. We are, somewhat, independents—somewhat. There is a Free Will Baptist State Association, and most Free Will Baptist Churches belong to it. However, up until ten or twelve years ago I didn't know there was such a thing, because we're isolated to a certain extent here in the mountains. But there is a state association and the state belongs to the national association. One time I went to our national convention which was held down in Raleigh [North Carolina] and there were thirty-six hundred Free Will Baptist ministers there.

REVEREND TED LANEY: We do now have two North Carolina Free Will Baptist organizations, if you remember, Brother Nations, Jr. Over in Durham County, eighteen thousand pulled out at once [and organized a separate church].

What was that split over?

REV. NATIONS, JR.: It was [within] an individual church. The big split came over majority rule. In other words, they had a split, they took it to court, and the court rewarded the minority in the church. And the minority who took the church was a very small minority. It was over majority rule—that's what it split over.

How are Free Will Baptists and Missionary Baptists different?

REV. NATIONS, JR.: The major difference between the Free Will Baptists and the Missionary Baptists is eternal security.

REV. LANEY: The greatest majority of Missionary Baptists preach eternal security; if you're saved, you're eternally saved, and can't be lost no matter what you might go out here and do. We don't believe that way.

REV. NATIONS, JR.: The Free Will Baptists believe that a person can be saved and then depart from God in their actions. [A person can be saved, then] live a riotous life, and in the end be lost. That's the major difference between Free Will Baptists [and some of the other Baptists]. We differ, also, on the arts of baptism and communion. For instance, if you belong to a Free Will Baptist church, and you move to where there wasn't any, and you wanted to unite with a Southern Baptist church, they would not accept your baptism. But if you're a Southern Baptist, you're saved, you've been baptized, and move into our neighborhood—or any neighborhood where there is a Free Will Baptist church—and maybe there is not a Southern Baptist church handy, and you want to come and unite with the Free Will Baptists, then you tell us you have been saved, and you're satisfied with your conversion, you're satisfied with your baptism, and we will take you in on that if your life proves it.

REV. LANEY: The Bible speaks of the free will. In other words, you by your own choice, and by your own free will have a right to accept Christ as a savior. You're not forced to or made to. You have your own right to worship. There is nobody to dictate or tell you that you've got to do this, that, or the other. He speaks of our free will often.

REV. NATIONS, JR.: We believe that each individual is a free moral agent in the sight of God, therefore having the right to choose; the right to be saved or the right to be lost. That's where the words "free will" come in.

REV. LANEY: All the old people that organized this association of Free Will Baptists are all dead and gone. That was back when there wasn't any automobiles or anything to travel with. They walked through these mountains and went all the way down into Georgia.

REV. NATIONS, JR.: They went to Georgia and got a charter and came back and organized the first Free Will Baptist church in this county. They walked!

REVEREND CLYDE NATIONS, SR.: I'm a man that can't read nor write my name. I thought I'd been called [to preach] for about six months, and finally I was on the floor testifying. I said I'd be preaching my first message over at the Alarka Post Office in the square Saturday—*I* didn't say it, the Spirit of God said it. I fought it, but I was on the floor testifying, and He said I'd be preaching at two o'clock on that Saturday. It was a great experience. It's something that I just about had to do. I can't read or write, but I organized three churches, built two, and pastored about five.

REV. NATIONS, JR.: I was saved when I was twenty-one. I was preaching before I was twenty-two. When you start talking about the calling of the ministry or the decision to go into the ministry, it's a very wide subject, especially in the modern times that we live in. For instance, let me say I was watching a national TV program on seminaries where there was people going to become preachers. Unless I have forgotten, there was sixty-some percent of the young men in three different seminaries that had never had a personal experience . . . that never had been saved . . . that never had a personal experience with the Lord. There were various reasons why they were there. Some had considered the work of a doctor, the hard long hours, and the money. They had excluded it because of the obligations, and the long hard hours. Some had considered the idea of a lawyer, and what they had to go through with, and the money they would make. And they considered the ministry, and what it involved, and the money they would make in the ministry. Therefore, they decided to go into the ministry. It looked easier. That's not why I am in the ministry, and not why I am a pastor. God was personally calling me. I was anointed, and when I use the word "anointed," I speak of the power of God. There was many hours I laid awake. I could vision myself preaching to congregations of people. I visioned people being saved under my preaching and this is how I felt God dealing with me.

REV. LANEY: As for myself, when I was sixteen years old, I felt the call of God. For five years, I guess I lived as rough and rugged a life as any man could live, fighting the calling wherein that I was called. I went through about any and everything that a man could go through with. [When I was] about twenty years old [I went to] a prayer meeting one evening. I didn't get renewed back up, or renew my covenant with God in the prayer meeting, but it was riding so heavy on me—the burden—that when I got home I made my way through the pastured fields, about a mile over into the woods. There, on my knees, I made things right with God. When I walked into the church that night, they stopped the choir from singing, and the pastor said, "Somebody has been saved today." I hadn't told nobody, and nobody didn't know it, or anything. But, he said, "I wish you would come on to the front and make it known." I couldn't wait no longer, and I walked to the front. As I went to the front, two went to the altar and got saved that night.

Still I fought the calling of God. I taught Sunday school lessons, I sang in the quartet for three or four years. Every way I worked for the Lord other than preach. It boiled down to the last thing, and there wasn't anything else to do. The load was so heavy. The burden was so heavy that I just couldn't go on with it. But when I went down before the church that evening, I got down on my knees and I began to pray. I said, "Lord, if You'll just lift this burden and help me, I'll do the best I can." I'm glad that He took it off. For thirty years in the pulpit, I've never regretted an hour of it.

Do you see any problems in the church today?

REV. NATIONS, JR.: I feel one of the great hindrances of religion— I'm talking about the born-again Christian movement—is to let the theological [differences of opinion] split the fellowship. I feel that

God is not at all satisfied with the fact that we let these differences divide us from fellowship. The unsaved portion of the world is watching. We're supposed to represent love, peace, and unity. We say we're supposed to be doing this under the influence of God.

Do Free Will Baptists speak in tongues?

REV. LANEY: The Baptists don't speak in tongues. Paul says in his writings that it's better that words be spoken in a language that can be understood than ten thousand words be spoken in languages that cannot be understood. The scriptures go on to tell us, concerning those that speak in tongues, let them have an interpreter that they might interpret to the congregation that doesn't understand. Now, take for instance, just yesterday I was at a funeral at the Church of God. I don't know how to understand it, but practically half the funeral was preached in what they call the "unknown tongue." Well, there was two-thirds of the people, or more, that was there that wasn't the Church of God people. They all came away just as dumbfounded as I was about it, saying, "Well, what did they say?" or "What kind of a funeral was it?" I'm not against it, but if a man preaches, let him have an interpreter. Now take, for instance, Billy Graham, the great evangelist here of America. [He] goes all over the world; but, you see, let him go to the foreign countries without an interpreter, and get up and start preaching over there in our language. What effect would that have on that congregation of people without an interpreter? But, through his preaching and a man [an interpreter] that knows what he is preaching, and is able to interpret to that congregation, there's thousands of souls that get saved. With an interpreter, I'd say [speaking in tongues is] all right; without it, no.

REV. NATIONS, SR.: I wouldn't want to contradict anything that Brother Ted said, but not anything says, "He that speaketh in tongues, let him have an interpreter." There's different kinds of tongues, and there's differences in the unknown tongue. The unknown tongue— no man understands it. We don't preach against it, and we don't practice it. But Paul said, as Ted said, "I'd rather speak in ten words with understanding than ten thousand of an unknown tongue that by my voice I may edify the church."

REV. LANEY: I went to a revival with two Holiness preachers. One of them, a real old gentleman, would preach every other night, and never did at no time, in no way, come with tongues. I mean, he preached to where everyone could understand it. But the young preacher . . . half his sermons the people didn't understand what he was saying. We had the privilege to talk to him one night before the services had started and we asked him about it . . . why he did it, or why it had come about. I'll tell you just exactly word-for-word what he told me. He said, "My sister went through college and took up a foreign language," he said, "and it's through her that I speak these words," he said, "and it's not from God." So, there's where he got his, because he was speaking some other kind of a language that he got out of college.

How do Free Will Baptists feel about foot washing?

REV. NATIONS, JR.: Yes sir, the Free Will Baptists have them. That's one part of their communion service. The women wash one another's feet and the men wash one another's feet. Some of the Independent Baptists are practicing foot washings now. The scripture is taken from one of the four Gospels—which one I don't recall right off . . .

REV. LANEY: All four of them has it.

REV. NATIONS, JR.: It's taken from Christ's teaching where He washed His disciples' feet and it's supposed to represent humility.

What are the Independent Baptists?

REV. NATIONS, JR.: You see, the Independent Baptists came out of the Southern Baptists. Do you know why? Independent Baptists are really just Southern Baptists or Missionary Baptists, but they came out because they could not support the work of the whole of the Missionary Baptists such as the cooperative program; in other words, the Independent Baptists support missionaries and mission work—home missions, foreign missions and so on—but they do not support the organization of the Southern Baptists. That's the only thing.

What is the Free Will Baptist's stand on abstaining from movies, ball games, and other worldly pasttimes?

REV. NATIONS, JR.: That differs in the preachers and the churches, it sure does. For instance, I like to go to football games and I do occasionally. I like to watch a softball game, and I do that occasionally. I've *not* been to a movie house since I was saved twenty years ago. Most of the Southern Baptist preachers preach against movie houses, and probably most of the Free Will Baptists preach against ball games.

REV. NATIONS, SR.: Speaking of the ball games and movie house, all of that . . . he says [the policy is] all in the preacher, which it is. I've been preaching twenty-seven years. I've not seen a ball game—football, basketball, baseball—and I've not been to the movies. I've set that aside. That's the way we both feel about it. I'll say it's not good to go; he says it's no harm. We work that a'way.

REV. NATIONS, JR.: We don't fight.

How do you feel about snake handling?

REV. NATIONS, JR.: Now let me tell you what I think about that one, and I don't mean to be comical. I pride myself in one thing, and that's not being critical of my preaching friends and brethren in opposite denominations. I pride myself because I've preached for nineteen years. In my business here [filling station/bait shop], I never criticize my competition next to me—I never do. You can't get one of my customers to tell you that they ever heard me criticizing my competition over the road. I pride myself in not doing that. I do that same thing in my church. You could talk to my church members; I never criticize. I don't think God is happy when we do that. I've been a Christian for almost twenty-one years, and the Lord has worked marvelous things in my life, and that's the truth. I oftentimes mention this in my preaching wherever I am—that I know God is for real because He has done so many things for me, when I gave Him my life, that I couldn't do for myself. I tried to be a better person; I tried to be a cleaner person. I made decision after decision that would backfire the next day. When I actually surrendered my life to the Lord, then He changed my life in the manner I'd been trying to, and I appreciate what He's done for me down through the years. But what He'd have to do to get me to pick up a snake, I'd have to be beyond myself, I grant you. I could not know anything about it or I would not do it.

REV. NATIONS, SR.: He answered for me and, I think, for most of the other Free Will Baptists. I'd handle a snake, all right, if his head was cut off and I had on gloves!

Do you believe in Divine healing?

REV. NATIONS, JR.: Absolutely; I believe that. Three weeks ago I had a true experience with that. I believe that God heard and answered prayers in behalf of a man that's fifty-nine years old. Ever since I've been pastoring my church, we've been praying continually to see this man saved. He went to the hospital and when they did surgery on him, they said that there was no chance; it was cancer of part of his stomach and his lower intestine, and they didn't see any hope. But they went ahead and sewed him back up after his surgery, and they kept him there trying to build him up until they could do surgery and take out the tumor. People kept praying and witnessing to him and now he's back on his job. Three weeks ago, he made an open profession in church. I believe it was a divine

act of God. Yes sir, I do. But as far as me being able to walk up
to you and laying my hands on you and saying, "I command You,
Lord, to heal this man"—I'm sure you've seen some of that on
TV or somewhere—no sir, I don't think we have the right to do
that. I do believe with all my heart that God hears a humble prayer.
I don't know of any greater medicine that I'd rather have if I was
real sick than to know that people who believe in the Lord were
finding time and a place to pray for me, pray for my healing. Yes
sir, I believe in Divine healing.

REV. NATIONS, SR.: We do preach the fifth chapter of James. Call it
for them, Brother Ted. . . .

REV. NATIONS, JR.: "If any among you are sick let him call for the
elders of the church and they'll anoint him with oil and the . . ."

REV. LANEY: ". . . prayers of the saints will save the sick and if they
have any sins, they will be forgiven."

*Is part of the worship service to invite those
desiring prayer for sickness to the front?*

REV. NATIONS, JR.: Not mine, no sir.

REV. LANEY: We have, yes, up at our church.

REV. NATIONS, SR.: We let them make that choice. If we're in church
and some feel like they desire prayer and want us to pray, we anoint
them with oil and pray with them. We don't ask them to come at
any time.

James says, "If any among you are sick, let *him* call for the elders
of the church and let them anoint him with oil. The prayers of
the saints shall save the sick and if he has any sins, they shall be
forgiven him." We practice that—but not as much as we used to.
We used to keep a bottle of oil sitting in the Bible stand or some-
wheres at all times, and if anyone asked for prayer, why, we'd pray
with them. But, they'd ask; we didn't ask them. Then if someone
was to send for me to come over and pray with them, if it was
fifteen miles, I'd go. I'd try to go believing what James said, "If
any among ye are sick, let him call for the elders of the church . . ."

REV. NATIONS, JR.: I think the general stand of the Free Will Baptists
is somewhat based on that one verse in the Book of James. I think
if you were going to say something about the stand that the Free
Will Baptists took, you'd probably do well to mention that they
do use James' Gospel quite a bit.

Have you, personally, ever seen anyone healed?

REV. LANEY: Yes, I have. I can take my ownself, just this past Easter.
A little over a year ago, I had a real heart attack; but up through

the Easter weekend, there was a blood clot somewhere in my chest in between my shoulder and my heart. Even this big artery was swollen until it was as big as my finger. Well, I went through all the weekend preaching, and I started a week of coming to the church and having prayer and nothing else at night—of a night, just a solid week of coming to church praying. I told some of my members Wednesday evening, I said, "If this don't move, I'm going to have to go back to the hospital and get something done." They said, "If you can, wait until prayer meeting's over tonight; maybe it'll be gone."

During that service, God heard and answered someone's prayer. Someone's faith reached God; or maybe three or four, or maybe the whole congregation, 'cause when I went to the trailer after service was over, I was feeling some better. I went to bed and I went to sleep right off. I got up the next morning and had not a pain, not a bit of swelling, nothing. There's not been any pains of the heart in any way since then. God hears prayers.

REV. NATIONS, SR.: When I was pastoring the same church that [Rev. Nations, Jr.] is pastoring now, there was a small child took sick and they rushed him to the hospital. They thought he was dying or at the point of death. We had prayer and in the next hour I told the folks, "I have a car sitting out there and it's full of gas. If any of you think that the baby isn't better, just get in the car and go to the hospital and see." The baby had improved and came home the next day. We were at church and we had prayer, and in an hour's time, when the service was dismissed [the baby had improved].

In three years, I've been in the hospital eighteen different times, myself. I'm a diabetic. I've been in there for bursitis, arthritis, and everything, and I've had many prayers prayed for me. Shortly, I'd come out. I'm still a diabetic; there's never been anyone prayed the prayer of faith that I'd be healed as a diabetic, but as far as arthritis, bursitis, and all that, why, I guess I'm about as limber as any sixty-six-year-old man.

Did Free Will Baptists have circuit preachers?

REV. NATIONS, JR.: Brother Henry Cochran, one of the first Free Will Baptists ministers [in this area] told me that at one time he used to leave the head of Alarka Creek and walk across the mountain and preach where I'm at—at the Sawmill Hill Free Will Baptist Church—on Saturday at noon. Then, he'd walk right over to the Almond Depot and catch a train, and ride over to Andrews, which is twenty-five miles on the train. He'd walk up to the Beaver Creek

River Baptist Church, which is about a three-mile walk, and have a Saturday night service. He'd stay all night there and get up on Sunday morning and walk across Atowa Mountain down into Graham County and have a Sunday morning service and a Sunday night service with them. Then on Monday morning, he'd walk out to Thompton and catch a train back to the mouth of Alarka, and get off and walk back, which is about five miles back to where he lives. He said he did that many times and got paid fifty cents on it for a round trip.

REV. NATIONS, SR.: Speaking of pastoring two churches, I used to come to Alarka on Saturday morning, preach Saturday night and Sunday morning, and I left to go back to Conley Springs and preached Sunday night and Wednesday night. I tried pastoring them two [which I couldn't do now]; I'd get up at four o'clock Saturday morning, rain or shine, sleet or snow, come this way and preach Saturday night and Sunday morning, and go back down there at Sunday night, ministering.

How often do you have services?

REV. NATIONS, JR.: We have service on Sunday morning, Sunday night, and Wednesday night.

What is the purpose of revivals and singings?

REV. NATIONS, JR.: A revival is to revive the individual. In other words, the man that's lost and don't know anything about the Lord, you don't revive him; you work toward getting him saved. But a revival is to revive the individual Christian; to bring us closer together in fellowship with one another and God. That's what a revival is for.

As far as singings are concerned, there is diverse opinions on what the singings really do. Used to be, I think, it was much different than it is now. The professional end of singing, I think, is hurting the gospel work more than it is helping it; however, up here we have singings. A great deal of time you'll get in one where the Spirit and power of God intervene, and people are drawn closer together in fellowship and love toward one another and in God. But, singing as a whole . . . there is certainly differences of opinion as to what it does really do.

Nearly every Saturday somewhere in this county, there is a singing. And you'll have your different groups. Most of the time, churches come together. One church may have a quartet or two quartets and a choir; for instance, the Alarka Baptist Church has two good gospel quartets. They're good, too. And they have a number-one choir. My church has a quartet and a choir. Most of the churches do, and on a Saturday night—any given Saturday night—somewhere in the county there is a gospel singing in a church. They tell me that they used to have a gospel singing convention on the courthouse lawn out here in the square in Bryson City every so often. Mostly, it consisted of church choirs and they had these old-timers that knew music real good. They had judges of the singings. They'd walk around and look over people's backs and watch the music as they sang, and they graded them.

PLATE 19   Mrs. Selma Mosely.

SELMA MOSELY, Black Baptist

Mrs. Selma Mosely, a member of the Ivy Hill Baptist Church, firmly believes in "reading and studying God's Word regularly." A Baptist and resident of the mountains all her life, Mrs. Mosely joined the church when she was eleven years old and has been actively involved in its affairs since that time. She has served as a Sunday school teacher, leader of the small children's "Sunbeam" group, and president of the "Missionary Circle." Although Mrs. Mosely never received any formal music or voice lessons, she serves as pianist and singer at Ivy Hill, crediting her musical ability as being "a gift from God." In fact, Selma came from a large family that included eleven children, many of whom were musically inclined. She remembers several of her brothers "picking up by ear" such instruments as the ukelele, accordian, and guitar. Mrs. Mosely strongly holds to her beliefs and faith in the Christian experience. In this interview she discusses her religion as being the real, sustaining force in her life.

KEITH HEAD

I joined the church when I was eleven years old. I attended church [and] different church activities during all my girlhood and as a teen-ager. My father was a minister. [Back then] when you were young, you were just taught to go to church and then you played in different activities. I was in the choir and I was teacher of the intermediate class in Sunday school and then [I] was in the prayer service—*that* I loved. That's really where I got converted—in prayer service. My father always led the prayer devotional. We had BYPU

(Baptist Young People's Union); I was president of that. Then we had a Junior Young Women Circle once a week. The older women had a Missionary Circle. So, it kept us busy. [I was] very active [in the church] all during my young life even up until this present year of 1977. I came here in Rabun County [Georgia] in 1947, [a year after I married]. I was here for just a few months until I connected up with the Ivy Hill Baptist Church. I've been a member ever since and I've been active in the church here ever since I've been here, and I've been here thirty years.

I try to stay busy [with church work]. When I had more youngsters, I organized a little club we called the Sunbeams. I went with the children—the girls and the boys. This went on until now it's almost run out and I don't have anything to work with. There is a little group now, but it seems they are not interested anymore. I don't know. When the change came, it really stunned me. I prayed and I said, "Lord, I never thought the time would come that I wouldn't have anything to work with." I don't know whether it was the generation gap, you know. When I was working with this last young crew, they got to where they didn't want to recite their pieces; they didn't want to learn them. And then they didn't want to read them. So, if you don't do one of the two, there's nothing for you to do. I used to have all types of programs on all different occasions like Christmas, Easter—different holidays. I would have programs for these children and we would have a real good time. I really, really hated when the time came that I didn't have anything to work with. Now, this other little group—the last group that I'm working with, they don't even bring their children to church. So, therefore, you can't work with somebody when you [can't] really get close to them. If I say anything to them I have to say it in the street because they just don't come to church. You can't get the message over. For a long time it was funny but sad—I would always invite them to come to church. I'd say, "God loves you, I love you, and I know the rest of them that come [do too]." This went on and on and then they got to the place when they would see me coming, instead of me saying it to them, they would say, "Miss Selma, we're coming to church." See, they beat me to the draw, but they weren't coming. I got the message real quick. Seems like they couldn't get the message when I was trying to give it to them, but I got their message. So, I don't say anything to them now. Very seldom ever do I invite them to church because the church is right there, and they know the doors swing on welcome hinges.

It's a sad picture. It's very sad, because I think of the young people of today and as I have my morning devotional every morning, I pray for the young people. I *love* young people. I *love people,* regardless, I just love people. You know, there is a better way than the wrong way. The right way is the best way. If one will accept Jesus Christ as their personal Savior—they should just give Him a try. They should find out for themselves.

I was talking to a lady last night over the telephone. I said, "You know, you think about the coming of Christ," [and He is coming again because He said He was]. "You think now when we leave this earth, we will be at the resting place until the resurrection, because He said the dead will be caught up at the first trumpet sound and that [trumpet's] going to be for the righteous." And those that are here on the earth are going to be caught up, too; that's going to be the righteous. He said, "It was appointed to man to die and after death there is the judgment." But there will be some [living] on this earth when He comes. Everyone is not going to be dead. So, I said, "It is worthwhile for anybody just to think about what the Lord promised us—life eternally." And I said, "Just think, there isn't going to be any more hatred, any more death; there isn't going to be anything but peace and happiness forever and eternity. He promised that to everybody, not one individual group, not one race. He said He had no respect of person." Isn't that wonderful when you just think about it? Heaven is going to be here on this earth. This is God's earth. John said he [saw] the new heaven and the new earth coming down, so it's got to be coming down; it's got to be here. To think that you're just going to live forever and eternity without pain, without sickness . . . He said no more tears. All of that is going to be done away with. This old body that we're living in—it's going back to the dust. From dust He made it and that's where it will return. The soul is what He wants. He said He has a new body for us and that body is going to be a perfect body. Mine's worn out anyway. It's filled with pains and things. Not too many people don't have pains with their bodies. You take the older people that live and have already gotten rackety, they're not going to have to live in those old bodies. He's got us new bodies. It's a wonderful life.

As I told you, I joined the church early, at eleven years old. I've not been perfect, but I've been trying very hard. I remember when I was converted. Back when I was a girl, they used to call for mourners. I don't know whether you all know anything about this or not because they have done away with this in all the churches. When you were a sinner, you went up to that mourner's bench and the Christian people would pray with you. I mean they would pray with you a week, two weeks, or ever how long it took until you felt like

God had forgiven you of your sins and that you were ready to accept Him as your personal Savior. There were thirteen of us, I remember very well, and we were at that mourner's bench about a week. Maybe we didn't understand or know [why], but we were there. We felt something had happened and the change had come. We had accepted Christ as our personal Savior and then we were baptized.

As I said, back when I was a girl, the older women had what they called a Missionary Circle and they would sometimes have an evening prayer service. I was always with the older group. I followed them to these meetings. I liked that. I would sing as a girl—vocal, not with the piano. God gave me the gift of singing and I have sung in church and prayer service until I have seen those old women shout and almost look like they were going to tear the building down. You don't see too much of that now. Back then people were really with it. You know what I mean? They were very active in Christ. Those old mothers and fathers were happy because tears would just be [falling]. As a girl, I said, "Lord, I don't have what they've got, and I want it. I want to know that You are alive! I want to move and I want You to move me!" I didn't want to be doing it on my own and faking it, I wanted to really know that He was a living Savior. I went to evening prayer service and, when they called altar, I went back [to accept Christ again]. When I came through that time, I understood the Lord more because I was older.

[Conversion] was the best [feeling], honey; there is no comparison. There is *nothing* in this world, *nothing* that compares with it. It doesn't last, and it couldn't, because I don't think man could stand it. You know, the Lord says He doesn't dwell with man at all times. Now this is what you call the Holy Spirit, when He racks that marvelous body of yours. I mean it is something. When it's all over, everything looks so new, everything is so different and you are ready—I mean, you let the Lord use you. You just open [your] mouth and He puts the words in. I mean the Lord will use you. That I know. I thought of the verse where Jesus was talking to Nicodemus. He said, "Nicodemus, you must be born again." Conversion and accepting Jesus Christ is kind of like a new born baby. You take a little baby, it's going to be nursed, breast fed or either bottle fed for maybe a year, and then the growth just keeps coming. Directly the baby is going to start crawling, and after a while, it's going to start trying to walk. This is Christian life. I mean, you can't get it all at one time. You've got to grow in it. The Lord tells us, He says, "My grace is sufficient to keep you." He will keep us. Then He said in running the race, be patient. So, we have to be patient. You just don't get all of this at one time.

They [used to shout] in services. Yes sir. You don't see that anymore. You think people now are serving a dead God, but God is
not dead. He is alive. You know He went to the grave, didn't He?
He stayed three days, but He rose. He is a living God. You can
go into church and people are sitting up just like monuments. Just
still. If you can't feel something, I think something's wrong. I think
you need to go back and ask God to give you that that will move
you, because He is a living God and He'll move you! You're going
to clap your hands and you're going to say "Amen." I go to churches
and say "Amen" and sometimes people look around, and I mean
you can see them looking. But it doesn't make any difference, because
when I hear the truth, you know I can witness. The Lord wants us
to be witnesses. He doesn't want us to be silent. He wants us to
let the world know He is alive. He wants us to talk, He wants us
to be active, He wants us to sing. He said, "Sing praises with a
shout!" This is what you don't see anymore.

[My father] was a minister and he was the superintendent of the
Sunday school and also of the prayer service. I've heard my father
preach and I've heard him pray. My father lived to be eighty-nine
years old. There were twelve of us [children]. I was the baby of
the crowd. So there was a large family. My mother was a good
Christian woman. She lived a very sweet life. I had a wonderful
mother and the Lord called her at the age of sixty-three, which
then [was old]. Now, in this generation, people [at sixty-three] are
not old. Not even at eighty. They say the "girls" of eighty. When
I turned fifty, I told my son, "I can remember when my mother
was fifty, she was an old lady. Now that I'm fifty, I don't really
feel old. I know I'm headed in that direction, but I don't feel old."
But she was old and at sixty-three she died.

I've been in [prayer] service with my father. I can remember the
first prayer that I ever prayed in public. I asked him, as a girl, I
said to him, "Papa, I want you to call on me to pray."

He said, "You want to pray?"

And I said, "Yes."

I was [so] looking forward to this all week I just could hardly
do any good, because I was thinking about Wednesday night prayer
meeting, when he was going to call on me to pray. Now, understand,
I didn't study any books or anything. You know, they do have books
and it's all right to study them. I believe in studying. But I didn't
study a prayer. I'll never forget that Wednesday night. I just kept
looking at my father. I'm sure he couldn't do any good [preaching],
because every minute I was just looking at him to call me. Eventually
he did call me. It frightened me so bad and I was so looking forward

for it [that], when I got down to pray the Lord's Prayer, I went through the first part of it and then it just left. It just went away from me. I couldn't even think of it. I knew the Lord's Prayer, but it just went away from me, and I finally said, "Amen" and got up. I was very embarrassed and I told him after prayer service, "Don't call on me anymore."

He said, "Yeah, I'm going to call on you again." He said, "You keep praying."

He knew I could say the Lord's Prayer, because back when I went to school, we had devotional of the morning and [we] said the Lord's Prayer and the Twenty-Third Psalm in concert. I guess it was just the excitement of being in public my first time. I kept praying until the Lord really let me pray. When my mother was sick, she used to call me to the room and ask me to pray for her. So, I've had a wonderful life. I've tried both ways. I've tried the wrong and I've tried the right way, and the right way is better than the wrong way. If anybody can accept Christ and let Him come into their life, He can make a beautiful life for them. The Lord has all of this beauty out here, and you know, people walk to and fro in this earth and never see it because they're blind to it.

Back when I was a girl, they used to have the revival services. They had one week of prayer. This was to get the Christians heated up and ready. Then, when the preacher came in, honey, he *had* to preach. Oh, yeah! That second week those Christians were really on fire! That preacher—all he had to do was hit the pulpit, and I mean he'd preach his heart out! He had to, because it was so warm you could feel the love and the Holy Spirit. He had to! There used to be some of the best revival services that I believe I've ever seen. And the young people, I mean they would come into the church. And most of the time, there weren't too many that stayed away from the altar, either. I mean they would come in and accept Christ, you know. But this is what has happened; they have taken this out of the church, you know what I mean? They don't have the altar call anymore. They say, "You come and give me your hand and God your heart." But I [think] that's why a lot of people in these churches don't have the love of Jesus. They don't know anything about Him because they never really went through the part to accept Him as their personal Savior. Their name is on the church book— they are members—and the churches are full of members, don't you all agree? They're full of members. "But my name's on the church book." But, see, that's not enough. We have to accept the Lord as our personal Savior. The most precious gift that has ever been given [was] when God gave His Son to the world. Wasn't it?

He gave His *own* Son that whosoever believeth on Him shall not perish, but have everlasting life. So this is what He has promised us and I believe it. I believe every word.

You know, I'm not a fanatic, but I try to be very religious in my everyday life. I want to live a good life. I want to live a life that will please God. Then if it pleases God, it will have to please man. It will just have to. Then if [man] doesn't agree with me, I'm just going to go on anyway. Yeah. I don't want to miss what God has promised for me, and what He promised for me, He promised for everybody. Everybody has this right, and this is what I really like about it. And this is what I tell my church people. In our Christian life, you don't have to be jealous of what I do and you don't have to be jealous of what the other person does, God has a work for every individual. A Christian family is like a puzzle—every piece has to fit in before the puzzle is worked. The Lord tells us, He says, "I'll pay you by your works." He said, "Behold, I come quickly and My reward with Me. I'll pay each man according to his works." Now He has a work for us. We don't go in just being a [church] member, we have to go in and then do the work that the Lord has for us. You know, there was a writer that wrote, "If you can't sing like angels, and if you can't preach like Paul, you can tell the love of Jesus that He died for all." That's so true. See, everybody can tell that. It's just a wonderful life. I'm going to tell you what the Lord said. I know you've read it, you've heard it. The Lord said, "Seek ye first the Kingdom and My righteousness and all things shall be added."

[After the revivals, we'd have baptizings] on the river banks, you know. Of course, now people have pools in the church, but back [then] you were baptized in a creek! Or a river, you know. I mean, honey, they would be lined up on the banks. It was just beautiful. Now when I was baptized, there were thirteen of us. That was a pretty good-sized baptizing. People back then would go to church, and at the baptizings, the people would be lined up along the banks. And those old ladies, honey, and the fathers would be shouting and praising God. Yeah. The deacon would carry one [person] at a time to the minister.

Most of the [baptizings were in the summertime] or in the fall. They never did baptize too much in the winter. Of course, when I worked at the hospital and the hotels, it was Sunday work and then I didn't get to go to service [and baptizing] as much as I'd liked to. You know, God said He chastened those He loves. He loves us all, but sometimes when you think you're getting away [from] or not doing the things that would be pleasing to God, something's going to happen. I'm going to show you what happened to me.

I was working [on Sunday]. I sent my money, but see, that wasn't enough. You don't pay in. He didn't say we were going to pay through. He said He was going to pay us by our works. I was sending in the money, but I was out there working. You know, I was stricken down in 1968 with phlebitis, and I laid for one year before I could walk. I thought I wasn't going to walk anymore. I had a lot of time on my hands, I had a lot of praying, I had a lot of crying and talking to the Lord. And after the doctors and nurses did all they could, the Lord healed me. It's been ten years and I'm not able to work anymore, not full time. I had to go on disability. I broke down at the age of forty-eight, so I was young. I wasn't old enough for social security, but I could get disability. The Lord has been good to me these [ten] years. He's let me know that He is the Way-maker. I thank Him because I haven't had to beg. Not a day. He said, "I will supply your needs." He didn't say my wants now, my *needs*. I thank Him. I'm grateful, and I think these years have put me closer to the Lord than ever in my life.

I really, truly believe in healing, because I've been healed so many times. I'm not a person that runs to the doctor too much. I've been healed by people coming in praying for me and I've been healed just talking to Him, myself.

[Years ago] a lot of the young people, if they got in trouble or depressed or felt like they needed somebody to talk to, would come to my father or he would go to them. All he wanted to know was if they needed him. He always tried to lend a helping hand and reach out for someone. This is my main goal. I think a lot of my father and, of course, of Mother, too. I know their prayers helped me through life. I know I'm not the best person in the world, but I'm not the worst. If I hadn't had Christian parents [who] disciplined me and pointed out that the way of the cross leads home, I probably would have been a worse person than I am. I probably wouldn't even be living for the Lord. Finding Him at an early age and being in a Christian home [with] a Christian father and a Christian mother helped me through life. It's really helped me.

Older people used to help one another with their children. If they saw your child do something, why, if they didn't whip you, they'd make you think they were going to whip you, and they *sure* were going to tell your parents. You were going to get the whipping! So you got it from your parents. But, you know, people are running away from that. They could see somebody's child out here fixing to kill one another [and they'll say,] "I'm not going to get involved. I'm not going to say anything. It's none of my business." And this is the way the world is going, and this is bad. This is bad. If I didn't know you, and I saw you doing wrong, I'd like to say something. To let you know that you're just doing wrong. You might not accept it. Sometimes I think if we got involved a little more, it would be a better world to live in. You know, I have a song, the title is, "If Everybody Was Like Jesus What a Wonderful World This Would Be." Everybody is not going to be like Jesus. But there are some that are trying to get like Him. I think this is the main goal. When the Lord saved us, He saved us to help save somebody else. He doesn't want us to be selfish. He wants us to spread His love and help people. This is my main goal. I love to reach out for somebody and do something or say something maybe to help somebody.

You know, when the Holiness came into North Carolina, my father and mother were the first people that opened the door for them. The little Holiness church that they have there now started in our living room in [Canton] North Carolina. They went from the little church—a plank church—to a big rock church. But it all started from my mother and father's living room. They were for [the Holiness church] and [they] went to the altar and kind of got saved and got live with it.

I went through it! We just stayed members in the Baptist church. Papa knew it was right because he was a minister. He had preached and he just got stronger in the Lord. They could speak in tongues, and my mother could, too. I'll tell you, they shouted the floor out in our living room. They had to put a new floor in it. They worshipped in our living room for two years. Over two years, and out of our living room went the Holiness church. It was Black, but now the whites and the Blacks congregate together and they have a wonderful time. See, I've been away from home a long time, but I go back every once in a while. They have a beautiful church. Everybody comes together now. Everybody is [a member of] his own church, but they do come together. Just like [our] church out here. We don't have any white members [and] over town they don't have Black members, but every so often, we can get together. All of God's people can get together.

I've had my feet washed. If I can still remember, it seems like this was something like an altar call, you know. They'd get them up there, [and] they'd take off the stocking and the shoe, and I reckon this really shows the love that you have for your brother or sister. You know the woman in the Bible . . . I guess this refers to what she did for Jesus. You know, she washed Jesus' feet with tears, and He was talking about the love that this woman had in her heart for Him, and no other one had offered to do this. This shows humbleness, too, to humble down to wash your feet. They'd just sing and pray, and they had these towels . . . it was something kind of on the order of taking the Lord's Supper. This kind of goes together. You could just feel the love running from heart to heart and, as they say, breast to breast. You can really feel love. I think we [should] get back to those kind of things like having a family altar with a Christian foot wash. I'm talking about the Christians now, and this is where it should begin. The Christian needs to get more involved and active. You know, there's scripture in the Bible where the Holy Ghost came in on people and they said they were drunk but they weren't drunk on alcohol, they were drunk on the Holy Ghost. I think a lot of us ought to get drunk on the Holy Ghost.

I've heard of [snake handling and drinking poison], but I haven't ever been in one of those types of meetings. I quote this scripture where the Lord says you can eat it or drink it and it will not hurt you, but you've got to be in the Lord. But you know, there have been people bitten out here from this snake handling. I wouldn't want to pick up any snake, because I'm scared of it.

Back when I was a girl, they had dances. They've always had dances. The dances have changed, just like everything else has changed. I look at the young people on the television dancing, [and] it's beautiful. They're doing more exercise—they've gotten more [physically] active than I guess we [were]. We didn't do all of that. I heard somebody on the television say they'd like to see the fox-trot. They did that back when I was a girl—fox-trot, Charleston, two-step, jitterbug—that was the names of the dances they had. Everything has changed. The girls and the boys used to dance together. The waltz, that was very popular. You find them doing that every once in a while, but most of the time they just single. Just everybody out there on the floor jumping, jerking, and a' hopping. It's all right. It's just different. The style of the girl's hair [has changed] and the boys wear the long hair. My mother used to braid my hair and she would wrap it. They used to say this would [make] your hair grow and mostly that's what we were wearing it for, but we would take this stuff off and take it down on Sunday and style it in some way. But life kind of repeats itself a little bit on the styles, the fashions, the hairdos and things. My father wore a moustache. The older men used to wear the thick moustache and kind of twist it at the end—kind of twirl it up. And they wore the little goatee on the chin.

[The church looked down on our fashions and dances a little bit.] I think they've always done that. The churches were kind of strict but they would talk to us and tell us. A lot of times we'd think [to ourselves] or say to another young person, [that] they were meddling or something like that, [but] you didn't say it to the older people. You just didn't let that go out. I mean, you respect people and you respect old people and the churches. The young people were young and [the old people] would say, "You're going to sow your wild oats." I guess you've heard that version. But when you get the wild oats sowed, you're apt to be through with that part of life. I think this is true. I don't think you can take young people and make old people out of them. In this age [the] young have so much to confront them. It looks like [life has] more to offer you all than it [had] to offer, say, back in my generation. So, this is why I pray so hard for the young people, because I've been young. We all have. We've been through that stage—one way or the other, we had to get through it. We have to pray for these young people and help them to get through that stage. After you get over that, life can be beautiful. You're going to learn more about life. Of course, some people never get through with it. You take some of these old people, [they] still have to do things they did back when they were young. Trying to repeat life! I [say] that doesn't make sense. You don't repeat it, you just keep going forward. I see a lot of them trying to repeat it, but that's not really good. I was telling the taxi driver the other day, I was telling him I didn't want to repeat life, but there would be a lot of things maybe I did coming through that I wouldn't have done [if I'd known then what I know now]. I'd try to make it a better life. But I don't want to go back and repeat what I've done. No, I want to look forward. We know what we've done in the past, but we don't know what the future holds. But we do know who holds the future.

[I think we're living in the last days, now.] I really do. According to what the Lord has told us, He said, "When [you] see these signs, you look up and know that your deliverance is drawing nigh." And, according to the Bible, we can look up and expect God anytime, because we are in the last days. We are in them. According to God's Bible—and I read that Bible, and I don't say "daily" because I don't do it in the day, I do it at night. I read that Bible every night. I search God's Holy Word and pray constantly, and then at times

I get the encyclopedia and I get my dictionary on the Bible, and I try to run reference. I believe in people studying God's Word. Paul told Timothy, "Study to show thyself approved unto God," so, I believe in studying. We [should] notice the things that God has told us and the signs that He has given. He tells us as you see the fig trees and the leaves, the winter and the summer, then [those are] some signs. He says when you see these things happening, just look up and know your deliverance is drawing nigh. I'm looking for it. He says, "Not even the angels in Heaven know the time." But He says, "Watch and pray." So, we know not the minute or the hour the Son of Man cometh, but He said, "Be you also ready." Just be ready. He isn't going to give us any warning. He's already told us everything He's going to tell us. It's up to us now.

PLATE 20   Mrs. Beulah Perry.

BEULAH PERRY, Black Baptist

In Foxfire 3, *students, Beverly Justus Phillips and Vivian Burrel, introduce Beulah Perry as "one of the most beautiful people we have ever met." Mrs. Perry is indeed that and more and we deeply value her friendship and support. As well as an extensive personality article that appeared in* Foxfire 3, *Beulah Perry has been featured many times in our magazines and books, aiding in our research on a great number of topics. We have documented her making baskets out of white oak splits with Aunt Arie Carpenter; she has given us recipes for cooking possum and told us how to dye cloth with various wild plants; she has told us of her remembrances of old corncob-pipe-smoking midwives and granny women; and she has proved invaluable help with her information on old-time burial customs and the care of animals.*

Most important, however, to Beulah Perry are her religious beliefs and her association with her Baptist Church and her relationship to God. Beverly and Vivian also relate in Foxfire 3 *that "her belief in God and the Bible are the main forces in her life. She was brought up in a very religious atmosphere and these qualities shine through." We are again pleased to feature Beulah Perry, this time in a religious context; a woman who is a living example of the Christian faith and ideal.*

KEITH HEAD

My grandparents died when I was about twelve or thirteen years old. My grandfather was a slave in his day. I don't know where he came from over in Africa. He was free by the time my mother was born. The people who had owned him gave him a little piece of land, about twenty-five acres. That sounded like just a garden spot then. The different white people would take a little bit of his land, and maybe another one would move in and take a little more, so eventually Grandfather wound up without any of it.

My parents were farmers. There were nine of us and I was the second child. We stayed on a big plantation; and then after we all grew up, my father bought a little place. I was raised on a farm and we had a good time. When I look back on when we were young, it seems like we had more fun than the young people do now. We had more leisure time.

We had six months of school a year, three months one time and three months another time. When it came time to work the crop, school would close. Then it would open again when we were through working the crop.

We went to church. That's one thing we did. You know, that's something that gets away with me now. My father and mother carried us to church and Sunday school, and now there's so many young people that don't even go to church, much less Sunday school. It seems so strange to me to see a mother and dad with four or five little kids and not taking them to and from church. We were raised up to go to church. On Sunday evenings we didn't do like children do now—running around. We played and had fun but it wasn't loud. It was quiet on a Sunday. We recognized the day as the Lord's day, so we had fun but it was in a calm kind of a way.

I was converted when I was nine or ten years old. I never will forget. There was a revival going on and when I was a kid, the parents carried the children to the altar. They'd have altar calling and the parents would carry their children to the altar. The preacher talked that night and said for the people to pray for everyone and that the Lord would bless us.

The next morning I went to get water from the spring for my mother. On my way to the spring I got to thinking about the meeting that night. I thought about what the preacher had said. As I was coming back [to the house], I set my bucket of water down and I prayed. I was in a little patch of pines about as big as these two rooms. Then something just happened. I didn't know what it was. I couldn't quit crying. I just felt good. I knew I was happy and tears kept coming. I went on to the house and I carried my water in, set it on the table, and Mother noticed something unusual about me. I don't know what it was unless it was the tears or my eyes [which] were red. I hurried out the door. But my mama called me, "Beulah, wait a minute. What's the matter?" She said, "Come here." I went to her and I told her I didn't know what was wrong.

I said, "I was coming on back from the spring and I stopped

and prayed, and I reckon I got happy." I said, "I can't stop crying."

As I was talking to her, the tears were coming down and she said, "Well, the Lord has blessed you. You've been converted." Mama took her apron and wiped the tears away, and she said, "You've been wanting to join the church. You can join now. When you join the church, you have to be a good girl."

So the next day or two one of the elderly ladies in our church came to visit Mama and I was in the kitchen, so I heard Mama telling about what had happened to me. This lady said, "I told you the other day that child was converted and to let her join the church. Now you let that child join the church tonight."

I've been a Christian ever since. My mother and daddy were Methodist. We were all born, raised, and converted in a Methodist home but we moved out to a community where there wasn't any Methodist church. There was only a Baptist church and the Baptist people wanted us to join their church. We talked to Papa about it and he said it was all right to join. He said, "The church ain't gonna save you. All God wants is a pure heart." He said, "It's nice to be in a church but when you're in a church, do right. If you ain't gonna do right, there's no need of joining a church." So we joined the church there. We were just raised up to believe that way. I guess I was about thirteen when we moved out of the community and joined the Baptist church.

I always wanted to be missionary and still, yet, I'd like to be one. Every once in a while I sit down and I think, "Sometime I'll get to go to Africa yet." Maybe it's just that I want to go makes me think that I'll get to go. I was talking to Reverend Letson, the Baptist preacher in town, and he said sometimes when we couldn't get to go places like we wanted to do, God had a mission here at home for us to do and just to do everything I could for the Lord and He would understand the rest. But I always wanted to be a missionary.

My father had an uncle who sold his little plantation and went to Africa (he and his whole family) when I was about ten or eleven years old. I wanted to go with them. One of the girls and me were good friends and I wanted her to tell her dad to let me slip off with them. She told her daddy and he told me, no, he couldn't do that—that it would break Papa's heart. He said, "Now you be a good missionary here at home and someday you'll get to come to Africa."

I haven't got to go yet and you know, I think sometimes the Lord always has had it so. [Sometimes when] we want to go to places, [if] we'll stop and do some little something around where we live that will help somebody else, that's a part of a mission. I think sometimes, "I may not go, but if it's God's will or had been His will, I would have gone." There's a mission around us. There's something around here I can do and the Lord knows I can do it better here than I could anywhere else. He had a purpose for it.

Back when I was a little girl coming along, we had those big revivals every summer for about two weeks. We just had preaching and singing and praying and church things. [There was] prayer meeting every night and maybe two or three of the elder people would testify, different ones singing and praying and telling about their conversions. There was calling to the altar and praying for people.

We didn't get to have our [revival] this year. We were building the new church. I have really missed it—it's kind of like you don't feel right when you don't have that revival. I hope we get to have one next year. I like church. You know, it's hard to get away from the way you [were] raised, isn't it?

Some of the rich people's churches don't make as big a to-do as we poor peoples do. They have a kind of dignity or something. They have their [church] meeting but it's just mild and in a quiet way. Some of them, not all of them, are that way and some of them just let the Lord use them in a big way like we do. Now you take the Holiness churches and the Black people's churches. Those churches and ours have church pretty well alike. We just have a big time. I don't know that you do get as much out of those quiet kinds of services. I guess the word of the Bible is strengthening to us.

We do go around to different churches and they come to ours for different meetings and things. One night another church had their Saturday night singing at our church and it was such a glorious thing. That's one thing about the people in different churches, they will come to the other's rescue. They will do that and I think that is the best thing there is. I think when God comes to get His church, He won't just get certain people. He wants all of those pure hearts; that's what He comes for and I think about that a lot. When God comes back and gets His children together, they'll be from everywhere—every church and nation. That's a glorious thing.

Roman Catholics

And I tell thee this is my turn,
that thou art Peter, and it is upon this rock
that I will build my church;
and the gates of hell shall not prevail against it . . .

Matthew 16:18–19

The Catholics represent a comparatively new denomination in the mountains but one whose numbers are steadily on the increase. In Rabun County, for example, during the last twenty years, the Catholic church has grown from a few members to several hundred. Other Catholic churches in small towns near here also show substantial growth.

To a large extent, Catholics reflect the newer population content of the mountains. Many Catholics, such as Lina Davis, who is presented in this section, came into non-Catholic mountain areas and realized a need for their own church. As Mrs. Davis points out, more and more Catholics became established in this area, for reasons including business and recreation, and thus the local church was born.

We feel that the Catholic Church is a strong force in the religious community, continuing to grow and add members, be they new converts or others moving in. As religious acceptance and tolerance take hold, the Catholics can look forward to productive and positive times ahead.

PAUL F. GILLESPIE

LINA DAVIS, Roman Catholic

Lina Davis, a member of the Catholic church, represents one of the newest denominations in our mountainous region. Mrs. Davis was born in central Italy and lived much of her childhood in Milano, the second largest city of that country. During World War II, she met and married John Davis, an American soldier, and they returned to the United States in January 1947. Mr. Davis is a practicing attorney and Mrs. Davis is actively involved in community volunteer service, including work with young people's organizations

PLATE 21   Lina Davis.

and the local nursing home. She is an active participant in the affairs of
her church and explains in the following interview how this particular Catholic
congregation came into existence and grew strong in this area.

KEITH HEAD

When I first arrived in Rabun County from my native Italy in January 1947, there was no Catholic church or Catholics living in the area. The closest Catholic church was sixty miles away in Gainesville. I attended mass in Franklin, North Carolina, [where] the Sunday services were held in a private home.

In 1956, Walt Disney arrived to make a movie, *The Great Locomotive Chase,* with a crew that was largely Catholic. The crew worked hard seven days a week and had little time to travel to North Carolina for mass, so the Bishop of Atlanta gave special permission for the Franklin priest to offer mass in Clayton. By this time a few more Catholics had settled in the area and after the Disney people left, mass continued to be offered in Clayton.

For a place of worship the parishioners had the use of the Community House or the Legion Hall. There were very few members; but, in the summertime, tourists increased attendance at services to between 100 to 130 people. Then, one day, as a miracle, a church in Pennsylvania decided they wanted to do something in the mission field and chose to build a much-needed Mission Church in Clayton, paying practically all the costs. In November 1961 the proud congregation attended the first service in their own little church. As time passed companies from northern states relocated in Rabun County, bringing along personnel and the parish grew from fifteen families to forty-five and is continuing to grow.

The pastor stays pretty busy. Besides St. Helena in Clayton, he serves also St. Mark in Clarkesville, and provides religious services at the reform school in Alto; and with the assistance of a nun, teaches religious education for adults and children during the week.

When I first came over and the church wasn't here, I went to [the Baptist] church with my husband. A few times I was sitting in there with a lump in my throat because of the things they were saying about Catholics in the church. I was thinking to myself, "that's not true," and I turned to my husband and said, "but that's a lie." Finally I quit going. After the people got to know me and after they saw my beliefs and they saw the way I felt about the church and how the church came in, you wouldn't believe the change that came from them toward the Catholics. In fact, now I don't even feel we are any different. [You see much more cooperation.] Now older prejudice is gone—I know it's gone. The Episcopalians went through the same thing when they came in. But, you know, the Episcopal is just like the Catholic, except their ministers can marry if they want to and they don't recognize the pope as their leader. You can go in an Episcopalian church and you think you are in a Catholic church.

It is amazing how the presence of a church can change the mentality in a community. I remember how friendly and kind the people were when I arrived in 1947. Nonetheless, there was bigotry and hostility toward the Catholic religion, which began to change only after Catholic worship began in the county. Then people began to show tolerance at first, then respect and finally full acceptance.

My husband is a Baptist deacon. It works out beautifully, and we let our children choose what they wanted. As they were growing up, I sent them to Sunday school at the Baptist church before we had the [Catholic] church here. They wanted to know why Mama didn't go to the Baptist church and I explained it. And so they asked me, "Why can't we go with you?"

I said, "Fine," so they came [with me] and they were happy. So all my children are Catholic. My daughter is married now to a Baptist and there is no Catholic church [where they live], so she goes to church with him, which is fine to me. As long as she goes to church, I'm happy.

In Italy, when I was growing up, 90 percent [of the people] were Catholic. We knew there were Jews and Protestants, but they were just a word to us. They never taught us in school—you see, religion was a subject in school like geography and history—we didn't know anything about anything. For us, people were people. When my husband, when we were starting to marry, I knew he was Protestant, so we went for the application to get married and, for the first time, the priest said, "Well, you know your husband is Baptist."

And I said, "So?"

And he said, "Well, you know you can't [marry]. You need the dispensation."

That was the first time that I knew that I couldn't marry another faith. But, it was easy. We made the application, went through the pope and we had permission. [Dispensation] is getting permission to marry someone of another religion. It was no problem. Usually, at that time, they made the parents sign that the children be raised Catholic, but we didn't sign; we weren't asked. My parents were more concerned that he was a good boy. My mother said she hoped that I would stay with my religion. It never crossed my mind to change.

Our belief in God is generally the same as Protestants, maybe the rituals differ. If you stand and we kneel, there is a difference like that; but it doesn't make much difference. We believe on the consecration of the bread and the wine. We have real wine; we just barely wet the lips.

We were often accused of worshipping the statue and idols. Still now, we hear about it. We Catholics have pictures [of Christ] in our home and the crucifix and pictures of Mary. But, if you take the youth today, they have their rooms full of Elvis Presley and this and that. Why can't there be a picture of Christ? Or a statue of Mary? I'm a fan of those, and why do we have to be criticized for it?

We consider Mary as somebody special because she is the mother of Christ. I was told by some people here that she is a woman like us. I say, "No, she's not a woman like us. She's special. She was Christ's mother." I do pray to Mary to intercede for me. To pray for me. We don't worship Mary and say, "Hey, Mary, make a miracle." We ask her to pray for us. We believe in the Trinity. We believe that Mary is a holy person. I pray to God, but every once in a while, I say, "Mary, please help me." I turn to her like I would turn to, let's say, my mother. I say, "Mother, help me." But my mother is a mortal and Mary, to me, is in heaven. God is the one we really pray to, but we just ask for the help of Mary.

We have saints, but these saints existed. That doesn't mean that we worship St. Francis and ignore God—they are just soldiers of God. They are an inspiration to us. Their lives were an inspiration to us. We try to follow their example.

[We do believe in purgatory.] In the Catholic doctrine, purgatory is defined as a condition of temporary punishment for those who depart this life guilty of lesser faults. In the scripture we read, "But I say unto you that every idle word that man speak they shall give an account thereof in the day of judgment." (Matthew 12:36.) It is holy and wholesome to pray for the dead that they may be loosened from sins.

As Catholics, we do believe that, in order to be saved, we must believe upon the authority of God—the truth that God has revealed. Our Protestant friends believe that God has given us the means to know what He has taught—the Bible. But the Catholics say that at the time of Christ, the Bible had not been written. Christ did not say "sit down and write the Bible and let every man read and judge it for himself." He sent His apostles throughout the world to teach and baptize in the name of the Father and of the Son and of the Holy Ghost. Jesus never wrote a line of scripture nor did He command His apostles to do so, except when He directed St. John to write the Apocalypse 1:11, but He ordered them to go and teach all nations. At the time the King James Version of the Bible was authorized, seven books were omitted, so our Bible has [these books].

All religions outside the Catholic Church teach that the Bible is their rule of faith and men cannot be saved without the Bible. But the Bible was written fifteen hundred years after Christ. Errors were made during the many translations, consequently it has been interpreted in so many ways that five hundred different religions were founded, all quarreling with one another about the true interpretation.

History says that Christ founded His church. In laying the foundations, He spoke to the apostle Peter and the recorded words are, "Thou are Peter and upon this rock I will build my church." He did not say, "Martin Luther, upon you I will build my church," nor did He say, "Upon you James, or you Joseph Smith, you will build my church, the Mormon Church and so on." It is not possible to believe that Jesus founded a church and then, after fifteen hundred years approved five hundred contradictory sects founded by such men as the above. Jesus said His church will never teach errors, John 20:23.

[Our priests don't marry] because Christ, the great exemplar of the clergy whose ambassadors they are, was not married. St. John the Baptist, eulogized by Jesus as "the greatest man born of woman," was not married. Also, being free from family responsibilities, they can completely dedicate themselves and their work to the church. There are different orders of priests—Franciscan and Dominican. They are all highly educated—they are all university educated, many of them have a doctorate. When they become priests, they take a vow of poverty. They barely survive; they don't suffer, but they have just barely the necessities to go on day by day.

They have to take the vow [of priesthood] three times. Between those three times, time goes by and they make their life pretty strict and miserable—to see if they are strong enough to take it. Halfway some of them change their minds.

Our priests have to keep secrets. If a priest's brother is accused of a murder and the real murderer goes to that very priest and says, "Look, I did it," the priest cannot go to court and say, "Look, my brother didn't do it—so and so did it." The priest can't, for any reason—even if he has to die, even if his own life is at stake—he cannot break the secret of confession. [If the priest has someone confess that they are going to commit murder], he can tell the person that is going to be killed. He can say, "Look, you are going to be killed, so watch it." But he cannot reveal who said it. It is the secret of confession.

Nuns also don't marry. When they take the vow, those are the rules that they find, so they have to accept it or leave it. I would be in favor of them to marry. I feel like that if they let them marry, we would have more priests now. Because some of them want to be priests, but at the same time they want to have a family and children.

[Catholicism in Italy is much like it is here.] We were *very* strict—as a matter of fact, too strict, until Pope John XXIII. He was a marvelous, beautiful human being. He was down to earth. For example, confession—[now] we don't have to [be confessed] if we don't want to. We believe that confession helps to put us in a state of grace as we approach to receive the sacrament of Holy Communion. On the day of His resurrection, Christ said to His disciples, "Whose sins you shall forgive they are forgiven." Consequently, to the descendants of the disciples, the pastors of churches, God has given the power to absolve (John 20:23), providing we have sincere contrition and repentance. We have to confess mortal sin before we go to communion. When I'm through with confession, I feel so relieved.

We believe in miracles. There's nobody like Catholics that believe in miracles. We have the Bible and I try to understand the best I can. But sometimes I interpret things on my own. Now I don't believe literally in Adam and Eve. That's my mind. That's left up to us. I question lots of things, but that is normal. For me, religion is the way you live your life—it doesn't do any good if you are Catholic or Baptist or whatever if you are rotten. It's your everyday life, to me. That's what religion is, to live a good, clean, fear-of-God life.

Church Of Christ

Are you sowing seed of the seed of the kingdom, brother, In the morning bright and fair? Are you sowing the seed of the kingdom, brother, In the heat of the noonday's glare? For the harvest time is coming on and the reaper's work will soon be done; Will your sheaves be many? Will you garner any, For the gath'ring at the harvest home?   (from *Christian Hymns*)

Simply, the Church Of Christ maintains that its purpose is to restore New Testament Christianity, and moreover, it is the contention of those making up this church that theirs is the same church that was established by Jesus Christ, in approximately A.D. 33. According to spokesperson Wayne C. Rawlings, who is presented here, the Church Of Christ does not and will not compromise with those from other denominations concerning many Christian theological beliefs. Here Mr. Rawlings explains the views of the Church Of Christ, placing emphasis on the concepts of restoration of New Testament teachings. He also discusses the role of missions in bringing the Church Of Christ to areas such as our own.

PAUL F. GILLESPIE

WAYNE RAWLINGS, Church of Christ

This interview with Wayne C. Rawlings, minister of the Clayton Church of Christ, needs little introduction. Here Mr. Rawlings presents the beliefs of the Church of Christ in a straightforward manner. He states that the purpose of the Church of Christ is to restore New Testament Christianity—the religious teaching of Jesus Christ Himself. He places much emphasis on the belief that the church is "not a denomination" and "has no part of a denomination." He perceives his church as being the only "true" church and sees denominationalism as something confusing and unpleasing to God.

Mr. Rawlings is originally from Maryland, leaving there in 1951 to serve six and one half years in the military. In 1958, he became "a New Testament Christian" and one year later he married Sandra Daugherty from Chattanooga, Tennessee. In 1973, after fifteen years in the appliance business, he decided to become a gospel preacher and began preaching part-time in addition to attending school.

The Church of Christ was established in this area in 1974, and Mr. Rawlings came here shortly after that time. He feels that mission churches, such as this one, are extremely important and that the Church of Christ is generally making great strides all across the country.

KEITH HEAD

PLATE 22 Sandra and Wayne Rawlings.

I am Wayne C. Rawlings, the minister of the Clayton Church of Christ. The Clayton Church of Christ has been in [Rabun County, Georgia] for approximately four years. The reason why we are here is to restore New Testament Christianity just like you find in the Bible. The Church of Christ is not a denomination. It has no part of a denomination. The Church of Christ is the Body of Christ, Ephesians 1:22–23 and also Colossians 1:18. These scriptures state that the church is the body of Christ. Christ is the head of the church which He purchased with His blood, Acts 20:28. The church is not an accident, like some people teach. There are certain religions that teach that the church was an afterthought in the mind of God. They go on this theory that God was going to establish a kingdom. Well, God did do exactly that; he established a kingdom which is the church. The church was in the mind of God before the foundation of the world, Ephesians 3:9–11. And through the church, God was going to make known his manifold wisdom.

It all goes back to the beginning of time when man sinned. God created man, and God gave man and woman an opportunity to serve Him, but man sinned—he was disobedient. From that disobedience, man was to die spiritually and physically. At the time they disobeyed God's command in the Garden [which was] not to eat of the tree of knowledge of good and evil. They disobeyed and partook of the forbidden fruit; they died spiritually right there. Physically, they died many years later like we do today. There is going to be death and judgment. Everybody will stand before the judgment seat of God and give account on how they lived on this earth. And how we accept God's Word will [determine] where we will go for eternity. God did not leave man in the dark, however, when he sinned. God said, "I will make a plan." That plan was going to be through Christ and through the church.

The Church of Christ is the oldest religion in the world. It had its beginning just as Isaiah prophesied, Isaiah 2:1–4 and Daniel 2:44. Isaiah said from the mountain of Jerusalem His word would go forth. Daniel 2:44 says God would establish a kingdom that would stand forever. Well, that prophecy in Isaiah and Daniel was fulfilled approximately A.D. 33 when the church was established in Jerusalem. Jesus established it. Because when you read the Bible in Matthew 16:18, Jesus told his apostles he would build his church. Between Matthew 16 and Acts 5, the church was established. When you read Acts 5:11, it says, "and fear came upon the whole church." Of course, the church was the people. That's the definition of the word church. Ecclesia [comes from] the Greek word meaning to call out—those that are called out of darkness into the kingdom of the Body of Christ. The word church and kingdom are interchangeable. The definition of kingdom is reign, rule, or government. When you accept God's plan of salvation in the Bible and obey it in its completeness, then you let Christ reign in your heart. In other words, the kingdom of Christ reigns in your heart. Christ rules—and I'm not talking about the heart that pumps blood, but the mind. In the New Testament, the word heart means mind. The church and kingdom is the same institution, it's the Body of Christ. It had its beginning in around A.D. 33, and Jesus Christ gave his apostles all authority on what to teach. And so we in the Church of Christ follow the apostolic teaching which Jesus commanded the apostles to teach. In Acts 2:42, it says those that were baptized on that day, about 3,000 souls, continued steadfastly in the apostles' doctrine and fellowship, "to the breaking of bread and the prayers." That is what we do. We follow that pattern just as it is recorded in the New Testament. So, the Church of Christ had its beginning in Jerusalem in approximately A.D. 33. It is the oldest religion in the world, and it's the only religion. It's the only faith, the only church, and so the church that I am a member of and others in Rabun County are members of, follows the pattern that God has given us to follow.

After the church was established and started growing, people went everywhere due to the persecution of the Christians—even in the first century when the church was started. They went into Sumeria and Judea and then you could say the uttermost parts of the earth. Paul went down through Asia Minor and Macedonia and even into Rome. And how the church got established in Rome no one knows, but if you read Acts, chapter 2, you see that on the Day of Pentecost, there were fifteen nations represented there and one of those mentioned was Rome. Evidently some of the Jews there from Rome on the Day of Pentecost were converted to Christianity and probably went back and established a church there. Not a new church but *the church*—the body of Christ. When they obeyed it, they became a member of the church. The church grew in the first century [and it spread throughout Europe]. It was suppressed by Catholicism but continued for a long time, and then in the seventeenth century, Alexander Campbell came from Scotland as a Presbyterian, if I'm correct. They came to a new world, America, and they studied the scriptures. They could see what they were taught and believed was wrong, and so they made a plea to go back to the Bible. And so, up through Kentucky, Virginia, and Tennessee, and even some parts of Georgia, they made a plea to the early pioneers to restore Christianity—to leave their denominations and go back to the Bible. There is a difference between reformation and restoration. Wesley and Calvin and Luther were more concerned with reforming the Catholic Church. They were on the right track. They knew Catholicism was wrong and they tried to reform some of their ideas. But before they completed their work they all died. A lot of things the Methodists, Presbyterians, and Lutherans practice—those three men said, "Don't do anything in my name, but give all the glory to God." They didn't want any Methodist church started—or any Presbyterian or Lutheran church. They wanted to stick with the Bible. Alexander Campbell was one of the early pioneer Christians that really went back to the Bible to restore Christianity. It started moving and more people started reading the Bible.

The strongest parts for the Church of Christ now are Tennessee and Texas, but the Church of Christ is going into all the world, as Christ commanded in the first century. As time moves on, there are people who are concerned about New Testament Christianity, and they are leaving their homes and going out and reaching these people. The reason why the church took so long to get here in north Georgia is because the members of the Body of Christ were negligent in carrying out the Great Commission. I can't apologize for that, and I'm not going to compromise it either. They just failed to carry out God's command. So, we are here in this area trying to get the people to read the Bible. It's hard because no one ever heard of the Church of Christ. It is not a new religion—it is the only religion according to God's standards. I don't say that to be boastful. I say that because we are to obey God rather than man. We are here to restore that, and I plead with people on the radio.

If you listen to the radio program, you know I challenge people to read and to see what God's Word says about religion, instead of what this man says or what that man says. We take it all back to the Word of God.

I don't think the Church of Christ was met with hostility when it came in. The church was established in 1974, and I made a visit up here and preached for them one Sunday and I found everybody friendly. They were well-received and I am well-received today. People are searching for the truth. It was pointed out to them what is the truth, and they obey the gospel. The only way a person can get into the Church of Christ is by obeying the gospel.

No one can join the Church of Christ. [You simply] accept Jesus as the Son of God and submit to baptism and have your sins washed away. There's no big emotional thing or waiting period or voting. When a person comes to the knowledge of the truth, they accept Jesus as the Son of God. They submit to baptism and are immersed in water. Between the time they go under the water and come up out of it, that's when God operates on them. You believe He will wash away all your sins. Jesus adds you to his church. No one does it for you. If a person comes in this door right now and says they have been studying the Bible and found that the Church of Christ is the true church and they want to be baptized for their remission of sins, well, I can't reject them. I don't have that authority and I will attend to their needs, which is baptism, and God adds them to His church.

Missions are important. We need to go back to the first century again. Jesus told his eleven apostles—Judas had already committed suicide—He was on Mount Olive, and before He ascended back to heaven, He told his apostles, "You are going to receive power." He wasn't talking to anyone else. They were the ones to receive the empowerment of the Holy Spirit. He said, "You are going to receive power, and you are going to be My witnesses. First in Jerusalem, then in Judea and Sumeria, and then in the uttermost parts of the earth." New Testament Christianity began just like Jesus said it would [in] Jerusalem, where the church was started. The persecution took it into Judea and Sumeria; then Paul went into the uttermost parts of the earth. Colossians 1:23 said everyone in the known world heard the Word preached in that first century. Everyone—thirty years after the church had its beginning, everyone in the known world heard the gospel. They all didn't believe it, but they heard it. We are to take the gospel into the uttermost parts of the world.

Christ is our head and we have no earthly headquarters. Our

headquarters are in heaven. In reality our citizenship is in heaven. Christ is the head of the church and He has set up His organization. We have no conventions, symbols, councils, or anything like that. Each congregation is autonomous or self-governing. Each congregation should have elders, deacons, teachers, evangelists, and then, of course, members. We don't have elders here because it is a new work. We don't have anyone qualified to serve as elders. In order to be an elder of a church, one has to meet the qualifications found in 1st Timothy, Chapter 3, and Titus, Chapter 1. The scriptures teach, in Acts 14:23, that every church is to appoint elders to oversee the work. Those elders are subject to Christ only. They oversee the work and they have to answer to God on every decision they make, so they've got to be absolutely sure that they're right. This is God's pattern. And even though this congregation here is supported out of Chattanooga, Tennessee, those elders in that congregation cannot tell us what to do up here. They can suggest things but they cannot *tell* us how to do things. They walk by faith, believing that I am going to teach by the New Testament. So they have faith in me as a minister that I will fulfill my responsibility and teach nothing but the word of truth. They cannot demand this and that. So each congregation is autonomous, but we work and cooperate with each other.

A preacher has no authority in the Church of Christ—elders rule, men that have been selected and are qualified. Deacons are under the elders and they are servants—that's what the word means. Some denominations have deacons that oversee the work and that is contrary to the teachings of the Word of God. They can make suggestions to an eldership, but they are subject to the elders. A preacher is subject to the elders. In the Church of Christ, a preacher is a member of the Body of Christ and all he has done is give up secular work and [become] a full-time evangelist. That is the only difference between myself and another male member here. I have no more authority than he has. I have given myself wholly to the Lord.

People have taken the verses about the handling of snakes out of context, Mark 16:17-20. Jesus was talking to the eleven apostles then. He had just given the great commission to them—to go into all the world and preach the gospel unto every creature. He said, "Now, if you believe—you see some of the apostles disbelieved even after the Resurrection, so He's still talking to the eleven—He said, "If you believe, you can go and handle snakes, handle fire, and drink poisons." Here's the clincher and the purpose, "And they went forth and preached every where, the Lord working with them and confirming the word with signs following." So the purpose for that was to confirm that the apostles were preaching the Word of God. That's all it was for. So the only way anyone could receive these miracles was for the apostles to lay their hands on them. But it couldn't be transferable. God gave these people these signs and wonders to do to convince people. Now, if I lived back then and they laid their hands on me, I could go out and do those things. But, see, I couldn't give it to you if you lived back there. The apostles had to do that. So when the last apostle died and the last man who had had hands laid on him by the apostle died, well, no one else could do it. So no one else today could do it. You can read 1st Corinthians, Chapters 12, 13, and 14 and it talks about the miraculous gifts. So there is no one living today that lived in the first century. And so there is no such thing as people handling snakes. They do it today, of course, but how many have died from it? Well, that doesn't prove your faith; that shows your stupidity and ignorance! I'm not going to pick up any rattler to prove my faith, because I prove my faith by my works. And my works don't include picking up snakes. The people who handle snakes say they can perform miracles, but they are using religion for personal gain.

I believe in Divine healing, however, because I pray for it every day. But there is a difference in Divine healing and what we call miracles. A miracle is something against the natural resources of life. God has set the world in its pattern, and a miracle is something supernatural. I mean if you came in here with one arm and I was a faith healer and I would restore [the other] arm, it would be a miracle. But praying for people that are sick, Divine healing from God can come about. We pray for Divine healing or healing from God. The prayers of righteous people, as James says, availeth much.

Speaking in tongues is again one of those spiritual gifts given to the apostles that's been done away with, because it ceased like the [other] gifts. When the apostles died and the ones in contact with the apostles died, it ceased. Tongues was just another language. They talked to people in their own language. There were fifteen nations assembled on Pentecost. Historians say there were three million people there that day and all different languages [were represented]. The apostles, through the grace of God, spoke in all the languages and everyone heard and understood.

[The Church of Christ] has services on Sunday mornings and nights and Wednesday nights and any other time we want to meet. We have gospel meetings, vacation Bible schools, and we cooperate with and support other Church of Christ meetings in other towns.

Our worship is according to the pattern—we have preaching and the Lord's Supper every Sunday like the Bible teaches. We're to listen to God and not change it because we think it ought to be another, certain way. For example, we don't have mechanical instrumental music in our worship because it is contrary to the teachings of the Word of God. So we don't use it. We do have an instrument; our instrument is our heart. We don't have mechanical instruments and there is a lot of discussion about that. There shouldn't be because the scriptures are plain. We do have songbooks and the Psalms. We are to sing melodies in our heart and the Psalms, spiritual songs. Psalms 23, for example, is a spiritual song. Anything to glorify God— that's the purpose. You can get beautiful music out of those Psalms.

I want to emphasize that [the Church of Christ] is not a new religion. I can't help but to say that we are the *only* church. If we are to please God, we've got to be a member of that church. I'm confident that if anyone will sit down and read [the Bible] they will see that. Because, I know. I was caught up in this any-denominationalism, and God was not happy with that. God is not a God of confusion. All of these religions cannot be right. Somebody has got to be wrong, so I will take my stand on the Word of God. I'll listen to what God says to me through the Word, and I'll apply it to my life.

If everyone would go back to the Bible, everyone would be a member of the Body of Christ which is the church. There would be no denominational religions whatsoever. Anywhere. This is what Jesus prayed for. I believe sincerely that what we practice is truth and truth can be found in the Word of God. Everything I say can be found in that Book. We ought to pattern our lives after that Book.

Episcopalians

Praise my soul, the King of heaven,
To His feet thy tribute bring;
Ransomed, healed, restored, forgiven,
Ever more his praises sing;
Alleluia! Alleluia!

It hardly seems possible that the Episcopal Church, with its formal structure, would gain a foothold in the southern Appalachians as a strong religious denomination. Episcopalians, however, did quite well in establishing churches in the mountains, and efforts such as those of Reverend Rufus Morgan, whose life work is presented in this chapter, greatly furthered their acceptance, growth, and prosperity in this region.

The story of Reverend Morgan, who has contributed to articles in previous volumes of *Foxfire*, is largely self-explanatory. Basically, he describes his religious upbringing, his education, which includes seminary studies in the city of New York and Ph.D. work at Columbia University, and efforts in beginning and revitalizing rural Episcopalian churches.

Reverend Morgan's endeavors were met with a great deal of enthusiasm by many inhabitants of the mountains. His accounts of these experiences represent a significant religious history of the Episcopalian movement.

PAUL F. GILLESPIE

RUFUS MORGAN, Episcopalian

Reverend Rufus Morgan, retired Episcopal minister, has been a close personal friend of many of us here at Foxfire for several years. He has also proved to be an invaluable source and contact for our publications, having his life story appear in Foxfire 4 and aiding us in our research on "Old-Time Burials" that formed an extensive chapter in Foxfire 2. Many of our readers are already quite familiar with this man who, at ninety-five years of age, continues to display tremendous strengths and an awe-inspiring love of life.

Because religion and a strong faith are central in Reverend Morgan's life, as was accentuated in the article in Foxfire 4, *it was necessary for us to draw upon that story to present his beliefs in this particular book. While we have used excerpts from that chapter, subsequent visits to the home of Reverend Morgan and discussions about his religious experiences have added depth to his story of ministry and work in the mountains.*

Reverend Morgan's life is uniquely remarkable to us in many ways: He pioneered several Episcopal churches in his area and still ministers to the small St. John's Episcopal Church near his home; until recently, he regularly hiked in the Nantahala Mountains and has been up Mount LeConte over 150 times; with the help of friends and neighbors, he recently built a log home to replace his old homeplace completely destroyed by fire; and he displays a calm but confident and powerful assurance about himself and his God. In

PLATE 23   Reverend Rufus Morgan.

Foxfire 2, *he says, "A Christian has hope and looks forward to being with Christ. The faithful servant of Christ lives on. . . . I like one translation that I ran across a few years ago in a passage from Saint John's gospel. The commentator gives us this translation: 'If any man observe my saying, he shall not notice this until eternity.' Then he goes on to explain. It's like a man sitting under a tree reading a book. As he reads, a leaf falls on the page of the book. And what does he do? Become disturbed? No, he brushes the leaf off and then goes on reading. And he said that death is like that. It has no more significance for a Christian than that leaf which falls on the page."*

Reverend Morgan has had a special impact on many of us.

KEITH HEAD

My grandmother Siler had been a Chipman before her marriage, and she was born in New York state of Canadian stock. She was brought up as a member of the Church of England in Canada; that's the same as the Episcopal church in the United States. She had a half-sister who had married and had come down to Murphy, North Carolina. My grandmother came down to visit her, and she met my grandfather. He lived over here in this valley.

She stuck to her Episcopal church, although there wasn't one here. The nearest one was over in Waynesville, forty miles away. When there were children to be baptized, she would take them over there. Then she let the bishop know that she was here and a member of the Church, and that she wanted to keep her contact with the Church. So the bishop would call that to the attention of any ministers passing through and they would come by to see her and give her the service.

My parents both belonged to the Episcopal church. They couldn't stay away from the church of their inheritance, and it wasn't long before we started services there in Murphy. My father was what they call a lay reader. He started the services in a room above a furniture store with a piano box serving as an altar. My mother was the organist and Sunday school teacher. My father conducted the services except one Sunday a month when a man would come out from Asheville and hold services for us. We had some neighbors in our community—Blacks—who had no religious instruction at all. Sometimes they'd be working for my mother and begin asking questions, and she would teach them. Very often she would gather them on Sundays onto our back porch and she'd have a Sunday school for them. Later, somebody enabled her to buy a little log cabin near our house which she used for a Sunday school for the Blacks.

In 1877, a minister finally came, Reverend John Archibald Deal. There wasn't any parsonage, so Mr. and Mrs. Deal lived with my grandparents, and I'm pretty sure that it was in this house in which we sit. My grandparents had gone to housekeeping in a log house—one of the old-fashioned log houses with two rooms under one roof with what was called then a dog-trot, an open space in between the rooms.

After Reverend Deal came, he began immediately to make plans for building a church, and it was the first St. John's Church here. The land was given by my grandparents, and with the help of money that he was able to get, as he said, from the North (I think he originally came from Connecticut), and from what gifts he could get here, contributions of materials and labor, they built the church.

According to his record, my mother was one of the chief contributors to the building of the church. She was just out of prep school, but at that age and at that time, she gave a hundred dollars toward the building of the church which was quite a sum for a schoolgirl. And she fed the carpenters while they built the church.

While the church was being built, there was an incident which is brought to my attention every time I think of St. John's Church. There is a marker up there at a double grave for Chief Cuttahsotee and his wife, Cunstagih. [They escaped] from the Trail of Tears and came to my great-grandparents' home. My grandfather visited them, read the scriptures to them, offered prayers, and sang hymns to the old man. While the new church was being built, the old chief died. He had requested to my grandfather that he be buried with the white man's burial. So, since my grandfather was giving the land to the church, he had him buried there. And the chief's wife, Cunstagih, died the next day. She wasn't sick—just passed. So she was buried there with her husband. I am always proud of my family's participation in that episode. Their graves are the most prominent in the St. John's cemetery. They have a large stone for a grave marker. We were friends of the Indians. Occasionally, not as often as I'd like, I come in contact with their great-granddaughter and great-great-grandchildren over there at Cherokee.

After St. John's was built, the Episcopal church just nine miles over in Franklin was started, then one in Highlands, one in Cullowhee, all over the place, because Mr. Deal was a very missionary-minded man. Another thing that he did during the expansion of his work was to establish a small church between here and Franklin for the Blacks. There weren't very many of them here, but he was a very practical man, and he built the church for worship, but also developed work for crafts, cabinet-making, and so forth. I used to minister to that congregation and last Sunday I had some visitors. After our service at St. John's, we were out there on the porch and a pick-up truck turned into the drive. This man came up with a bundle in his hand. He was a member of that Black congregation. While I had charge of the church down there, he loved rabbit hunting, and would very often give me a rabbit he had killed, so that was what he had. He had a rabbit that he wanted me to have that he had had in the deep freeze and then his mother-in-law had made some jelly and pickles, and she had sent that to me. I keep that contact. When their minister happens to be away, I go down still and hold service for them. The man who came up from Columbia, South Carolina, to teach cabinet-making built various things for the church, including a baptismal font for St. John's. He got inspired to go into the ministry and he told me (he was very young when he came here) that he studied under Mr. Deal for twenty-three years before he could get far enough along to be ordained for the ministry in the church, and he worked in and for the church until his death just a few years ago.

The time came when I wanted to go off to school, because at a very early age, I determined I wanted to be a minister, I guess largely under the influence of my mother. She probably influenced me more than anyone else. We shared appreciation of flowers, beauties of nature, that sort of thing, a very great deal. I admired her for her devotion to the church in so many ways. She played the organ; she taught Sunday school. She let me know very early in my life that she would like very much for me to go into the ministry. She told me about a prayer when I was sick with typhoid fever and the doctors didn't expect me to live. She gave herself to prayer in addition to her ministry to me physically, and she said that if God would spare me, she would do what she could to give me to God's service, and that had a real influence on me.

We didn't have any high school over there then, so I tried to find some high school that I could attend by working my way. For a few months I went up to Andrews, the next town in the county. I did the chores—building fires, chopping wood, whatever came handy—for my board. I still remember the whistle of the local tannery before daylight. That was a sign to get up and do the chores before school. And then I also went to a school at Micadale, a church school outside of Waynesville, and lived in the home of the local minister, who had several scattered churches, and I did the chores there for my board. My oldest sister was teaching in this school. She wasn't so much older than I, but she had gone to a preparatory school operated by our Aunt Lucy down at Hickory, so she was ahead of me more than her years would indicate. And then those schools didn't prepare me to go very far. I went to the Waynesville High School, a public school. One year I boarded with the local Episcopal minister and looked after the church, sweeping it, building the fires, mowing the lawn, whatever came up. And another year, I boarded with the same sort of arrangement, with a Mr. Thomas, and did the milking, the fire-building, and other chores around the place. During the summer I would get whatever job I could—driving a team sometimes to haul material for paving the main street in Waynesville.

Some things follow you in life. James Thomas, the man with whose family I was staying that winter, was a descendant of Bill Thomas, who was a white man but adopted by a Cherokee Indian chief, so he was always interested in the Indian's plight. When the government hunted out all the Cherokees they could catch from these mountains, they finally gave up and just had to let the rest of them go. Later Bill Thomas asked permission to get from the Indians the little bit of money the government had allowed them for taking over their property, to buy a tract of land to settle these Indians on. The government gave him permission and so we have what is called the Indian Reservation of the Eastern Band of the Cherokees, which authorities say isn't technically a reservation, because it is owned outright by the tribe of the Eastern Band.

Anyway, I stayed with this family and a baby was born to the Thomas family. The mother was a staunch Episcopalian, and she asked me to stand as sponsor, godfather of this baby, Sarah. I still keep in touch with Sarah who lives in Waynesville. That friendship with the Thomases has continued to be very dear to me.

I enjoyed those years and did better than I expected to in school. When it came to the year of graduation, which I think was through the tenth year, rather to my surprise I had an average for the two years I was there of 99. It was the only creditable grade I ever made. And, of course, being the highest grade in the class, I was valedictorian. I remember one event that rather embarrassed me at the time. I prepared my valedictory speech and then I had to practice it. I wanted to hear what it sounded like, and I couldn't very well practice in the home where I was staying, so over across the creek that runs through the town, there's a ridge and I went over there to practice saying my speech. One evening I was over there on the side of the ridge and I heard voices down below. I wondered who was there and what they were coming up there for, so I waited. They called and I answered, and they came on up. I found it was some folks who had a feeble-minded son who would get out and yell and call, and they thought I was he. I think they were somewhat dismayed that I was out there in the twilight saying my speech.

While I was there, I had a little practice in church work and Sunday school teaching and then I became what we call in our church a lay reader. The folks in the church there at Waynesville thought that I could help out, so although I was just a high-school boy, I got a license as a lay reader. Most of my work, besides Sunday school, was holding service in the Black church over on the other side of town. I enjoyed that very much. I always had a liking for people of other races, whether Blacks or Indians or whomever.

I remember once the minister got me to go over from there to

Cullowhee to hold service in the St. David's Church. The principal member in the church was old Colonel Davies, who was a Welshman. I went over and held service and the old colonel was also a lay reader, and he wrote to the minister in Waynesville, telling him that he didn't think it was necessary for the minister to send that high-school boy to hold services—that he could hold services just as well and save the trouble.

Well, I graduated there in 1906, and that summer I got a job with a lumber mill, Soco Flume Company, over on Soco Creek on the Indian reservation.

Then I went, contrary to the expectation of some of my friends, to Chapel Hill. They thought I would go to Suwanee University of the South, which is a church college. But I thought since I was planning to be a minister, I ought to have experience with people who are not church-connected and who are not planning to go into the ministry, so I went into the University of North Carolina.

I found it very difficult there for two reasons: The sort of high school that Waynesville had didn't prepare a man for college and so I had to make up almost a year during my freshman year; and then I had to earn my way. I found that more difficult than it had been in high school, but with what work I could get, sweeping up buildings and tending fires and acting as sexton to the church, I managed to get through with the help of summer work.

One summer while I was there, in 1909, the Bishop asked me to go to Canton, a papermill town, and start a Sunday school there. Because we had no church there and no church building, we rented a tent and called it the St. Andrew's Tent Sunday School. Later on the church was built there and they took that same name.

Part of my work there at Chapel Hill was looking after the church. I would build the fires and sweep out and ring the bell. One morning I was feeling down in spirits and I needed the communion service— at least I felt I did and I still think I did—which was to be at seven-thirty in the morning. I rang the first bell thirty minutes before the service was supposed to start; then I rang the second bell just five minutes before and the minister wasn't there yet. In a few minutes he came rushing in, saying he had slept late. Nobody else came to the service. He said, "Well, since there's nobody else here, we just won't have a service this time."

That was a terrible disappointment to me and I've thought of that a great many times when there were just perhaps one or two or three for an early communion. I've been very much pleased to go ahead with the service if there was just one.

Well, I graduated from there in spite of the hardships. That was the hardest period of my education. Then I considered the matter of seminary and university work, and again I wanted to go somewhere besides my own local habitat. I decided to go to the seminary in New York City, a general theological seminary. I don't approve of what the arrangement was there entirely, but it helped me very much. In the churches there in New York City, they get so hard up for qualified Sunday school teachers, they'll pay seminary students for teaching or acting as secretary or doing social work in the church, and so besides the scholarship I got at the seminary, I got paid for that sort of thing.

I got along very well, not making any outstanding marks, but I enjoyed it. I played handball at the gym we had there. I played basketball, but I didn't get along very well there, because I didn't know much about it and I was too rough, I guess, for the authorities. I got penalized quite often at it, but I did enjoy it.

While I was there, there was a mutual arrangement (and still is) between Columbia University and the seminary. The seminary was way downtown, 20 Street and 9 Avenue; Columbia was up on Morningside Heights. I had to go by elevated train back and forth. I studied there as much as I did at the seminary. The course at the seminary is three years, but at the end of that time, I managed to get a fellowship at the seminary. I was ordained deacon in Spring 1913, and I got a job during that fellowship year at a small church right near the seminary as assistant rector at St. Peter's Church. I had a very pleasant year there.

The minister with whom I lived one year when I was at Waynesville had gone back to his native state of Vermont. He had a church up there in Swanton, Vermont. He invited me to come up and help him for the summer, 1912, while I was still at seminary. I went up and helped with the Sunday school; painted the church roof; various other things. Then I discovered that it was just out of the kindness of his heart that he had invited me to come up. He didn't have enough work for me. So I got a job in the marble mill down by the Asisqua River and I worked there in the drafting room practically all summer. I enjoyed getting down to the river, and then sometimes out onto Lake Champlain in a canoe after work was over. I'd take a sandwich along and share it with the mosquitoes, of whom there were plenty.

So I worked there until nearly time to go back to the seminary. When I told the mill authorities, they offered me a permanent job in the mill at a salary of more than I received for the first several years in the ministry.

The winter before, I had met a young lady in New York. Her

family had a summer home up above Gloversville, New York, and
we thought we were pretty much in love. Her family invited me to
come by on my way back to New York City and make them a visit
in their summer home. I went, going down through Lake Champlain,
Lake George—a beautiful trip. We got to talking things over and
her mother didn't like the idea of her daughter marrying a minister.
Her mother was something of a climber, and so she talked with
me and with her daughter. She said, "I won't allow it, unless Rufus
will promise to do all that he can to get the best position that he
can in the ministry." Well, that's not my idea of the ministry. She
would like to have had me a bishop or something of the sort, and
I wasn't about to do it. So the young lady said, "Well, whatever
Mother says, I have to do."

I said, "Well, if that's the way you feel about it, it's all over as
far as I'm concerned."

So I went next morning down to Gloversville which is above Al-
bany, bought a frying pan and a blanket, almost nothing else, and
started out walking it off. I walked from there to Boston, 217 miles,
sleeping out at night, averaging more than 40 miles a day. I got
to the outskirts of Boston and found a restaurant and got supper.
I had walked 43 miles that day. Then, when I had satisfied my hunger,
I went out and looked for a policeman to inquire the way to the
nearest "Y." He gave me directions and then as I started off, he
noticed that I was a little bit stiff, and he said, "Look here, fella."
I stopped. He said, "Have you got money enough to get out of
here on?"

I told him I thought I had. I still tease some of my Boston friends
about their trying to run me out of town the only time I was ever
there. So I toured Boston that day on a sightseeing bus and that
night I took the boat, the Fall River Line, down to New York, back
to the seminary.

I was studying at Columbia University aiming for a Ph.D. in Political Science. I met most of the requirements, but I had never studied
German. I had taken a lot of French and Latin and Greek and Hebrew—never good at any of them—but I had never had any German.
My sister, Lucy, had been at the Deaconess School on the Cathedral
grounds there near Columbia University and I was in and out there,
and she or somebody told me there was one of the students there
who had studied German, lived in Germany for several years, and
she heard that I needed German and she volunteered to help me.
That broke up my doctorate, and I married her instead of learning
any German to amount to anything. I never did get my Ph.D. Later,

the seminary there awarded me an honorary STD (Doctor of Sacred Theology), which is the only one that I ever received.

The school at Penland was my interest when I started out in the ministry. While I was still in the seminary studying for the ministry, the man who was bishop over this section of North Carolina, talked over what I wanted to do, and I told him I wanted to come back to the mountains to do what I could here. He gave me a choice. The Episcopalian church had a school founded in 1842, Valle Crucis, in what is now Watauga County. It was first started as a training school for ministers, who wanted to go to work in the rural section, especially in the mountains. Later, it was changed into a boarding school for mountain girls that would train them as they would like to be trained, but who didn't have money enough to go off to school. He offered me the choice of that position in this old established school or a farm at Penland, where a man had tried to establish a school for mountain youth and had failed to make a go of it. He had just planted some apple trees on it because the one at Valle Crucis had done so well.

I chose Penland because it was virgin territory so far as the Episcopal church was concerned and I could determine the policy of it. I had been at Valle Crucis one summer studying, intending to write my Ph.D. thesis on that community and one phase of the work there really distressed me. That was the "old clothes room" where people from the cities would send their old garments to be given or sold to the people—the so-called poor mountain whites. I didn't like that approach. I preferred the idea of training the mountain people in things that they could make a living at themselves and give them a sense of dignity.

So, as I said, I chose Penland and called it the Appalachian Industrial School. I spent the summer of 1913 here, although I was going back for further study at the seminary and Columbia University; then I came back in the spring of 1914. I fixed up an old log house there quite comfortably—it was a plain cabin. Then there was an old farmhouse on the place and I made it over into a school building with space for a couple of teachers to live and the classrooms. During that first year or two, we did what we could to put in plumbing. There wasn't any electricity then. We bought a site down on the Toe River, intending to put in a power plant for ourselves and the community.

We started in giving the first students, who were boys, a chance to work there on the farm—working in the orchard, helping with the plumbing, putting in a pumping station for the water, pumping it up to the buildings. We put up a building we called Ridgeway Hall, and then put up a simple, but more suitable, building for a family than the log cabin. Later on, it was used as a dormitory and the people who followed me named it Morgan Hall. Instead of continuing as I had planned it, a school for boarding pupils, learning farming, orchardry, and so forth, they discovered there was a greater need for smaller children from broken homes, etc., and so it was run by Mr. Peter Lambert for a number of years. Then the church felt that the public schools and orphanages were adequate to take care of that type of work, so this was discontinued.

All the time I was planning with my sister, Lucy, to put in crafts, reviving the old hand-weaving, spinning, basket-making—teaching the women of the community these arts so they could earn money for things they needed in their home—to give them a greater feeling of worth. But after I had been there for four years, I felt that I would have to leave Penland. The bishop wanted me to travel, raising funds, and begging money, going to Philadelphia and New York and other cities in the North. There were others doing the same kind of thing and I was having to follow them. I didn't appreciate the methods some people used, and I felt that I couldn't do this.

Penland continued with Lucy heading it up. She had already taken some training in Chicago in weaving from a Mr. Worst. Later he came down to Penland to help her set up additional weaving classes. Then she got a lady, one of the few original people who is still there, to do the spinning and weaving, and she trained the local women in some of the crafts. They were then able to do things that they couldn't do otherwise—improve their houses, make curtains for their home, give their children dental work, and do all sorts of things that made life somewhat better. One of the first things that she did was to have a log-raising where the men came in and brought logs to make this log house for the weaving and spinning, and basket-making and other crafts. Then she worked valiantly replacing one building that was on the property that had burned down, and erected a stone building that they called the "Pines." Then the men helped build a larger log building that is still used, and of course the women helped by feeding them.

Instead of remaining as a community project, which she intended it to be, people began coming to take training from outside. They'd learned about the school, because Lucy had to market things that were made there in order to purchase the materials and run the school. She attended the general church convention, which meets once every three years, in New Orleans in 1925, and took some of the materials, articles that had been woven. I was a delegate to that convention so I went down and helped her all I could in the marketing. After that, she went to various other conventions and people got acquainted with what Penland was doing until, before she retired, people were coming from forty-eight different countries besides all over the United States, some to learn the crafts and some to teach.

I went down to South Carolina and ministered to three small churches in neighboring towns for a couple of years. During that time, there was the flu epidemic of World War I.

That was 1918 and I was thirty-three years old. I lived in the little town of Barnwell, a characteristic lower South Carolina town. Sherman had come through during the Civil War. He used the Episcopal church to stable his horses. I also had churches in a little town south of that, much newer, Allendale, and another town about the same distance, fifteen miles, maybe. Each one had its points of interest. They were the old South Carolina type of communities. There in Barnwell, soon after I came, I was to have an evening service. I went down to the church and rang the first bell half an hour before service, turned on the lights, got ready and, five minutes before the service, rang another bell, and nobody came. Well, I am rather a crank, I guess, about promptness, so I waited about fifteen minutes after the time for the service—no congregation. So I just turned off the lights, closed the door, and went on up the street. I met a group of the congregation. "Why, Mr. Morgan, what's the matter? Not going to have any service?"

I said, "I intended to, but there wasn't anybody there at service time."

"Well, we were going to church, and thought we had plenty of time."

So I went back and held the service. After that, they were prompt.

One thing that interested me there, because that's low country with sandy soil [is that] instead of just digging a grave for a funeral, they dig it and then a brick mason builds up the walls of the grave for fear it will cave in. Then after the casket is in place and the service over, he builds an arch above it, so that it is encased in brick. That was quite new to me, of course.

The school authorities where I was living in Barnwell were without a principal for the high school. They asked me to pinch hit for them. I said, "Well, provided you get a man just as soon as possible." For the whole year, they didn't find anybody else. Workers were scarce. So I did church work and the school work together, and during the flu epidemic I ministered through the Red Cross and saw more people die, I think, that year than I have in all the rest of my life. I ministered to the people out in the country and in town, and then to the chain-gang Blacks, who lived in metal vans. I couldn't see why they didn't freeze to death.

I went from there to Chester, South Carolina, a mill town, and was there for six years. Then I went to Columbia and there I was executive secretary and general missionary for the diocese of upper South Carolina. I visited churches that had been closed or without a minister and did various things—reorganizing congregations, etc. After five years of that, I became rector of St. John's Church there in Columbia. I enjoyed ten years there. They had a comparatively new stone church, and were still in debt, and the vestry wanted me to jump right in to raising money to pay the debt on the church and on the pipe organ. I said, "Are they pressing us for the debt?"

"Well, not exactly. There it is and we're paying interest on it."

I said, "As I understood it, you called me here as your spiritual leader, and that's what I propose to try to be. If we take care of the spiritual life, the money part will take care of itself."

So we went ahead and built up the work in the Sunday school and the congregation. I spent ten very pleasant years there.

One thing that I remember with a great deal of pleasure. I did some planting around the churchyard. There were some great stones that had been left over from building the church and I managed, with some help, to get them arranged in a circle serving as seats, and very often we'd have our young people's meetings there in that circle. I planted some roses back of the seats and later, after I had left, they put up a parish house right where that circle was. Some of my friends who were interested in flowers and gardening rescued one of the roses, took it home and when they had an opportunity, they gave it to me, and it's growing out here in front of my porch. I planted another rose there next to the church and I have started cuttings from it and have them growing here. Another thing that I did—those of us who are interested in flowers and trees formed a dogwood garden club and we planted dogwood trees along many of the streets and there at the church.

During the time that I was there, I served also as business manager for our summer conference grounds, Canuga Lake, outside of Hendersonville. I had no experience in that sort of thing, but somehow we worked it out. I had had young people's camps for the church in various other places before we took over Canuga Lake on an option. We tried it in 1928, and liked it well enough and were able to raise enough money to purchase the buildings and twenty-five-acre lake and four hundred acres of land. Fortunately we had a good dietician and other help. That first summer there were heavy rains and they washed out the dam to the lake. We had to have that rebuilt.

I've kept in contact with many of the boys and girls. Some of the men have gone into the ministry; one or two have become bishops. It renovated the life of the youth of the church in the Carolinas, especially. Some came from other states.

We would spend summers there at Canuga, except I would go back down to hold services at St. John's Church. All that time I was homesick for the mountains, and the work in this section here had gone down terribly. I heard the minister at St. Agnes' Church in Franklin was leaving, so I got in touch with the bishop and I came up to take charge of the work.

The first day of November 1940, a very significant day in our church calendar, All Saints Day, was the day I returned to Franklin and Macon County, North Carolina.

The work in this section had gone down, mostly through neglect in our church and in some of the others. We treat the country work as a step-child; do not support it, do not send good men, so some of the churches that our first ministry here in this area had established, had been abandoned, some of them torn down. I wanted to begin to get them on their feet, so I could reestablish them or establish new ones. Bishop Griffin told me, when he asked me to come, to take charge of the church in Franklin, St. Agnes', and the Church of the Transfiguration in Highlands, and temporarily hold services over at Murphy. Well, that's a stretch—from Highlands to Murphy—of about eighty miles. So I started in with that and then I saw other needs.

The man who was conducting service at the Black church, St. Cyprians', lived in Asheville and came over to Franklin once a month. I asked them if they wouldn't like to have service every Sunday, and I gave them services. The church in Sylva was being neglected, so I called it to the attention of the Bishop. The next year, 1941, the minister who had been serving it from Waynesville resigned and went to Florida. So the Bishop said, "You see what you can do with it."

So I took charge of it. They had no minister and the church had been closed at Cullowhee, so I went over there and for the time being, as the church wasn't suitable to have service, I held services when I could at the Student Union [at Western Carolina University].

Then I had some funds that people had given me when I left Columbia, and I spent about $400 just patching things up, so that the building wouldn't deteriorate. Later I got the women of the national church to give me $10,000 to renovate the church and add a wing for students' activities and meetings.

Then I discovered that the Episcopal churches never had a service over at Cherokee, and since my people had always been friendly with the Indians, been interested in them, I started going over there and finally built the church from other gifts from the women of the church amounting to $20,000.

I built another church over at Murphy, a Black church, and started a little congregation which has been abandoned since over at Andrew's. I knew that I couldn't do an adequate job, but I wanted to start things going, and there are six of us working now in that same territory—eleven churches that I had charge of when I had to retire.

I don't think I've told you about my present love, which has been my love ever since I was born, St. John's at Cartoogachaye.

The first Episcopal minister came to Cartoogachaye in 1877. At the urging of my grandmother, the bishop sent him. He came without anything tangible to work with or to work on. He and his wife lived with my grandparents until he could get a log house built about a mile from here. That's right across from where St. John's Church stands. The stipend, or salary, in those days was very, very small. He would teach in the subscription schools—that is, people would send small sums to send their children. He would teach during the week, then minister on Sundays. The first church that he undertook to build was right across from where he lived in his log house. My grandparents gave the land, two acres, and according to his records, my mother was an outstanding contributor. She was just recently out of St. Mary's School at Raleigh. I don't know where she got the one hundred dollars to give toward the building. She fed the carpenters who worked on building the church.

That was the beginning of Mr. Deal's work. Afterward, he built various other churches; one in Franklin, one in Highlands, one in Cullowhee, one over on Shooting Creek in Clay County, some which have disappeared.

The Reverend John Deal says in the preface of the book, *Parish Register,* that he went north to get money to help build the original St. John's. He came in 1877 and he built the church about 1879. The first wedding that was performed in the church was that of my father, Alfred Morgan, and my mother, Fanny Siler, according to the records. My parents were married in 1881 and my oldest sister was born in my grandparents' house in 1882, and then I was born there in 1885. I was baptized in the church.

It was only about six years later that my family moved over the mountain to Cherokee County. I remember that quite well. As far as St. John's was concerned, it went along fairly smoothly until that first minister, Mr. Deal, retired about 1909. There is no further record of services there, but the congregation went down through neglect, mostly, of the church and I can't find out just how long it stood. After the building was torn down, the place was neglected, and the people who had loved ones buried there—most of them moved the graves. There were a few left, those of Chuttahsotee and his wife, Cunstagih, and my mother's grave and two infants', and Mr. and Mrs. Gillespie, Mr. and Mrs. Oliver, and just one or two others. People supposed that the church grounds would go back in to wilderness and that would be that.

While I was living in South Carolina, I heard that the church authorities were planning to sell the land where the church had been. I wrote to them and asked them to please not sell it, but if they did, to give me the chance of buying it because, when the graves were moved, some of our relatives wanted to move my mother's grave and the two infants', and I protested, so they didn't. I started, whenever I could on vacations, before I moved up here, clearing out the underbrush and dreaming of building a church back. Just by raking and scraping, getting up what materials I could, I started the building and we held our first services there in 1945. I had moved back in 1940. We have continued since with just a handful. Last Sunday, for instance, we had seven in the congregation. Sometime in the summertime, there will be twenty-five or thirty. The church, with crowding in, will hold about forty-five people.

I had to retire from the other churches officially when I was seventy-two, because that's our age limit in the Episcopal church. So that's been my only charge since that time—from seventy-two to eighty-nine. I say my only charge because there is another little chapel that we've finally built, nine miles beyond St. John's in Rainbow Springs. I'd been holding services in the remnant of an old school house, one room, and then the people over there, the few of them wanted a church. We had no money for it until 1962. We got together enough stone and started building just a very small chapel, which is an open-air chapel—no walls to it—just a stone floor and stone altar, with locust posts to hold up the roof. The wall around the floor is high enough to sit on. During the summertime, we hold services up there, from May to October. That cost only a little over one thousand dollars to build, but I took that out of the offerings that St. John's had given.

In regard to money, St. John's is unique in the way of a church. We do not take up collections as they do in most churches, except when the bishop is here. We always give to the bishop for his discretionary fund, the offerings when he is here, so in order to have it, we pass the plate. Otherwise, we just put a handmade pewter plate on the organ and those who know our custom and want to put in something, they put it in after the service. So there's enough to take care of our expenses and to make a missionary donation to the church. I do not and never have had a stipend or a salary [from St. John's].

As I grew older, about four years ago, I think, I realized that I couldn't be on hand there many more years and I began to think about what would happen to St. John's after I died, or became disabled. So I got a lawyer, a relative of mine, to incorporate the St. John's Donor Foundation, in order to start a fund and make it grow as fast as possible for a background fund to help look after somebody who would volunteer to do the same thing I've done just to serve in a voluntary capacity to hold services up there after I'm gone. Well, that fund like the cemetery fund is not to be spent, the principal, but only the interest, and since it is for the continuance of the work after I die, even the interest is not to be spent until I have to give up.

Not long ago, a member of the church, who had been very faithful, died. She and her husband had volunteered to clean the church every little while, to repair the cushions, do various jobs that they saw needed to be done, and then after a while, she brought her tape recorder to the church and recorded the services. After her death, we received several gifts from five to twenty-five dollars in her memory for this fund. I have a friend down in South Carolina who, when she has a friend who dies, instead of sending flowers, sends a small check in memory of the friend, for that fund. So it's slowly growing. If we get a gift not designated for anything special, we just add it to the fund.

The present church has been used about the same length of time that the old church was used. In the record for the old church, there were eight weddings recorded. Recently, I performed the forty-first wedding in the present church.

There are various things that are of interest to me. One is that a few years ago, I realized that people in my family would wonder what kind of marker to put at my grave, so I decided to make that decision for them. I got a lovely stone back in the mountains, got the monument man to put the lettering on it, and to erect the stone where I want to be buried.

We try to minister to people no matter what church they belong to. We have people buried here who are Baptists, Roman Catholics, Presbyterians, Christian Scientists, whatever, but *before* they die, we try to minister to them, too. Sometimes we have groups who come in there asking my permission for meditations who are on a retreat, and sometimes they request that I give them a holy communion service and I do. I don't question to what church they belong. I am just happy that I can minister to them in any spiritual way. That has been my interest so far as the church is concerned here in these latter years.

I am quite handicapped. I've got to the point where I can hardly read at all unless I use a very strong lens, so I read the portions of scripture over and over again through the week to memorize the passage, and then I'm ready on Sunday to conduct the service. Sometimes I get what we call a lay reader and he will help to read the lessons or the songs in a service. I can't memorize all the songs, so when I lead them, I choose some of the shorter ones that I have memorized in times past. I hold services there twice most Sundays—Communion at 8:00 Sunday morning and Morning Prayer, or Litany, at 11:00, and then in the summertime a third service at 4:00 in the afternoon in the Chapel of the Ascension up on the mountain. Naturally, I can't tell how long I can continue but I am on the lookout for somebody who, after he retired from the active ministry, will take over on the same basis that I've been carrying on these last few years.

I haven't mentioned a couple of things that gratified me. One is several years ago, maybe twenty-five years ago, I was chosen as the rural pastor of the year for the state of North Carolina. This was not denominational but out of the whole bunch, and that pleased me. And after I'd been out of the seminary for thirty years, the General Theological Seminary from which I graduated awarded me the honorary degree of Doctor of Sacred Theology, and that's the reason that a good many people call me "Doctor."

But many of those who knew me before I received the doctor's degree just call me Mr. Morgan. Some of them have the habit of calling me Uncle Rufus, or if they are approaching my age, of course they call me Rufus, so I come to any of the calls. Some people call me other things that I do not like so well. Some call me Preacher Morgan and that seems to indicate that a minister doesn't do anything but get up and preach once a week. I think a minister's duty is much more than that. Some people call me Father Morgan and I don't like that because Christ somewhere said, "Let no man call to thee 'Father.' You have one Father, Who is in Heaven." But in certain areas of our church, the ministers encourage people to call them "Father"—Father Smith, Father Jones, etc., because they like the formality of it, the distinction of it—the old idea of the Middle Ages of "father confessor," but I don't like it. Christ's reason, as I gather it from the scripture, gave instructions to keep His followers from being proud. Most of us like the distinction of being noticed by people, and if they call you "Father," you sit up a little straighter and no matter how high you go, even the Pope of Rome (that's what pope means, papa, father), I don't think it ministers to the spiritual humility. Christ always taught humility. When James and John, the two brothers, wanted special places at Christ's side when His kingdom was established, He rebuked them. He said it was not His to give. It was for those who earned it.

The building of this new four-lane highway has distressed me. And all that goes with it. I've sometimes said that I wish a bulldozer had never been invented. I can say that with a good deal of conviction. There is much in our present world that distresses me, because it seems to me that the emphasis on the part of modern man is exactly contrary to the standards of Christ.

I've been on the radio recently on the local station for morning devotions. I took the very simplest thing that I could think of for my subject—the Lord's Prayer. One morning I spoke on the petition for material things: "Give us this day our daily bread." Not overflowing bins, not millions of tons for our own profit, but give *us*—the people who *need* everywhere, and let us realize that it's given to us to supply our *needs*. I quoted St. Paul, "Let him that stole, steal no more, but rather let him labor, working with his hands that he may have to give to him that needeth." And then Christ: "Be not anxious for your life, what ye shall eat, or what ye shall drink, or yet for your body, what ye shall put on."

And that, to my way of thinking, is exactly contrary to what we are actually engaged in now. We are beginning to discover that that can't satisfy our needs. The fact that so many people are held for ransom is an indication that the people who are trying to get it from the millionaires, realize that the millionaires shouldn't have it. And the hijackings are in the same category, and the scandal in our government is in [it]. It's all the result of man's being completely occupied in the thing that Christ told us not to do. Of course, it leads to the downgrading in our estimation of God's creation. In building our roads, we are influenced by politicians, by big business, by people who make the modern machinery to grade the roads. They grade the roads in order that man might have higher speed. We come up against the situation that we have, for we've just been over-reaching ourselves, cheating ourselves, by going too fast, too far. Yes, that sort of thing is distressing.

Sometime back I went in to see a lawyer to get a deed made, giving to my daughter and her husband their part of my property. I have very, very little. I bought some of it for around twenty-five dollars an acre. A man from Florida sometime ago wanted to know what I would take for it. I said, "It isn't for sale."

"Well, if I offered you twenty thousand dollars for this little tract, would you take it?"

I said, "No, it's not for sale, any more than my children are for sale."

"Well, I think I could get twenty-five thousand dollars for it for you."

I said, "No, it's not for sale."

Well, of course, it's for sharing. My daughter and her husband—he's retiring—are moving back here and I'm giving that part of it to them. I love my place, and I've planted most of the trees and the shrubs and other plants on it. I've loved each one of them, and that's what it means to me—it's God's creation. We go roughshod over the whole thing. The business people and those who live on business are against the idea of saving those things or establishing wilderness areas. Our local newspaper *fights* against the idea of wilderness areas, which might be kept for our descendants in all their primitive beauty and grandeur, because it will take a few dollars of our tax money which comes back to the county when we cut down the trees in the national forests. It's that sort of thing, you see—we're just in it for the dollar, for the accumulation to ourselves, regardless of the destruction that we're bringing on our world.

But I hope we'll wake up in time. In the meantime, I walk along the trails in the Smoky Mountain National Park and my companion stops and he says, "Listen to the silence." We had left the bulldozers, speeding cars, other machinery, down here. We go up there where there's peace.

What brought me back to these mountains was my heart. My mother loved them intensely, as had my grandparents and great-grandparents. It was just inbred. I've loved this place all my life.

When we used to come back and forth from Cherokee County, over here where the county line is marked (between Macon and Cherokee Counties), coming this way, we'd get down and kiss the earth, because we loved it so. When we'd go back, we would get down and kiss Macon County good-bye.

These last years, since 1940 to 1974, have been particularly happy, both within the church and in my relationships with other people in activities that I've been able to carry on—climbing mountains, studying God's hand in His creation, and the increasing number of friends—it's all been very lovely.

A little question in our prayer book, in the section called "Offices of Instruction" is: "What is your bounden duty as a member of the church?" The answer is: "My bounden duty is to follow Christ, to worship God every Sunday in His church, to work, to pray and to give for the spread of His Kingdom." And if you want it expressed in a prayer, I can think of nothing finer than that which is called the Prayer of St. Francis of Assisi: "Oh, Lord, our Christ, may we have Thy mind and Thy spirit, make us instruments of Thy peace. Where there is hatred, let us sow love; where there is injury, pardon; where there is discord, union; where there is doubt, faith; where there is despair, hope; where there is darkness, light; where there is sadness, joy. Oh, Divine Master, grant that we may not so much seek to be consoled as to console; to be understood, as to understand; to be loved, as to love; for it is in giving, that we receive. It is in pardoning that we are pardoned, and it is in dying to self that we are born to eternal life."

I've been trying to live by that.

Jehovah's Witnesses

"And ye shall be my witnesses, saith Jehovah." (Isaiah 43:12)

The following section is comprised of several combined interviews with those who are called Jehovah's Witnesses. This group came to the mountains in the thirties and forties and have established themselves as a strong religious entity. Among other practices, they are known for their well-organized and persistent evangelism, much of it door to door, spreading their message with a variety of printed materials.

Jehovah's Witnesses arrived in this area with basic beliefs somewhat different from those of the already established fundamentalist protestant groups. Some of these beliefs, including the refusal to submit to blood transfusions, the nonrecognition of a literal burning and fiery hell, and rejection of traditional Christmas celebrations, have made Jehovah's Witnesses to some extent controversial and opened the way for vocal and lively theological debate.

When we approached Jehovah's Witnesses in this area regarding interviews to be conducted by *Foxfire*, they were quite receptive, and we were generously welcomed into their homes and biblical discussions. It is hoped that this composite of recorded visits will explain the basic tenets of the beliefs of this group and clarify parts of the doctrine that have caused Jehovah's Witnesses to be controversial.

PAUL F. GILLESPIE

ERNEST CLARK has lived in this area for seven years. He and his wife, Patricia, have two daughters, Cindy and Amy Clark. Ernest is self-employed and in the construction business. The ministerial work he does is completely voluntary and without pay.

RUTH STOCKTON and her mother, Reppie Jones, also appear in this interview. Mrs. Stockton became one of Jehovah's Witnesses in 1951 and Reppie Jones joined and was baptized a year later. Mrs. Stockton and her mother were among the first Jehovah's Witnesses in this region.

KEITH HEAD

PLATE 24   Ernest Clark.

ERNEST CLARK, RUTH STOCKTON, and REPPIE JONES, Jehovah's Witnesses

ERNEST CLARK: My parents were Jehovah's Witnesses when I was born; in fact they met in a Kingdom Hall. That was back in '41, so I've been one of Jehovah's Witnesses all my life, although I haven't lived in Rabun County that long. I guess Ruth here was probably one of the first witnesses in the county.

RUTH STOCKTON: I became one of Jehovah's Witnesses in '51. I studied briefly with a lady from Florida, and my reason for studying with her was because she started a study with my young sister and younger brother and I was curious to find out just what she was teaching. This was by permission of my mother; but I thought that I really would like to know exactly what she was teaching these children. I became very interested because this woman was so very intelligent in the scriptures. I studied with her a period of eight days and then continued to study on my own for about seven or nine months and was baptized in Atlanta.

REPPIE JONES (Ruth Stockton's mother): I became one of Jehovah's Witnesses after Ruth did. I was a Baptist. I was born and raised in the Baptist Church. I was baptized as one of Jehovah's Witnesses in '52.

RUTH: Yes, I was baptized in '51, you were baptized in '52. I taught my mother the Word.

REPPIE: At that time we didn't have a Kingdom Hall. We had the

PLATE 25 Ruth Stockton and her mother, Reppie Jones.

books and our Bible courses in my home. In a year or two we had a Kingdom Hall in Tiger and we had out meetings there.

RUTH: I knew of no other Witnesses except in Franklin, North Carolina, and I had contact with the Watchtower Bible and Tract Society through them, because after I became a Witness I wrote to the Society and they recommended that the Franklin congregation get in touch with me, which they did. Shortly after that, I think about a year after I was baptized, there were Witnesses from New York who came into this county and worked over a period of two or three months. A couple of them stayed with us over a year and the congregation was formed by them.

ERNEST: Usually the situation with any congregation is that when there's people available they send a special missionary, or we call him a special pioneer. That is, a full-time worker of Jehovah's Witnesses. Didn't they send one of the special pioneers here?

RUTH: Yes, a special pioneer was sent to me and the overseer of the congregation in Franklin was sent to me and so I received immediate contact. It is by contact with another person who has this understanding and they teach another and they teach another and they teach another . . .

So missions is a very important part?

ERNEST: Oh yes, definitely so. Lots of times, as the people are availa-

PLATE 26 Ernest and Pat Clark with their daughers, Aimee (left) and Cindy.

ble and make themselves available for this work, they don't even need any interest in the territory, they will simply move there. Some of these missionaries are sent out in a very formal way. They are allowed six months' training in Brooklyn and they are given a definite assignment. They are given a meager financial help—only above and beyond their basic living expenses if they can't earn enough locally through their own work. Then there are others who are able to work part time and serve part time and this would be more like what I called the special pioneer service, where the other is a full-fledged missionary where he doesn't work secularly at all. He devotes one hundred fifty to two hundred hours a month, in the house-to-house preaching activity. They wouldn't have any time to work.

RUTH: Basically though, you must understand that most of the Witness work is done by people who receive this Truth and feel the need to express it to other people. This was the case of the lady who studied with me. She was not a special pioneer; she had this truth in her heart and felt the need to express it. And so wherever she went, she took it. And this is the way that most Witnesses are made, it's by other Witnesses who feel the need to express what they have learned.

ERNEST: Its very beginnings will help you understand how it's expanded. To give you some idea, back in the early 1870s a little Bible group was formed in the basement of this man's house. His name was Charles Taze Russell. And they started a study of the

Bible. They had all been group members of the nominal religions—the Baptists, the Catholics and so forth—and I suppose the biggest change they made when they started studying the Bible, was their thinking on where people go after death, the state of the dead, the trinity doctrine, and teaching of hell fire. This is where they saw that there was a need for them to withdraw from what they'd been learning in the churches and they started studying. This was in the early 1870s. Charles Taze Russell was a prime mover of the group; he became the spokesman. By 1879, he'd published the first issue of the *Watchtower*. That was a hundred years ago and in those one hundred years it's never missed one issue of publication. It was only last year that it went from the original nickel a copy to a dime a copy. So for ninety-nine years it stayed a nickel a copy. Anyway, basically, to give you an idea, he printed that first *Watchtower* in 1879 and it says here in the brochure, *Jehovah's Witnesses in the 20th Century*, that "by 1880 scores of congregations spread from that one small one and in 1881 Zion's *Watchtower* Society was formed. In 1884 it was incorporated with Russell as president and the name was later changed to what is called now the Watchtower Bible and Tract Society."

In other words, a hundred years ago it started out with one person, really, the one that had the idea to have this group come into his home. The brochure says, "By 1909 printed sermons were syndicated in newspapers and by 1913 they were in four languages and three thousand newspapers in the United States. They distributed books, booklets, tracts and Bibles by the hundreds of millions." We're only talking about a few thousand people back then. And interestingly, about the Society it says, "In 1912 they began to work on the *Photodrama of Creation.*" The *Watchtower* Society pioneered the use of motion pictures with a soundtrack on it. You know, they were right in the beginnings of the film industry. It says, "Showings started in 1914 with thirty-five thousand seeing it daily." And there are copies of that still in existence and still being shown. My father was privileged to see some of these films.

Since the 1800s the growth of Jehovah's Witnesses has been phenomenal. In Brooklyn, New York, where the headquarters are now, buildings have been built and have been purchased, for the purpose of nothing other than to produce Bibles and Bible literature. Two thousand individuals live at the world headquarters. They provide their own dormitories for them. They're all people that have proved themselves in the congregations and are recommended. They're spiritual-type persons. The people who work in these offices only receive twenty-five dollars a month. They're all given room and board. They get twenty-five dollars a month for their personal necessities. And, when I'm talking about twenty-five dollars a month, I'm talking about from the president of the Watchtower Society down to the person that empties trash. Everybody gets the same amount. So there's no chance for any greed; there's no chance for any prestige; there's no selfish reason for a person wanting to go there other than to serve his Creator. I think most of the ones there are young men from eighteen to thirty-five because of the tremendous amount of labor to go into the printing presses, and so forth, and the handling of the large bundles; they use the women where they can, where they can handle things. Anyhow, they have a tremendous printing organization.

The worldwide work is directed from Brooklyn, the world headquarters. At Brooklyn they have a governing body consisting of sixteen people. These are men who have been associated with the Bible and Jehovah's Witnesses for fifty or sixty years.

RUTH: They've been with it for more than half of the whole time it's been.

ERNEST: In order to have a group of buildings like that and to operate it in the United States, you've got to incorporate. You've got to have some legal governing body. We have a legal corporation, it's entitled the Watchtower Bible and Tract Society of New York, Incorporated. That is simply set up to comply with the law of the land. But that is not what governs Jehovah's Witnesses. Rather these sixteen spiritual men, who have been appointed because of their abilities as Christians, they basically are the ones who are responsible for the information we read in *Watchtowers, Awakes,* and other Witness literature.

They are the governing body of Jehovah's Witnesses. Right from the headquarters in Brooklyn they appoint the elders in every one of the 42 thousand congregations in the world. So there's no in-between. Under them the world is divided into something like seven or eight zones—the entire world. So under them there's appointed a zone overseer, then those zones are broken down into branches of which there are branches in most of the major countries in the world. At these branches many have their own printing facilities to print the *Watchtower,* books, literature, and so forth, in their own language. Whereas it used to all come out of Brooklyn, but now they're deversified. Within the branches then, there are districts. For instance, one branch serves the entire United States, the Brooklyn branch. It's broken down into districts of which there are thirty-

five to forty, say, in the United States. Then a district is broken
down into circuits. And there's an overseer over the district and
then there's a circuit overseer. The circuit overseer is the one we
come closer in contact with.

He comes around on an average of about every six months. He
has eighteen to twenty congregations. It takes six months to go to
each one; he spends one week with each. Usually they are married,
but not always. Some pull their own travel trailer. Others stay in
homes of Witnesses in the area. They move to a new congregation
every week. You have to be dedicated to do that.

While the circuit overseer is in the congregation, the body of
elders meet at least a couple of times during the week with him
and discuss the spiritual needs of the congregation—what it needs
to build it up—and, of course, the circuit overseer's main reason
for being there is to take the lead in making disciples. He goes
out and knocks on doors with us. The president of the Watchtower
Society, he goes out in Brooklyn and knocks on doors. So, there's
no one above anyone.

How are the local congregations financed?
ERNEST: You can go to any one of the 42 thousand Kingdom Halls
in the world and there is *never* a collection plate passed. *Never* has
been one. We don't even own one. We have, in the back of the
Kingdom Hall, a little box that says, "contributions for the Kingdom
work." And there's not the feeling pervading that everyone's watching you put money in. It's anonymous. In other words, you could
go to the Kingdom Hall all of your life and never put a thing in
and I would never know it, he would never know it, no one would
ever know it. There's no pressure.

*What about pressure from headquarters? Is there any requirement, an obligation
to give money?*
ERNEST: None. If we have more money thàn we need to pay local
expenses in our Kingdom Hall account, and if we wanted to, and
the congregation voted by hand count, we could send the excess
to the Society to further the preaching work.

Don't you have to send some of it in?
ERNEST: No. There is no tithing. There is no financial obligation.
Some people, when they die, will their estate to the Watchtower
Society. But we have no external source of money at all. And this
is what makes it so amazing.
ERNEST: I said that the president of the Society receives the same

twenty-five dollars a month as does the one that cleans the floor. The reason, of course, obviously is that the entire structure is trying to be patterned after early Christianity. That's its basis. We had to organize and incorporate to meet the laws of the nation to publish books and magazines; simply, it's the law. But—you see, by everyone earning the same amount of money, there's absolutely no reason for anyone to have any feeling of superiority.

Of course, anyone among Jehovah's Witnesses who is out on the road, as a circuit overseer, that can't hold a full time job, has to have some financial help, but the help is absolutely meager. For instance, the circuit overseer is the one who we most totally relate to and he goes around to the congregations in several states. Now this man is allowed to apply to the Watchtower Bible and Tract Society for I think it's ten dollars a month. Now you picture it—he's providing his own gas, his own home, everything; and he can apply, if he wishes, for ten dollars. "Well," you say, "so how does he make it?" Now most of these who're out on the road are ones who have no savings anywhere, they just go from week to week. But when they're with the congregations, the congregations know this, and we try to show our appreciation for them by helping them out. Nobody goes up and says, "Here's ten dollars for so and so." Everything's done anonymously.

The Scripture, I think, underlying this is Matthew 6:1–4 which says: "Take care not to practice your righteousness in front of men in order to be observed by them, otherwise you'll have no reward with your Father in Heaven. Go making gifts of mercy, do not blow a trumpet in front of you just as the hypocrites do in the synagogue and in the streets that they be glorified by men. Truly I say to you, they are having their reward in full. But you when making gifts of mercy, do not let your left hand know what your right is doing, that your gifts of mercy may be in secret; then your Father who is looking on in secret will repay you." So each witness feels a personal obligation to give of themselves; they don't need to be solicited or begged, or to have people stand up and ask them to. They give freely of what they have.

Let me ask you something. If every preacher that you know of now—any preacher in Rabun County, Georgia, the States, in the world—if every preacher's salary from the church was suddenly cut off, stopped today, how many do you think would stay in the ministry? I've asked some that and they've said, "Well, my minister'd probably quit." You can turn the same token around and say to the two hundred thousand ministers of Jehovah's Witnesses, or elders, if you were to cut their salary off, how many would quit? Well, that'd be a ridiculous question because they're not getting a salary anyway. Revelation 22:17 says: "The Spirit and the Bride keep saying, 'Come, let anyone hearing come, let anyone thirsting come, let anyone that wishes take life's water free.' " Also Matthew 10:8 says, "you receive free, give free." And so this is why our ministers aren't paid and why contributions are made in private.

RUTH: The furthest thing from my mind would be what the elder puts in the contribution box. And he wouldn't even think of asking what I put in; it wouldn't ever occur to him to ask me.

ERNEST: No. It's never been asked of another Witness.

RUTH: What our heart moves us to do, we do. Without being asked to do it.

ERNEST: 2 Corinthians 9:7 says, "Let each one do just as he has resolved in his heart, not grudgingly or under compulsion, for God loves a cheerful giver." And this is really what our stand is.

Does each congregation have an appointed minister?

ERNEST: As I said, we have elders. 1 Timothy, chapter 3, and Titus, chapter 1, lists the qualifications of an elder. He needs to be the husband of one wife, be a good teacher, and so forth. Among these elders, we have a presiding overseer. There's nobody over anyone. The one who is the presiding overseer simply is someone who, if the group of elders got together, obviously, someone has to chair the meeting. Right? Somebody has to have the initiative to call the meeting. The overseer changes each year, but will always be an elder. The body of elders has oversight over any functions at the Kingdom Hall, and they especially take the lead in preaching the good news of the Kingdom. That's God's purpose for his servants at this point in history.

Let me read to you the very last words of Jesus, when he left the earthly scene. He said: (recorded at Matthew 28:19,20) "Go therefore and make disciples of people of all the nations, baptizing them in the name of the Father and of the Son and of the holy spirit, teaching them to observe all the things I have commanded YOU." And that's really what it's all about. That's why we have such a tremendous teaching program.

We offer to anyone, a free home Bible study course, to anyone who wants it, we will come to their home absolutely free of charge. I think last year one and a half to two million families allowed us to come to their homes. We study with these folks—use their own Bible in their own home. They can ask questions. We spend an hour a week, when they want it. And this is why Jehovah's Witnesses have been so successful in baptizing as many as we have. And, again, like I said, it isn't just a matter of a person saying: "Well, I want to be baptized." He has to meet the Bible's qualifications. So, we study the Bible with them and help them make these needed changes. You have to be morally clean. And so, when you're talking about an organization that's grown like ours has, it's simply the appeal of the Bible truth, the reasonableness of what the future holds for man, the Kingdom hope of living here on earth forever that appeals. We don't hold church bazaars, we don't hold church suppers, bingo games—we don't have any of that. Only things that have to do with the Kingdom interest ever come over our platform.

The body of elders preside over our meetings. Again, it is not haphazard. We have five hours of meetings, five different meetings during the week, some of which are combined. All the ones who attend—all the congregation members know exactly what's going to be studied—can prepare ahead. So there's no surprises when you get there. The elders handle the basic teaching parts—that's why they're elders, because they have the "art of teaching."

Are there any educational qualifications?

ERNEST: No.

RUTH: We have a theocratic school in which even our overseers can engage and enroll if they want.

ERNEST: But there's no termination to the length of the school—there's no graduation. It's a continuing process . . .

RUTH: It last forever . . .

ERNEST: The women also participate in this school, giving talks to others under the directions of the overseer. The men generally give talks directly to the congregation. These last five or six minutes each. For some of them it's simply a Bible reading, with an explanation of that portion of the Bible. Some of the talks come from the Watchtower Society's printed publications. Constructive counsel is given. The whole idea is to try to become fluent so we can present the message to people at their doors in the best way possible.

RUTH: . . . to learn the most we can about the Bible in order to present it to others so that they can learn also.

ERNEST: So when these students give their talks, not only do they learn from the information they have presented, but they also learn *how* to present it. Listen to some of the titles: "How could a God of Love Destroy the World?" "Is the Bible Really Inspired?" "Should Life Be Saved At Any Cost?" The talks consider everything about life. For example, a mother and child and the doctors' dilemma of who are they going to save, the mother or the child. "Was the Church Built Upon Peter?" "Are Adornments Proper for Christian Women?" "Why Smoking Is Not Pleasing to God." "Is the Devil the Evil Within Us?" "Why do the Witnesses Refuse to Salute the Flag?" All these are subjects that we take up and discuss and anyone is welcome to attend.

And so our meetings are very informative. We discuss ways in which we can serve the Creator as in the scripture we read there about making disciples. We rehearse among ourselves; we demonstrate ways in which we can teach other people the Truth. That's what it's all about. We want to influence people to see what we have found. We would be selfish if we didn't. If we think it's so good, what kind of people would we be if we didn't share it? Really, what is more pleasing than to think of an earth where locks and keys will become a thing of the past? Doctors, hospitals, ambulances, police, and armies, will become things of the past. Graves will be no longer needed. Just let your mind wander a minute—to think of what it would be like if we had only God-fearing people left on earth. And this, to us, sounds good. This is what we want; this is what we're looking for and this is what the Bible promises. It's not a dream. It's the new earth that the Bible actually promises at 2 Peter 3:13 and Revelation 21:1.

We have no displays of emotion in our meetings. Our meetings, the best way I can describe them, are Bible study discussion in an organized way. Everything that we do is basically all pointed to helping us keep the command Christ gave to his apostles, to preach the good news of the Kingdom. (Reading) "Jehovah's Witnesses are taught to try to be exemplary as citizens of the state, exemplary as Christians in every way that they possibly can." They try to inculcate this in their meetings. It's all done in a very up and up way. Just like Jesus. When he would get together with them and talk to them, what would it amount to, really? Discussion. Like in the Sermon on the Mount—it was basically where he would teach them. And so as far as any basic display of emotion, it's almost nonexistent in our meetings.

Do you have a definite conversion experience?

ERNEST: No. We grow in this. Some people believe in the baptism of infants. We feel that baptism is the expression of one to do God's will. We're saying that we're dedicating our life to the service of our Creator. Children, they're obviously not in a position to do that. They don't even know what God's will is. And so, as one studies the Bible with Jehovah's Witnesses, he simply comes to appreciate and grow in that knowledge. And you could ask any one of the 2.2 million Jehovah's Witnesses in the world, "When were you saved?" or "What was the date of your conversion?" and you won't get a date. Let's simply say it's just a matter of learning. It's just about like if I asked someone, "When did you become a man?" What date would he give? What we feel so far as one's being accepted for baptism among Jehovah's Witnesses, it's not on the length of time that they have studied the Bible, it's not on how much they know. It's what's in their heart. We try to make that the prime thing.

We believe in complete immersion. I think the Baptists believe in that too. We have baptisms whenever we have local assemblies and at our national assemblies in the summertime. It basically consists of a talk about what you're doing and the Bible's definition that you're dying to your old former course of action by being buried in the water and coming forth to a new life. So it's really just a beginning, it's not the end of something.

I'll touch on just a little bit about communion, which is once a year. We have about a thirty-minute discussion about the new covenant that was made with those who will go to heaven to be with Christ. It's a serious matter. The talk is given. The cup is passed and a prayer said. We don't do it weekly, daily, or monthly. We feel that it's like an anniversary or something—it comes up once a year. I'm not trying to minimize its importance. It's most important. It's the only celebration that we observe. We don't observe Christmas, Easter, or any of the celebrations that the nominal Christians do. They have pagan origins; they are not found within the Christian teachings. The only one that Christ said to keep is the memorial of His death. He didn't ever say to "keep the memorial of my birth." Did He?

If you go to any Witness's home, you'll never see a Christmas tree. And we have good reasons for it. I think you're aware—all you have to do is read the newspaper at Christmastime. It admits the whole pagan background of everything—the mistletoe, the tree, the star, and all that. Check sometime. You'll find December 25th was the worship of the Day of Saturnalia. It had nothing to do with the day of Christ's birth. It had to do with sun worship. He wasn't born near then. Many know that, but what do they do? They tell their children lies about Santa Claus and about Jesus being born that day. We figure we're going to tell our children the truth.

RUTH: They might ask, "Well, is God real?" "If Santa Claus is not real, is God real?"

ERNEST: See. And so it spawns atheism, is what we feel. It can have an influence. I've never been given a Christmas gift because, remember, I said my parents were Witnesses when I was born. Obviously, our children have to feel a bit of hurt at that time, but they don't miss anything by missing Santa Claus. We give them gifts all through the year. We don't have to wait for one day. We do things with them. So it's not that they're left out.

Do Jehovah's Witnesses ever have churchings, excommunications?
RUTH: Yes, we do.

How does that take place?
ERNEST: What the Bible says is, "quit mixing in company with anyone called a brother that's a fornicator, a greedy person, idolator, reviler, drunkard, or extortioner. Remove the wicked man from among yourselves." So, what we would do if a person continues in the practice of sin—these are major sins we're talking about—drunkenness, fornication, idolatry, reviler, extortioner—then a letter is read publicly over the platform in the congregation. It simply states that this person is guilty of unchristian conduct. It's not spelled out. It simply says that his conduct is unbecoming a Christian and it gives the name of the person and that's it. That person then is welcome to attend any of our meetings in the congregation, which is open to the public any time. We do not seek out his fellowship and association in any way, shape, or form. He's not recognized in the congregation even if he should raise his hand. This is where we're carrying out "remove the wicked man from among yourselves."

We realize from the Bible that reinstatement back into the congregation is based not on the amount of time that's elapsed and not on the gravity of the sin, but on the repentance of the individual. So if the person can convince the body of elders that he's truly and sincerely repentant through his actions and through what he says, he can be reinstated. Some have been reinstated in a month or two.

Everyone is treated the same and the elders, when they meet with individuals, they try to put themselves in that person's shoes. And they try to extend every avenue of mercy that they can. And you can believe when a person is disfellowshipped out of Jehovah's Witnesses organization that that person absolutely didn't want to stay in. That's about what it amounts to.

If you evaded your taxes and were caught by the law and were punished for it, certainly the congregation would raise a question about it if you continued it and weren't repentant. If you are caught

PLATE 27   A congregation of Jehovah's Witnesses.

breaking any of Caesar's laws that did not conflict with God's laws, the congregation would certainly want to talk to you. Why? Because we're commanded to keep Caesar's law. If you continually broke the speeding laws and received ticket after ticket you'd not be setting a good example. But the whole idea is that Jehovah's Witnesses have one of the cleanest organizations in the world; I mean morally and physically clean. The Bible says that the elders are charged with the responsibility to keep it that way. So when a person appears to challenge the cleanness then they have to be removed.

RUTH: The opportunity to remain is there even after a person has committed sin. When they show a hard attitude that is unresponsive to what God wants them to do, then they're put out. And rightfully so. We expect to be. We know that we will be. It's a deterrent to sin.

How do Jehovah's Witnesses feel about the use of tobacco and alcohol?

ERNEST: Our basic reason for not smoking is not for health reasons, because the surgeon general said it is dangerous, but because the Bible said that we're supposed to present our bodies as clean and acceptable sacrifices. And it's an unclean habit. How can you present an acceptable sacrifice to God if you've got a diseased body? It's really, we feel, tantamount to suicide; it's slow suicide, isn't it?

RUTH: . . . you're injuring something precious that God has given you.

ERNEST: Smoking has always been completely out of vogue among Jehovah's Witnesses. It was never a disfellowshipping offense up until about ten years ago. As the Society researched the derivations

PLATE 28 Carl Friebus conducts a question and answer discussion using the *Watchtower* magazine on Sunday morning.

of tobacco and smoking they found it to be associated with spiritism. The Greek word "pharmacea" has to do with drugs. Of course, now we use drugs in a medicinal way, out of a drug store, but originally these drugs were used by the priests in pagan ceremony and worship. And, of course, tobacco is a drug. There's no question about that. And it has a tremendous effect on the body. In fact, some have said that tobacco's even worse than some of these hard drugs to break the habit.

Jehovah's Witnesses may drink in moderation. It's a matter of personal choice, but they don't get drunk. Drunkenness is what the Bible condemns, not drinking. Jesus' first miracle was to turn water into wine.

Jehovah's Witnesses, by not accepting a lot of these accepted things—like drunkenness, immorality, use of tobacco, and so forth—are actually protected. Jehovah's Witnesses are not known to be dying from lung cancer. Because they don't smoke. They don't die of cirrhosis of the liver. They don't have venereal diseases. So we have a tremendous protection by staying within the confines of this organization and associating with people who think like us. So, this is why we encourage close association with ones that think like we do. This is why we have such a brotherhood.

Do Jehovah's Witnesses encourage higher education?
ERNEST: We try to eliminate education that will not enhance our worship with our Creator. We encourage a full high school education. We do not encourage, in all cases, a higher education past that. The main reason is that if a person applies himself in high

school, he should be able to learn to read and write well without any problem. Additionally, we encourage a specialized education that Jehovah's Witnesses provide. We probably have five to seven different types of schools that we operate now. We have no seminary. If you recall, there are scriptures where Jesus—what was it they said about Him?—they said that He didn't study in the schools. That was recorded at John 7:15. We find that in some colleges there's considerable atheistic-type curriculum that a person is exposed to—evolutionary and atheistic. And, we feel our children don't need that.

RUTH: They need the basic training in learning to make a living and they need training in learning to be a disciple of Jesus; these are the two things in life they have to learn. So, whatever they need, technically, to do this is all the education we feel they need. They need a lot of education in spiritual warfare.

What are those six or seven schools that you talked about?

ERNEST: We have the continuing theocratic school within every congregation, of which anyone can join up. There are very few requirements. Then, from time to time, they send instructors out from Brooklyn for schools where only elders are picked to attend. I went to one of these schools for two weeks and it was two weeks of solid instruction. Nothing new, nothing startling is brought up, simply a review of the basic Bible truths that elders need to know. Then we have a school for a group that we call pioneers. These are the ones who—say, for example, Ruth—found that she didn't have to work full time and could devote ninety hours a month to knocking on people's doors, to declaring the good news. This is a requirement to be what we call a pioneer. In other words, he's basically spending his full time in the work and in strictly talking to people about the Bible. Then these have a special school. Out of that group certain ones are selected with the ability and the availability to go to other areas, like Rabun County was years ago when there were no Witnesses here, to serve as special pioneers. These go to a school. Then out of that group, they invite some from the pioneer group in general to what we call a Gilead School, which is held in New York. That is with the view to sending them overseas on missionary assignments. And they are strictly full time. These are the ones that go and live in branch homes or missionary homes in various countries and work as missionaries generally. All of these schools we're talking about are above and beyond the five hours of instruction that we all receive every week.

RUTH: You could stay right here at home as a Witness and get a very good education in the Bible. You don't have to go anywhere.

ERNEST: We're encouraged to spend time in personal study before each meeting to know what's going on. And then the elders take the time they need to spend in preparing lectures, talks, discussions and, I'm telling you, in the life of a Witness, most Witnesses, there's not enough time in the day for them is what it amounts to.

RUTH: I can say that I believe truthfully that the knowledge a Witness has depends upon the Witness himself, how well he applies himself, because the education is there for him and the help is there for all of them. They have all the help they need to be just as good as they want to be. And this is locally and everywhere else and I believe that they are the best educated people, as a group religiously in the world.

How do you feel about faith healing?

ERNEST: We don't practice any form of faith healing. We feel that it was a power that God gave to his son, Jesus, and Jesus gave that power to his twelve other apostles and a few other people, and we feel that when those people died that power left the earthly scene. This what the Bible says at 1 Corinthians 13:8–11. In order for the Christian church to get established, it needed something to show them that this was really from God. And so they had these acts of what Jesus did, like resurrecting people, healing people, speaking in tongues, which amounted to no more than speaking in a different language. So, it served to establish the church in the doubters' minds. And so, what happened when Jesus would heal somebody? It would go like wildfire, wouldn't it? They'd come flocking by the hundreds and thousands to him. So it served a purpose. Because Jesus—how long did he preach? Three and a half years. And yet look what he did in three and a half years. Look what it's still doing today! He's still the most popular religious figure on earth, isn't he?

RUTH: But it was, as Paul explained, at 1 Corinthians 13:13, that these gifts, being able to do these things, would pass away and the Christian church would be identified by three other things— love, faith, and charity and the greatest of these is love.

So you don't believe in any kind of healing?

ERNEST: We will accept most any kind of medical treatment for healing with the exception that we don't take blood transfusions. We don't take them because of a scriptural viewpoint and yet we find a tremendous amount of support in the hazards of taking blood—hepatitis, for instance, and venereal diseases have been transmitted that way. And the post-operative recovery of a person taking blood can take much longer. But the Biblical view is our real reason, not the medical view. The Bible says at Acts 15:28,29—"abstain from blood." This was necessary for Christ's followers.

Also the Israelite law said that when you killed an animal, you had to drain him; you couldn't eat the blood. Remember that? That was the law. There was no question about it. If they found an animal that had been strangled they weren't allowed to eat it because the blood hadn't been drained. Anyway. People say, "Well, you're not feeding on it, you're putting it into your veins, but, really, that's just a way of bypassing the stomach—it goes into the stomach. In fact, what's it called? It's called intravenous feeding. If your doctor told you to abstain from alcohol, that you were going to die if you kept drinking for some reason or other, would you go and start injecting it into your veins and say, "Well, Doc, I'm not drinking it." No. You see. It's the same idea.

Remember that one thing that I said one of the talks was on? "Should Life Be Saved At Any Cost?" Life, apparently, according to the Creator, shouldn't be saved at any cost. Because if you have to break a law of God to save a life, then it shouldn't be saved.

RUTH: And, we're willing to die for that.

ERNEST: Yes. So, if we're on an operating table and the doctor says, "You are going to die if you don't get blood," while we respect his opinion as a doctor, we still ask that our rights as individuals be obeyed and that we not be given blood. We'll take the consequence; we're prepared. Here's the thing about it. We feel that if we go ahead and take that blood, there's a good chance we could die anyway. There's no assurance, is there? What about your conscience? If you go ahead and take that blood and die, how might God view you? If it really is against the law of God? Whereas, if you don't take the blood and go ahead and die, at least you have a better chance for a resurrection. It's the long run we look at, not just the immediate future.

The Bible says the life is in the blood. Recall, they never ate meat before the flood; they were never allowed to eat meat. Do you recall what the prohibition was after the flood? He said, "you can eat all the meat you want," he says, "but don't touch the blood." Now, that wasn't just a Mosaic law, that was the way it was before the law of Moses.

PLATE 29 This old photograph, approximately forty years old and supplied by Ernest Clark's father, Ernest A. Clark, shows a group of Witnesses preparing to spread the good news of the Bible using photographs and recorded messages.

RUTH: There's another point, too. Have you ever thought that God, who made the body, knows what's best for it? In Acts 15:29, for instance, it says we're to abstain from blood and it adds a couple of words that might interest you, "it adds good health to you." Could it not be that God, in His providing these things in the Bible for us, is actually protecting our health? We view it even today, that He is.

Listen to what God told Noah, at Genesis 9:3,4. He says, "Every moving animal that is alive may serve as food for you. As is the case of green vegetation, I do give it all to you. Only flesh, with its soul, it's blood you must not eat." Notice how the word soul is used here? It's the life of a person. That is the representation of life. It's been called the "river of life." So, God holds blood sacred. Remember, it was the blood of Christ, wasn't it, that was so sacred there at the altar. And so this is why we feel that if He told them not to eat animal blood, how much more so human blood?

Do you believe in foot washing?

ERNEST: We don't have the practice of foot washing at all. Jesus did do it, obviously, as a sign of humility, true humility. The thing about it, when Christ did it, He wasn't trying to put on a show. When He washed the feet of the disciples, it was just the custom in those days. They'd come in, it was all sandy, they wore sandals in those days, and it was their custom that somebody'd get the wash-pan out. They were hot and dusty, so they'd all pull their sandals off and somebody'd wash their feet. Well, this time when they met, nobody offered to do it and there was a need. Jesus just went ahead and did it; it wasn't a show of piety on his part.

Let's try to look at it like the Lord's Prayer. Some people reiterate the Lord's Prayer word for word every day of their life. We look at it more as a model prayer. We don't repeat those same words, but the basic ideas. And this is the idea about washing one's feet. Piety can be shown in so many different ways, you know. Jesus, He only did it once in the Bible that I know of, in three and a half years of His ministry. So it wasn't a monthly practice, or a yearly practice; there's no account made of it.

How do Jehovah's Witnesses feel about the scriptures Mark 16:17 and 18: "And these signs shall follow them that believe; in My name shall they cast out devils; they shall speak with new tongues; they shall take up serpents; and if they drink any deadly thing, it shall not hurt them; they shall lay hands on the sick, and they shall recover"?

ERNEST: All right, let me read to you here [he reads from the *Watchtower*] " 'A zealous member was bitten by a rattlesnake Sunday night during a snake handling ceremony at a rural church and later died,' so reported the *New York Times*. Only four days earlier the *Times* told of a woman dying after being bitten twice by a rattlesnake, September 16th, at the Jesus Pentecostal Church. 'Snake Handling Sects Survives in Appalachians,' quoted the *Times* feature. It showed pictures of snake handling done by members of the Holiness Church of God in Jesus' name . . . Why do these people make snake handling a part of their worship? Because in their authorized versions of the Bible, Mark 16:17 and 18," which you just read, reads, "And these signs shall follow them that believe . . ." Is that really what the inspired Bible teaches? An experience of the Apostle Paul might seem to indicate this. When he was shipwrecked on the island of Malta, a viper fastened itself on his hand as he was gathering kindling wood. When nothing happened to him, the natives began saying that he was God. But did Paul go out of his way to collect poisonous snakes in order to handle them? No. Nor do we read anywhere in the Greek Scriptures (that's the same as the New Testament), where any of Christ's followers did so. So what purpose is served, it may well be asked. What purpose does religious snake handling serve?

"All the miraculous gifts that God bestowed upon Christ's early disciples served very practical purposes." So, really, we're getting into all these things. "Curing sick people, raising dead persons, making lepers clean, dispelling demons. Even the gifts of tongues. On the Day of Pentecost, this gift of speaking in tongues enabled

PLATE 30 Elders for Jehovah's Witnesses. From left to right: Visiting elder, Henry Southworth, from the Asheville (N.C.) South Congregation, and local elders, Joseph Cardeira, Carl Friebus, and Jerome Schott.

Jews coming from more than a dozen different lands to hear the magnificent things of God in their own language. Later it was to be used for the edification of the Christian congregation. What they're saying here is when people speak in tongues today it's jibberish. At Pentecost, when the disciples got up and started preaching to the crowds, they were able to speak in the tongues of others, ones that were there so they could understand. That was the gift. But today, when they're speaking in tongues, it's not just in a foreign language. It's an unknown language.

The Apostle Paul stressed that no one should speak in a strange tongue unless an interpreter is present so that everyone could benefit from it. That scripture is First Corinthians 14:28: "What is to be done then, brothers, when you come together? One has a psalm, another a teaching, another a revelation, another a tongue, another an interpretation, but all things take place for upbuilding." Again, a preacher talks in an unknown tongue, is it going to be upbuilding to anyone in the audience? It wouldn't seem like it, would it? You don't even know what he's saying.

It goes on. [He continues to read.] "There are other matters to consider. If the words . . . at Mark 16:17,18, about handling snakes and not being harmed authorized Christians to do so, what about the other things mentioned in those verses? Should not Christian followers also be able to drink poison and not die? And what about

their being able to cure people merely by the laying hands on them?"
It says, "to what conclusions do all these questions lead? There
must be a mistake somewhere. In fact, that's what nearly all modern
Bible scholars have concluded." And this may be a revelation to
you, namely that these words—and not only these words, but all
of what appears in Mark 16:9–20—were not written by Mark, but
were added by a later hand. [Reading again] "On what grounds
do scholars so conclude? On both external and internal evidence."
It says, first of all, there is the telling fact that the oldest and most
highly regarded Bible manuscripts, the Vatican 1209, do not contain
this section. Now there's something to that. Those verses are not
in the oldest manuscripts we can find. What does that say? That
they were added later, possibly. "There are also a number of ancient
manuscripts that contain a short ending of about one verse beyond
8. Other manuscripts contain both conclusions." So, some manuscripts end with verse 8, others have a short ending, others have
a long ending and some even give both endings. "In addition to
all this testimony of the Greek manuscripts, all of which combines
to cast doubt on Mark's having written anything beyond verse 8,
there are a number of the oldest versions or translations that do
not contain the verse in question.

"What if all this evidence were true that this was never even part
of Mark's writing? Doesn't that lend even further credence to that
fact that it's not for Christians to do?" Let's face it, the Bible you've
got in your hand, that was printed in 1611 by the authority of King
James of England. That was some sixteen hundred years since Christ
and the apostles were on earth, wasn't it—fifteen hundred and some
odd years, we should say. All right, in those fifteen hundred years,
do you think that's the same Bible that Christ used? What do you
think? That Bible, just like this one and every other one that we've
got, is a translation of a translation. And I'm not trying to discredit
the Bible in any way, but here's what we've the advantage of, since
1947. Have you ever heard of the Dead Sea Scrolls? Do you know
what that's done for Bible scholars? It's been absolutely amazing.
Recently they've found some they think are even older.

Let me read you Benjamin Wilson's comment on the King James
Version of the Bible. Benjamin Wilson was not one of Jehovah's
Witnesses. This is what he stated: "In the year 1604, forty-seven
persons learned in the languages were appointed to revise the translation then in use." So you see, they already had a translation; they
were just going to revise it. "They were ordered to use the Bishop's
Bible as a basis for the new version and to alter it as little as the
original would allow, but if the prior translations of Tyndale, Cover-

PLATE 31 Young members of Jehovah's Witnesses at a Sunday morning *Watchtower* study.

dale, Matthew, Cramer, Woodchurch, and the Geneva editions agreed better with the text, to adopt the same." They were saying the one that agreed more, use it. [He continues reading.] "This translation was perhaps the best that could be made at the time and if it had not been published by Kingly authority, it would not now be venerated by English and American Protestants as though it had come direct from God." It's a translation just like everything else we have—subject to errors.

This is what Wilson goes on to say: "It," talking about the King James, "has been convicted of containing over twenty thousand errors. Nearly seven hundred Greek manuscripts are now known and some of them are very ancient, whereas the translators of the common version of the King James had the advantage of only eight manuscripts, none of which were any earlier than the tenth century." This was written in '42 before the Dead Sea Scrolls were even found. So what he's saying is they only had eight basic manuscripts to make the King James from. They have found manuscripts now dated back before Christ was ever on the earth. When they read, they find that the King James had verses 9–20 in Mark that wasn't in those. So you see how the human tendency is, that once you've got something, how're you going to admit to yourself that it really isn't what it should've been? A man who would simply say, "Well, it's in my King James," and not consider the evidence that this scripture was probably spurious and added later—if that's the case, if you blind yourself to it, it can affect your worship. Because what if God didn't want Christians to be handling snakes? Is that really what Christianity is all about, handling snakes and drinking poison? It doesn't appear like it, does it?

Are there any major doctrinal differences between Jehovah's Witnesses and other religions?

ERNEST: Really, I'll tell you, there are very few doctrines, basically, that Jehovah's Witnesses agree with the majority of other religions on. And we like to point out the reasons. Let's consider a few of the teachings, and you will see some of the differences. Well, [he reads] hardly anyone would disagree with the first one. The first one is, "The Bible is God's word and is truth." The second one is, "The Bible is more reliable than tradition." Now the third one is, "God's name is Jehovah." I've noticed some of the ministers on the local radio using it occasionally. You'll find among Jehovah's Witnesses, if you ever come to the Kingdom Hall, it's used as often as the word "God," or maybe even more often. One of the things we feel is a mistake among most of the churches of Christendom is that they don't really understand what the name means and the importance of it. There're several scriptures in the Bible that show that really a Christian's salvation is dependent on knowing the name of God. You ask the average person, "What's our Creator's name?" and he says, "God" or "Jesus." Our contention is that the word Jehovah is a name, where the word God is a title or position.

First Corinthians 8:5,6—what does it say? "There are many Gods and many Lords, but to us there is one God and one Lord, Jesus Christ."

RUTH: And we think we need to differentiate between the two and to set Jehovah's name higher than all the others.

ERNEST: This is one of the commissions Jehovah's Witnesses take to heart, take literally. They feel that the glorification or the sanctification or the honoring of the name of their Creator is absolutely number one. This isn't saying that they do it perfectly and a hundred percent. They try. They're imperfect just like the Baptists, like the Catholics. They try, you know, in their lives.

RUTH: The word "Jesus" means "Jehovah Saves."

ERNEST: It means Jehovah is salvation. You know, any word in the Bible that you ever see that ends with "jah"? That's a shortened form of Jehovah. Have you ever heard the word at Christmastime, "Hallelujah"? It means "praise Jehovah." How many people sing that and don't know what it means? We're trying to get people to know the meaning.

PLATE 32 *Watchtowers.*

RUTH: Our point on it is, many people not knowing Jehovah's name and not knowing the importance of Jehovah are actually rendering worship that belongs to Jehovah to Christ.

ERNEST: In the Bible, in Exodus, the third chapter, it says, "And God said unto Moses, 'I am that I am,' " and that's the literal meaning of the letters JHVH. When the Hebrew text was received from whatever manuscripts that were available, all the scholars of the world had to work with was these four letters, JHVH. Those are all consonants and no vowels, and scholars changed it into readable language.

One of the major differences between Jehovah's Witnesses and other Christians is what the ultimate destiny of the God-fearing person is. To the Baptist, there are two destinies to the average person . . .

RUTH: Heaven and hell . . .

ERNEST: You see, this is probably one of the biggest disagreements that people have with us when we go to them—we don't believe that we have an immortal soul. You see, there's no such word as immortal soul in the Bible. Did you know that? Yet you hear it constantly, don't you? The immortal soul? You've heard that term? The two words are not found in conjunction in the Bible. You see, you have to believe that a person's soul is immortal in order to

PLATE 33 Copies of *Awake!* and the *New World Translation of the Holy Scriptures.*

believe in hell fire. Because what good would it be for God to send you to hell fire if you're truly dead and don't know anything?

Here're some basic reasons why we believe this. God saw fit to create man. The Bible says He created us in His image, didn't He? All right, remember how the first man was made? This will give us a clue as to what we are and where we're going when we die. Let me read it to you. It says, "And Jehovah God proceeded to form the man out of the dust of the ground and blew into his nostrils the breath of life." And it says, "And the man came to be a living soul." Now there really is the basis of the whole thing. According to that formula—He's telling us how He made man—There are two basic ingredients, the dust of the ground and the breath of life. Now when He combines those two, what did He say He made? Man became a what?

RUTH: Living soul.

ERNEST: Did you catch that? But do you know what ninety-nine percent of the people read into that? God *gave* him a soul. Now is there a difference or not? If my wife said, "I'm going to go make a cake," she doesn't go get the flour and the sugar and all the ingredients that goes into a cake, she doesn't put it all together and then put a cake into it, does she? It's simply a result of the combining of those things. In other words, after you've combined all of these things and put it in the oven, you have a completed cake. What happens if a person dies out in the desert? Their body goes right back into the atoms and molecules of the ground. So what is it then about man . . . it says here, it says that "he *became* a living soul" as a result of God's breathing His breath into him.

Now would it shock you for me to tell you that animals are souls too? Genesis 1:20 and Numbers 31:28 says that they are. Ruth was taught for forty years that man has a soul instead of *being* a soul. We believe that we *are* the soul, as long as we are living. As long as we have the breath of life. We honestly believe that when humans die that they simply are out of existence. NOWHERE. The only chance a person has of living again is if you're in God's memory and He chooses to resurrect you at the Last Day as the Bible says.

Hell, as far as Jehovah's Witnesses are concerned, is simply wherever your grave is. It could be six feet under the ground, it could be in a fish's belly if you died out at sea. That could be your hell, your grave. Remember when Jonah was thrown overboard? Let me read you from the King James Version, what he said and where he said he was. They found out that Jonah was the sinner among them causing the waves so they cast lots and threw him overboard. Jonah 2:2 says: "Then Jonah prayed unto the Lord his God out of the fish's belly," and notice where he's at, now, he's already been swallowed, "and said, 'I cried by reason of my affliction unto the Lord, and He heard me. Out of the belly of hell cried I, and thou heardest my voice.'" Now, do you you suppose he was feeling the flames of hell licking up around him inside that fish's belly? That doesn't really seem reasonable, does it? What do you think he thought was really going to happen to him? He thought he was going to die there, didn't he? That's what he thought was going to happen.

Now, to Jehovah's Witnesses, it seems more reasonable that hell is simply the abode of the dead, simply a state of non-existence, it makes more sense that this is where Jesus was for parts of three days. Then, what did God do at that time? He restored him back to life.

Let me show you another scripture that will help to reinforce that. Ecclesiastes 9:4–10, and listen, it says, "For to him that is joined to all the living there is hope: for a living dog is better than a dead lion. For the living know that they shall die; but the dead know not any thing, neither have they any more a reward; for the memory of them is forgotten. Also their love, and their hatred, and their envy, is now perished; neither have they any more a portion forever in anything that is done under the sun." Then dropping on down to verse 10, it says: "Whatsoever thy hand findeth to do, do it with thy might; for there is no work, nor device, no knowledge, nor wisdom, in the grave, whither thou goest." Remember, the word "grave" means hell. Notice what it says? That the dead know nothing, they don't have any more wisdom, knowledge, work, or device. And so, if there is no consciousness, then there can be no fiery hell, can there? Otherwise, what would be its reason for being? And you recall when God made Adam and Eve there, back in Genesis? He put them in the Garden of Eden? Remember what He told them? "Be fruitful, multiply, and fill the earth." And then he laid one restriction on them; remember what it was?

THE TREE. . . .

ERNEST: and what did He say would happen to them if they ate of the tree?

THEY'D DIE. . . .

ERNEST: You mean he didn't tell them they'd go to hell and burn forever? See? That's what people read into it. But we just can't see it; it's not there. He never promised them that "I'm going to burn you forever and ever because you ate from the tree." In fact, what He actually said was: "dust you are, dust you will return to."

This is what Romans 6:7 says, "For he who has died has been acquitted from his sins." So you see, once you die, you've paid the penalty for sin. That is it. It's not burning forever and being tortured. So that's why God then can resurrect them on the basis of Christ's ransom, you see. Because he paid the price.

Do Jehovah's Witnesses believe only 144,000 people will be chosen by God to be resurrected on the final day?

RUTH: Many are confused about the 144,000. This is because they have no concept of anything more than heaven and hell as man's final destiny and they leave out the earth, which the Bible does not do. The Bible shows that the earth was to be inhabited and would be here forever. So they have no other place for their people to go. They say there either has to be a heaven or hell. And certainly there's going to be more people alive than 144,000, so they get hung up and that number angers them because they think "there's no chance for me if there's only 144,000." But actually there is a great number of people destined, more than anyone can number, destined to live on the earth. And by leaving out the earth, they leave out God's hope for mankind. Earth will be brought back to the paradise condition that the Garden was in.

ERNEST: In other words, you see what it's getting back to? What God had originally purposed. For man and woman to live on the earth, to fill it with a righteous race of humans and to enjoy life forever. You see, the only time God ever told Adam and Eve that He'd terminate their life was if they disobeyed. So, what would be the alternative or the opposite of disobedience and death? Obedi-

PLATE 34   The Clark family at the Kingdom Hall.

ence and life, wouldn't it? And he never promised them, "Well,"
He says, "listen here, Adam, if you live and don't eat of that tree
for a thousand years then I'll take you to heaven." He never promised
them that, either, did He?

The reason for the Kingdom of Heaven was to rule over the earth.
The Bible shows Christ made a covenant with them that they would
be kings and priests over the earth. That's recorded at Revelation
5:10 and Luke 22:29. And think what a situation we've got here.
Here's a man who'd been on earth serving as our king and there's
the underkings and underpriests—a 144,000 people who have lived
on the earth—what better representation would you and I want in
heaven than somebody who's already lived as a person? So then
our feeling is that those 144,000 plus Christ are the only ones that've
ever been promised heavenly life.

You see, nobody really went to heaven before Jesus, did they?
Think about that for a minute. Isn't he the one that opened the
way?

RUTH: The Bible says of man born of woman there is none greater
than John the Baptist and that he that is least in the Kingdom of
Heaven is greater than he is. This was said because John died before
Jesus opened the way to heavenly life. I think it's Hebrews 11:13
that says that they never received the promise but still the promise
is there for them, that they will be resurrected in God's due time
and brought back to live.

ERNEST: In other words, this 144,000 that we're talking about began
to be numbered clear back when Jesus died. So, all of Christ's apos-

tles were part of that—those who died after him. That's why that scripture Ruth mentioned awhile ago says that the lowest angel in heaven is still greater than John the Baptist, because he never went to heaven. And can you think of anybody more worthy to go to heaven, if you were to list those worthy, than John the Baptist? He opened the way for Jesus, baptized Jesus. He never became part of the 144,000. So this 144,000 have been selected for the past two thousand years.

Ruth's husband died about two years ago. As much as she loved her husband, she doesn't feel that he was sent to heaven. You don't have that feeling at all, do you?

RUTH: No.

ERNEST: So she realized and actually is comforted in knowing that he, no doubt, will be resurrected back to the earthly scene. And frankly, most of Jehovah's Witnesses, the 2.2 million that don't profess to be of the heavenly class, have a longing to live here on earth forever. We feel that this is what we were made for.

So during the thousand-year reign of Christ's Kingdom—which Jehovah's Witnesses feel is not in the long distant future—the Bible shows that all the earth, literally billions, probably, will have the opportunity to be resurrected and then to be able to learn the Bible truths without having the sin of Adam being charged to them. It's already been paid.

What happens if the end of the world comes, say in my lifetime or your lifetime?

RUTH: Jesus says that as the days of Noah were, so it will be at that time. That's one good expression for this because it shows that many were taken alive into a whole new—well, the earth was here, but it was a cleansed earth at that time. So this was an example; that was a miniature picture that Jesus gave of how it will be at the end of the system of things.

ERNEST: So this is where the majority of mankind will live. As we said, the billions who have died and maybe the millions who will live through the Battle of Armageddon and *never* have to die, they will form the nucleus for the new earth. And then those as they are resurrected back in an orderly fashion will be able to be taken care of, see? Housing, education and so forth will be available to them. Then, of course, the Bible shows that at the end of a thousand years man will be retested, but under completely different circumstances. This time he'll be tested just like Adam was; the perfect human with the influence of the devil. The devil will only be let loose right at the end of the thousand years. And he will accomplish some of his purpose.

During the thousand-year reign in Revelation, the 20th chapter, notice what it says is going to happen here, it says, "I saw the dead, small and great, stand before God; and the books were opened, and another book was opened, which was the Book of Life; and the dead were judged out of those things which were written in the books, according to their works." Then it says, notice? "And the sea gave up the dead which were in it." Now think about that for a minute. Remember a while ago I said when you die, if you die out at sea, that could be your hell or your grave?

RUTH: So these people in hell are dead. That's what the Bible says.

ERNEST: But now if those people were condemned to eternal torment, have you ever heard of anybody ever getting out of hell? Is there a concept of that ever known? To my knowledge, I've heard them say . . . when you go to hell you're there forever basically. But here it says, "death and hell delivered up." Again, how can death deliver up something? Is it a tangible thing? It's a state of being, isn't it? It's a condition, isn't it? Then this is what we say hell is, or the grave, it's a condition of the dead. And notice what it says here, "death and hell delivered up the dead which were in them; and they were judged every man according to their works. And death and hell were cast into the lake of fire." And then it's all cleared up in these words, it says, "This is the second death."

RUTH: And this second death is God's judgment. These people will be dead forever.

ERNEST: So once they've been resurrected back, if they prove unworthy then for life, under the system where the devil isn't there to influence them, where they no longer can say, "Well, I'm just a sinner like Adam," then they will be removed from the earthly scene to never ever experience a resurrection. But, it simply says it's the second death. And it used such terms here as "death and hell were cast into the lake of fire." Well, how can you cast an intangible thing into a lake of fire? You can do it simply by removing death from the earth, can't you? Removing the plague of death.

RUTH: That's what the Bible says in 1 Corinthians 15:26 that "death will be destroyed."

ERNEST: And in Revelation the 21st chapter, verse 4, it says, "God will wipe away all tears from their eyes; there will be no more death, neither sorrow nor crying nor pain be any more; the former things have passed away." This is our hope for the future and what we feel will be the answer to the prayers of righteous ones everywhere.

INTERVIEW AND PHOTOGRAPHS BY LARRY CARTER AND RICKY WEAVER

Methodists

The World, the devil and Tom Paine;
Have tried their best, but all in vain,
They can't prevail, the reason is,
The Lord defends the Methodist. . . .
They pray, they preach, they sing the best
and do the devil most molest,
If Satan had his vicious way,
He'd kill and damn them all today.
They are despised by Satan's train
Because they shout and preach so plain
I'm bound to march in endless bliss,
and die a shouting Methodist. . . .*
(Frontier Methodist hymn)

The Methodists and their brand of religion were well accepted in the mountains. Church related activities of this denomination appealed to the people, as evidenced by the recollections of those who appear in this section:

E. L. ADAMS, 100 years old and a Methodist preacher, remembers strong, spontaneous, and enthusiastic revivals.

JULIE McCLURE, 105, recalls the "protracted meeting" and old camps where "they had the best meetings in the world." She adds that "back then when you got religion, you kept it; people lived right."

CONLEY HENRY discusses "all day singings" and "dinner on the grounds."

LEONARD VISSAGE, who joined the Methodists in 1914, remembers a footwashing at his church and other "wonderful, wonderful times."

E. C. PRESLEY, a Baptist who turned Methodist when he married, talks of the time when those two denominations worked together and combined their services.

In contrast to these warm reminiscences, several of those interviewed express concern over a perceived change in the attitudes and practices of Methodists and the religious in general. Conley Henry, for example, worries about the new, more liberal stands on open marriage, abortion, and women in church pulpits; Leonard Vissage, in a more general way, questions the dedication and convic-

---

* William Warren Sweet, *Religion in the Development of American Cultutre, 1765–1840* (New York: Charles Scribner's Sons, 1952), p. 158.

tions of younger generations. These concerns are indeed real to many and will most certainly receive future consideration in not only Methodist circles but all denominations.

In general, Methodist theology has been and will continue to be appealing to a great number of individuals. Those like E. L. Adams and Julie McClure are living examples of its impact on religious life in Appalachia.

PAUL F. GILLESPIE

E. L. ADAMS, Methodist

E. L. Adams, a Methodist minister, is the second oldest person interviewed for this study. At 100 years of age, Reverend Adams remembers when the Methodist Church was composed of two major groups, the Northern Methodists and the Southern Methodists. Reverend Adams began his ministry around the year 1900 and traveled a country circuit to different Northern Methodist churches in the mountains. He recounted when the two branches of this faith combined and happily added that "the combination churches did a heap better work than they did when they were separated."

While many Protestant individuals and groups are adamant that their particular theology and beliefs represent the only true way, therefore ruling out any spirit of cooperation, there are others, including Reverend Adams, who have always believed that churches of different denominations should work together in their ministry and outreach. He, himself, preached in several different churches. He says, "It never made any difference to me whether I was in a Northern Methodist pulpit, a Southern Methodist pulpit, or a Baptist pulpit. I was just preaching to folks and I always had a good congregation." This short interview exemplifies this spirit of mutual cooperation as Reverend Adams discusses his ministry.

KEITH HEAD

I was raised in a very religious home. My father was a preacher, and I grew up under the influence of the home. We had family prayer twice a day. I always went to Sunday school, and I joined the church when I was eight years old. I was baptized by immersion in a small fish pond [near] where I was raised. They've always used some pond or some stream. The church I joined was the Congregational Methodist church. There is no difference in the Congregational Methodists and the regular Methodists except the Congregationalists select their pastors, and the regular Methodists serve their pastors [to the churches] from the conference. I don't remember any special experience that I had except I was leading prayer and Sunday school and things like that by the time I was nine or ten years old.

I had the idea I was going to be sent as a missionary. I finally made up my mind and decided that what the Lord wanted me to do would be [foreign mission work]. The impression I got [from God was], "You are right where I want you." I was at Young Harris [Georgia] teaching and preaching at these country churches. I felt that the Lord wanted me to preach. I commenced preaching by the time I was twenty-one or twenty-two years old.

I usually preached in the country churches under the pastor of the Young Harris church. I was the junior preacher. At the beginning, there were four Southern Methodist country churches and four Northern Methodist churches. Back during the Civil War, there were as many folks in this country that went to the Federal Army as went to the Confederate Army. When the war was over, more folks had been bushwhacked and killed in this country than had been killed in the army. You can understand what a division there would have been. So the two churches were separated. The Northern Methodists had one pastor that came here. Finally, when the Northern Methodists became weak, and on the occasion when they didn't have a pastor, I went and preached if they invited me to. Finally the Northern Methodists appointed me over their country churches. It wasn't long until the Northern Methodists were wanting to combine with the Southern Methodists, but I held them off until the conferences did the combining. We consolidated some of those Northern Methodists with the Southern Methodists, and some Southern Methodists with the Northern Methodists. The separated churches were then combined. The combination churches did a heap better work than they did when they were separated. It never made any difference to me whether I was in a Northern Methodist pulpit, a Southern Methodist pulpit, or a Baptist pulpit. I was just preaching to folks, and I always had a good congregation.

I never made any difference or felt any difference between folks, regardless of their profession. In the churches where I preached, I had the Holiness that came in to help with the singing and praying. I will give you this illustration: I was running a revival meeting and a Holiness preacher and his wife came along. They tried to run a meeting in one of the Methodist churches on the head of Hightower where I was pastor. The folks didn't want them in there. The regular organized churches didn't give them much encouragement. They came on down to this other church [where I was running the revival], and they told me they'd like to attend my services if I didn't object. I said I didn't object to anybody. They were good

PLATE 35   Editor, Paul Gillespie, and Reverend E. L. Adams.

singers and I put them at the head of the singing and leading prayers and one thing and another; both he and his wife would pray publicly. So time ran along, and it came to the end of the second week [of revival]. I had about a dozen that had joined the church. About half of them wanted to be immersed and about half sprinkled; they had their choice. There was a pool in the creek right down past the church that all the denominations used. So I set [the time to baptize] at Sunday morning at nine o'clock for the ones to be immersed.

There was a schoolhouse right close to the church. When I went down there to put on clothes that I didn't mind getting wet, this Baptist preacher was in there changing his. He was going to baptize a woman that wanted to join the Baptist church. There had come up a squabble in the Baptist church as to whether she'd have to be re-immersed; I'd immersed her [before]. The leaders of the Baptist church had decided, according to the law of the Baptist church, she'd have to be re-immersed, and by a Baptist preacher. I wasn't a Baptist preacher. Some of them had said if my baptism wasn't good, then they didn't know why. But they went according to the law and she had to be re-immersed. About a month before, he had set that [same] Sunday morning to baptize her in that pool beside our church where I was going to baptize. Well, this Baptist preacher was in that schoolhouse changing his clothes. He began to apologize and said he hoped he wasn't interfering with me. I said, "no," that there was never any interference concerning worship, no matter who it is.

Well, I had this Holiness preacher and his wife to sing, and the Baptist preacher and I went up together to the pool, and we arranged it this way: I was to go in first and he was to lead my four (I believe it was four) in to me to immerse them and lead them back. And when he came in with the fourth one, I'd go out and lead his one in [for him to baptize]. [While he was baptizing his,] I got over to the other end of the pool, and I thought I put my foot on a rock. I sort of put my weight on it to shove it down in the mud and it proved to be a mud turtle! I held him down there until we got through, and then we went to the schoolhouse [to change clothes]. I said to this Baptist preacher, "Brother Jones," (I don't remember what his name was) "did you notice anything unusual when you went in there?"

He said, "No."

I told him about that mud turtle and he broke out in a big laugh. He said, "You certainly are getting things together. You got a Holiness preacher standing on the bank singing his heart out, and joining in with a Baptist and Methodist preacher at a baptizing. They were all there, but I had no idea there was a Hardshell Baptist around!"

The attitude of one denomination toward another certainly has [changed]. The attitude of the Protestant church toward the Catholics certainly has changed [for the good]. My attitude is this: There is one God, one Bible, one Savior, one Holy Spirit, and God is the heavenly Father of everybody.

The world is getting better. You see, there's an attitude in all the different denominations; the leaders of the various divisions in the churches of the world today are nearer together than they used to be. I've set down over here in a Baptist church when a Baptist preacher would turn around toward the "amen" corner and make a statement that if you weren't immersed and didn't belong to the Baptist church, you didn't have any chance to get to heaven. Now, that's all quit. Of course, the denominations give the people the best chance to join what they want to and what they believe. You take the people of the world. The leaders of the main nations right now are getting together and settling their disputes. They're settling by mutual understanding rather than by war. I've lived long enough to see a heap of changes.

PLATE 36 Mrs. Julie McClure.

JULIE McCLURE, Methodist

Julie McClure, who we learned about through an article by Barbara McRae in the Franklin (*North Carolina*) Press, *has the distinction of being the oldest person we have interviewed for this publication. Mrs. McClure was born October 1, 1875, in a log cabin near Hayesville, North Carolina, the daughter of Matilda Johnson Coleman and George Coleman. Both of her grandfathers were immigrants to this country, one from Ireland and one from Scotland.*

At 105, Mrs. McClure possesses a great awareness and, even though she is hard of hearing and her eyesight is not what she would like it to be, we were intrigued that she could remember so much about her earlier experiences, particularly the ones of a religious nature. It seems that those were the most vivid and she attaches much significance to them.

Mrs. McClure has lived in the mountains all of her life and has witnessed many traditions that have been on the decline or vanished altogether over the years. For example, her mother carded wool and wove material for clothing; her father tanned hides and made shoes. She emphatically pointed out that "he even made his own wooden pegs for those shoes." As true of many mountain families, they also made such things as soap, candles, and molasses.

Julie McClure also remembers aspects of mountain religion that have nearly disappeared; she talks of old-time "protracted meetings" and the fact that the Sabbath Day was strictly and rigidly observed. She clearly remembers her conversion experiences and being baptized. Mrs. McClure admits to being a "proud Methodist" for just about all of her 105 years and it pleases us to have a person of her age and Christian experience included here.

KEITH HEAD

I got religion on my own feeling. I went [to church] ever since I was big enough to know what going was. I can go right to the spot today where I got saved at a protracted meeting. We called it a protracted meeting back then. Old-times, you know. Old-fashioned times. That's what I love. It was on the side of the road going home [that I got saved]. I was fourteen years old. I joined the church at that time, the old M. E. Methodist Church, and I've belonged to it ever since. Sure did.

I was sprinkled twice. The first time I was sprinkled at home. I remember that, too. I was small. The preacher came by from the campground and stopped to speak with me and my little sister. Old preacher Campbell was his name. Gray-bearded. He was going back home from the camp meeting. My father came out and hung me up and spanked me for running [from the preacher]. Carried me under his arms and the preacher sprinkled me. Then when I got religion and went to join the church I was sprinkled again. They sprinkled me in the church. I was always a Methodist.

It used to I'd never heard tell of [anything but Methodist]. It's the truth. The old M. E. Methodist Church is the first church that I can remember and that's been a right long time, you know. It's been there ever since the world's been standing, I reckon. I wouldn't ever part from the Methodists. That's right. I know all about it.

I knew [the church] to have camp meetings [with] tents built around a big arbor. Back when I was nine years old, I went there. My father had a tent built there. Nothing bothered it but the Methodists. The Methodists were the ones that run it. It had a big, long arbor and you had to go out there and hear preaching. The people would move there. Take their rations with them and move there and stay for six weeks and run that meeting. I remember all about it. I was about nine or ten years old then. I can remember back then better than I can now.

Used to have the best meetings in the world. I'm sorry they tore the camp meeting up. I'll tell you, those camp times were the best times you ever saw. People took their own rations down. They didn't go and buy it; they raised it in the fields and gathered it up and took it there to feed the people at the campground.

They had good [revivals] too. They had them in the daytime and of the night, too. Now they just have a little of the night. They'd work in the field until meeting time and then they'd go with just what they had on and have preaching at twelve o'clock [noon] and then they'd have meeting of a night.

Never saw but one woman in my life have the Holy Ghost in the Methodist church. She'd come to Sunday school every Sunday. She'd dance and testify in Sunday school. She was Methodist and that's what she did every Sunday. She said she was sanctified.

Back then when you got religion you kept it. People lived right. They wouldn't grind coffee on Sunday. They wouldn't churn on Sunday. They wouldn't bake bread on Sunday. They sure did live straight. My mother raised two or three loaves of bread every Saturday and it done 'til Monday.

I was raised to go to church. I was raised in a religious home. I had four brothers and two sisters. My father stayed upstairs and in the night when he'd get ready to go to bed, he'd come downstairs and have prayer. I always went to Sunday school and meetings. I was raised religious.

I can remember when my mother made my dresses to my ankles and I had to wear them there. She'd make my step-ins to come down, you know. And I didn't think that I wanted to wear them down there long. When I'd get to school, I'd roll them up. I'd pull them [down] before I got back home. They'd make them nice, you know. They'd put trimming on them. I thought that was a little too tacky. I didn't like it.

[We never did play cards either.] Pshaw, no! I remember burning one deck they brought in my house after I was married. My mother would never have that thing in her house—a deck of cards. That's the devil's work.

[People today] ain't got what they used to have, I don't believe. I feel that way. Times ain't like they used to be. No, there ain't nothing like it. I just feel the end of time ain't far off. I believe that the Lord's coming. I know we're in the last days. The Bible's about fulfilled. It's already fulfilled.

PLATE 37   Conley Henry.

CONLEY HENRY, Methodist

We met Conley Henry quite by accident. On a hot and humid summer day while we were on a general search mission for religious material, we happened by old Double Springs Methodist Church. Its mere appearance suggested an interesting historical significance and we stopped at little stores and houses looking for some of its members. We were directed to the home of Conley Henry who welcomed us warmly amidst the noisy barking of dogs not yet convinced of our intent. After running a power cord out onto the cool porch from inside the house, the tape recorder was turned on and Mr. Henry began telling us about his church and his beliefs. As this interview will indicate, Mr. Henry was frank, open, and extremely straightforward.

Born August 13, 1909, in Jefferson, Georgia, he has since lived most of his life in the mountainous regions of Georgia and North and South Carolina. He joined the church in 1918 (which at that time was composed of both Methodist and Baptist members) and he has closely watched it and others develop since that time. There are many aspects and problems of our society that concern Mr. Henry, but through his testimony, it is indeed evident that he is honest in his beliefs and steadfast in his faith.

KEITH HEAD

My wife and I both were born in Georgia. I was born in Jefferson right out of Gainesville. I've lived in and out of this country practically all my life except from '36 to '42 when I worked with the National Park Service. Then in '42, the war came on and, of course, we were all facing the draft. In '42 I worked on the farm right here for about a year. In '43 I went to work for the United States Forest Service [in Montana]. Later in '43 I was drafted. I went into the army in January, '44 and left a wife and two children, as many did.

[I don't remember when I was first introduced to the Methodist Church.] So many years has happened since that. I was born in 1909, you see, and [my conversion] was along in the 1920s. I joined the Greenstreet Methodist Church in Gainesville at the age, I daresay, around twelve years. Both my sister and I became members. The pastor there was Reverend Mack Eakes.

My wife's people have been members of [Double Springs Methodist Church] ever since there's been a church out there. She was a Mongold. And from this book of the church [he holds up church record book], you'll see [the name of] William Mongold. The church was established on September 9, 1858, as a union church. The deed was executed by Eliot M. Keith and Alexander Bryce, Sr. [In the deed] Lewis Moorehead, Ron Fretwell, and Gambel Brazeale [were named as trustees]. The lot contained ten acres, more or less, and it was deeded for the cause of religion. Up until the late 1940s, both the Baptist and the Methodist faiths worshipped at this church. Up until just late years, it was always known as Double Springs Methodist Church, not Double Springs United Methodist. We don't call ourselves "united." In fact, there's still a legal question, which is open to controversy, as whether we actually have become the United Methodist Church or not, because we became United Methodist and we didn't know it.

They had some awful hot times out there at that church when it was a union church, and we're still having some trying times yet. [The friction] wasn't between the two denominations, it was between Baptists and Baptists and Methodists and Methodists. There was practically no friction between Baptists and Methodists. We've always figured that the friction that came about was a family friction rather than a denominational friction.

In the late forties, the Baptists pulled out and built a church of their own. And just until very recently, in the last year, they called their church Double Springs Baptist Church. There was some other Double Springs Baptist churches on Oconee County [South Carolina] and they saw fit to change their name to Mountain Rest. Mountain Rest Baptist Church. Now, the cemetery out there [Double Springs cemetery] is just as old as the church is. It's a union cemetery. There's people of all faiths buried out there. People that don't belong to a church at all. There's Methodists and Baptists.

It was [common then for Methodists and Baptists to worship together], because that was the only church out here. People from Pine Mountain [Georgia] came and worshipped. In fact, Baylus Nicholson, whose name is listed right there, is a man from up at Pine Mountain. One of the Baylus Nicholsons (now there's several Baylus Nicholsons, it was a common name among Nicholsons), this Baylus is the father of one of the beloved Rangers in Rabun County [Georgia]. I know you've heard of Forest Ranger Roscoe Nicholson. In fact, the Coleman River Wildlife area [has] a monument to Roscoe Nicholson [because] he was the first ranger on that district. Out there at that church in the early days, some slaves saw fit to stay with their white people when they were freed; in fact, that was the case with my wife's mother. There was a slave that stayed with her and they always spoke of her—now, this word would be forbidden now—she was known as Nigger Mary, and Nigger Mary, no doubt, had worshipped out here at this very same little church.

I can remember one expression that my mother [learned from] a particular old lady that was there [who was], no doubt, very, very devout. She said, "May the Spirit of the Lord descend on this congregation like fire going through the broomsage." Now, you know what broomsage is, don't you? Now, when fire goes through broomsage, it goes in a hurry, don't it?

They [used to get] quite emotional and shouted. They had another little expression that always brought a little bit of laughter to us. This particular individual, she was evidently shouting and she became so emotionally upset that she fainted. And you know how it was in the old days when anybody fainted, why, they all crowded around—just a big crowd around 'em. So someone began to walk in and push 'em back and says, "Boys, stand back, stand back," (and they called her Sal). Says, "Sal's got to have air, God or no God!" So, you'll agree with that, wouldn't you? Now, those things have been handed down to me. As the saying goes, "The truth it may or may not be." But the two things that I said, there's nothing sacriligious about them if you take it seriously. There was a person there that fainted, and the fellows didn't know much about first aid then. The man knew that she had to have air, and he began pushing them back 'cause "Sal's got to have air, God or no God."

In the present Methodist church out there now—perhaps one of the failings of the church, I'd say, [is that] we haven't had a revival out there at that church in ten or fifteen years. We used to have them many years ago. My wife's in there; she'll sort of coach me a little on that. They had revivals and at times we'd have a Baptist minister for one revival, and then on another revival, we'd have a Methodist. That, you might say, is one of the failings of our church now. I was talking to an eighty-year-old citizen yesterday (his name's mentioned on [the church record]—he's a Vissage), and he said the last revival we'd had there was about ten or fifteen years ago.

MRS. HENRY: Yes, I can [remember that]. We had a week of it and we'd have a morning and an evening service. Everybody'd get happy.

MR. HENRY: Lots of times those revivals would be in August. Yeah, hottest time there was, and they'd have a morning session and an evening session. Some of the ones that attended those revivals, they'd call it "roast 'n ear religion."

MRS. HENRY: We didn't have the camp meeting or the brush arbors. The Methodists and the Baptists out here did not have it.

MR. HENRY: [We'd] have a protracted meeting and it would last two weeks. It was the custom then to invite the preachers home to dinner. They'd stay in the home while they were here. Now that was back in horse and buggy days. In fact, right across the road from that old church there used to be a hitchin' rack. They'd tie their horse or their mule up to a swinging limb. That's been in memory of my day. I can remember when they had the horses. People came out there and they had dinner on the grounds. They'd just spread the tablecloth down on the ground and put the food down on the ground; of course, we had ants, yellow jackets, and things like that to contend with just like we do now. Some of those old trees out there could tell you more about it than I could if they could talk.

The first homecoming that I know of anything about was this hundredth homecoming August 10, 1958. The pastor then was Reverend Robert J. Howell.

We've survived several storms in that church out there. Some have not been too pleasant. Along in 1958, they wanted to move that church—move the church from its present location over to Highway 28. A good many of the older members didn't want to move and some of the younger day generation did. We took a vote on the thing. We thought we were outnumbered and apparently the good Lord took a hand in that. That took place somewhere around 1958, because this man [Robert Howell] was the pastor of the church. Anyhow, we went to see the district superintendent, B. B. Black, who was down here in Anderson, South Carolina. He made us the commitment that they'd never make the proposal to move our church

100th Anniversary
HOMECOMING PROGRAM

Sunday, August 10, 1958

Double Springs Methodist Church
Mountain Rest, S. C.

THE REV. ROBERT J. HOWELL
Pastor

PLATE 38

PRELUDE

CALL TO WORSHIP

INVOCATION

HYMN: "HOW FIRM A FOUNDATION"   46

AFFIRMATION OF FAITH

WORDS OF WELCOME

RESPONSIVE READING SELECTION 341 "THE HEAVENLY HOME"

GLORIA PATRI

SCRIPTURE LESSON

SILENT MEDITATION

PASTORAL PRAYER

THE LORD'S PRAYER

OFFERING

HYMN: "SWEET BY AND BY"   199

SERMON.................... ... REV. WARREN T. GREENE

HYMN: "GOD BE WITH YOU"   277

BENEDICTION

POSTLUDE

The entire offering received today will go into the
building fund of the church.

HISTORY OF DOUBLE SPRINGS CHURCH

The Double Springs Church was organized as
a "union church" in 1858. On September 9, 1858,
Elliott M. Keith and Alexander Brice, Sr. executed
a deed to Lewis Moorehead, Bryan Fretwell, and
Gambrell Frenzeale as trustees, conveying a lot
of ten acres. The consideration was for: "Cause
of Religion". It is significant that no sect or
denomination was mentioned. For about 90 years
the Methodist and Baptist worshipped together.
In the late 1940's the Baptist built a church,
and since that time this building has been used
solely by the Methodist congregation.

Mention might be made of the names of some
of the early members, both Baptist and Methodist.
Among them are Lewis Moorehead, Bryan Fretwell,
Gambrell Frenzeale, Abel Robins, Ransom Hunt,
Andrew Keys, William Mongold, Charley Hunt, Robert
Crisp, A. J. M. Billingsley, S. G. Herndon, W. G.
Russell, Baylis Nicholson, Simpson Moseley, Billy
Lyles, George Simms, Jacob McCall, George Killian,
W. H. McGill, James W. Vissage, Tyler Gillespie,
Lawson Brown, Harriett Pell, Mary Barker and her
colored girl, Sue Sarker.

The original building was remodeled in the
early 1900's with the cement steps being added in
1948. The Sunday School Rooms were added in 1961
with the present remodeling program beginning
July 1, 1964.

PLATE 39   Opened Program for the One Hundredth Anniversary of Double Springs Methodist Church.

again. It's never come up again about moving that church anywhere.

Singing was a popular thing; in fact, they would have an all day singing and then dinner on the ground. They'd come from Pine Mountain all up in there. The all day singing and dinner on the ground was quite common. They didn't have any trouble then [in getting people to come sing]; in fact, I can remember when they used an organ out there. It hasn't been but just the last thirty or forty years or longer that they had a piano. They always used an organ. All day singing and dinner on the ground . . . that was the order of the day. And Baptists, Methodists, and the ones that belong to the big church—meaning the ones that didn't belong to any church whatsoever [all came together].

MRS. HENRY: They would have groups, quartets, and the congregation.

MR. HENRY: Along in the year they [had singing]. We had a pastor here just before the one we have now and he told a little innocent incident. He said that they had a quartet, and he said they had a quartet of *six*.

He told another little interesting thing that happened in Pickens County Court. Now this was in Pickens County, South Carolina and the pastor's name was Reverend Edgar Grant and he'll verify this very story. He said that this particular court, why, as they'd call their name to see whether or not they were present at the court procedures, why [the judge'd say], "When we call your name, we want you to answer with a verse of scripture." So this one would answer with one verse and the other with another and they kind of began to run out of shorter verses. They called on one and he recited as his verse, "Jesus wept." You know, that's the shortest verse in the Bible. Called on this next man and he'd just about run out of verses. He made like he didn't know too much about the verses in the Bible, and this [first] man said, "Jesus wept," so the next man answered, he said, "He sure did."

Now we've had some pretty rough characters around that church; in fact, there has been one of the doors that has been replaced. On one of the original doors out there, there was about a .32 caliber bullet hole. I won't make any statement whatsoever about who shot through the church door. I don't know who did it; all I know is hear-say, and that don't go. Now, why they did it . . . it might have been because he was happy . . . riding a horse or a mule . . . and he decided he'd just shoot at something. [Maybe] he didn't intentionally intend to shoot at the church, but the hole was in the door for anyone to see and was for many days. It is not in the present doors. It happened sometime when there was no worship services at the church. Part of the [church] history that we're not proud of . . . a lot of the people that worshipped out there, they made whiskey—or said they did.

MRS. HENRY: [They'd have church trials.] Church 'em.

MR. HENRY: Church 'em. That's the term they called it.

MRS. HENRY: They've done that out here in this union church—the Baptists have.

MR. HENRY: I don't reckon we've ever had any Divine healing out there or snake handling. There was none of that speaking in tongues.

I don't know how they did about taking communion. You see, the old Methodists believed in open communion and the Baptists, you might say, have closed communion. But if there was ever any friction between the matter of taking communion between the Baptists and the Methodists as long as there was a union church, I never did hear of it. I never heard of anyone being refused communion in this old Methodist church. That's one point of difference now between the Baptists and the Methodists. Of course, the immersion is one thing and sprinkling another. Another [difference] is exhortation. The Methodists don't believe in exhorting anyone to join the church; they apparently didn't.

But, of course, now there's so many things at the Methodist church that I don't agree with and among them is the open marriage, the stand on abortion, and the matter of the Panama Canal—turn it over to the Panamanians. I was in Panama in World War II. And another thing is segregation. The old Southern Methodist Church, which is the only segregation church that I know of, best represents my views on the church. In fact, my father who died in Georgia and was buried up here at Rabun Gap cemetery, told me just as a child, he felt like one of the biggest mistakes the Methodist church ever made was when they united with the Northern Methodist Church. It had to have been somewhere around '36 to '42. I think it was somewhere in '39. Well, '39 was rough times in this country. It was rough times.

The present United Methodist is, in my opinion, on the wrong track. Another thing is gun control. I am not a racist. I am not a racist. I'm saying that twice. If you allow me to select my Black associates and friends, I may be more familiar with them than just the run of the mill Black people. Yeah, if you can select, but to have the Federal government to say I've got to take them in my church or listen to them worship, I think they're exceeding the boundaries of reason.

I've always considered myself like the book written many years ago about a man without a country, and I feel like maybe in this, I'm a man without a church because so many of these new varieties of the United Methodist Church I don't go along with. As to why I was a member of the old Methodist church, I believe in open communion. I believe that if a man wants to be sprinkled, sprinkle him. If he wants to be baptized, baptize him. If he wants either or both, that's all right. I am . . . let's see . . . let me count how many generations . . . my great-grandfather, my grandfather, my father . . . I'm a fourth-generation Methodist. That's right, and my son's fifth, but we can't go along with this United Methodist. Now, we may have to because we haven't another way to go.

Some of these more liberal preachers have shifted from the regular Apostles' Creed that we repeat in the morning worship, the altar worship. They've been using another creed, and we've always been reared to use the Apostles' Creed. And that's one of the differences in the present day United Methodist Church and the old church that we knew. Here's the old acclamation of faith also known as the Apostles' Creed: "I believe in God the Father Almighty, maker of heaven and earth and Jesus Christ, His only Son, our Lord, who was conceived by the Holy Spirit, born of the Virgin Mary, suffered under Pontius Pilate, was crucified, dead and buried, the third day arose from the dead, ascended to heaven and sitteth at the right hand of God the Father Almighty and thence He shall come to judge the quick and the dead. I believe in the Holy Spirit, the Holy Catholic Church, the Communion of Saints, the forgiveness of sins, the resurrection of the body and the life everlasting." Now, the new United Methodist Church has substituted another creed. That's another thing we don't understand—why the new United Methodist Church does not continue to use the old Apostles' Creed. Some of them don't recognize the Virgin Mary.

Another thing [is] they do not adhere to the Bible. The United Methodist Church does not adhere to the King James Version as strict as the old Southern Methodist Church does. That's one of the basic differences in the two set-ups. Another thing that the Methodist Church is lax on now—and it just makes my blood boil every time I hear it—and that's homosexuality. Yes siree. And the question of homosexuality is, and you refer to the Bible, it's recognized as a sin. Very clearly and there's no compromise on it whatsoever if you adhere to the wording of the Bible, which any one of us can understand—which is as simple as a simple directional sign on the highway—we can understand what the Bible stand is on homosexuality; it condemns it as sin. But, yet the United Methodist Church is weak on it. It takes a weak-kneed stand on it. And I dare say, if some of the poor souls that's buried out here in this Double Springs cemetery knew that the stand was being taken, they'd roll over in their graves; in fact, the liberal stand is one of the biggest objections that I have to the United Methodist Church now. Maybe we can tolerate the segregation or the integration. We can tolerate the integration, because we've got the same Lord. We have the same Maker and we're trying to go to the same place. We can tolerate that. But asking us to tolerate open marriage, abortion, homosexuality is just more than I can stomach. Too liberal . . . absolutely too liberal. And may I add women preaching in church pulpits . . . King James Version plainly forbids such.

In some instances [people] have [gotten away from the church]. [Our church is] moderately strong, but few in numbers compared to Baptist faith. Double Springs Methodists are allergic to night air and revivals.

PLATE 40   Leonard Vissage.

LEONARD VISSAGE, Methodist

After our visit and interview with Conley Henry, he suggested we meet and talk to one of his friends, and "old-time" Methodist, Leonard Vissage.

When talking about religion today, Mr. Vissage's general tone is one of caution and concern. Over eighty years old, his personal faith remains strong and steadfast but he senses a lack of spirit in the church and longs for the time when brotherly and sisterly love was regularly practiced.

In this interview, Mr. Vissage discusses certain aspects of mountain religion that have greatly declined in practice over the years. Though he misses these practices and feels that Christians and their churches are becoming lax in attitudes and forms of worship, he points to the fact that these changes could very well be setting the stage for Christ's return. He says, "I think the Spirit is leaving the churches; in fact, my Bible says in one place of His teachings, 'Without a falling away, I will not come back.' That's why I think He's getting ready to come back, because it's going to be a wonderful experience. . . ."

KEITH HEAD

I joined the Methodist Church in 1914. At that time it was a union church. They split up and the Baptists pulled out and built that church up above it.

I've seen some wonderful, wonderful times happen in that church. I wish I could see some revivals like we had back then, but the Spirit has just seemed to have left the churches. I don't know why. I've seen my own mother shout up and down that aisle when I was a young child. You don't see it any more. They don't go for it and they wouldn't accept it. If you hollered "amen" over there, I guess they'd think you were crazy.

Those days are gone. There's been some drastic changes, but I can't say that it's for the better. I think the Spirit is leaving the churches; in fact, my Bible says in one place of His teachings, "without a falling away, I will not come back." I tell you there's been a drastic form of falling away! That's why, I think, He's getting ready to come back, and I look forward to His coming back because it's going to be a wonderful experience. I'm eighty years old and I know I haven't got much time to stay here, but like I told the fellow the other day, "I've got a home up yonder that's much better than this one. I want to go to it. I've got so many friends and relatives that has gone on and I believe they're waiting on me."

I'd advise anyone—you boys, now I don't know you, but if you're not born again, that's the next step you'd better do. That's the only way that can get you up yonder. Christ says that you've got to be born again. You can't explain that verse to most people. He had a hard time explaining it to Nicodemus. Nicodemus was an old, high Christian that thought he was it. He knew all about it but Christ told him, "You must be born again."

Nicodemus said, "How can I be born again? How can I go back in my mother's womb?"

Then Jesus explained that you had to be born again of the Spirit. They don't teach it too much now. They don't teach it in the Methodist Church. We have quite a conflict over here in the church now simply because I feel no spirit in there. What we need to do is get back on the old track. Go back to the old King James Version and live it and preach it and practice it and then your church will grow; your church will be something that you can be proud of.

[People used to take good care of each other like the Bible says Christians should.] They loved one another. I can remember back in these mountains where I was raised over here—most everyone was farmers. If anyone needed something done, it was done. Say you had a big crop of corn and it had rained and the grass was taking it, you wouldn't have to worry because your neighbors would take care of it for you. If there was a sickness in the family, they'd do it. That's brotherly love. Where is it today? You don't see it. It's gone. If you get anything done today, you pay for it. You pay dear for it. That's the way I'd like for it to be [again]. You won't see it and I don't expect it.

It's really sad when you get to studying about it. It's really sad. There was at one time an old lady that lived down here and that old lady was quite a character. Everyone in the country knew her and everyone loved Granny Martin. She didn't profess any religion, but I tell you right now, if anyone got sick, Granny Martin went and she stayed until they got well. If you needed her, she was there—they won't do that now. Her husband died and she had one boy that never would work and she'd get in quite a jam once in a while and people would help her. I remember one winter that she didn't have anything to feed her animals. She came over to the house; she called my father "Fuzzy Bill" because he wore his whiskers in the winter. He'd quit shaving in September and wouldn't shave until May. She said, "Fuzzy Bill, you're going to have to go get my stock and bring them over here and keep them or they're going to perish to death!" Well, we always had plenty of feed, kept a lot of stock, and sold plenty of feed, so we had plenty of grain. So we came and got them. One of them was an old jackass and he'd wake you up in the middle of the night hee-hawing! I was a kid and I remember those things. The way back then was the way God wanted you to live. You live for the Lord through other people.

I was saved in the home. We moved from up here in 1906. We moved to town. My father wanted to go down there and raise cotton—you can't raise cotton up here; it won't open. You can grow it as high as your head, but it won't open. I was in my second year of school and they were running a tent meeting right across the street from where we lived; in fact, the visiting preacher was staying at our house. The preachers would come out and eat dinner and go back and stay in a room. They were studying and praying until time for service. Just before service, they'd come out and walk around—maybe around town before service. Oh my, the people that was convicted in that meeting! I got under conviction—that was 1910—and I just fought it and I wouldn't do anything about it. I went through that meeting and I felt every minute like I was going to die, and I got sick. Well, the Sunday school teacher and my youngest sister, one night about one o'clock, were sitting on the side of my bed and the Lord made a new creature out of this old boy. Yes, sir. I never will forget it. I could go back right now and put my hand in the corner of that room where it happened sixty-something years ago.

I'm telling you! That's the most wonderful experience! You can't never experience anything like that. No, sir, you won't! I was a new guy; I was a new creature. Old things were passed over and gone and everything was so beautiful, so light and so beautiful! Instead of a sick somebody, I was a well somebody and I haven't had any more trouble. I've never been in the hospital and I've never stayed in the bed two days since then. Up until then I was a sickly kid. I was ten years old and only weighed sixty pounds. The Lord is a wonderful Lord.

I've done a lot of things I shouldn't have done during this time. I've not lived as close to God as I should have. I went against Him lots and lots of times, but I'll tell you right now, when you're born into that family, there isn't any getting you out of it! I was born in the Vissage family in 1896, and I was born in God's family down there in town in 1910 and I'm still in that family and there's no getting me out of it!

Did you have revivals back then?

Oh, boy. They'd last generally two weeks. I've seen so many revivals in my life that I couldn't point out any special one but one. I had a sister and a brother that got saved in a revival just the summer after I was saved. It was a Wesleyan Methodist preaching. They run a revival and the church wouldn't hold the people any night. When they made an altar call, they got there! There was a man preaching that had killed a man. He didn't mean to; he hadn't done it on purpose. He was born again and he was called to preach. All he could do about it was just cry, but he made one of the most dynamic preachers that I've ever heard. When that man got up behind that pulpit, you could feel the power. During that meeting there was a girl [who got saved] and I never will forget it. She was just a young woman and she got under conviction and she just wouldn't go [up to the altar]. Right up to Saturday night she wouldn't go. Finally she got up and started and just about the time she got up within a few feet of that altar, she fell—she pitched forward. That girl was lying there at one o'clock the next day. They got the doctor with her and they couldn't account for it. Well, about two o'clock Sunday evening, she came up from there and she came up shouting and everyone in the village heard her. She made one of the most wonderful little missionaries that was ever in the African country.

Have you ever been to camp meetings or brush arbors?

Yes. I've been to numbers and numbers of brush arbors. They had brush arbors all around in this community when I was a boy. It might be a Baptist or a Methodist [meeting] or maybe they'd all join together. That's what they used to do. They'd have a meeting and everybody went.

They'd make little benches to sit on. They'd put that brush up there to knock the sun off of you and it'd turn a light shower if it would rain, but if it rained pretty hard, you'd get wet! From six years old and up I can remember brush arbors. It's been forty or fifty years since I saw a brush arbor.

Were there any singings in this area?

Sure. I had a bunch of cousins that lived over yonder at Highway 28 and that whole family was musicians—five girls and two boys. They all played their own instrument and they all sang their part. Old man Doc Vissage was a bass; old man Lee Vissage was a baritone. Now old man Doc, I'm telling you, now he could get down under the floor with that old bass! I've never heard anyone sing like they did. They'd go all over the country and I'm telling you right now, when they went to a meeting, they really packed the churches. That's one reason—and I'll tell them right now—why we don't have better services than what we have right now. We're not singing those old hymns. We're not singing them like we one time did. They're not putting the spirit in it! Now that's it! They get up there and sing some old thing that hasn't even got any music in it, I don't think. They sing two or three hymns and let the preacher get up there and talk about something besides the Bible mostly. That's not worshipping God! You show me a church that has a dynamic choir and I'll show you a church packed with people. That'll do it.

Have you ever seen any foot washings in the Methodist church?

In 1948, our preacher just pulled up and left and we didn't have a preacher, only someone to come in and preach for [a few services at a time]. We wanted to get a preacher. So myself and two other men went over into the Ebenezer section to a church over there to talk to that superintendent and see if he'd get us a preacher. He said, "Let me study it for a week." The next week he told us, "Well, I can send you a young man. He still lacks a little bit of being out of school and he'll have two churches." John Don Hayes was this boy's name. He was a good man—a good boy—and I really loved him. Now, he was on fire for the Lord, that boy was! He was a good preacher and he could play the piano and sing. We were talking over there in my living room one day—me and a friend of mine—and John came down there. We were discussing the way [the church] used to be and [John] said, "Let's have a foot washing."

I told him, "Now you're talking."

Next Sunday night after service, he says, "Let's have a foot washing."

I said, "All right. Do you want to wash my feet or me to wash yours?"

And he said, "We'll wash both."

Well, I tell you, I was surprised at the people that joined it. I'll tell you right now, we felt the Spirit, too! Now that was the only time I've seen it happen in the Methodist church. Whether they used to do it, I can't say, but I know that we did.

Have you ever known anyone to be healed?

Well, it happened to me. Doctors used to come to our house once or twice a week [to see me] before I was born again. I don't guess I've taken a half dozen doses of medicine since then. There isn't anything the matter with me. I can't see good. I've lost my sight, but I'm getting old and that's natural. I can get about as good as I ever could. I can climb one of these mountains about as good as I ever could. Who's doing it? I thank God for that! I don't thank man. I thank Him for everything we have. Without Him, we haven't got anything—not even the air we breathe. I know God can heal. I know He can.

We had a preacher over here and he preached his last sermon just a few weeks back. He preached a real sermon over there one Sunday on Divine healing. Well, it surprised me. I hadn't heard a Methodist preach on Divine healing in forty years, maybe longer, but he did. I said, "Brother Grant, you sure surprised me."

"Well," he said, "I can't help it, brother. I'll preach it as long as I preach. My mother was healed and I know He can do it. I'll preach it as long as I preach."

I told him, "Glory to God for you!"

He said, "I'll preach it as long as I preach and if they don't like it, I'll quit."

That's the kind of man I like to hear! Stand up for God's Word!

Denomination doesn't make one bit of difference in the world to me. If a church is working for the Lord, I'm for them; I don't care what they call themselves. Baptists, Methodists, Church of God or what, I'll be there just the same as anyone else. I'll help them all I can because we're all looking to go to the same spot. This here denomination stuff just won't work.

I wish people would go back to the old Bible, get right with the Lord and live by that old Bible. We'd have a lot better country. There wouldn't be any friction between the churches.

The Bible says "My Spirit will not always strive with man" and it's not. It's getting away from us. What's doing it? They're not preaching that word right. They're not born again. They're making a career out of preaching now. That's why it is. I hate to see it so bad. I have grandchildren and I have great-grandchildren, but as time goes on, they're going to come up in this and they're going to be led astray, these grandchildren and great-grandchildren. I don't know what's before them.

PLATE 41   E. C. Presley.

E. C. PRESLEY, Methodist

While en route to an interview in western North Carolina, we stopped at a small post office to make sure our directions were clear and accurate. As we were talking to the friendly postal worker, we happened to mention our religious study. He immediately told us about his father, E. C. Presley, and his many years of association with the church, and offered to call and set up a meeting so that we could talk with him later that day. We gladly agreed, the interview was set up and, after getting our initial directions clarified and a hand-drawn map to Mr. Presley's home, we were on our way.

Mr. Presley proved to be as cordial as his son. We set up our discussion on the front porch and Mr. Presley began recalling his religious experiences. A Baptist for 52 years, he is now a Methodist and said that the two denominations always got along in his area, remembering "union" meetings and joint homecomings between the two.

E. C. Presley is concerned that other present day activities are keeping people away from the church. He also senses a change in the overall mood of the church and its people, but at eighty years of age, he maintains the faith that has sustained him all of those years—a faith that becomes more important to him each day of his life.

KEITH HEAD

The churches are not like they used to be. We've debated a whole lot about whether they're in worse shape or better shape. Back when I was a young man and went to church that was about all there was to go to—that or the movie. Now there's a ball game somewhere nearly every night to watch and there's TV and so many different things to go to. I think people get carried off with a lot of this stuff and maybe go a little too far with it.

I joined the Baptist church when I was sixteen years old and I'm eighty years old now. I was a Baptist fifty-two years and then I joined the Methodist church. I like them just as well as I do the Baptists. My wife was a Methodist. We moved down to this community and they don't have union Sunday school and church here, so I just joined with her so I could go with her to church. I changed because she don't drive the car and it would've been a botherment [to attend different churches].

The Baptist people and the Methodist people cooperated together fine. I don't know as where they ever had a dispute or an argument. My folks were all Baptists and I guess that was the reason I joined the Baptist church. Our Baptist preacher and our Methodist preacher were holding a series of [union] meetings and I got converted during one of those meetings.

We had a Sunday school and I attended it. I got a diploma from the Baptist people. I passed the examination capable of organizing a standard Sunday school—that's what the Baptists called it then. I was superintendent up there at the Baptist church for ten years. We'd have Sunday school at the Baptist church for three months and then we'd go to the Methodist church and have Sunday school over there. I've been the superintendent over at their church lots of times when their superintendent wouldn't be there. If he wasn't there, why, I'd take over. [The superintendent] had to take up Sunday school and see that all the classes had a teacher. If one class was short of a teacher that Sunday, well, you had to either get a teacher or teach it yourself. I've done both. I've found teachers when I could and when I couldn't, I'd teach myself. A Sunday school superintendent has got a right smart of a responsibility to run a good standard Sunday school.

The Sunday school was actually the only thing [the Baptist and Methodist churches] combined on, except when they went to have a series of meetings—a religious gathering. When they run a meeting, they'd all come together then and have their meetings together. The regular preaching day, we'd go to the Methodist church for their preaching. They just had preaching once a month then. It isn't like it is now. When we Baptists had our preaching day, they'd come over to our church.

We'd have a revival up there about once a year. We'd either have it at the Methodist church or the Baptist church. We were all union. I think they have a homecoming together yet up there at Speedwell

[North Carolina]. That's where most of our people's buried. We go nearly every year. I don't go out as much as I used to except to church here. It's just a quarter mile from here out to the church. I believe in going to church. I always did believe in it. I went to church all my life. Oh, I've missed a few Sundays along—sickness or something like that—it can't be helped. Back then I knew people to ride horseback two and a half miles to church on Sundays. I don't know whether anyone would do that or not now. If they've got a car they might drive that far, if they've got a good place to park and don't have to walk too far!

Back when I joined the Baptist church, our church only had preaching services once a month. We had two days of it. [The preacher] came twice to the church, once on Saturday and then on Sunday morning. Now, they've done away with that Saturday meeting. Now we have preaching every Sunday morning. If our preacher can't make it, why, he'll get a preacher from Lake Junaluska, a retired preacher, to come over here. Our preacher has three churches and he tries to preach at every church every Sunday. That makes it awful hard on him. I wish our church was strong enough to where we could hire one pastor to be there every Sunday, but the church doesn't have enough paying members to do that at this time. He's trying to preach every Sunday at all three churches. That makes it awful hard on a preacher. I don't see hardly how a preacher can hold out. The First Baptist Church here in Sylva [North Carolina] has preaching every Sunday. They have just one preacher to supply the church. They have a lot of members and they're well able to pay a preacher just to have one church. That's what I wish we had, but we're just not able to. What members we have out here, we just can't pay a preacher in full. We have to split up with some of the other churches.

[The Baptist church] used to have singings. It was usually on Saturday night or Sunday evening but that's kind of faded out of the picture, I believe. They still have a few, but they're scattered wide apart. They sung more old-time hymns then. That's what I liked—the old-time singing. Old man Jeff Moss used to teach singing schools. I went to one one time; I couldn't sing. There isn't no singing to me! I can't keep a tune.

I have been at a few places where they'd have judges [for a singing competition] and the judges would decide which one was the best quartet or class. Different communities had their own quartets. Up at Glenville [North Carolina] every September there'd be quartets from about three or four states come in and they'd compete against each other. There was a class come from Nashville, Tennessee up there and they brought a little organ. They'd play this organ and sing. I've seen other classes with guitars. Each class usually had their own music and sometimes a class would sing without music. They don't think it's right to have a banjo in the church. The banjo and the fiddle's mostly for dance music. Neither church don't back that up. They had some real good singing [at Glenville]. This was a high school building where they were holding [the competition] and if you didn't go pretty early, you didn't get a seat. They went all out for it in that day and time. It might be different now, I don't know. There's so many other things to go to.

[The church has changed in many ways.] The Baptist people, way back yonder, used to try people and turn them out of the church. I don't know as the Methodist ever did that—not since I've gone to them they haven't, but I've seen people tried up there in the Baptist church and they'd be dismissed from the church for something they'd done. I don't think the Baptists do that anymore. I think that they've decided it's better just to take their name off the book and drop it at that, instead of getting up in front of the church and trying people. That isn't fair. I don't think that that's right. It's embarrassing. The preacher would bring [up the trial case in question] and then they'd be certain witnesses. It was like it was a real trial. If they found them guilty, they'd turn them out of the church. The ones that liked these people didn't want them turned out—they had their friends—but still, the crowd run it over the one or two families and they turned them out anyway. Like say . . . a girl in the community gets pregnant. Well, back then they'd take her up and try her; generally, they always convicted her and turned her out of the church. Now that's a Baptist church only. I never seen that in the Methodist church. The Baptists don't get their members up and try them and turn them out as I know of anymore. I haven't heard of it in a long time.

When I first started going to a Baptist church, they had foot washings. They don't do that anymore. I remember going to one foot washing up there—I hadn't joined the church then—I was very small—but I went to this foot washing. A member of the church would pull his shoes off and I'd wash his feet or he'd wash mine. I haven't seen that in church in years and years. I never did see it but one time and that was in the Baptist church. I never did know of the Methodist church having a foot washing.

Back then you'd have a series of meetings and people would get happy and shout. You could have a meeting going on for two or three weeks and they'd have it every night and every day and there'd be a lot of people'd get happy and shout. They shouted in both churches back then, but you hardly see anybody shout anymore in any church.

There's another thing in the Baptist church that's changed a little. You know they used to believe in closed communion, the Baptist people did. They've changed that. The Baptist people will come over to our church and they'll take communion with us. Well, back yonder years ago, a Baptist wouldn't take communion with the Methodist church, but they've changed that now, and it's different than what it used to be. That's the three things that's changed in the fifty-two years I belonged.

I tried to live right a long time. I've made lots of mistakes, but I never did give up faith. I've always held onto my faith. In these late years, it's more serious now than it was back when I was in the prime of life. I'm taking it more serious now. I don't have too much left to live for. I'm eighty years old now and don't have many more years left. I've been on borrowed time ten years and I'm trying to live every day just like it might be the last day.

Pentecostals

Jesus has a table spread
Where the saints of God are fed
He invites the chosen people, come and dine
With His manna He does feed
and supply our every need
Oh how sweet to walk with Jesus
all the time.
"Come and dine," the Master calls us, "Come and dine"
We can feast at Jesus' table all the time
He who fed the multitude, turned the water into wine,
to the hungry calleth now, "Come and dine."

Similar to the Baptists, Pentecostals constitute a large denomination characterized by diversity in the form of a number of Pentecostal types or subgroups. All Pentecostals, however, share common beliefs, one of the most important being that each Christian should strive to "be filled with the Holy Spirit." Evidence that this important event has occurred in one's life is revealed by "speaking in tongues," the utterance of an unknown language. Among other places in the Bible, "speaking in tongues" is referred to prominently in the second chapter of Acts, a book in the New Testament. This subject is thoroughly covered in the interviews that follow.

Pentecostals are in other ways distinctive, believing that they can receive other supernatural gifts. For example, they believe that some can be given the ability to prophesy, to heal, and that a select few can interpret the act of speaking in tongues. These gifts are also referred to in the New Testament, I Corinthians 12–14.

This collection of interviews represents two Pentecostal schools of thought. Included are the Church of God, a large and influential denomination in the mountains, and the Fire Baptized Holiness Church. Those speaking for these groups were most receptive to our inquiries and we strongly feel that some of this publication's most vivid accounts and recollections are included herein.

PAUL F. GILLESPIE

RAY DRYMAN, Church of God

Ray Dryman, my great-grandfather, was the first person we interviewed concerning mountain religion and that interview was, I suppose, largely responsible for the conception of this book. I had intended to do an article for the magazine on the experiences of Grandpa, but after some discussion with Paul

PLATE 42   Ray Dryman.

and other members of the Foxfire staff, the idea of a more complex and complete book on religion was born.

Known to practically everyone in the Scaly community as "Uncle Ray," at age ninety-four he is the oldest member of that community. Grandpa helped usher the Pentecostal movement into Scaly and was largely responsible for the building of the Church of God there. Although he was never overly vocal in the church, his strong presence was felt by preachers and church members alike. Like a patriarch, he has always been one of the "cornerstones" of the congregation and many are the times I've seen him going down the road, walking cane in hand, to the church about a mile from his home.

Although Grandpa has recently suffered a stroke and can't read the Bible daily as he had done for so many years, he still has the strength to occasionally attend the church he has loved so well. We feel that Grandpa is the true essence of the religious experience in the mountains and we thank him deeply for inspiring this publication.

KEITH HEAD

I was married in 1910 and I got saved about eighteen months later. It was in 1911, I guess. They had just run a Methodist meeting down here at the Methodist Church and I got under conviction and I was saved. I felt real good. I was hoeing cabbage when I got saved. I was hoeing and just got real happy. Wasn't anybody there to hinder me. That was at home—down here at my old home-place.

There is a lot of difference in the church now and back then. Back then, if anybody didn't keep the teachings of the church, they'd turn them out. Now they don't turn anybody out. I don't know of anybody being turned out down here in a long time. Bessie, my daughter, was turned out of the church for cutting her hair. [They said] she was disorderly and broke the teachings of the church. This was the Pentecostal Church. They had a modest line of dress. The women were supposed to dress modest. Back then they wore dresses down around here [between the knee and shoetop]. They had to have old high top shoes; there weren't any slippers worn much then. And they didn't wear short sleeves. Anybody knows what modest dress is and not to follow after the world.

In what other ways could you "follow after the world"?

By going anywhere that's worldliness—these old bathing places and these old ball games. I don't know what you might say, but they aren't good places to go anytime. There's all kinds of people there and it's not a good place to be. I wouldn't go to one at anytime.

Do you remember when you went from the Methodist Church over into the Holiness Movement?

Yes, I was superintendent of the Methodist Sunday school and this fellow, Frank Miller, came along. We went to school together and he had come into the Holiness way—the Church of God. He was running a meeting out here at his granddaddy's. I was fixing to make a crop. He came along there in April on the road. I was at work by the fence. He stopped and got to talking. When he got ready to go, he said, "Ray, come over there to preaching."

I said, "Where is preaching?"

He said, "Over at Grandpa's, tomorrow evening."

I said, "I don't know. I might come over." So I came on down to Sunday school at the Methodist Church. I said to H. O. Penland, "Let's go out and hear Frank Miller preach and see what he's got to say. He grew up with us, you know. He was a good boy, never had any trouble, a fine boy." So we went out there and he preached. He commented on the Church of God but his main theme was sanctification and the baptism of the Holy Ghost. They believed that a person under the Spirit could handle snakes—pick up a snake—if the Spirit was on them and directing it. Well, I read the Bible and I didn't doubt that; if the power of the Lord was on a man, he could do *anything!*

So the next Sunday, I decided I'd like to go back. I figured that was about the best I'd ever heard and I got to reading my Bible to see. I had a New Testament—a brand new New Testament— and I got to reading that and went back there again and then I got to following his line. It was every bit Bible, but I'd never heard it preached before. [The Holiness doctrine] got up sort of a stir in this country and I said, "Fellers," I said, "they're right about it, they're preaching the Bible!"

I saw where I missed it. I sure had an experience. When I got the Holy Ghost, I was just going along down the road right [about where the Holiness Church is now], praying and meditating and the first thing I knew I was speaking in a new language. I reckon some people get it one way and some another. But that's the way

I got it. I never was gifted in tongues but speaking in tongues is evidence of the Holy Ghost. That's what they did on the Day of Pentecost.

It wasn't long until they had me rolled out down there [at the Methodist Church]. They told me they didn't have much use for me down there. My church and everybody in the country fell out with me and so I quit the Methodist Church; just quit going. We had a time then. You never heard such a fuss. My folks all got mad at me. They just about disinherited me for a while. Because I went the wrong way they thought! I never did get many of them convinced [that I went the right way]. They didn't like the idea.

They [also] ran the [people that went to Holiness meetings] out of the Baptist Church and told them not to come around there. Toliver Vinson got the Holy Ghost and he went up there to the Baptist Church and told them he would talk a little bit with them. They told him not to come back up there with that kind of stuff— didn't want any of it around there. I heard him not long ago, said they never had ask him to come back and he never had gone!

The Holiness first held their services in people's homes?

Yeah, at old man Watkins' and from there they came to Jim Kell's and had church. They had church there at my house. I had an old store building and let them preach there, too. Just here, yonder and about, you know—everywhere you could get in and preachin'!

Then I asked H. O. Penland up there about buying a lot [for a new church]. He said he'd sell it to us. I went to the brethren and they said, yes, that we would buy it. I think we paid a hundred dollars for it if I remember right—a half acre of ground. The church got it [the money] up. We just made it up. I remember how many members—eight or ten. Henry Miller and Meade Kell built the church and me and old man Miller hauled the lumber in from Rabun County to build it.

Do you believe in Divine healing?

I've seen people that said they were healed. I remember old lady Ledbetter was healed. I know of a child that had diphtherial croup that was healed. It was at the point of death and it never did use a bit of medicine—back over here on the Lloyd cove. They used to—the Church of God used to—call for people to come in and pray when they got sick. Well, they do yet. The church is not strong as it used to be in that line. They kind of drifted back. All churches have gone off. People had church back when I was growing up. People don't live the good life like they used to. They've got too heady and high-minded.

How do you feel about snake handling and the handling of fire?

[Snake handling] is all right if you have the Lord directing you. But you better be careful and don't try to handle snakes if He isn't in it. But God has all power. The Hebrew children went through the fiery furnace and they came out. I've known people that has handled snakes. More than just one, too. I've known one fellow to get bit. In the early days of the church, they would handle snakes. Frank Miller got bit—the preacher got bit. They started to kill the snake and he said to hold on. I reckon he thought the Lord had given him power to pick it up. He picked it up and it bit him on the arm. A big rattlesnake. He got pretty sick but he never did take any medicine. The next Sunday he was preaching. They never did take him to the doctor. They just prayed for him.

I've seen people handle fire. When we had that meeting there in my home, we had a lit fire there—it was a cold day. There were three people that handled fire that day. Just reached in there and picked up those coals and held them in their hands. No sign of fire on them. No sir, it never burned them. That convinced Toliver Vinson that people could handle fire. He wasn't a member—he was just a sightseer. One fellow rubbed his hand along on the blaze. His wife was scared to death. She just knew his hand was burned off. Didn't even singe a hair on him. He just sat there and rubbed that fire and looked back over the congregation and grinned and talked in tongues. That's right. That was convincing, you know. When a fellow stands there and sees anything like that done, he knows there's something to it.

How do you feel about foot washings?

I've never been to a Holiness communion but what we didn't wash feet—all but one of them and that was down yonder at Gainesville. They had communion and they said nary a word in the world about washing feet. I said, "Well, that's peculiar. I never knew Holiness people but what didn't wash feet." I went to another foot washing before that one and I'll tell you what I think—now I don't know—but I think I know what the distraction was. Down here at Prentiss at a communion service they washed feet. Bee [his daughter,] was down there and there were lots of members—there is a big congregation in that church. The women and men went into different rooms. They went in there and washed feet and I said to Bee, "Bee, boys, you had a crowd of them washing feet in there, didn't you?"

She said, "No, we didn't have many."

I said, "Why?"

"No," she said, "they all had on panty hose and you couldn't get to their feet!"

Did people shout when you were in the Methodist Church?

Yes, they shouted! I've seen them shout, Methodist people. There was one fellow in my recollection that came here and preached. Let's see, his name was Sam Perry and he came here to run a meeting. He was a Wesleyan Methodist and he'd preach sanctification. Boys, I'll tell you he *preached* down there. I guess I was about eight years old, maybe nine. They had a tear-down over there in the Methodist Church. Boys, there were all these [people]. I don't know who in all and those women just threw that snuff winding. Nearly everybody quit using their snuff. That old man, Raleigh McConnell, got religion in that meeting and he got up and down that aisle there just as flat of his back as ever you'd seen a fellow—just like he was dead. He was knocked right under that power, right there! That was in the old Methodist Church. It's been torn down.

[I remember another time] in Ashbury—down at the Ashbury Methodist Church. They were having a revival down there. This Gudger fellow [was there]. He was sort of an idioty kind of fellow; wasn't all there. But he was a pretty good old Gudger. [He was] a small fellow; I don't guess he weighed over a hundred pounds. [Anyway,] everybody was getting happy and shouting; old man Gudger was back at about the middle of the church sitting right next to a window. [People] were just crowded in all around him and he said, "Give me room," he said, "so I can shout." It was in the summertime after dark and a couple of the boys just picked him up and set him out through the window out in the yard. And they said he just cussed that thing! He had room then!

Could you tell us the story about Uncle Boos?

That was at the Church of God. They were having a testimony meeting down at the Church of God. Old Uncle Boos stayed out there at old man Watkins' but old man Watkins had died and Boos' sister's boy just came in there and kind of scrounged the old man, Boos, out. He went down to old man Miller's to live with his sister. [Anyway] they were having a testimony meeting and all the people were around testifying and after awhile, old Uncle Boos got up to testify and he said, "Well, I just don't know. I've been hammer-pecked, hen-pecked here, yonder, and about and I don't hardly know where I'm at and I don't really know if I've been saved or not." And he said, "I don't believe I've ever been sanctified and I know I don't have the Holy Ghost." He took off up the aisle just shouting. Tickled me to death!

PLATE 43   Toliver Vinson.

TOLIVER VINSON, Church of God

Toliver Vinson is another one of those who pioneered the Pentecostal move-
ment into the Scaly Mountain Community. He has always been one of the
leaders of the church and has taught the adult Sunday school class for many
years. He and his wife, Ruby, are still closely tied to this community as are
many of their children and grandchildren.

It takes a dedicated person to stand up to adversity and disapproval from
one's friends and associates. Many years ago a riff existed between the "main-
line" fundamental churches and the newer Pentecostal movement and we admire
Toliver Vinson because, in spite of that riff and the disdain of many of his
peers, he stayed with and remained faithful to the Pentecostal movement. Later,
as the different churches tolerated each other more and started cooperating
toward the reaching of a common goal, Toliver Vinson became one of the
most respected members of the community.

KEITH HEAD

I was saved in the Baptist church. I was also sanctified there in
revival and received the Holy Ghost *before* I came to the Church
of God. Claude McConnell and a whole bunch of boys were praying
on the altar and I was praying with them. The first thing I knew, I
went kind of limber and I knew there was something happening
and I was sanctified right there. A few days before the revival was
over, I received [the baptism of] the Holy Ghost.

My daddy used to say he was praying for a double portion [to be saved and to receive the baptism of the Holy Ghost] and I used to tell him that if he got a double portion he could hardly live. He couldn't make it! But in a revival up there [at the Baptist church], he got so far along that he was in a trance or something—he was that way for about a week. He was the happiest man you ever saw and he couldn't do his work and I told my mother, "Don't worry about him. We'll do the work. Let him enjoy himself and have a good time." So he must have got a double portion!

They started preaching "Holiness" here [at Scaly Mountain] about 1914 or 1916. When it [the Church of God] first started out it was up there at Ray Dryman's in an old store building. They used to have a post office there and I attended their meetings when I was about twelve or fourteen years old. There was just one door and one window and they had a table and a lamp, one of those kerosene lamps, on the table. There were so many shouting and carrying on. I was a little excited and afraid. I thought about jumping out that window! I knew that if I jumped out that window, I'd knock the lamp out! If I'd knocked it off, people would've been in the dark. I always wanted to [be as well mannered] as I knew how to and not hurt anybody. I decided to stay with them. That was about the best thing that I could do. Everything quietened down after a while and my nerves did too, a little bit!

Why did you leave the Baptist church and join the Holiness movement?

The [Baptist] church just about made up my mind for me. They said I'd have to leave off that speaking in tongues and so forth if I stayed with them. They said their conference just wouldn't put up with it. The deacons talked with me and they said that if I'd leave that speaking in tongues off that I could stay with them. I told them no, I wouldn't do that because the Lord had given it to me and that I appreciated them and loved them and loved the church but I wasn't compromising with them or anybody else.

The only bad thing that happened after they asked us not to be there speaking in tongues [occurred at a revival]. The [Baptist] church had a revival and invited us back and everyone was welcome. There were quite a few Pentecostals there and a lot of people were in prayer. Brother Lawrence Talley and myself were praying and probably speaking in tongues. We used to wear those little sailor hats—straw hats—and they were hung up there [toward the front] somewhere. The preacher got hold of one and sailed it across toward a bunch of us. He might have been throwing it at Lawrence Talley but it hit me. It hit me right across the forehead; of course, it didn't hurt much. That was the only physical thing that happened. That was kind of surprising; I'd thought a lot of the preacher but there was something wrong with him or he wouldn't have done something like that.

Do you remember when the old Methodist church was up here in Scaly Mountain?

Years ago, I saw those old lady Methodists "dance" and their hair would get down and almost pop and crack. They'd dance and run the benches just like Pentecostals do now. I've seen them jump from one bench to another. Looks pretty scary in a way. It's enough to excite a lot of people, kids and so on. In a way, it's kind of unbelievable to anybody that doesn't know anything about it. They'd get in the Spirit and if that's what they wanted to do and what the Lord wanted them to do, it's all right. I don't want to do something like that, but I wouldn't condemn it.

Can you remember any revivals?

I remember—I guess it was in the forties—we had a revival that lasted for six weeks and it looked like the whole country was going to get saved. They had big revivals all along. The old church building would reel and rock when the people'd shout and carry on. My dad used to be pretty hard on the "Holiness." He'd say it was of the devil—all that speaking in tongues. After that big revival, he never was hard anymore. He joined the Church of God. He was a member of it when he died.

They had those [camp meetings] but I didn't go to them. They had buildings [for them] over at Hayesville and Shooting Creek. They used to have conventions about the same as camp meetings that'd last about two or three days but those old camp meetings would last about a week or ten days—a brush arbor or something like that. The only thing [like that] that I ever went to was an outside tent. They used to have quite a few of them at Clayton and Mountain City. One fellow out there at Mountain City bought an old tent that had quite a few holes in it. When it rained, you had to hunt a place where it was dry. I heard him say one time that when anybody got blessed in that tent, he got blessed, too!

Have you ever seen anybody handle fire?

Up there at Ray Dryman's we were having a cottage prayer meeting. We had it quite often and there were a lot of people there and Ray always had a big fire and hickory logs [burning]. [He had] a big old fireplace and that thing was really red hot. Of course, I was new in the Pentecostal way. They got to shouting and speaking

PLATE 44   Keith Head and
Toliver Vinson.

in tongues and so forth; there was three or four or five, maybe,
and they'd just dip into those big logs that were on fire and pick
them up. After it was over with, I wanted to be sure that they were
doing that. I had some of the boys go out on the porch. [They]
had water out there and I had them to wash their hands. Their
hands were pretty smutty and [after they washed], their hands were
just as clear [and unburned] as mine.

I've seen a half dozen at a time going right into the fireplace
and picking up those logs and not getting burned. We used to have
a log stove in the old church [Church of God] up here with a pipe
running out and that thing was about red hot and it was about to
fall over. Some of them caught that thing and carried it around
there and put it back on. You don't see that much anymore.

How do you feel about handling snakes?

People have handled snakes. It can be done; it's the Word. It's
supposed to be done in its place and for a purpose—the right time
and the right place and so forth. One of our neighbors, years ago,
got bit and was in pretty bad shape but they say he handled snakes
after that. I'd have to be right knocked out before I'd handle any!

How do you feel about Divine healing?

I've seen people healed. It doesn't take long. The Bible teaches
that it's not an amount of words or a lot of speaking—the Lord
hears [anything]. I went to my sister's and she'd been sick and in
the bed for a week. I went in and I said, "The doctor has already

come"; and you know, she rose out of that bed and went to shouting and helped to fix lunch that day.

I was over at Hayesville one time at a convention and this man's wife was sick. He was a representative of the county and he invited me [and another man] to take dinner with him. His wife was sick and had been in the bed for about a week. I thought, "Boy, what are we going to do about dinner." He'd invited us for dinner.

He said, "Let's have prayer; my wife has been sick for a week or more."

So we prayed for her and she got up and helped her husband fix our dinner for us.

Ruby, my wife, had a bad pain and she could hardly work. Her side was hurting some way and Brother Larry was preaching and a lot of people began to shout; it seemed like electricity or something went all over the building. He believed in Divine healing; he's probably got the gift of healing. Anyway, there were a lot of people healed and they said for everybody to join hands. I could feel something. It seemed like a light above sunlight went through the building and Ruby was healed. She hasn't been bothered with that pain in the side anymore. It was just like electricity—went right through us. There were a lot of people holding hands. There must've been six hundred, eight hundred people there.

I'd [also] like to tell you about my dad. He could stop blood; I know he could. The last few years that he lived, when we'd kill a hog, we'd just about have to send him away from home. The hog wouldn't bleed and would hardly die. He wouldn't say he could [stop blood] but you'd tell him an animal or a person was bleeding and the biggest part of the time it'd soon stop. I know that to be a fact. We boys tried to get him to tell us how it was done and he said he was only supposed to tell one person. My daddy would forget sometimes, and he'd get my mother to read the verses to him; they'd get off in the room somewhere. When he had a good memory, he'd know it. But after he got old, he'd have my mother take a Bible and go off into the room and she'd read the verse or verses, whatever it was. He'd go places; maybe a horse or cow or something would get cut. Maybe a cow would get her udder almost cut off and about bleed to death. They were always taking him [to stop blood].

I've known people that weren't even saved to stop blood. They'd use some verse from the Bible so I guess it'd be all right. You know, anybody that honors good, even if they are a sinner, the Lord will honor them. That's what the Bible says.

PLATE 45   Granny Reed.

GRANNY REED, Church of God

I have been acquainted with Granny Reed, as she is best known, for quite a while. I remember, as a young child, going with my family to the Assemblies of God camp meeting at Cullasaja, North Carolina. There in the old sawdust-floored tabernacle nestled near the slow, lazy Cullasaja River, the rafters would seem to swell as the people offered their prayers, praises, and the "songs of Zion" unto God. At some point during the service, "testimonies" would be given. Voluntarily, people would stand and publicly tell what God had done for them. Then Granny Reed would get slowly to her feet and as all eyes focused on her, she'd begin, "Children, I've been walking with the Lord many a year now. . . ." When she finished, there were few dry eyes and even fewer sad hearts in the congregation.

Granny Reed is ninety-four years old. For a long time she was a Baptist, but now she is a member of the Church of God in western North Carolina. Those who have come to know Granny Reed love her simply because of the love she shows toward them. I have never seen her without being greeted with a warm hug, and hearing her say, "God bless you." Granny Reed is a testimony and a credit for both the Church of God and Christianity.

KEITH HEAD

I have been a Christian about seventy-eight years. I'm ninety-four now. I was converted when I was twelve years old. It's been a long time. Then it wasn't like it is now. We didn't know anything about the deep things of God. We just knew the born-again experience. And we really did have a born-again experience in those days.

I never had thought about being a sinner. I never had thought about it. I was going along a little barefooted girl. We always went barefoot until we were in the teens in those days. I was going along and kicking up sand and playing, you know.

My daddy said "huh" like that. When he said that, I knew he wanted to say something. I said, "What is it, Dad?"

He said, "You're old enough to know what you're going to church for, instead of playing along like that."

I stopped and I thought, "Well, does Daddy think I'm a sinner?" I began to study about it. I thought, "Well, him and Momma pray for me every night and I'm a child of God surely." I stood there and waited until he got in front of me and I dropped in behind him and started on toward the church.

I cried till I thought I couldn't cry. I thought, "Oh, dear God, I'm a sinner and I'll be left here. Mother and Daddy goes to heaven and I'll be left." It troubled me to death. These days, children don't pay any attention to things like that. But, oh, it broke my heart. I went on into church, I had a little cousin; her daddy was my mother's brother and he was a preacher. He was preaching. I went in and scrooched down beside of her and said, "Zadie, if you was to die, would you go to hell?" Me and her was the same age.

She said, "I don't know, Rosie. Papaw prays for us every night and I never thought nothing about it."

I said, "Daddy thinks we're sinners. He thinks we're old enough to know what to do."

She said, "I guess we are. We're twelve years old."

We sat there awhile and I said, "I'm going to the altar when they call. I ain't gonna risk it another night, for Jesus might come tonight."

She said, "They'll make fun of us and us barefooted."

I said, "I don't care. I'd rather be made fun of than to go to hell."

She said, "If you go, I will."

So whenever they had the altar call, we went and just knelt and cried. We didn't know how to pray or nothing. In a little while, they broke up [the meeting] and we didn't get saved. Oh, how bad I was troubled. I went to the church door and I said, "Uncle Isaac, do you care if me and Zadie don't go home for dinner?"

He laid both of his hands on our heads and said, "God bless you, children. Stay if you want to."

So when they all got out of sight, me and Zadie (we was right by the river at the old Brush Creek Church) went up the river to an old sheltering rock and we walked in between them rocks. I looked at her and said, "Zadie, do you know how to pray?"

She said, "No, I don't. Papaw does the praying."

I said, "I don't know how. For Daddy and Mother both prays. And I don't."

We stood and looked at each other for a while and she said, "Well, we could say, 'God, be merciful to us a sinner' for we're sinners."

We knelt and prayed and cried. We didn't know what to say except "God, be merciful to us sinners." We cried and cried and when they came back to the church, we ran down to the river and washed our faces and pushed our hair and went on into the church. I never heard anything the preacher said, I was so anxious to get to the altar to get saved before dark, because I didn't want to risk it after dark. Jesus might come, I might die, and oh, I couldn't stand it. I never heard anything said. And the minute they called the altar call, we went. We went and we prayed and we prayed. I was praying so hard and Zadie was too. After a while she jumped up and came flying to me and said, "Oh, I'm saved, and God's going to save you."

Well, I thought I was the vilest sinner on earth. He's saved Zadie and he ain't saved me. That made me worse than ever. I liked to cried my heart out.

I said, "God if you don't save me now, I'm going to die. I've done everything I know how to do and I don't know anything else to do." When I said that, an awful feeling came over me. I was mashed down low and lower. I couldn't hear them singing or nothing. I felt like I was going through the floor. All at once, it begun to come up like that. And when it come up, there I was standing in the floor. Everything was as bright as sunshine. I jumped just as high as I could. I jumped and grabbed Uncle Isaac and hugged him. My daddy was just parting the people trying to get to me. Well, I thought they was the prettiest people I'd ever seen in all my life. Never after that did I doubt my experience. I know I was born again.

Well, I was determined to live in His steps. All my life I've wanted to live in His steps. And when anyone asks me to go to a show or a ball game or place of music, I would just say, "Now would Jesus go there if He was here?" No, He wouldn't be there. He'd be somewhere else, praying or reading or doing some good to people. I never have been to a ball game or a theater in my life. I've just tried to follow in the steps of Jesus.

As quick as the light of Holiness came into this country, I was there. The Lord spoke to me and told me to go or I wouldn't have gone, because I didn't know what kind of people they was and I was afraid of them. But you know, I was almost dead. I was sick. I was awfully bad off. I had an abscess in my side and I'd been operated on, but it didn't do any good. I was going to die. I knew I was. I had my family, two boys and a little girl. I said, "Lord, I hate to die so early and leave my family. My little girl needs me so bad, she's so sick all the time."

You know, whenever I told the Lord that, I just laid there a little while and He spoke to me in an audible voice and said, "Go down to the Holiness tent meeting and I'll heal you."

I didn't know it was the voice of the Lord. It scared me so bad. I looked all over the room. He'd never spoke to me in an audible voice before. I looked everywhere and there was no one around. I lay there just a-trembling.

I stayed till the next morning, laid there studying about it. Next morning, I said, "That didn't sound like a wicked voice. It must have been the Lord."

But why would He ask me to go to that place—a Holiness place? They're wicked people (for I thought they were). I'd been taught that! All at once it came again, "Go down to the Holiness tent meeting and I'll heal you."

I said, "Lord, I ain't able." I couldn't raise up without fainting. I was awful bad off.

He said, "I'll make you able." And that was the last I heard.

I thought to myself, "If that's Jesus, I'll put my feet down on the floor and try it and see and if I don't faint, I'll know that it's Him." Well, I got out on the side of the bed and I turned myself this and that a-way. I didn't feel like I was going to faint, and I said, "Now, Lord, if it's you that's leading me in this way, let me walk in the living room there and sit by the fire." I got up and walked, but I was stiff and sore. I walked in there and sat down.

My mother-in-law, Mother Reed, was waiting on me in there. She looked in and saw me and said, "How come you ain't in bed? Who brought you in here?" She knew I couldn't walk.

I said, "The Lord." When I said that, she thought I was out of my head. She ran out and called my husband. He come in and I told him about the Lord speaking to me.

He led me right on in and he said, "Well, go to the Holiness church. We'll go down there if He promised to heal you."

And I said, "Yes, we'll go." I was still afraid to, nearly, but I went. That's where I got into the light of Holiness; it's been about fifty years. I never got healed until I got the baptism of the Holy Ghost for I didn't ask to be. [The preacher] just had his healing services on Friday night. After I went down there on Friday, I thought I was going to get healed that day. They had cards to give out and the ones that had cards went up to give them to him and stood in line. I didn't have one and I didn't go. Oh, I was disappointed so bad. When he got through praying for the sick, I could just feel down there to see if I was healed, and I'd say, "No, I'm not healed. It's still there—that sore place." I studied about it.

When he got through, he said, "Everybody that's sick and afflicted, hold up your hand." Well, I held up my hand real high. I was afraid to let it down; afraid he'd miss seeing me. He came to me and handed me a little card and bowed and went back.

Well, I had to go home with that. I didn't know nothing else to do. When I got home I read that card. "Are you saved? Have you been baptized with the Holy Ghost? How long have you been sick? Do you believe God can heal you? Will you read your Bible and pray daily?"

I said to my husband, "I don't know how to answer this card. I can answer every one but there's a distinction here between 'Have you been saved?' and 'Have you been baptized with the Holy Ghost?' There's something else to it some way. I reckon I have been baptized in the Holy Ghost. I was baptized in the Father, Son, and the Holy Ghost."

He said, "No, Rosie. There's something else to it. I'll tell you what to do. I'll take you down there Monday morning and let you stay with your Aunt Minnie (she lived right there by the tent) till you find out something about it before next Friday." Next Friday was the healing night.

Sunday morning I was so heartsick about everything, I couldn't eat a bite. I said, "I don't want nothing to eat." I went on to my aunt's and told her not to fix anything for me to eat. I wanted to know something about the Lord before I eat anything more. I just got convicted to death! I never eat a bite for three days and nights. The first night of the revival he preached about the baptism of the Holy Ghost and I've never in my life had my eyes opened so. It just struck me that I'd die or have that gift.

I said, "Lord, here I am. Been a Christian all these years and thought I was walking in the steps of Jesus and I ain't even halfway started!" I felt awful about it. I went on fasting and praying and on Tuesday night—that was three days and nights that I had fasted— I went in there and told the Lord that now I was ready for the baptism and I said, "Now You give it to me. I'm setting way back here in the tent and nobody won't know that I'm wanting it."

Well, it came down just like a shower of rain. It was like a funnel in the tent just r-o-o-a-a-r-r-i-i-n-n-g. I fell over on the bench and my lips felt like they were an inch thick. I said, "I won't disturb." And when I said that, it just left me like that. Then I sat there a little while and I said, "Lord, did I imagine all of that?" I never had such feelings in all my life. I said, "You didn't get mad at Gideon for putting out a fleece twice. If I ask You to send it one more time, then I'll know it's You." And it come again.

Right then the preacher was saying to everyone that wanted the baptism to go into the prayer room. Well, I said to the entire congregation, "Come on, children, this is of God. I done asked Him."

I went in there. There wasn't no room at the benches. They was all lined up. I just knelt down right in the middle of the floor and received it.

Oh, yes Honey. They turned me out of the church and wouldn't have a thing to do with me. My own people wouldn't ask me home with them. First time I went to my own church, I thought I'd be the greatest help to them in the world, and they just turned their backs on me.

I went up through the old field. I was walking by myself, all alone. My daddy was against me; everybody was against me. I went on to the top of the mountain and looked back over the mountain and I said, "Lord, if nobody in this earth speaks to me anymore, my daddy nor nobody, I'll walk these hills alone with You. I'll never turn back." I'd cried all the way up the mountain. I was heartbroken because they had treated me so dirty, and I hadn't got to where I didn't have a lot of feelings, then.

When I said that, the glory of the Lord came down on me and just wrapped around me a sheet of love. Oh, how happy it made me. I shouted all the way down. I never cried anymore about my church. He took it away. But they turned me out.

They didn't know any better. My poor old daddy said I'd sure land up in an asylum—I'd gone plumb crazy. Yeah, he thought he'd have to send me to the asylum.

But my mother just accepted every bit and got the baptism in my house. Oh, she was like me, she wanted all the Lord had for her. My daddy was good, but he was scared to death; he thought it was some kind of strange doctrine. But before he died, he said he saw the light. He said he knowed it was right.

I was brought up in a good Christian home. They had their family prayer, and they made us go to church and never thought of nothing but doing right. I never heard my mother nor my dad say a dirty word in my life nor never seen nothing wrong out of them. They was good people. My daddy thought that the only religion in the world is the Baptist. He just thought that was it. But Mother could see a little further in the distance.

I said one day, "Mother, what does it take to be holy? I don't do nothing wrong." I thought the Holiness people didn't eat meat

back then. So I said, "I don't care about meat. I can do without
that. Why can't I be holy?"

Mother said, "Honey, there's something to it I don't understand,
but if we keep reading and praying and trusting God, one of these
days we'll find out what Holiness is." She knew we should be holy.
But my daddy thought it was holy enough to be Baptists.

[The Holiness] didn't indulge in the worldly things in life. They
didn't think it was right, and I don't yet. I don't think we can be
two people. I think we either have to belong to God or not at all.
I think we have to turn loose of the things of the world that's got
any foolishness in it at all, because the Bible says that all that is
not good is bad. If you don't find any good in something, there
isn't any use to partake of it.

There was a little girl, and sandbones had eaten her backbone
out to where she was in a steel brace, and she hadn't put her feet
on the floor to stand up for seventeen months. She was sitting in
a wheelchair with her steel brace on.

They drove the car up to the tent and raised up the tent close
to where the preacher was preaching where she could listen at him
preach on Divine healing. Well, the preacher was boarding at their
house, and he went on home that night. When they came back and
started to carry her out of the car, the preacher said, "Just let her
alone. She's going to walk to the house tonight."

And he went around and laid his hand on her and prayed a few
words—he didn't ever pray but just a few words—and she leaped
out of that car and ran to the house! She ran in and she ran upstairs
and jerked that steel brace off and put on her clothes. She went
into every one of the bedrooms of her brothers and woke them
up and told them what God had done for her. She's still alive yet!

Oh, I don't know of the healings that took place up there. They
brought one woman from the hospital that they'd given up to die,
and the preacher went out to the car and prayed for her and she
was healed perfectly. There's been lots of healings since.

I've prayed for people and they was healed time and time again.
But it seems like these days that it's harder to get through to victory.
I don't know why. I went to a little baby that was dying of diphtheria
and its little head was swelled up and its eyes was rolled back in
its head. They was going to take it to the hospital, and they had
to wait for the train to run before they got there. They thought
the baby was going to die before the train got there, so they called
for me. I never had seen the people. I ran down there and I asked
the Lord as I went on, did He want me to pray for it secret or
out loud. I said, "If You want me to pray in secret, You cause the

woman to ask me to lay my hands on it. I know You're going to
heal it, Lord, but I want to know how to pray about it."

So when I went in, she was holding it. The baby was about two
years old and you couldn't see nothing but the whites of its eyes
and it was gasping, trying to breathe—couldn't breathe hardly at
all.

And the mother said, "Lay your hand on its little neck and see
how hard it is. It's like a rock." And I knew then so I just lay my
hand on its neck and began to rub and say, "Thank you, Jesus"
in my heart. Every drop of that swelling just oozed out and the
fever left. That little thing popped its eyes open and looked at me
and laughed. It jumped down and out its mother's lap and run
into the kitchen, got a stick of stove wood, and it came back pecking
on the stove and looking at me and laughing. It hadn't seen me
before but it was tickled to death. It knew something had happened!
It was well from that day on.

The man come in and he said, "What in the world happened?"
The baby was just playing and laughing and running around me.

Mrs. Blair said, "Miss Reed just laid her hand on its neck and it
got well in a few minutes!"

And he said, "Well, there ain't no use to go to the hospital, is
there?"

I said, "No, your baby's all right, Mr. Blair. It's all right."

I never told them what happened and next morning, I felt condemned about it. I didn't know what to do so I went back and
asked her if she knew what made the baby well. And she said, "You
prayed for it."

I said, "Yes, Jesus healed it." Then I told her how God did work
through people.

[*Editor's Note: Shortly after our interview with Granny Reed, she phoned
to tell us about a vision she'd had and to see if we wanted to record it.
Keith and Wendy went back to her home and she related the following experience.*]

I was very sick on my bed. I told Jesus I wouldn't pray that night.
I was so tired and sick I just said, "Lord, remember all my objects
of prayer. Keep Your loving hand on them for good, and all the
churches that are trying to please You." Then I turned over with
my face to the wall, and my eyes got wider and wider, and I felt
all disturbed inside. I looked up and said, "Lord, what is it? I don't
feel like I will ever go to sleep." It seemed that I had died a natural
death, and I was carried to the entrance of heaven in the arms of
angels, very softly. I did not see anyone. But I stood on my feet. I

opened my eyes and looked, and there stood Jesus. I looked from His head to His feet. Oh, I can't express it! I just cried out and said, "Oh, how wonderful, wonderful, wonderful You are!" I said, "Lord, I have been looking for You and been praying for You to come and stop these awful wars and crime, and bring peace on the earth. But You didn't come."

Well, I said that, and He moved up to me as the wind swept Him, and laid His arm around on my shoulders, and looked straight into my eyes and said, "No, I didn't come. The time is short, but My children are not ready."

Oh, how sad He looked! I said, "Lord, I thought all Your children were ready."

He said, "No, no. Very, very few."

I said, "Why, Lord?"

He said, "They have too many weights to overcome and too many spots on their garments. They won't be able to rise and meet Me when I come in the clouds of Glory, for I'm coming for a church without spot or wrinkle."

Then I said, "Lord, if they are Your children, what is their spots they haven't overcome?"

He said, "Hate, jealousy, grudgery, selfishness, pride, and the cares of this world. They are all wrapped up in the world until they are ashamed to be called a Christian." He looked at me and said, "I am sending you back to the world to tell My children to repent, and need filling with the Holy Spirit. For the time is short, and My children are not ready."

I said, "Lord, please don't send me back! I want to stay with You."

But He said, "Not now. Go back and warn My children the time is short." Then He vanished out of my sight.

I looked all around and I was in my bed—I felt of my pillow to see if it was real. There was no sleep for me that night. I cried and talked all night. I said, "Lord, I can't tell it. They will all say that I am crazy, or dreamed it, or imagined it, Lord. I just can't tell it."

So, next morning, it was all before me all day. But I didn't speak about it, and that night it all happened again. I died, and I was carried to the entrance of heaven again. He told me the same thing. He told me to tell all the churches I could. And He looked at me so kind, and said, "Can I trust you?"

And I said, "Yes, Lord. I will tell it if no one believes. I will tell it." And I told even the Baptist church, the Assembly, and the Church of God, and all that will listen at home.

My granddaughter asked me, "Grandma, what will Jesus do with those that won't repent and overcome?" And the Book of Revelations opened at the third chapter and I said, "Honey, this is what the Bible says, 'He that overcomes shall be clothed in white reignments and I will not blot his name out of the lamb of the book of life, but I will confess his name before My Father and angels.' "

And she said, "Oh, their names will be blotted out if they don't repent." I pray to God His children will repent before their names are blotted out. Remember, time is short.

This all happened to me about three years ago. As I write this all down, I know I will not be here long with my brothers and sisters to warn you. As I write this, I trust someone will be glad. Please forgive my bad writing. My age is eighty-six in six months. I've been a child of God seventy-three years, and have loved every minute of these years. God bless all who read this. You're in my prayers, and God bless all.

PLATE 46   Reverend Jake Quilliams.

JAKE QUILLIAMS, Church of God

Reverend Jake Quilliams, a preacher for the Church of God, is known far and wide for his dedication to his faith and church and his ministry to those of all beliefs and denominations. Reverend Quilliams is a modest man who works quietly and diligently within the community. He strongly believes that he is an instrument of the Lord here on earth to help all people and to preach the fundamental teachings of the Bible and his particular denomination.

Reverend Quilliams has been associated with the Church of God for many years but his work is not confined to that church. He has been known for many years as a twice-daily visitor to the two area hospitals and without being forward he makes himself available for ministering, counseling, or just plain talking. In addition to his regular services at his church, he preaches weekly at the local nursing home and has a radio program including area singers every Sunday afternoon. He holds many revival meetings and other special services and conducts funeral services for those of all denominations.

Reverend Quilliams is adamant concerning his beliefs and is a powerful spokesperson for the Church of God in this area. His unwavering faith and encompassing knowledge of the scriptures combined with his friendly attitude and tremendously helpful ways make him one of the most respected members of our community and we were extremely grateful when he offered to discuss with us particular aspects of his denomination in our study of mountain religion.

KEITH HEAD

I was called [to preach] when I was just a boy. I was about ten when I got called by the Lord. During rainy days, I would get up in the barn loft and make me a little Bible stand and do like I was preaching. One day—I never will forget—doing like I was preaching and my dad walked in. He said, "Son, what are you doing?" He didn't understand [at that time]. But I felt the calling of the Lord upon me then and I realized I was to preach. I could see by a vision multitudes of peoples back when I was a boy and I was preaching to them.

When I was sixteen I received the Baptism of the Holy Ghost and was saved. The Church of God came into the community of Cartoogachaye and began to preach in a little log cabin. My oldest brother and I would go to these services. Back then [some] people were against Holiness, worse than they are now. When they came into a community other denominations would fight them. They didn't want their children to go to these services because of what they [Holiness] believed in. I'd go to these services and would see how the Lord worked and how the power of God would fall. [It would fall] so strong in that little log cabin that it would actually shake the little building. It scared my brother; he thought it was going to fall from the pillars. People were shouting all over that place. People would get saved and sanctified and full of the Holy Ghost—just like Pentecost. Then [and there] I saw the Holiness were right. Those people had something that I didn't have.

So at the Cartoogachaye Church of God there was a revival. I was sixteen. Howard Speed was the pastor and Clarence Elrod was the evangelist. I remember that very well. I was good and saved but I knew there was something more for me. It didn't make any difference how long it took—I was going to stay until I got satisfied. I didn't understand the Baptism of the Holy Ghost, didn't understand the Church of God—didn't know anything about it. It was new to me, but I knew those people had something that I didn't have. I began to seek the Lord that night and I began to pray. Some time after midnight—I didn't know what time it was—I told the Lord I was going to stay. It didn't make any difference to me if it took a week. I was so hungry and thirsty after God; I hungered after the Holy Ghost so much that I saw the Lord all night long. I prayed and I'd get happy and I'd shout and other people stayed with me all night. I didn't know it until it was all over with; they told me. When you get real salvation and the Spirit, you lose sight of everything worldly. You have to die out with the world and be filled with the Spirit. I received the baptism along that morning about daybreak. The Lord blessed me and I would get happy and they told me I went all over the church. They'd get me down in one place to pray for me and I'd get up and run off! Some of them asked the pastor, "Why don't you pray for him?"

He said, "I'll tell you what. If you catch him and hold him, I'll pray for him."

I went all over the place. I was shouting and having a good time. I'll never forget that morning; along about daybreak I was laying under the bench. I came to myself and I was speaking in a heavenly language, an unknown tongue that I had never talked in before. I didn't know what it was all about. I didn't understand the Holy Ghost like I do now. I didn't understand it but I knew it was something that I never had before. I knew it was the power of God.

The Holy Ghost is a gift. A lot of people don't understand speaking in tongues. They condemn it by using a verse of scripture there in Corinthians. Paul said, "I'd rather speak five words in my own understanding than ten thousand words in an unknown tongue to the church." But he also said that when you're speaking in an unknown tongue, you're not speaking unto man but unto God. When you're speaking in tongues, that's one language that the devil can't understand. When you're talking in this heavenly language, direct to the Father, the old devil has just got to sit back. He can't understand a word you're saying. Because it is a direct line—the devil and nobody else knows what you're saying.

Also, during that night—let me go back—I argued with the Lord. I told Him, "Lord, I'll do anything but preach." Because I thought about it and I had just a third grade education and I felt I wasn't capable to preach.

The Lord said, "You obey Me and I'll give you the Holy Ghost. I'll fill your mouth. Don't worry about the message or preaching. You obey Me and I'll fill you with the Spirit." So I obeyed Him. I went on home that morning and everything was so wonderful. Well, it was like living in a new world. Even the birds sounded sweeter. I went home and [at that time] I was helping my dad make acid wood to make a living. They were already up. Mother already had breakfast on the table. I told Ellen, my sister, "I've been telling you what those people had and now I've got it. I've got the Holy Ghost." About that time the power of the Lord fell and I got happy and shouted all over that living room and when I got through I looked around and my sister wasn't even there! Scared her. I didn't even eat any breakfast that morning. I didn't want any. Dad came back from the barn where he was feeding the cows and the horses and said, "Son, get your ax. We're going to make acid wood today." I'd stayed up all night long. It didn't matter to me. I couldn't have slept if I had gone to bed anyway. I was so full of the power and the Spirit, I couldn't have slept anyway. So I went on to work that day. We'd take an old crosscut saw and cut the logs in two. He'd pull the saw one way and I'd pull it the other and tell him about what the Lord had done for me and I'll tell you, that was the sweetest day.

That night Daddy said—I was seventeen and back in those days children minded their parents—"Son, you can't go back to that church tonight." I'd have died if I hadn't got to go. I said, "Daddy, I've got to go." He kept on fussing at me and said for me not to go but I got ready and went on. That was the first time I ever disobeyed my dad. But I felt that the Lord had given me the Spirit. The Lord wanted me to go on and I started out then and began to obey and began to go to church. That's where I got my start.

Then I went to the army; I was called when I was eighteen. I went into the army and stayed twenty-seven months. I stayed nineteen months overseas. While I was overseas in Manila every chance I would get, I would preach. So over there in the streets of Manila— that city was tore all to pieces when we went into it—I'd have street service. People would gather around and we would have a time. I never will forget—one day we were standing by an old building and I didn't know it was a Catholic church and the Father came out and he said, "You're going to have to leave. This is our property." While I was next to their church, there were boys fighting on the other side of the street. I didn't argue with him, I just walked across the street to where those boys were and kept on preaching. The fight stopped and they all scattered and some of them came to listen to me.

Back when we first started out, they would throw rotten eggs at people in the [Holiness] churches and break windows and shout at them. Let me tell you a little experience I had when I pastored my first church at Tessentee. That was the first church I pastored. We started in a home, a lady's house. The crowds got so big we had to get a tent and pitch it outside. That's where the church got started. During our revival, people fought the Holiness. They were going to see that the Church of God wasn't going to get in that community. So we were in this good revival and we were going to have a homecoming on a Sunday. I never will forget it; me and the evangelist were out in the yard and we were working on the tables and the deputy sheriff came up. They came up in the yard and wanted to know who we were. I introduced myself and they knew who [the evangelist] was.

He said, "We got warrants here to serve on you and the preacher.

The community got you for disturbance and they want you to close this revival out. If you don't close it out, I'm going to have to take you in."

The evangelist said, "All right, I'll tell you when we're going to close this revival out. When God says quit, we'll quit."

They stood around a few minutes and went on into town and that was the last we heard of them. They must have had the transformer because they threw the lights out on us—we didn't have any lights. So we just turned the cars and made lights and had service all the night. We had the power company to turn them back on the next day. That wouldn't stop us so the preacher's car was sitting beside the road and while we were preaching, they pushed his car off the side of the road into a potato patch. They were that much against us. We found out that the ones complaining and the ones that took the warrant out lived three miles [from where we were].

We have many Holiness movements that are not a part of the Church of God [as I know it, and all of this confuses people]. Our Church of God doesn't believe in handling snakes. It's more of a put on of a show because the Lord said, "Thou shall not tempt the Lord thy God." That's just like going across a freeway and just throwing yourself in front of a big truck. You've got more sense than that. You've got more sense than to take up a poisonous snake. So that's the differences.

There are a lot of good things we believe in. We believe in foot washings. Most of the Church of God churches have them every quarter but you can have them as often as you want. We believe in the Lord's Supper and foot washings. Men washes brothers' feet and sister washes sisters' feet.

We believe in Divine healing. I've known of people getting healed. I've prayed for a lot of people. Do you know Granny Eller? She got cataracts on her eyes. And we prayed for her here the other night and they disappeared before long. She went back to the eye doctor and the eye doctor wanted to know what had happened to her. She's up in her eighties and now she's getting so she can see better. It's a miracle work of God. You have to have faith in God.

[When I came into the Holiness way] I was just a different person. The Bible says that you become a new creature in Christ; old things are passed away. I was washed clean and purified and the Spirit dwelled within me. It's hard to explain the gift of the Holy Ghost. You've got to be sincere and really want this.

PLATE 47 Student Editor Keith Head, Brenda Lee, and Reverend
Charles Lee.

CHARLES LEE, Fire Baptized Holiness Church

*We found Reverend Charles Lee's church before we found Charles Lee.
While riding on back roads in the far northwest mountainous reaches of South
Carolina we passed a sturdy-looking church with a sign in the grassy front
yard that proclaimed, "Fire-Baptized Holiness Church." Since we had never
heard of this branch of the Pentecostal church, our curiosity was greatly aroused
and we began stopping at nearby houses in search of someone who could
discuss and elaborate on Fire Baptized Holiness beliefs. At the second house,
an elderly lady told us about Reverend Charles Lee and gave us directions
to his home.*

*After Reverend Lee learned of our study, he was glad to answer our inquiries
concerning his beliefs. And even though he represents one of the lesser known
groups within the Pentecostal movement, our interview with him, and our
attendance at one of his church services, made us understand the important
and significant theology of the Fire Baptized Holiness. Since we began our
friendship with Reverend Lee, we have noticed more of these particular churches
coming into being in our area.*

*Reverend Lee speaks for a church that holds to conservative beliefs and
traditions. A Fire-Baptized Holiness preacher since 1952, he now discusses
the principles held dear by him and his denomination.*

KEITH HEAD

[When I got saved about 25 years ago] it was just true conviction of the Lord and His working upon my life and calling me. Just like anybody else getting converted and being saved. I got saved when I was in the Navy and then I received sanctification about two or three weeks later. Then in about two more weeks, I was baptized with the Holy Ghost. I received the call to preach on a Thursday night [after] I was converted on a Sunday night.

When I was just a child, I went to Holiness meetings and I knew that God had His hand upon my life but I didn't know I was going to be called to preach. I didn't know that because nobody knows the future. But whenever I got saved and then began to mend my ways and seeking the Lord and praying, why, the Lord began to open up the way. I knew that it was God's will that I preach. I just knew it.

I knew when the Lord was dealing with me. I was laying on my bed that night and I couldn't sleep. My mind was troubled. I knew something was wrong. I was praying and meditating to myself. Not out loud, you know. No emotional fit. I was just laying there praying, talking with the Lord. The presence of the Lord was great and I knew it was He. The Spirit of God moved in my mind. Well, I felt like the Lord had something for me to do, but I didn't know what it was. I was troubled. Like I say, I couldn't sleep another half minute in that condition.

[When I first recognized the call to preach,] I just didn't feel like I could do it. Just like Moses, you know. When the Lord called Moses, [Moses] said, "I'm slow of speech. I can't do it." The Lord says, "I'll give you a spokesman." The Lord gave him Aaron [Moses' brother] to speak for him because he was a much better talker than Moses was. Well, I felt like *I* couldn't do it. And I knew it was God dealing with me and I knew I'd *better* do it. I didn't know at the time the Bible says that the gifts and a calling of God are without repentance. God calls a man to preach, there's no way of getting around it. It's got to be done if you please God. You don't have to, but you could be lost—go to hell [if you refuse it]. [I felt I couldn't do it because] I'm a nervous-like fellow, always have been a little bit nervous and hurried up, but yet, the power of God, the Holy Ghost, gives a man boldness, you see. I told the Lord I would preach. I accepted it and I went to sleep just like that [he snaps his fingers], instantly.

When the Lord called me to preach, it seemed like the Bible came before me and the pages were being turned like something coming off a press. Just like a newspaper coming off a press. I saw later on that when I was preaching the pages of the Bible would

be in my mind and they turned like [they did in my vision] because
I preach fast. I can't preach no other way except fast. You've seen
some people that can just talk and rattle it off with no trouble at
all? When I get to preaching, why, it just comes to me.

Where did the name "Pentecostal Fire Baptized" come from?

In the book of John's writing, we find where John the Baptist
came preaching in the wilderness saying, "repent ye, the kingdom
of heaven is at hand." Well, he went on to say that Christ, the
Messiah, would come and He did. Then the Law was fulfilled. John
went on to tell the people, "I'm not the Christ. He that cometh
after me is mightier than me," says, "He shall"—*shall,* you know
what shall is? He *will* do it, you see. It can be done; it will be done.
That's the way you use shall. Well, he said, "He *shall* baptize you
with the Holy Ghost and with fire." Well, you see, they took the
name "fire" and "Pentecostal" because we believe in Pentecost like
in the book of the Acts of the Apostles. Pentecostal Fire Baptized—
that's what it means: "He shall baptize you with the Holy Ghost
and with fire."

When [Christ] baptizes you, you'll know you're baptized. When
you repent, you become as a little child. The Bible says—3:3 of
John says—"verily, verily I say unto thee, except you be converted
and become as a little child, you cannot see the kingdom of God
or enter heaven." When you're born again, that's repentance. You're
on a level with God as a little babe then. You're forgiven of your
actual transgressions of sin which man commits.

Sin is in a two-fold manner. The Bible speaks about it as the
Adam nature. Sin, man inherited from his forefathers because that
nature is in a man. That's what causes a little child to lie to his
parents. He's got the Adam nature in there. You take your child
or anybody's and you tell it not to do this and not to do that—
you've got to watch a child. That sinful nature is there. "Adam's
sin" we call it. Man failed back there in the Garden of Eden at
Creation. He transgressed the Law of God. He fell from a holy
state which he was created in. When man was made there wasn't
anything wrong with him. He was perfect because the Bible says
everything God created was good. There wasn't any flaws in him.
Adam and Eve sinned there in the garden and transgressed the
Laws of God willfully—willfully because God told them not to. When
you repent, you ask God to forgive you of your sins. All right, you're
born again. You pray. The Spirit of God is renewed in you.

We teach [conversion and sanctification] as the two works of grace
and the Baptism of the Holy Ghost as a gift of God, a promise of

God which Christ promised to His disciples. Speaking in tongues is a sign of the evidence that you have received and been baptized by the Holy Ghost—that's the initial evidence that you know you've got the Holy Ghost. We teach sanctification as the second definite work of grace. It is, like I say, a work for you to do yourself, on your part and then as you continually grow in the grace and knowledge of the Lord Jesus Christ after your conversion, you *can* be sanctified. By appropriating faith and grace in your heart, God can sanctify you as a second definite work in a moment like that [he snaps his fingers]. You know about it when you're sanctified just as much as you knew about it when you got converted.

How is the Pentecostal Fire Baptized Holiness Church different from other Pentecostal churches?

Basically our Bible preaching of doctrine would be the same thing as the Pentecostal people because they believe in regeneration, sanctification, Baptism of the Holy Ghost, and Divine healing. All these Holiness movements teach that. Basically, the fundamental teaching is the same thing, but the government is different in our church.

I'll tell you when the body was organized as a group of people. It was in 1919, November 21. These two churches, the Free Will Baptist and this body of preachers that already called themselves Pentecostal Fire Baptized preachers because they preached the Holy Ghost, they got together over here in Georgia as a group of preachers and formed the church conference. [They] organized and got together and fellowshipped and made a covenant and that's why we're named the Pentecostal Fire Baptized Holiness church.

[Our conference includes churches in] four states: North Carolina, South Carolina, Georgia, and Alabama. We've got one church in Virginia and it's kind of in our conference.

What services other than morning worship do you hold?

We have revivals, camp meetings, and watch night service. [Watch night service is] the last day of the year and we stay [at the church] until the New Year comes in. We sing, pray, and preach and invite other people in.

We had a homecoming the first Sunday in June. [At homecoming] we have regular services or invite a former preacher in or someone to preach for us that day. Then we have dinner on the grounds. People come in from other churches and we eat together. After that, we sit around, clean up, go back in the church and start singing. Just let the Lord have His way.

They have some [special] singings sometimes. People come in

from other churches and sing. We just invite the people in that wants to come.

We believe in feet washing. [The service is] not necessarily regular, like on a schedule. Somebody suggests that we haven't had a foot washing in some time and that we ought to have a communion service and foot washing. We have foot washing when we have the communion.

Have you seen any people healed?

I've been healed. I went to the doctor and was told I needed surgery but I was prayed for the Lord healed me. I know some people that's been healed of different things but I've never personally seen too much of such instantaneous things like [are] in the Bible. I've never seen too many healings but I know healing's real and a man's got a right to believe in Divine healing and trust God for the healing of his body and not to have to take any medicine. He might suffer some things. The Lord don't do everything that you want done right away but He does heal. Healing's real. You can't explain it but you can know it when you get healed and you can receive it.

A lot of these people are preaching Divine healing today and commercializing it, sort of speaking, making money off the Gospel. A man ought not to make money off the Gospel. He ought to preach it free. He ought to give it willingly. He ought not use it commercially like some of these preachers are preaching across the land today; telling people that they got so much power and they got this, that, and the other. Well, certainly some people's got power. We don't deny people having power with God. But still, they ain't got *that* much power. They just can't heal everybody, because they're doing it more or less for the gain. That's the way they're deceiving the people. The Bible says "this know also, that in the last days many false prophets would arise and deceive many and deceive the very elect if possible." Christ said "go not near, have nothing to do with it." There's people claiming that they got more grace than anybody's got. But God's not limited to no person; it's for whosoever will. You've got just as much right to call upon the Son as I have— anybody has, whoever they are, because they're human beings and that's all.

We believe in people living right to get to heaven. That's the purpose of preaching the Gospel—not to just have a place of entertainment. [Church] is to be lightly taken. It's to be really considered as a work of God. Churches today, why, they have these fellowship homes and they have all kinds of get-togethers and things. Churches are doing just like the schools are doing—for the entertainment of the people. We believe in getting the presence of the Lord there and having the power of God in our midst and the Lord a'working, because, without that, you can have ten thousand or a hundred thousand people gathered together like in a ball game and the Lord not be in the midst.

Did they ever "church" people in the Pentecostal Fire Baptized Holiness Church?

They have "church cleanings" they call it. People come before the church like Matthew tells us. People fall out with one another. They can't get along. Somebody teaches something or other that's contrary to our teaching, you see. They call in the boards and get together and decide upon it and go talk to the person and ask them the trouble and try to settle it within themselves. If they can't, then they have a church meeting.

Here're the general rules: "No person shall be admitted unto the full fellowship of this church who is not in full accord with the teaching of the same. He must give satisfactory evidence, aside from his own testimony, that he is regenerated, groaning to be sanctified, and seeking the Pentecostal Baptism of the Holy Ghost. In accord with these professions all who remain with us take as their rule of conduct the Word of God and shall conform outwardly as well as inwardly in their daily walk and conversation to its simple teachings (Galations 6:16). We are commanded in God's Word not to be unequally yoked together with unbelievers and to have no communion or fellowship with the unfruitful works of darkness such as oath-bound secret societies, labor unions, social clubs, corrupt partisans, and politics (II Corinthians 6:14, Ephesians 5:11). Be not conformed to this world (Romans 12:2), but come out from among them and be ye separate (II Corinthians 6:17). He will turn away from those who are the form of Godliness but deny the power (II Timothy 3:15). To cleanse ourselves from all filthiness of the flesh and Spirit (II Corinthians 27:1) such as use, growth, and sale of any tobacco of any form, use of morphine or intoxicants," Coca Colas and things like that. This does not apply to minors who are forced to do so by their parents in obedience to them; wives who are forced to do so by their husbands. "Foolish talking, jesting, use of slang language [is forbidden]. Abstain from the appearance of all evil such as attending fairs, swimming pools, shows of any kind, including television." We deem it a violation of these rules for a member of our church who is the head of the house to allow a television to operate in his home. If they break these rules we feel like they're not in harmony with our teaching, so they might turn somebody out of church [for breaking them].

Most of the Fire Baptized Holiness still don't go to shows and ball games?

That's right. We don't go to ball games. I used to be a great football fan. I never went to baseball much but I loved football. I have not been to a football game in twenty-five years.

I have never owned a television. I have never bought one. I remember when television was invented. The first one I ever saw was in New York City in a bar in 1948. They just had come out and there weren't any down here in the South. They didn't come out till about 1951 down here. When television came out only places like that bar could afford one at that time.

[Some of the church members are less strict now.] They used to not go to [movies] but now they got television in their homes. Well, that's the same thing; it's just an improvement of picture shows. That's all a television is. They show a lot of pictures and movies over television. Nobody can't tell me about television because I know when they first came out. And I know they're evil. Even the government says that they're defiling and harmful and that they're warping up people's minds. Education is good, but it's not going to make the world better. It's good for people to have some education—I haven't got much—but it's destroying our human race and our country as far as the morals and everything's concerned. It's destroying our people. Just like ball games and things. It's all right for children to get out here and play ball but when they get out here and try to take one school against another—they get out there and this fellow, he's "booing" for this and the other fellow's "ahing" for this and they get in fights.

[But the church is] still pretty much the same. [Our rules for living are still strict and] that's the reason why you won't have as many people [in the Pentecostal Fire Baptized Holiness Church]. There ain't many people willing to abide by it. That's why we don't have [a large membership] and that's why we've had [splits within the church] over the years. At the end of World War II, about 1945, they had approximately seventy-two churches throughout the four states but now we have thirty-five churches.

Do members still dress conservatively?

We don't go indecently exposed and put on display like the world does. We don't believe in wearing shorts, halters, and pants for women. People didn't used to do that twenty-five to thirty years ago. You'd see a few people [in shorts, for example] around the house, but they wouldn't do it [in public] then; but now people's going nearly nude. That's contrary [to our beliefs]. Of course, it's people that's not Christians. Some may be claiming to be Christians but they're deceived.

The high school had this ruling—they said it was required of all people to take physical education. [My daughter] refused it, she didn't take it. She wouldn't put on a pair of shorts. They wouldn't give her a diploma because they said it wouldn't be right. Well, they discriminated against her, see. She had a B average and twenty-one units and only eighteen was required but they didn't give her a diploma. They only gave her a certificate.

Holiness people were really persecuted years ago. People used to take tents out to preach and maybe they'd cut the ropes and things on the tents. I could take you to people that really don't like Holiness today. They're church people but they don't like Holiness in no form, no fashion. I know some of them personally. But as for me, there ain't nobody harmed me or nothing. I know older preachers [who were persecuted]. There's one fellow [whose life was] threatened back years ago. I knew him. He's dead now. They used to throw eggs and things at people walking down the road and people going to church. People didn't like them. They'd call them "old holy rollers" and things like that. I know that to be a fact.

To be a Christian, you've got to do different from the way the world does. In this "are the children of God manifested from the children of the devil." Now, somebody's serving the devil. Somebody's living in sin. If they weren't, why, there wouldn't anybody be lost. Everybody's not going to be converted. No sir. People are preaching that this old world's getting better all the time; it's not getting better, it's getting worse all the time.

People don't believe the Word of God; they'll turn deaf ears and turn away from the truth. They say, "No, it don't take [faith and dedication]. You're wrong; you're a fanatic." They say, "No sir, preacher, I'll do what I want to. I can do as I please." That's what the world'll tell you. Anybody'll tell you about it, especially if they've not made a decision to follow God. People are bickering, they're growling, they're not content, they're not satisfied. As much as we have today. When I was a child, I didn't know what living in a brick house was. I can remember walking five and six miles to church. Now you can't get folks out in an air-conditioned automobile [to come to church]. They want to go for a ride on Sundays; they want to get their boat. They're going to do what they want to do. They're a servant of sin. Look at how they dress. We're [supposed] to pattern our life after Christ.

The world's not being converted today. There's a few folks getting saved but there's not many folks getting religion—the kind that's pure and undefiled, like the Bible says. You get out here and you look at people. You go into town and look at the people and see how they're living. Well, they're ungodly. They haven't repented and been born again. They're not serving God; they're serving the flesh. According to the Bible, if you live and serve the flesh, ye shall die. The Bible says "for the wages of sin is death, but the gift of God is eternal life with Christ Jesus."

Everybody believes in God, or tells you that they do, but they don't believe in Jesus Christ, the Son of God. He is great and His power is sufficient to cleanse them up and keep a man from sinning. Some people don't preach it. They say, "Oh, you've got to sin a little all the time. You can't help but sin." But [he reads] here it says, "He that committeth sin is of the devil." "Whosoever," listen to this, "is born of God doth not commit sin." Now, that's the Word of God. It's in there. If you're doing the will of God, you wouldn't want to do wrong; you don't want to commit any evil. No vile will come out of a man's mouth. You can't be a Christian and use profanity at the same time. If a man uses profanity, there's something wrong with him. He's not got the grace of God. That's why we say you've got to be sanctified because when you get sanctified it cleanses a man up and puts love in his heart for God.

Presbyterians

All people that on earth do dwell,
Sing to the Lord with cheerful voice;
Him serve with fear, His praise forth-tell;
Come ye before Him and rejoice.
For why? The Lord our God is good,
His mercy is forever sure:
His truth at all times firmly stood,
and shall from age to age endure.
                    (Old Hundredth, *Genevan Psalter*)

Three Presbyterian ministers are presented in this, the last section on mountain denominations. L. B. Gibbs, who came to Rabun County in 1926, rode a circuit, ministering to a number of churches. He has preached in several southern states and remains active in church affairs. Clyde Hicks presently rides a circuit consisting of several churches, continuing a tradition long existent in local religious history; Sid McCarty, advocate of interdenominational cooperation, also supports the Charismatic movement, a new phenomenon he discusses in this chapter.

Presbyterians would not typically come to mind when discussing "mountain religion." Characteristically, they do not handle snakes, conduct foot washings, or hold lengthy revivals; and their orderly services are usually run by well-educated ministers. Presbyterians were, however, among the first to come into the mountains, and their influence has been far reaching. Therefore any religious study such as ours, without inclusion of this denomination, would be incomplete.

PAUL F. GILLESPIE

L. B. GIBBS, Presbyterian

Reverend Leonard Burns (L. B.) Gibbs is an obvious and logical spokesperson for the philosophy and theology of the Presbyterian denomination. Reverend Gibbs was born into a Presbyterian family on November 20, 1901, in Jackson County, Georgia, the son of Leonard Hamilton Gibbs, a farmer, dairyman, and orchardist, and Minnie Elizabeth Burns Gibbs. In 1912, he became a member of the Presbyterian Church and later, upon completion of his theological studies, was ordained and became a member of the Presbyteries of the Presbyterian Church of the United States. Reverend Gibbs has contributed greatly to his community and is respected by both young and old, Presbyterians and those of other denominations. His record of church ministry is indeed impressive as he has served a number of churches in the mountains of Tennessee, Virginia, and Georgia. Two extensive interviews were done with Reverend Gibbs and we found that he was always ready to carefully, patiently, and intelligently answer our inquiries.

KEITH HEAD

PLATE 48   Reverend L. B. Gibbs.

I became a member of the church when I was about eleven years old. I couldn't tell you the exact date of my conversion. There are a great many people who are unquestionably born again and are believers in Christ who can't put their finger on any certain day. If they grew up in a Christian home where they were taught about the Bible from childhood, a lot of times it is more difficult for them to put their finger on a date, and that's my case. I can't, but I did become a member of the church when I was about eleven.

I first came to Rabun County [Georgia] over fifty years ago at the end of my first year in seminary, expecting to spend the summer. Instead, I stayed twelve months and after that, I was back in school again for two years. In 1929, I married and we came to Tiger to live and were there for eight years, then we moved away. We came back again in '49 and lived here until '56 when I was pastor of the Presbyterian churches in the county, including Rabun Gap [Presbyterian Church] both times because we had only one ordained minister in the county at that time. A little over six years ago I retired, and we came back here to live. I'm still preaching as a supply [minister] in two of our churches, at Tiger and Wiley. So altogether, I have twenty-two years in Rabun County stretching over a period of fifty years.

Were your folks Presbyterian?

Yes. Both my father and mother were Presbyterians. I grew up in Habersham County [Georgia] and was a member of the Cornelia Presbyterian Church until I was ordained in 1929, when I became a member of the Presbytery. In the Presbyterian church, a minister is not a member of the local church but belongs to the Presbytery, which is the area organization.

How did you feel you were called into the ministry?

I never had any audible voice tell me that I ought to go into the ministry or any blinding vision or anything like that, but I felt that that was the place where I ought to work. I came to a very definite decision about that. There were a good many other things that I thought of as a boy when I was growing up, as most boys do, I think. But I came to the conclusion that the ministry was the place where the Lord wanted me to be. I think that's why I'm here.

How were the Presbyterians accepted when they first came into the county?

When I came, there had been Presbyterian work going on here for five years, so it was not absolutely new. But generally, I think the church was cordially received. There was some feeling on the part of some people, I think, against our branch of the church, perhaps; but, generally, I believe there was a good spirit in the county.

Could you explain about your circuit preaching?

Let me go back to the time when I first came to Rabun County in 1926. Our work in the county was very new then. There had been a minister here for five years, and he had just moved away. The Tiger church was the first one to be organized and then Wiley and the Boiling Springs Church in Persimmon, the name of which was later changed to King Memorial. So when I came in 1926, we had those three organized churches. We had a preaching point in the Timpson community out west of Clayton and one on Betty's Creek. In both of those places we were using the school building at that time as a building for our services. I would usually have a service in the morning and a service in the afternoon, and maybe another service at night in order to get around. Of course, I was not able to get around to every church every Sunday in those days.

Our church at Rabun Gap was organized in 1929, after the Nacoochee and Rabun Gap schools were merged, and I became the pastor of that church as well as the others. In the early fifties, the Clayton church was organized and the Timpson group, where we had a preaching point, was organized during the fifties. So that made six churches in the county altogether, which is what we have now.

What one main point distinguishes the Presbyterian doctrine from the doctrines of various other churches?

The Presbyterian Church holds to what is known as the Calvinistic interpretation of the Bible, which gets its name from John Calvin, who lived during the time of the Protestant Reformation. He systematized a statement of the teachings of the Bible as he understood them. He didn't invent it, I believe, but he did make a systematic statement. It goes back to St. Augustine, who lived in the fourth century and, I think, to the Apostle Paul in the first century. I believe that Calvin gives us a good and dependable statement of the Bible's teachings, and his system of doctrine is centered around the great truth of the sovereignty of God, God's right and God's power to do whatever's good in His sight. If you start with that, the other things fit around it. So that would be the central theme of the Calvinistic understanding of the Bible.

Have Presbyterians veered away from that one idea much during recent years?

There are people in the Presbyterian Church who interpret it more liberally now, I think, than they did, say, a few decades ago. Officially we still hold to what is known as the Westminster Confession of Faith, which was formulated by the Westminster Assembly in England in the seventeenth century. That was adopted by the

Presbyterian churches of the world as their statement of Bible teachings. We do not require of members of the church an acceptance of the Calvinistic understanding of the Bible. This, really, is required of ministers and officers in the church. A man is examined as to his knowledge of this system of doctrine and his acceptance of it before he is ordained to the ministry by the Presbytery, or before he is ordained as an elder or deacon in the local church. There is, on some points, some latitude of interpretation, but an acceptance of the system is required of men who are ordained to the ministry. I use the word "men," actually, now in our church, women can be, and some are, ordained to the ministry and the diaconate and the eldership, but the far greater majority of church officers are still men. We require of people who come into the church only an acceptance of Jesus Christ as their Savior, and their profession of their willingness to live for Him in the church.

Where does the word Presbyterian come from?

It comes from the Greek word "presbutoros" which is the word for elder in the Greek language. We find elders in the churches in the New Testament under the leadership of the apostles. They chose elders in the churches. That word is brought almost bodily from the Greek over into the English language with just slight changes.

Has the government within the church changed?

Basically, it is still the same. There may not be as close oversight of the local congregation, in a great many cases, as there used to be, but the organization is the same. The Presbyterian church is a church governed by elders. It gets its name from that fact, not from the fact that it holds to the Calvinistic system of doctrine. The minister is a teaching elder and the other elders in the local church are called ruling elders. The minister also has a share in the government of the church, and the ruling elders have a share in the teaching of the church, but they're named as they are from the predominance of their responsibility. The elders of the local church are organized into what is known as the session. The pastor, when he is installed as pastor, becomes moderator of the session by virtue of being the pastor of the church, and the ruling elders are all members of the session. Now that body has the oversight of the whole life and program of the local church. Then there are deacons in a great many of our churches, not in all of them. Many of them get along without a deacon. The deacons exercise a spiritual ministry, but [they also] have to do with the material side of the churches' life: the offerings, their collection and their distribution; the property of the church;

the buildings and grounds; looking after the poor, and so forth. So those are the officers in the church.

We believe in the organic unity of the church as a whole, and so the local church is a part of the presbytery, which is an area organization. When the presbytery meets, it is made up of the ministers who serve the churches in that area or who are serving in some other capacity, maybe as a teacher in a school. All the ministers who belong to that presbytery and a ruling elder from each church of the presbytery together constitute the presbytery. It convenes to carry on the work for the area and the oversight of the churches that are in that area. Two or more presbyteries make up a synod, which is a larger area. Here, we belong to the Synod of the Southeast, which is comprised of Georgia and South Carolina. The highest body is the General Assembly of the Church, which includes representatives from all the presbyteries within the church.

Are the churches here in the same presbytery now that they've always been in?

It has been the same for quite a good many years. There are seventeen counties here in Northeast Georgia [included in] the Athens Presbytery. Many years ago the boundaries were changed sometimes, maybe a county was added on or cut off and put over in another presbytery, but it has been the same now for quite a number of years. Any churches of our branch of the church are organized within that area belonging to the Athens Presbytery.

Do emotions play a large part of people worshipping within the church?

Generally speaking, the Presbyterian church in its services is less emotional than some other branches of the church. I believe that has been true all down through the history of the church. But that does not mean that we do not recognize the emotions as a valid part of a person's makeup. The gospel is an appeal to the emotions as well as to the intellect, but generally, the Presbyterian church has stressed less the emotional side than some other branches of the church have. I have not seen a great change, I think, in the churches where I have ministered in that respect during these fifty years.

Do you think there has been spiritual change?

As far as my experience goes, it has been largely the same. There are times in local churches when there are deep spiritual movements, maybe a revival meeting may stimulate the emotions of people, but on the whole course of the life of the church, I think it has remained pretty much the same.

Are there any differences between the old church and the new church?

I could mention two or three things. One is the change in the position of the church in regard to the ordination of women. That is only a fairly recent thing, several years ago, but recent as the history of the church goes. The church adopted this stand: First, that women could be ordained to the office of elder and deacon; and then to the office of the ministry. (I think it was later. I'm not sure. It could all have been done at the same time.) There are not a great many women ministers in our church. There are more elders and deacons who are women. That has been one change.

I think that there is, in some places, more laxity in these days in the interpretation of the Bible. [There may be more laxity] in the application of the Bible to daily living than there used to be, but I'm not sure that I could say that that was general. So, I have not seen any tremendous changes, I think, in that respect. More liberality, perhaps, in the interpretation of the Bible now than there was fifty years ago, but still [there are] a great many conservative ministers in the church and conservatism within the local churches, too.

What is the physical structure of a typical church?

I don't know that there was any characteristic type of structure that marked the Presbyterian church as different from others. Of course, years ago, many of the churches were only a single room, usually, pretty squarely built, and they had no Sunday school rooms. In the church where I grew up at Cornelia [Georgia] when I was a boy, we had no separate rooms cut off; the classes just met at different spots around in the sanctuary. It has been characteristic of Presbyterian churches in this general area, that we have had the pulpit in the center rather than on one side. Some branches of the church, for example the Episcopal church, will usually have a lectern on one side from which the Scripture is read and the pulpit on the other side where the minister goes to preach his sermon. There are some Presbyterian churches that are doing that in recent times, but the older ones had the pulpit in the center, which, I think, is characteristic of the church's putting the Bible in the central place in the life of the church. They typified that by the position of the pulpit. There was really no characteristic type of architecture, I think, that would mark the Presbyterian church as different from others.

How did the congregations pay their ministers years ago?

When I first came to Rabun County, the churches were very young. The Tiger church was organized in 1922. The minister had come there to live in 1921. The Wiley church was organized in 1924. Those churches were small in membership and money was not plentiful. There was little economic opportunity in the county, almost no industry at all, you could say practically none, so it was difficult for the people to make a living. The Presbytery and the Synod paid the greater part of the minister's salary; the churches paid only a very small part of it back in those days. This was considered home mission work, so most of the support for a minister came from the outside. Now in the years that have passed since then, industry has come into the county; there's employment for everybody who wants employment, and the churches have benefited from the fact that the people have more money. So now, the people in the churches give much more liberally than they used to and the churches are able to carry a greater share of the support of the minister. The Presbytery still assists in the support of the ministers in some of our churches in Rabun County, but there has been a tremendous change in that respect.

Do you think that congregations were more dedicated years ago?

I believe that the attendance in most of our churches was better years ago than it is now, but I'm not too sure that that means any less dedication of the part of the people who do come now. You see, fifty years ago the roads in the county were very poor, few people had automobiles, there was no television, there were very few radios, and I think, then perhaps, some people went to church because that was the only place to go. There was little competition. They'd gather there with the rest of the community and see their neighbors and friends there. Today, there's so much more competition. It's easy, for example, for people to get in their car and go to Six Flags [an amusement park near Atlanta] if they want to; or they can stay at home and listen to services on television with a more eloquent preacher than they'll hear in their own church and better music than they'll hear in their own church, in most cases. So, I think that those things have seemed to cut down on church attendance, but I believe that in all our churches there are faithful, dedicated people who are there because they want to be there to worship on Sunday morning and who are not distracted by these diversions that have come in.

Did the churches prepare for holidays?

I can remember that back in my boyhood in the church where I grew up, the Sunday school would have a Christmas tree. I remember that distinctly from my early childhood. I don't believe the emphasis was placed on Christmas in the services of the church as much then as it is now, or on Easter, either; but in our churches here in Rabun County since the early days of our work here, we have had special things at Christmastime and we have come to give more attention to Easter in recent years. Some say that those are pagan holidays that have been brought into the church, but it is a time when, without being pagan, we can think especially of the Lord's coming into human life in the birth of Christ and of the resurrection and the meaning of the resurrection. We do try to emphasize those things at those seasons.

Were there any other special services, such as watch night?

Not generally. As far as I can recall, we have not had any watch night services, for example, in the Presbyterian churches here in our county. I don't remember them from the days when I was growing up in the church. I don't think those are without their use at all. I think they may be very useful services, but our people have just not gone in for that kind of service, really.

In most of our churches in the county, we have had, from time to time, evangelistic services or revival services, special efforts to bring people to an acceptance of Christ as Savior and to come into the membership of the church, and to strengthen the lives of those who are already in the church; but those, with Easter and Christmas and daily vacation Bible schools in the summer, have been our stronger points in regard to special services.

We've had Bible schools in the county for many years. One change that I have noticed there is that when we lived here, for example, in the thirties, we always had young women to come in from the outside to help us in our Bible schools. They did most of the teaching, along with the pastor, himself. There were quite a number of college students who came to us from Florida State College for Women, year by year and some of them have had a continued interest in the work in Rabun County. Now, the people who have grown up in the church take the leadership and go ahead with those schools.

Did the Presbyterians ever have homecomings?

We have had those from time to time. I remember particularly, the King Memorial Church in Persimmon has had such services. I don't recall a homecoming service in any of our other churches in the county. There may have been some but I just don't remember any of them. [At homecoming] there would be a worship service with a sermon in the morning and dinner at the church, and, maybe in the afternoon, singing.

One thing that the Tiger church particularly has done is to work with the other two churches in the community, the Baptist and the Methodist church, in some union services. There was a time years ago, where we had union evangelistic meetings. We'd have a minister from the outside invited or maybe the three pastors would just preach in rotation in those meetings, which would be held in one or the other of those churches. Now at Tiger we have a union service every fifth Sunday, which comes once a quarter, and we rotate among the three churches. Sometimes, one of the pastors preaches; sometimes we have an outside minister to come in and preach. Once a year at that union service, the one that occurs in the summer, there will be a dinner at the church, but we do that only one time a year. That gives a good spirit of cooperation among the churches in the community. For four years now we have had a joint communion service on Thursday of Holy Week. That was begun at the suggestion of the Baptist minister and was begun in the Baptist church. We rotate among the three churches and we're back again this year at the Baptist church.

How is communion taken within the Presbyterian church and has it changed over the years?

There are two methods of actually serving the communion that I have known of. Generally, and always in our churches here, the people have sat in the pews at their regular place in the church and the communion is administered by the pastor, but it is served to the people by the ruling elders in the church. Then the pastor serves the elders after they have served all the other members. In one of the older churches in our presbytery, the Hebron church out from Commerce, they set up some long tables down in the front of the sanctuary between the pews and the pulpit and put chairs around those tables. When enough people will come up to fill up all those chairs, then the elders will serve communion to those. They get up and go back to their places and another group will come up and sit there. We generally have communion once a quarter and usually on the first Sunday in the quarter.

Do Presbyterians object to having musical instruments in the church?

In my lifetime, I have known of one minister who did not believe in having musical instruments in the church because, as I recall his attitude, they were not commanded in the New Testament. Most Presbyterian churches do have musical instruments. We believe that an instrument can be an aid in worship. [We believe] that the music in the church ought not to be a matter of show, it ought not to be just a performance, but it ought to be an act of worship. So, we use the instruments to encourage and aid the people in their singing. We believe that this can strengthen the worship of the church. So, we do have musical instruments in the church. They used them in the Old Testament. If you read the Psalms you'll see them over and over again. Occasionally [singings] are held in Presbyterian churches. Our people have not stressed them as much as some other branches of the church have, but once in a while we have had them.

Do they ever have camp meetings?

Yes, the Presbyterian churches have done that in the past. There is still one place in Georgia which has had camp meetings for years. They have little cottages now for the people to come and live in. They don't usually come and put up tents. That is at Camp Smyrna, which is between Atlanta and Covington, where that practice is still carried on and has been for many, many decades.

How do Presbyterians feel about foot washing?

I have never known of a foot-washing service in a Presbyterian church. Our understanding of the practice of foot washing is that there are two sacraments within the church, the sacrament of baptism by which a person is admitted into membership of the church, and the sacrament of the Lord's Supper which is the sacrament of fellowship. We do not believe that the Lord instituted another sacrament when he washed the disciples' feet and said, "As I've done this to you, you ought to do this to one another." But we believe that He was setting an example of service there. It was customary for a servant to wash the feet of guests when they came into a home because they wore open sandals and they walked on dusty roads and their feet would be dusty. In hot weather, they'd be hot and grimy, so it made for the comfort of the guests for a servant to wash their feet. Jesus was giving an example of service to His followers and we think that what He really meant by that was this: that we should be willing to render any sort of service to a fellow Christian, any sort of service that's needed. It's not customary in our country for a servant to wash the guests' feet when they come in. We wear shoes with socks, and our feet don't get as dusty and tired. If it were customary to do that in this country, and there

PLATE 49   Student Editor Keith Head, with Reverend L. B. Gibbs.

were no servant to do it, I'd say the host ought to do it. But you
see, it isn't customary here and we believe that He was giving an
example of voluntary service rather than a forced servitude. So,
we believe that we ought to be willing to do anything for other
people that they need, and some duties would be far more disagree-
able than washing another person's feet. But if they need it, we
ought to be willing to do that.

How do Presbyterians feel about snake handling and taking poison?

I haven't known of them doing that in any Presbyterian church.
As it happens, I mentioned this very thing in my sermon last Sunday
when I was preaching on the temptation of Jesus, where He was
tempted by Satan to throw Himself down from the pinnacle of the
temple and come down and do an amazing thing in order to give
people a sensation and encourage them to follow Him. The devil
there quoted Scripture when he tried to induce Jesus to do this.
He said, "If Thou be the Son of God, cast Thyself down, for it is
written, 'He shall give His angels charge over Thee to bear Thee
up in their hands lest at any time Thy dash Thy foot against a
stone.'" That's from the 91st Psalm. If you go back there, you'll
find that the devil quoted that verse exactly right, but he took it
out of its context and he made it mean something that it doesn't
mean at all. When you read the Psalm, you see it's written about

a person who's trusting God and trying to do God's will, not about a person who's trying God out to see how far he can go and get by with it, and there's a great difference between those two attitudes. I think snake handling, as far as I can see, seems to be trying to do a sensational thing, to work a wonder before people to stimulate them to believe. I don't believe that Jesus ever yielded to that temptation to just work a wonder before people to make them believe. His miracles were ministering to human needs and He did many things that were signs of His deity, but He never yielded to the demand for a sign to just prove that He was more than a man. Sometimes people asked Him for such a thing and He didn't do it. So, that is my personal attitude about snake handling or intentionally drinking poison. Now I believe that the Lord may have preserved me a lot of times from being snake bitten when I didn't even know there was a snake around. But if I had seen a snake and stuck my foot out there in front of it and expected the Lord to save me from it, I think I would have been acting very foolishly.

What's the church's stand on Divine healing?

Generally, in the past, I don't think the Presbyterian church has had healing services. There may be some that do that now; I'm not sure. I believe, and I think most of the ministers and most of the people in our churches would subscribe to this statement: that whenever we are healed, that is the Lord's doing. He can do it with means, that is by the use of surgery and medicine and the care of doctors and nurses; or if it's His will, He can do it without means, do it directly in a special way. I think that doctors and nurses are a part of His gift to us, and we believe in using their services, but if healing results, I believe that's God's doings. The doctor can't make you well. He can help provide the conditions under which you may get well, but he can't make you well. I believe that God answers prayers. I have no question that He has healed many people directly, without any means, and that He heals a great many people with means, doctors, medicine, and so forth.

What do you think about speaking in tongues?

I believe that the speaking in tongues on the Day of Pentecost was a speaking in known languages by persons who had not studied the languages and learned them; as if I, under the influence of the Holy Spirit, could get up and begin to preach in French, which I've never studied. I think that that's what happened on the Day of Pentecost, because there were people there who spoke a great many different languages and that was a means of spreading the

Gospel to those people while they were there and enabling them to take it back home. Now Paul seems to be talking about something that may be different from that in some of his letters. I noticed, though, that Paul, instead of exalting speaking in tongues to the first place among the Gifts of the Spirit, puts it down toward the end. He, himself, said that he would rather, I think, speak five words in a language that people could understand than ten thousand in an unknown tongue. I believe those are the figures that he uses, something like that. He also lays down the prescription that if somebody speaks in tongues there should be somebody else to interpret. I have never had an urge to speak in an unknown tongue. That's something that I simply don't understand because I've never experienced it. If those people are really being led by the Holy Spirit, then they have a right and a responsibility to do that; but, personally for me, it would be just a human effort rather than anything that God would do through me. I have a question about a lot of the speaking in tongues in these days, as to its value to the church.

Have you seen any of the Presbyterian people shout?

That has not been as common in the Presbyterian church as it has been in some other branches of the church, which does not mean that we question the validity of the emotional side of a person's life. We believe that it is important. Presbyterian services have been more along the line of instruction in the Bible; giving the people some solid truth to carry away with them. We believe that there is a legitimate appeal to the emotional side of a person's life, and if his emotions are not moved, he may never be moved to do anything about what he hears. There's been less open expression of that in the Presbyterian church than in some other branches of the church, which doesn't mean that we would find fault with other people because they do it another way. I don't remember that I have [ever seen anyone shout].

Do you, personally, think that hard times cause people to come to church?

I think that in many cases, some special difficulty or bereavement or sorrow has helped to bring people into closer contact with God and so with His church. I can think of cases where that has been true. In the case of some others, it doesn't seem to have that effect. So it's varied. You couldn't give any answer that would be universally true in regard to that question.

I can think of one particular case where a young son of a family died, and I believe that in that particular case the church has really strengthened the life of the mother of that son who died. I think of that one particularly. I think that there are many cases where that is true where the loss of a loved one or some particular hardship has tied the person up more closely to the church.

Did Presbyterians persecute the Holiness?

I don't believe I have ever known of anything that you could call persecution against the people in the Church of God or those of the Holiness persuasion. We differ with them in some respects, but we accord to them the same privilege we ask for ourselves, the right to interpret the Bible as we understand it and [the right] to practice it according to our understanding of its teachings. We differ from a good many other groups, but we would stand up for the privilege of practicing the Bible as you believe it.

What is the attitude of the Presbyterian church toward other churches?

There are groups that pass under the name of churches in our day who do not hold to what, I believe, are the essentials of the Gospel. In our churches where I'm serving now, we affirm our faith every Sunday morning in the words of the Apostles' Creed, which is a good statement of belief. The Westminster Confession of Faith is much longer, but I subscribe to the Apostles' Creed without any question. I believe that what it says is true. If people subscribe to that creed, they may not express it in exactly those words. I don't think the Baptist people would have any great difficulty with the Apostles' Creed if we used the word "universal" instead of the word "catholic"; and they wouldn't have any objection to the word "catholic" if they understood what it means, "universal, worldwide." It doesn't mean Roman Catholic Church, although I believe that they are Christians in the Roman Catholic Church, too. Where we agree is on those things that I believe are essential: the existence of God as a personal God; the Trinity, God the Father, Son, and Holy Spirit; the coming of Christ into the world as the Son of God; His giving Himself for our sins; the necessity of our repentance and faith in Him. If we agree on those things, I would say that there is much more that ties us together than there is that separates us. Our church believes in cooperation with other branches of the church.

PLATE 50 Reverend Clyde Hicks.

CLYDE HICKS, Presbyterian

Reverend Clyde Hicks, Presbyterian minister, is quite familiar with the ways of the old traveling preacher. His father was a circuit-riding Methodist minister who "had as many as seven churches at one time scattered over north Georgia." Reverend Hicks himself pastors three churches and he travels to them each week for services.

Clyde Hicks grew up a Methodist and, in one of the churches of his patient and understanding father, he preached his first sermon at the age of twelve. Several years ago for "personal and theological convictions," Reverend Hicks became a Presbyterian and along with his outside business interest, he hopes "to spend the rest of [his] life serving these churches."

Reverend Hicks has a sensitivity to the issues, problems, and needs in our community and he has made a commitment to help out wherever needed. His wife, Dolly, teaches at the high school in our county and they add positively to this community. We were impressed with Reverend Hicks's straightforward and well-thought-out answers to our questions and we appreciate greatly his cooperation.

KEITH HEAD

I was brought up as a Methodist. My father was a Methodist circuit rider. He had as many as seven churches at one time scattered over north Georgia. I don't know how he managed them; [he had] three or four services a day. We had a morning service, a couple in the afternoon, and an evening service. I'm a son of a preacher and [I preached] my first sermon when I was twelve years old. In one of his churches, [my father] was brave enough to let me preach and I preached on Jonah and the whale. I got Jonah in that whale, to Ninevah, and under the gourd tree praying to die in about five minutes. This is when I started. As a twelve-year-old boy, I started preaching—as a child, in a child's way.

I was converted in what a lot of folks would call an emotional atmosphere and it was an emotional experience as well as a faith experience. I don't think anyone can be in love, for example, and not feel it. I'd hate to have my wife say, "I love you but I don't feel it." Now, we don't go by feeling, it's a faith thing but there are times, like love, that religion has a feeling. It'd be a pretty pitiful situation if it were without any real emotion. I had a conversion experience at the age of seven in a little schoolhouse in Rex, Georgia. There was an independent, community wide, interdenominational meeting going on, commonly known as an evangelistic meeting. They used to call them "protracted meetin's" in those days, a term that is no longer used. They call them "crusades" now. This protracted meeting was going on in what the Methodists used to call the "old fashioned way"—"kneeling on my knees and praying through." Everyone was praying with the adults—the big sinners. They thought little Clyde was not a bad boy but I felt I had the potential of all the evil the big folks had, I just hadn't done it yet. God convicted me. I felt a call to come to Christ, confessing my sins and, by faith, accepting Him and it became a viable experience.

Shortly after, in fact, less than a month after, I felt called to the ministry. I'd been called all the time; I'd been feeling this. I'd preach to the dogs and my brothers, anybody who would listen to me. We'd get under the house and I'd use a five-gallon can as my pulpit. I'd preach to my older brothers and they'd laugh at me. Finally, nobody would come, so I'd take my dog up and pray for him. I was doing that when I was about four and it just grew on me. After I became converted and really came to realize Christ, then I felt that I must preach. It's been that way all of my life. That was one of the things that kept me clean as a young boy. Rather than going out and doing what a lot of the fellows did, I was able to keep pure in terms of sexual purity and moral behavior. Drinking, smoking, things of that nature were never a part of my life. I always heard Mother's prayers and felt the impact. It changed my life.

Prayer was a daily thing at Mother's knee. [I was one of] eight kids and they'd let me pray first at Mother's knee. I well remember it as she always prayed for me, time and time again, with tears falling on the top of my shaved head. I well remember the times she prayed,

"Make Clyde Your boy." She'd lay her hand on me and kiss the ball of my head. I'd long been asleep. I prayed first and by the time everyone got around, I'd be asleep. She'd usually wake me up and pray for me last and I've felt the tears on my head many times. This was one of the guiding lights that kept me clean as a young man.

God clinched it in an emotional experience and I can remember when. I drove down a stake, you might say, and I know when and where for me it happened. I wouldn't say that that's required for everybody. Whether you're on your knees or standing is secondary. It's [the] position of the Spirit that counts.

I was pastoring in a Methodist church when I became Presbyterian—about thirteen years ago. About four years ago while praying, I felt the vision—dream, conviction, whatever you want to call it—that I would be pastoring at least two or three churches in Rabun County. Nobody knew it but God. I knew it because He told me. So, purely on the face of that feeling, I decided to buy a business here from [a man who is] a Presbyterian elder. Realizing the need of a ministry, an ordained ministry, an on-going ministry in small, struggling churches that can't afford a pastor, he was quite anxious that we work out an agreement. That's why I'm here. I became a "tent-maker" minister and made my own way and served the churches.

Now my father was not only a circuit rider during the forties, but he was also a farmer and an upholsterer. His motivation was to have a business [in order] to serve his churches. This is my motivation. I wouldn't be in business for the sake of business. It's secondary to me. My first commitment is to God and to my churches.

Each of my churches has around twenty-six members. I have Clayton Presbyterian, Timpson Presbyterian, and King Memorial—locally [it is known] as the Persimmon Presbyterian but actually it is the King Memorial, a log church built in 1928.

How long have the Presbyterians been in this area?

Tiger Presbyterian Church is the mother church and I think it goes back to around the turn of the century. It was then and still is a member of the Athens Presbytery. It started in Tiger and then it branched out. The youngest church in the county is Clayton Presbyterian Church.

How is the Presbyterian Church governed?

A Presbyterian church has basically four courts. [First, you have] the session, which are local ruling elders. There are two types of elders. The ordained minister is a teaching elder. Those who're not teaching ministers are elected by the congregation and are ruling elders. They govern the church, elect persons to membership and have authority within the local congregation. The [second] court is the presbytery which is constituted of a number of Presbyterian churches, with their sessions, within a convenient geographical proximity. Then [third], you have the synod which is constituted of a number of presbyteries over a much larger area and [fourthly] you have your general assembly.

[The church government] hasn't changed since the beginning of Presbyterianism. It goes back to the New Testament concept. The word "presbytor," meaning "elder," is a Biblical word used by Paul in some of his letters to Timothy. The elders are in charge of the church, actually. The pastor is the moderator of the session, or Board of Elders. As pastor, I have a vote if I want to use it but I don't have to. I do not run the church at all. The affairs of the church are conducted in behalf of the congregation by the elected rulers or ruling elders.

Were the Presbyterians well accepted when they came into this area?

I was not here [when they first came in]. I would not think, however, that there was a great deal of hostility because we [now] have six churches serving six communities. That, in itself, would be a testimony of the acceptance by those communities. Mr. L. B. Gibbs, [who] was pastoring in the 1920s in Tiger, rode over the mountain on a horse to establish the Timpson church, which I am now pastoring. At this moment there is no hostility between the Presbyterians and other churches that I know of. It's a beautiful relationship and has been. We sense that we are all a part of God's vineyard; [none] of us has an exclusive claim on God's vineyard.

Have you seen any changes within the church since you became Presbyterian?

[Yes. For example,] our presbytery launched, through the Lily Foundation of Chicago, a rural "self-help" type of program. Our presbytery is one of the three places in the United States and the only one in the southeast [where this is taking place]. The foundation adopted the Athens Presbytery's rural churches in Rabun County as a kind of test project on strengthening the rural church. All the churches have had congregational inquiries [with] the people divided into small groups. We entertained and answered questions on what we can do to help ourselves. Now out of that, of my three churches, one gave their feeling and they seem to be quite satisfied. Another gave their feelings and they're still agonizing on certain issues on how to improve their situation. The third has started a Wednesday evening gathering. They had always thought the preacher ought to come do it but when I did go and do it, there was little or no interest. Now they've had [Wednesday evening service] going for about eight months. They meet together for Bible study. For example, they will study next Sunday's Sunday school lesson, then come back and restudy it Sunday. They'll all take the lesson, read it and study it. Then they go home and prepare for next Sunday's lesson. [They'll study] about twenty minutes, then they'll sing about twenty minutes, then they'll have about five of ten minutes of prayer—praying around. This is part of the revitalization of the church, part of the change. It's a new spirit.

[In the past] the Presbyterians never looked upon the "tent-making" ministry as very important. [But] it finally dawned on the officials—both the presbytery and the general assembly—that the country churches don't need anything fed down from the headquarters. They need something from the grass roots up. And the emphasis now in the Presbyterian church is that rural churches need to be free. Give them all the support you can and not just financial support. The presbytery is encouraging self-help and is helping rural churches in grants for improvement of the facilities and some pastoral support. But [the self-help idea] is to encourage men like me, who left a comfortable pulpit, to secure a business or to go into some profession, such as teaching or social work or into some agency within local governments and at the same time, to give of himself and encourage the people to do what they can do. So, what they call me now is a "tent-maker" minister. The Baptists have had this secret all the time and they've been ahead of the Presbyterians. Presbyterians are just now catching on to the concept. So this is what I am and what I expect to be. I hope to spend the rest of my life serving small churches.

What special services do the Presbyterians hold?

Our rural churches are distinctly rural with rural traditions such as homecomings and singings. Down at Timpson, they have a singing once a month. They're open to meet there as a community. The little churches in the rural areas are also used for community activities and if people want to get married in them, they can.

We have homecomings. It's just a traditional type of homecoming with dinner on the ground. They call it an "all day singing with dinner on the ground," but it's not really. They have a morning service with maybe a guest speaker or former pastor and then they have a big dinner on the ground. After that, they go up and sing a little bit. Just meet and generally get together. It's a good thing.

[Some Presbyterian churches] have what they call "preaching missions." They don't use the term "revival," but the country churches still say, "Let's have a revival meeting." And that's what they do. They get somebody to come in and preach Monday till Sunday and give invitations to "get saved."

Our churches have Bible schools. Mr. and Mrs. John Hull are proponents of assisting small churches in Bible schools. They come in the area with about fifty young people from all over the nation and hold Bible schools. Now, this year we did not [have Bible school] that way. We did not use them. And this is a change, too, [since] for the last three years we have been conducting our own Bible school. This means the people are getting educated to do it; they're not depending on someone else to come in and do it for them. But now, from time to time, we have this available to us. But Bible schools, Sunday school, morning worship, singings, homecomings— these are the big things and they serve the needs of the community.

Do Presbyterians outwardly show emotion in their worship?

You do not find a great deal of emotionalism within the Presbyterian church. Usually within the Presbyterian church you could sense a depth of feeling and even be moved to tears but not shaking tears; not the kind of outward expression that you would find more freely in some of the Baptist and Methodist and Pentecostal churches. Methodists used to be called "shouting Methodists," but you don't see many shouting Methodists anymore. Presbyterians and Methodists are usually about the same tone.

[In our worship service, my congregations] appreciate the pastor opening the invitation [to come to the altar] by singing "Just As I Am" just like they do in the Baptist church. When people come down, I make it clear that they're not coming down to join the church but that they're going to become a Christian. [When] they come down, if they are seeking Christ, we take them to the council room and deal with them personally with scriptures and prayer. If they want to join the church, they can come down and make it known that they'd like to transfer their membership. We believe in the council room. Bringing people to Christ should not be done before a gawking congregation. It ought to be in extreme privacy. This is another Presbyterian concept. I've led a number of people to God in the privacy of a study after the morning service. People, however, still like to see others coming down and publicly witnessing to their faith. That's a part of the rural Presbyterians' practice.

Incidentally, the Presbyterian concept of the altar is not a rail. You won't see an altar rail in Presbyterian churches. The Presbyterian concept of the altar is where you meet God, that's the important thing—when and where you meet God.

The Presbyterian church has always emphasized the intellectual approach to religion. This is not to say that the others didn't emphasize it but the Presbyterians have built a good theological base. They have always carried the idea that one must not only inspire the soul but one must also teach the mind to give it something to hold on to in an hour when one is not so spiritually inspired.

Do Presbyterians baptize?

We reject the concept that you're not baptized unless you're immersed. First of all, we are baptized in Christ by a faith experience. I would not be one, for example, to say that Quakers are not Christians because they have no form of baptism. Baptism, basically, is an ordinance that Christ instituted but I think Christ would be the first to use logic to say if it takes soap and water to clean your skin, it certainly takes more than water to cleanse your soul. The soul cannot be cleansed by physical baptizing. If so, then your soul would be temporal and the soul is spiritual.

Our method, primarily, is sprinkling [which] goes back to the Old Testament. You'll find that the government of the Presbyterian church is an Old Testament government, the old Hebrew government, as is our baptism. It's a kind of sacrifice—the sprinkling of the blood of the sacrifice on the altar. It's a kind of reliving of the Old Testament experience. The concept of pouring is not forbidden nor is immersion. Our concept of baptism is that it ought to be in the church as a part of the church worship experience. We believe first one ought to believe in Christ and baptism should follow one's profession of faith. One is a Christian first, by faith, and baptism is a seal of one's experience in Christ. One Sunday morning I baptized four in a congregational service and then delayed the service to a mill pond where we baptized two more by immersion. And I held them under until they got soaking wet. I wanted to make sure that they were real good and baptized!

We encourage [sprinkling babies]. When a baby is sprinkled, he becomes a non-communicate member of the church. The word "non-communicate" is important because it means he can never hold office, he can never vote, he can never participate in any active way other than attending the services of the church and the ordinances of communion and baptism. He can never participate in any active way in terms of business until he professes his own faith. This gives the church a kind of in-road, and this commits the parents in the presence of the congregation. It commits the parents and the church to a mutual concern and conviction to pray for the salvation of that child. So, being a member of the church is not actually salvation but is a way for the church to say, "We have you on a special prayer list and we will stand by you and surround you with prayer, hope, and faith until you come to the age of accountability." When children make their own profession of faith as they become older, then they can confirm the vows of their parents at their infant baptism or can be re-baptized if they want to. I encourage them to be re-baptized because I believe if a man is going to experience baptism, he ought to know what it is for himself and he doesn't know it as a child. There's nothing to forbid him to affirm his baptism and not to be re-baptized. That's been the stand of the Presbyterian church.

It's not a free ticket. The emphasis is really for a public commitment on the part of the parents. They affirm their faith at the moment of the baptism of the infant. It puts those parents on record before the world that they believe in Christ and are going to rear their child Christ-like. It also puts the church on its toes by assuming, through a covenant relationship, their responsibility to pray for the child. The parents and the church enter a covenant on the behalf of "little Susie," and they're going to stick with this little girl until she comes to the knowledge of her own salvation through Jesus Christ. This has always been part of the Presbyterian concept. This is why a lot of kids grow up in the church and stay with the church because there's a common bond established during infancy.

How do Presbyterians feel about speaking in tongues?

Technically and theologically we do not deal with the issue of tongues at all, although the Charismatic Movement, which is a modern, interdenominational movement of tongues, is very strong in certain areas of the Presbyterian church, but not in this county. I personally and theologically do not agree with those who accept the concept of tongues as the single—and I emphasize "single"—evidence of the Baptism of the Holy Spirit. I do not think it's Biblically or intellectually sound—nor theologically sound. Be that as it may, I've often said that if God tells a fellow to stand on his head and that's the way he can best be blest, then let him stand on his head! Presbyterians have never been that concerned over the theological issues to the point of grieving the Spirit. A man has rights, as God gives him the understanding to interpret these things; although, theologically and Biblically, I do think, probably, the tongue movement and the Pentecostals are not totally scriptural in some things. But that's my personal opinion and I do not condemn them. They probably would not think that Presbyterians are totally scriptural, either.

Do you practice snake handling?

No, no. I don't know if that even goes on in the county. Now, Presbyterians do not permit it. I don't think the Pentecostals, in this area, even permit it. This is where total literalism of scripture can get you in trouble. This is why I personally believe that you have to read the scripture in the light of the time in which it was written and if you take it out of its context you're in deep trouble. So that's why I am not a literalist in the sense of total literalism of scripture. Snake handling doesn't make good sense to me and it's not essential to prove your faith. But if I were a literalist in scripture, I'd probably do like some of those. But I think that's one case where I wouldn't be literal. A total literalist is often inconsistent. And this is one of the areas of inconsistency. Even good Baptist brothers who are strongly literalist in scripture don't handle snakes.

Do you believe in predestination?

Some of the Calvinists, the early Presbyterians, believed strongly like the Primitive Baptists: What is to be will be and you can't change it. Well, we have what we call predestination. I do not accept the position that some are chosen to be lost and some are chosen to be saved in the sense that God looks at you and says, "I like you, I'll take you. I don't like you, I'll not take you." God would be unjust to do that. But I believe that there are conditions in which the concept of predestination are couched. I do believe in predestination. I do believe that it's a Biblical doctrine. It's a question of interpretation. My concept of predestination—it might be different from other Presbyterians—is that there is a law of cause and effect. Did God predestine Ninevah to be destroyed? He said it would be. He told Jonah that in forty days it would be destroyed. Was God lying? Ninevah was not destroyed. He spared Ninevah. Did He lie? No. The condition of their destruction was if they did not repent. The law of cause—if they repent not, they die; the effect would be that they would die. If the cause was a good cause, the cause of repentance, they would live. This is the simple approach to predestination.

How do you feel about Divine healing?

Oh, I believe in Divine healing. We've had this experience. It's part of the scripture even as speaking in tongues is part of the scripture. I don't reject tongues as unscriptural. I do, however, reject the emphasis on tongues as a *single* evidence of the baptismal spirit. That's what I reject and that's what scripture rejects. You see, speaking in tongues is one of the spiritual gifts. There are nine gifts in the scripture. And the speaking of tongues is only one gift. The gift of healing is another gift. Yes, I have laid on the hands. I have anointed with oil. Presbyterians normally do not practice that, but, you see, I have a Methodist background as well as a Presbyterian-Calvinistic background. I feel like I have the best of both, which gives me a broader spectrum than one who's been reared a Presbyterian all his life and has never seen anything else. I've been on the Methodist side. I am now on the Calvinistic side of theology. I have seen the Methodist emphasis, which is experiential religion and the Presbyterian emphasis [which] is intellectual, theological religion. [The Presbyterians are] swiftly giving expression to the concept of experiential religion. They've never ruled it out, of course, but they've never been as emotionally expressive as they are today. So, I think that's a change in the Presbyterian church. While the other churches have come from emotionalism to a more theological stance, the Presbyterians have done just the opposite. Now I think they're meeting. I really think they're meeting.

Have you ever seen anybody healed?

Sure. In fact, my last church I pastored as a Methodist, I had a lady that had facial neuralgia. She was to have her face operated on. She asked me for the laying on of hands, which is scriptural in the 5th chapter of James and she took it literally. I called the elders of the church around, we laid on the hands on her head, she knelt, we prayed and as we prayed, I felt the power going through my hands just like electricity. It went right through my hand and went right into her head and I felt it. She just jumped and quivered all over. Suddenly she lifted up and said, "I'm healed," and she'd been healed. She is today. She never had the operation. Now, I did not do it; God did it. I was an instrument of God's healing. Healing is one of the nine gifts. But I would be very radical and very narrow to say you have to have this one gift or you don't have God's spirit, that [without it] you don't have the baptism of the Holy Spirit. If you read the 12th chapter of 1st Corinthians, Paul talks about the gifts, but in the 13th chapter, he says, "but, gentlemen, seek the best gifts," and he enumerates them, nine. I presume Paul enumerated them according to importance. But then he said, "Seek the best gifts and yet I showed you a more excellent way, the way of love." Yes, I believe in healing.

I kept a little vial of olive oil in the pulpit in the event someone asked for this, because many people take the scriptures literally in everything. I think if you do that everytime, you can be in difficulty. But that, of course, is a great debate in the church. At any rate, I believe literally what the Bible says on healing and I think you can be healed. My wife, in fact, is an example of it. She was healed of cancer about ten years ago. And she's healed today and we cease not to thank God every week. Hardly a day passes we don't thank the Lord, because God did this. You see Presbyterians can be healed, too. We're all God's children if we know Jesus.

Do you think people are falling away from the church?

From my experience, I do not believe the church is fading. Our churches have been holding their own programs. In fact, Timpson is growing; King Memorial is holding its own. It's an older community, but it still has a great number of young people and quite a few young adults. The one thing that doesn't change basically is the church. Your school changes, the government changes, your politics change, your social concepts change, but your rural churches still believe in and preach Jesus Christ as the hope of the world and that hasn't changed. As long as people can experience the warmth of their religious faith, it won't change. As long as the pastors can preach from experiential religion. If a guy comes in and all he's got is intellectual training and theological training with no heart in it, it'll be like hitting an anvil—he will be the one to crumble. I've seen so many come and go. These young boys think they're going to convert the world to a new social order. Their sense of evangelism is to change the social fabric of society, but our belief, and the Bible teaching still is and has been and shall always be, that it is Jesus Christ who changes the world through people who are converted to Christ. Because the world is still made up of people, individuals, and if you don't change individuals, you don't change the world. So that hasn't changed, I don't think, and if it has, I'm not willing to admit it. I've been at the preaching business twenty-six years now and I hope to be at it till I'm eighty. I believe in it!

PLATE 51　Sid McCarty.

SID McCARTY, Presbyterian

Sid McCarty, a devout Presbyterian, is a supporter of the Charismatic move-
ment which is finding its way into non-Pentecostal churches. The Charismatic
Movement places emphasis on the empowerment of the Holy Spirit and is
usually evidenced by glossolalia, or speaking in tongues, or sometimes by healing.
Although he loves his church and its ideology, Mr. McCarty regularly attends
meetings of other denominations and believes strongly in interdenominational
cooperation. Mr. McCarty has served his own church in a number of capacities
including elder, Sunday school superintendent, teacher, and sponsor of the
church's young people's organization.

KEITH HEAD

When I was about thirteen, I joined the Presbyterian church;
mostly because my dad thought I was old enough and it was the
thing for me to do. But really, there was no change in my life at
that time. A few years after that, I went off to school in a small
community where there were only two churches, a Methodist and
a Baptist church. At that time, the Baptist people decided to build
a new church, so they tore down their old church. The Methodist
people invited the Baptist people and everyone else to come worship
in their church during this time. While we were all worshipping
together, they decided to have a revival. I remember that one day

our math teacher gave us about twenty problems to work and hand in the next day, but he said, "Anybody that goes to that meeting will be excused from working these problems." So, the whole math class was there that night! That was the night that I went down and gave my heart to the Lord, along with several other young people. I remember, after the meeting, the preacher said that he'd like to talk to us, so we went up. Something I remember he told us was if we ever got in a bind, all we had to do was call on the Lord and He'd be right there to help us.

[I had a friend who was] an older boy than I, and smarter; he made better grades, and I looked up to him. Well, the next day he came up me to and said, "Boy! that was a crazy thing you did last night."

And I said, "What do you mean?"

He said, "When you went down there last night and gave your heart to the Lord. There's not any God. That's just something people have cooked up in their own mind, just to satisfy themselves and make themselves feel better. But, really, there is no God. When you pray to the Lord it does no good. It's just foolishness."

Well, I didn't pay too much attention to him, but still, what he said had its effect. I was living on a farm at that time and one job that I had was to ride a horse way back in the mountains to check on and salt the cattle. They had free range then, and I was supposed to go one morning on a certain day. [One morning] they told me I couldn't go that day, because they had to plow the horse that I was planning to ride, so I said okay. In a little while the blacksmith came to the farm and he had a day's work there. And, boys! he was riding the prettiest saddle horse that I ever saw. They told him what had happened, and he said to me, "Now, you take my horse and go check on the cattle; but you've got to be back here at a certain time, because after I quit here, I have a full day's work to do at home, and I've got to leave here then. If you can't get back here by that time, don't go." I told him he could count on me. I'd be back. So, I borrowed his horse and rode way back in the mountains.

I remember passing the last house and it looked like nobody was home. I went on quite a ways and I came to the pasture where the cows were. I let the bars down, led the horse in, put the bars back up, walked around and checked the cattle, and put salt on the various rocks. Everything was okay, so I decided that I might as well go on back. I started to catch the horse, and, boy! as soon as that horse saw me coming toward him, he wheeled and ran. That didn't disturb me much; I figured I could catch that horse, although

I didn't have a rope or anything to catch it with. I decided I'd just make out like I wasn't interested in catching him and walk up close to him, and all of a sudden jump and catch his bridle reins; but I couldn't get closer than ten feet to him before he'd run! So I got a long limb off of a tree there and I decided that I'd push it along the ground, get it so close to him, and twist it in the bridle reins and catch him that way; but he saw that limb coming at him and he turned and ran. Then I decided I'd take that long limb and I'd hem him up in a corner of the fence and catch him that way. I got him hemmed up in there and he saw that he was hemmed up. He run right over, hit that limb, knocked me down, and just kept going. I tried everything I could; I just couldn't catch that horse. I remember I sat down on a rock and I thought the situation over.

I thought about going down to that last house that I'd passed, and see if I could get some help—maybe somebody'd have a rope or another horse. Then I figured by the time I walked down there and got somebody and walked back up to where I was, it'd be getting dark and I never would catch that horse after dark. So, I gave that up. My time was running out, and I didn't know what to do. I thought about what that preacher said. He said, "If you ever get in a bind, all you have to do is call on the Lord, and He'll help you." Then I thought about what my buddy said. He said, "Aw! There's not any God! There's no use to pray to Him." Then I figured, now's a pretty good time for me to find out which one was right. I didn't know too much about praying, so I just said something like, "Lord, if You really do exist, and if You really do answer the prayers of Your people, please help me catch this horse." And, boy! I hadn't said any more than "amen." I was sitting on a rock and there that horse was a'grazing. The bridle rein had went down over the side of his neck and formed a loop right on the ground. [When] I got up and took one step toward that horse, his left forefoot went right into that loop. Then I jumped at him. He threw his head back first thing, and that drew that loop right up around his foreleg. He stood up on his hind legs, and he saw that he was in a trap. He just stood right still for me to come and untangle him, and I took him home in a hurry! Next day, I looked up that old boy who told me that there wasn't any God, and I told him what had happened. He said, "Ah, that was just a happen-so. That'd have happened anyway." I figured that he hadn't been under the same experience; he hadn't been trying to catch that horse.

I left that country about then and to my knowledge, I never did see that boy again. Three or four years ago, I was reading the obituary column in the *Asheville* [North Carolina] *Citizen* and I saw where that same boy had just died . . . and they called him "Reverend," Reverend so-and-so. Somehow during that time the Lord had got to that boy, and he had turned to be a preacher.

How does it feel to have a conversion experience?

I think the difference in my feeling after I was converted was that I had an entirely different outlook on life. Before then I didn't consider education or living my life for a purpose was important. But after then, one of my teachers—all of my teachers—noticed the big difference in me. I never failed in any course I ever took after that. I began to live my life for a purpose after that. That was one of the biggest differences. And after then, I always went to the Lord about any important decision that I had to make. I began to depend on Him for guidance and protection, prosperity, and everything that comes with it.

Does the Charismatic movement in the Presbyterian Church involve more emphasis on the Holy Spirit and speaking in tongues?

Yes. It's a new thing. There are those who are involved in it; there are those who are afraid of it and run from it; there are those who are indifferent. There is a group of Presbyterians known as the Presbyterian Charismatic Communion. They had a meeting a month or so ago out in California, and there were over five thousand that attended, whereas when all the representatives and everybody come to the General Assembly [meeting] of the church, there's only about fifteen hundred to two thousand who attend those meetings. But over five thousand attended this Charismatic meeting. The biggest change I see in the Presbyterian Church is their acceptance of the Charismatic movement, and that has brought some changes in it. As far as I can tell, the worship services are about the same. In the individual lives, I think, Presbyterians are more emotional now than anytime that I've known.

What is your feeling about the Holy Spirit and speaking in tongues?

I think it's a gift of the Lord. I think it's available to His people if they want it. I don't think He forces it on anybody. I think it's certainly a way in which we can praise the Lord more effectively than we can with our mentality. When we speak in tongues our little mind and mentality is not standing there editing everything we say. Praising the Lord through Holy Spirit . . . the Holy Spirit is refurnishing the voice, but God is furnishing the language and what we say.

A lot of people say and believe that everybody is filled with the Holy Spirit when they are converted. I think when we are converted, we do receive a measure of the Holy Spirit. And I think, generally speaking, the Holy Spirit is given by measure; some people have more than others. One person may have more at one time than he would at another time. The Bible tells us that Jesus was given the Holy Spirit without measure. I think when we are converted, we are led by the Holy Spirit to seek the Lord and to accept Him. The Bible speaks of Baptism in the Holy Spirit, and that's the way I like to refer to it, because that's the way the Bible refers to it. I think when we're Baptized in the Holy Spirit, we may speak in tongues at that time, or we may not. Most people, I suppose, believe that you do speak in tongues. I think when I received the Baptism in the Baptism in the Holy Spirit, I didn't know anything about speaking in tongues.

I went down one night to Georgia [to hear a Pentecostal preacher]. I was sitting there before the service had started, and no one had said anything. Nobody had prayed, nobody had sung, nobody had preached. We were just waiting for the service to start, and this man came in, walked up on the platform and put his Bible on the pulpit. He laid his hands over his eyes just a moment, and prayed for just a few seconds. As he did that there was a heat wave started at the top of my head and went right down over my body, just like that. I didn't know what was happening and I began to weep. I didn't know 'til sometime later that that was what happened when a person received the Baptism of the Holy Spirit. But it was a long time after that—several years—before I actually spoke in tongues freely.

How do Presbyterians feel about Divine healing?

The Presbyterians, certainly, believe in praying for the sick and I think we believe that the Lord answers prayer. Since the Charismatic movement has come into the church to such an extent, there're many, many instances where people have been healed physically through prayer. We believe that—I certainly do. The church also believes and teaches that a person can be in torment physically and one way the Lord might heal that person is to take him right out of this life into a life that has no suffering. He's healed that way many times.

[I've seen people healed.] My wife used to have arthritis real bad. She'd have to roll out of bed. Many times I'd just have to dress her and button her clothes for her. She could do her hair, but with real bad pain. We went to Charlotte [North Carolina] one time to a healing meeting—the first one I'd ever been to. It was one of Kathryn Kuhlman's meetings. During the service Kathryn Kuhlman said, "There's somebody up in the balcony who's been healed of arthritis, and somebody over there of bursitis." Then she said, "The Lord tells me that everybody who has arthritis in here can be healed. Just claim your healing." I was sitting right by [my wife,] Betty, and she poked me and said, "Look here! Look here!" She could move her hands just like that, and her arthritis was gone. She claimed it, and she's claimed it ever since. That's been six or seven years ago, I guess. She doesn't have any now. She was healed.

I saw hundreds of people healed there, not only of arthritis, but all kinds of stuff. There was a little girl who had polio. She was in body braces, and she couldn't walk or anything. Her mother took her up on stage and she said she felt that she was healed. Kathryn Kuhlman told the mother to take her in the dressing room and remove the body brace and bring her out. She did, and her mother just about had to carry her out. Kathryn Kuhlman, I remember, put her arm around her, and said, "Now, let's walk across the stage." She walked across with her help, but could hardly walk. [When they walked] back, [Kathryn Kuhlman] said, "Now, let's go a little faster, and a little faster." About the third or fourth time, Kathryn said, "Now, you try it, yourself, by His help." [The girl] kind of wobbled across the stage by herself, and then she said, "Now, go a little faster by yourself." And, about the fourth time, I'll tell you, that young'un was hopping and a'skipping, and throwing her arms, running back and forth across that stage just like she'd never been sick or anything. There were about five thousand people there. I remember Kathryn Kuhlman said, "Now, can anybody in this audience refuse to praise the Lord now, over this?" She said, "Let's praise Him by singing 'How Great Thou Art.'" And, boy, I'll tell you, it sounded like that roof was coming off. That was some meeting!

I think that the Lord is pouring out His Holy Spirit in these times, more than He has anytime in my lifetime. I think He is pouring out His Holy Spirit now more abundantly than anytime since the early church or since Pentecost—maybe even more now than at Pentecost. When I say "more," I mean certainly upon more people. At Pentecost there were just a hundred and twenty people, but now there's millions and millions of people throughout the world, not just around us, but over the whole world.

THE CAMP MEETING

"Camp Meetings, Camp Meetings, O glory, glory."
PETER CARTWRIGHT
(METHODIST CIRCUIT RIDER)

Historical Overview
By Bill Leonard and Paul F. Gillespie

The religion of Appalachia has preserved one of the unique phenomena of American religion, the camp meeting. Born in frontier Kentucky around 1800, the camp meeting became a vehicle of civilization, conversion, and social interaction in what was often the coarse, lonely and, the preachers said, godless life of the American wilderness.

The history of the camp meeting has already been examined in this volume (see the chapter on the Christian Churches). The earliest gatherings occurred in Kentucky under the leadership of Presbyterian preachers such as James McCready and Barton W. Stone. They soon involved preachers of other denominations until Presbyterians, Methodists, Baptists, and even an occasional Shaker could preach their particular gospel, secure converts and found churches out of the camp meeting experience.

Yet the camp meeting was more than a religious gathering. It was a social event for which folks traveled great distances. Most meetings lasted five to seven days and travelers had to bring supplies for a lengthy stay. Here persons bartered for goods, traded and raced their horses, argued politics, and became acquainted with their "neighbors." Here, too, men and women observed frontier courting rituals and many marriages began at the camp meeting. The songs and shouting, the unity of common meals and common prayer created a bond which was vital to the development of community on the frontier.

Religion was the dominant factor, however, and as the camp meeting became institutionalized, it became an important part of the religious life of the South and Southeast. Individuals who experienced religious travail during the year might wait for months before "camp meeting time" could provide the necessary solace for the soul. Persons fighting against the call to conversion often found that the enthusiasm of the camp meeting swept them over into the ranks of the elect. Those converted in earlier camp meetings returned year after year to renew the original zeal of brighter days and stronger faith. The camp meetings soon became homecomings when the people of God, spread out across the mountains, came together to rekindle the fires of faith and strengthen the bonds of friendship.

With time, many of the early camp meeting sites became permanent camps as land was set aside for the perpetual use of the faithful. The Methodists were particularly active in the establishment of permanent camp meeting sites. Indeed, by the mid-nineteenth century, the Methodists had become the chief proponents of the camp meeting experience in America. When doctrinal divisions damaged the ecumenical spirit of the camp meetings, other denominations sought new ways of conducting revivals within the local churches. The Methodists, however, continued to conduct camp meetings, often in the same locations. Eventually, permanent buildings were erected on many of the sites and a schedule was developed, particularly active in the summer months.

Present-day camp meetings usually are organized around a schedule similar to that of the frontier. There are few activities beyond preaching, worship, and visiting with friends. The day revolves around a series of services from morning to night, divided by meals and an afternoon rest period. Services are presided over by the "camp pastor" but a variety of preachers may be asked to speak at the services.

Congregational participation continues to be important in modern camp meetings. Singing is loud and enthusiastic with soloists, and choirs providing "special music." Sermons urge conversion on the unsaved but also stress the responsibility of those already converted to grow in faith and Christian maturity. Invitations or "altar calls" are usually given at the end of each service in order to provide prayer and counselling for those seeking spiritual comfort.

Throughout the week there is also a sense of community as friendships are renewed and Christian fellowship shared among all who are present. Tears are shed, prayers are offered, and faith is renewed. As these interviews indicate, the camp meeting continues to be an important time of religious and social rejuvenation among many Christian groups in Appalachia.

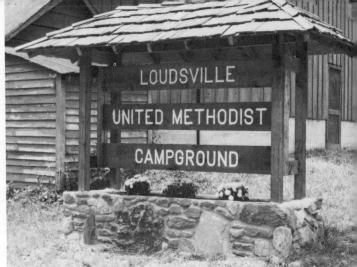

PLATE 52

PLATE 53   Porter Glover.

LOUDSVILLE
UNITED METHODIST CAMPGROUND

Porter Glover

The Loudsville Campground has been here right at a hundred and fifty-seven years. The first camp meeting was held around 1833, and it's always been a Methodist institution. It had its beginnings when the first settlers were coming to this part of the country and it's believed the name is derived from a gold miner named Loud who prospected in the area in the early 1830s. The original land upon which the permanent arbor still exists was owned by Major Frank Logan and he deeded this land to the trustees of the campground in 1850. Additional land was deeded to the campground trustees in later years; in 1894 by the White brothers, Will, John, Frank, Henry, and Charlie. In 1949, approximately one acre was deeded by Mrs. Ben Ledford in the memory of Ben Ledford's parents, Tom and Helda Ledford. In 1966, Pearl Simms deeded about one acre so that the campground would own all of the land that it was using.

Before these permanent arbors were built, they had what was called brush arbors. Of course, I never have seen a brush arbor as they were used only in the very early years of the camp meetings,

PLATE 54   The permanent arbor at Loudsville is an example of the typical architectural structure of arbors.

but I talked once to an old lady who said she would carry water to those that were working on the brush arbors. So they did exist and they were probably constructed somewhat like the permanent arbors, although not as big. A covering of brush and branches would be supported by posts and the sides were open. They would have their services under there. I would imagine that the brush would deteriorate from year to year and they had to do it over a lot. All of this work eventually led to a more permanent arbor that used split boards or shakes as a better lasting roof.

In 1905, the arbor was extensively renovated and for all practical purposes, rebuilt. It has been said that Tom Ledford dragged rafters for over two miles using just the front wheels of a wagon as a means of conveyance. Beams were hand hewn and the whole thing was covered with hand split shingles. In 1920, a metal roof was put on and it lasted until 1948. In that year, the present structure we have was built. It was dedicated by Bishop Marvin Franklin. This arbor was well built and has existed like this year in and year out. Like the old brush arbors, the sides are open for good ventilation. However, the trustees store the pews or benches and they are brought out each year for our camp meeting. We also put down a load of fresh woodshavings under the arbor for each camp meeting.

The yearly camp meetings would always be held in late August, but lately we've changed it so as not to conflict with schools which are opening earlier. At first, camp meeting would begin on Wednes-

PLATE 55   Another campground's meeting place, the Mossy Creek Campground arbor.

PLATE 56   The "tents" surround the campground on all sides.

day. Then for a short time it started on Tuesday and now it opens on Monday, running through the next Sunday. I remember when people would come in their wagons to camp out. Back then, most all of the service goers would camp out the entire week here. Many built small, simple log cabins or "tents" to camp in from year to year. "Tents" like these, are still in existence today with many being permanently owned by the regulars of the camp meeting faithful. People would bring a coop of live chickens, fresh produce, other vegetables, and meat. Some of these things were kept in nearby branches or covered earthen pits to keep cool. Milkcows were even brought along to the camp meetings. At first they had a public well for the tent holders and visitors. The business of taking buckets and going to get water provided the young men a way to help the young ladies in doing their chores and gave them an opportunity to talk to the ones they had been eyeing. I'm sure many courtships had their beginnings on trips to and from the spring or well. In 1939, wells were dug in convenient places and hand pumps installed. In 1954, an electric pump was installed and a water line laid to the rear of all the tents. The people began to furnish their tents with hot-water heaters and stoves. In 1961, a sewage system was installed and most tent holders built bathrooms within their structures. These tents—or maybe more appropriately, cabins—now have all the conveniences and some use them as weekend and vacation retreats. There are over fifty such tents now and many are two-story.

A lot of local preachers came to the camp meetings and many good, soul-stirring messages were heard. There were testimonial meetings and people shouted as they talked about their religious experiences. We still have good camp meetings here although people are quieter than they used to be. But even back then in the old days, there were those who thought all the people were hell-bound. A long time ago somebody told me that on the last day of camp meeting in August 1886, a preacher by the name of Newt Austin prayed and asked for an earthquake to shake people up and make them change their ways. So on Tuesday night following the close of the camp meeting the earthquake came and it scared people. They quoted one of the old preachers, Lou Allan, as saying, "Damn Old Newt Austin."

Somebody told me another story that supposedly happened in 1896. A pastor by the name of Cowan recommended that the men sit under one side of the arbor and the women under the other. This was opposed at the tent-holder's meeting. John Henry Brown and his girlfriend, Miss Lora Turner, came in and sat together. The campground marshalls, Mr. Hughes Allen, Jim Morris, and Riley

PLATE 57   A prayer bench is located near the pulpit under the arbor. The earthen floor is covered with straw.

Helton, promptly asked Mr. Brown to move across the aisle. Instead, he just left the arbor and his girlfriend followed him. Then others had trouble when they were ordered to move. Otis Hensley was ordered to move, but he refused and the marshalls removed him by force. In escorting Mr. Hensley off the premises, one of the lawmen, H. Riley Helton, was somehow stabbed. By the time of October court, tension had mounted so much, someone set fire to a row of tents and all the southside burned. This incident ended the separation of the sexes!

Of course, in the early days it did not take as much money to operate the campground. In 1910, for example, the records show that the total collection for the week was $18.00. Now it is not uncommon for the campground to have an expenditure of $5,000 or more. Most of the revenue comes from those who tent and others who come to the services. Visitors are good to help defray the cost of improvements and expenses for the camp meeting week.

We have a good camp meeting each year. The district sends several preachers out here for the week and we have several services each day. There are over fifty tent holders and on Friday and Saturday nights, this arbor is full. The camp meeting is something out of the past that has continued on and on.

INTERVIEW AND PHOTOGRAPHS
BY CAROL ROGERS

PLATE 58   Ocie Allison.

Ocie Allison

I was born and raised three miles from here and have been coming to this camp meeting for ninety-some years. I'll be ninety-six years old next month. I was baptized right over there [near the front of the arbor]. I was sprinkled and I remember I was just a little girl and my little brother, John, was getting baptized at the same service. The preacher had poured so much water on me and I was crying because I was afraid that the preacher was going to drown him!

My grandfather's brother, Frank Logan, donated the land for this campground and I had an aunt who said she was five years old when it started. I don't remember the brush arbors—they were long gone before I started coming here. But my aunt said she remembered them. There has been a camp meeting here every year since the early 1830s, except for one year during the Civil War. That may have been the year Sherman came through, I don't know.

People would come to the camp meetings back then in wagons and tie their stock to the trees. People would kill beef and bring it around here to sell. They would put the meat and other things that would ruin in jars and bury them underground to keep them from spoiling. Other things have changed a whole lot, too. When I first started out, we had to carry our water from the spring. We cooked on woodstoves in the tents and there was no electricity. For lights in the arbor, we had pine knots burning on top of dirt-filled stands made of logs. We had two on each side and one up at the front. After that we used oil lamps and kerosene lanterns.

I remember they had trouble at one of the camp meetings. They made a rule that men and women couldn't sit together and some of the men didn't like it. Some kind of row broke out and the sheriff,

PLATE 59   The Loudsville United Methodist Church is across the road from the campground.

who was an unusually large man, was stabbed on Sunday night. Nobody knew who did it! Something like that didn't happen a whole lot and we have always had wonderful camp meetings since I've been here. It's earlier [in the summer] now because of school but people aren't tenting like they used to. The tents used to be full but there aren't as many here now.

INTERVIEW AND PHOTOGRAPHS BY CAROL ROGERS

CULLASAJA ASSEMBLY OF GOD
CAMP MEETING AND CAMPGROUND

PLATE 60   The Cullasaja Assembly of God Tabernacle.

A DAY OF ACTIVITY: ASSEMBLY OF GOD CAMP MEETING as documented by Foxfire students, Keith Head and Wendy Guyaux.

7:30 A.M.: PRAYER BELL. A number of the campers gather in the tabernacle to have several minutes of prayer.

8:00 A.M.: BREAKFAST. Cafeteria.

10:00 A.M.: MORNING WORSHIP AND CHILDREN'S CHURCH. Most of the campers are present for this service. Total present will number one third expected at the evening service. (Many participants work in the surrounding area during the day and come to the evening services.) The morning workshop and children's church is similar to the evening service described as follows.

PLATE 61   Inside the tabernacle, benches are lined up on the sawdust-covered floor.

PLATE 62

PLATE 63   The ministers at the altar.

12:30 P.M.: NOON DINNER. Cafeteria.

1:15–7:30 P.M.: TIME OF PHYSICAL AND SPIRITUAL RELAX-
ATION. This period is spent in recreation and visitation among
campers. Some people go to the tabernacle to pray or play the
piano and sing. Supper is usually eaten shortly before the evening
service begins.

7:30 P.M.: EVENING EVANGELISTIC SERVICE AT THE TABER-
NACLE.

A. All the preachers in the congregation are asked to come to
    the front. The congregation is asked to stand and they sing
    "Walking with the King." Some of those in attendance praise
    the Lord with audible prayer as the song ends. The evangelist,
    Brother B. H. Clendennon, from Texas, walks into the taber-
    nacle praying and then comments on the great spirituality
    of the song. The congregation responds with a hearty
    "Amen." The song leader, Brother Hooper, implores the con-
    gregation to stand and as they sing more of the song, people
    in the congregation raise hands and clap hands. At the conclu-
    sion of the singing, people praise the Lord vocally and raise
    hands.

B. Brother Hooper asks the congregation to praise the Lord
    on behalf of the people's needs and, asking if needs have
    been met, he encourages the congregation to "give the Lord
    a handclap."

C. Brother Cookman, the District Assemblies of God Supervisor
    from Dunn, North Carolina, talks about the story of the Ro-
    man Catholic who came to the camp meeting to get the Bap-
    tism of the Holy Ghost and how the man gets sawdust on
    him from being "slain in the spirit" on the last day. Brother
    Cookman comments on giving and then the offering is taken
    up in Kentucky Fried Chicken buckets while someone sings
    a "special"—"Since Jesus Passed By."

D. A young man gives his Christian testimony and Brother Cook-
    man asks others if they have experienced the Lord. Many
    respond by raising hands and shouting "Amen." A series
    of songs then follows, including "He Signed the Deed," "Be-
    cause He Lives," "I Found Reality," and "Jesus Is Lord of
    All." Brother Cookman continues by telling about the man
    who came to the camp meeting the previous year to poke
    fun at the Pentecostals. He was converted and he will be
    coming to the present camp meeting to share his conversion
    experiences. Brother Cookman comments that if one "gets

PLATE 64   Special singers lead the congregation in hymn singing.

PLATE 65

PLATE 66

PLATE 67 The visiting evangelist, Brother B. H. Clendennon, begins the evening revival service.

PLATE 68

PLATE 69

close to the fire, he or she will get burned." The congregation responds with laughter.

E. Claudia Cookman, Brother Cookman's daughter, sings a special song, "The Family of God." Brother Cookman announces that his daughter is getting married and that people may not get to hear her sing again. A man in the congregation shouts, "Let her sing again!" Brother Cookman, quickly and humorously, responds with a "Thank you!" His daughter sings "Peace," a song that she has written but has never sung before an audience. After she finishes, much emotion is evident and people applaud.

F. Brother Cookman introduces the evangelist, Brother Clendennon, who is from Texas. Brother Clendennon talks about the morning service to be held the following day and about offerings which have ranged from $10.00 to $2,000. He goes on to introduce his wife and a camp supervisor, who knows that it is her birthday, leads an energetic rendition of "Happy Birthday."

G. Brother Clendennon begins the sermon with the text coming from the eleventh chapter of Matthew. He stresses the need for Christians to be forceful and after a very moving and powerful exhortation, he asks the people to stand and worship God. Emotional and spiritual fervor is quite in evidence and many, including those seeking the baptism of the Holy Ghost, go to the altar. Brother Clendennon calls for the Christians to come and pray and soon the altar is filled with people raising their hands, shouting and praying. After a period of this activity, the service comes to an end and the campers prepare for their night's rest.

THE TRADITION
OF SHAPED-NOTE MUSIC

A History of Its Development

By Edith Card

Singing schools and shaped notes. Singing conventions and gospel sings. These are musical phenomena about which a vast segment of American society is totally unaware or grossly misinformed. This does not mean, however, that the folk involved are small in number or isolated geographically or that this culture is in danger of becoming extinct. On the contrary, singing gospel songs by means of shaped notes is flourishing throughout the country. The exponents of gospel song gather regularly to sing from the latest publication as well as to enjoy old favorites. These "sings" are not only musical events, but also social affairs and, for many, an expression of religious faith. American youth throughout the country have "discovered" gospel songs. They sing them because it is fun and, along with ethnomusicologists and folklorists, recognize them as a vital part of American culture.

But what is a gospel song, how did it originate, and what are shaped notes; how do they differ from traditional musical notation, and what is the purpose of singing schools?

Singing schools originated in eighteenth-century New England, being promoted by the clergy in an effort to teach their congregations to read music and thus restore some of the musical heritage that had perished with the first generation of settlers. In the meantime, the congregations had developed their own style of singing. Everyone was expected to participate in singing the Psalms. No musical instruments were permitted to assist the singers in remembering tunes or harmonies. As time passed, tunes were forgotten or altered and the congregation added its own ornamentations and harmonies at will.

With the increase in illiteracy, it became necessary to provide assistance in the Psalm singing for those who could not read. The problem was solved by having the minister or clerk read or sing a line of the Psalm which the congregation sang after him. This prac-

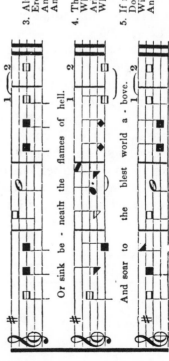

FRENCH BROAD. L. M.

Wm. Walker.

Slow.

1. *High o'er the hills the mountains rise, Their summits tow-er toward the skies; But far a - bove them I must dwell,

2. Oh, God! for - bid that I should fall And lose my ev - er - last - ing all; But may I rise on wings of love,

Or sink be - neath the flames of hell.

And soar to the blest world a - bove.

3. Although I walk the mountains high,
Ere long my body low must lie,
And in some lonesome place must rot,
And by the living be forgot.

4. There it must lie till that great day,
When Gabriel's awful trump shall say,
Arise, the judgment day is come,
When all must hear their final doom.

5. If not prepared, then I must go
Down to eternal pain and wo,
With devils there I must remain,
And never more return again.

6. But if prepared, oh, blessed thought!
I'll rise above the mountain's top,
And there remain for evermore
On Canaan's peaceful, happy shore.

7. Oh! when I think of that blest world,
Where all God's people dwell in love,
I oft-times long with them to be
And dwell in heaven eternally.

8. Then will I sing God's praises there,
Who brought me through my troubles here,
I'll sing, and be forever blest,
Find sweet and everlasting rest.

* This song was composed by the AUTHOR, in the fall of 1831, while travelling over the mountains, on French Broad River, in North Carolina and Tennessee.

PLATE 70

tice became known as "lining out" and continued as a traditional way of singing Psalms long after it was needed to offset the problem of illiteracy. The singing of the Psalms became even slower than before, but the pauses at line endings gave the singers even more opportunity to indulge in vocal ornamentation, which, by the way, was considered by the singers to be a musical accomplishment. Cotton Mather described the resulting sound as a "jar in his ears."[1] The clergy persisted and attempted to solve their problem by instituting singing schools promoting "regular" singing by note. The singers enjoyed their vocal freedom and at first resisted efforts to change, citing as reasons that the singing school was a scheme to get money; it caused people to stay out late at night; the syllables used were blasphemous; and the young people liked it, therefore it must be sinful.[2] Eventually the singing school became not only an educational tool but also a popular social institution.

And what about those "blasphemous syllables"? The syllables had to do with reading music and singing accurately. They were not the invention of the New England singing masters, having been utilized in England before the Pilgrims arrived in America. The syllables had been printed with the music of all of the major metrical psalters in England from the sixteenth century as well as in the *Genevan Psalter*.[3] They were printed under the notation in the ninth edition of the *Bay Psalm Book,* the first book printed in North America, and this edition contained the first music printed in this country.

The syllables, *fa sol la mi,* were used to identify the notes in the scale. There had been numerous scales developed by the Church from medieval times, but only a few were in use in the eighteenth century. Predominant among these were the major and minor scales. They differ from each other in the arrangement of intervals between adjacent notes, thus producing very different melodic possibilities. These scales usually consisted of eight pitches, the eighth being a higher repetition of the first. A syllable was assigned to each of these notes. [Ed. note: The interval between *la* and *fa* and between *mi* and *fa* are small intervals, called half steps, whereas the other intervals are whole steps.] The major scale was *fa sol la fa sol la mi.*

Ex. 1. Major scale with syllables.

The minor scale was *la mi fa sol la fa sol la.*

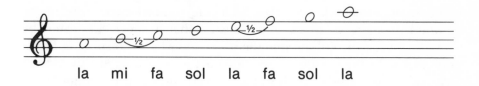

la   mi   fa   sol   la   fa   sol   la

Ex. 2. Natural minor scale with syllables.

In order to match the melodic range of a song to a singer's vocal range, the scale upon which the melody is based must begin on whatever pitch the voice can accommodate. The notation of scales must sometimes be altered to achieve the pre-set pattern of the scale, hence the use of signs to show this alteration: a sharp (#) raised the pitch; a flat (♭) lowered it. However, if the singer knew the scale syllables he could ignore reading alterations in notation, since the intervals between the syllables remain constant whatever the scale or wherever it might begin.

The singing school taught that skill of reading the musical staff, reading rhythm, singing by syllables, and singing harmony parts. In addition, the singing school fostered the development of instructional materials, books containing music to be used as lessons for the above skills.

The New England compilers, men of limited musical education but knowledgeable about the tastes of their contemporaries, applied themselves to this task with gusto. Their books contained hymns, psalms, odes, and anthems as well as the usual introductory section of "Rudiments of Music." This music was written for three or four parts each of which moved independently of the others. Since it was to be sung, each part was written on a separate musical staff. The compilers, who were not familiar with European rules of harmony, wrote parts that they considered interesting to sing and sounded good to them. The resulting harmonies bore little resemblance to European art music.

Following the Revolutionary War, many musically trained immigrants came to America. They quickly dominated the musical scene in the cities and ridiculed the compositions of the earlier settlers and their singing schools. In the cities, singing societies and choirs using the syllables, *do re mi fa sol la si do,* then in vogue in Europe, replaced the singing schools. In the rural areas and in the South, the singing school and the *fa sol la* syllables retained their popularity.

The two sets of syllables, *fa sol la* and *do re mi,* came to represent two conflicting cultural trends.[4]

Americans have always been known for seeking short cuts in the performance of their activities. Learning to read music was an extended process, so it was not unusual that a short cut would be sought. At the turn of the nineteenth century two enterprising Philadelphians, William Smith and William Little, provided this benefit by inventing shapes for the *fa sol la* syllables: a right triangle for *fa;* an oval for *sol;* a square for *la;* and a diamond for *mi.* These shapes were substituted for note heads but retained their rhythmic characteristics and were placed correctly on the music staff.

fa   sol   la   mi

Ex. 3. *Fa sol la mi* shapes.

The use of the shapes rescinded the necessity of learning the lines and spaces or those altered notes shown by sharps and flats.

fa   sol   la   fa   sol   la   mi   fa

Ex. 4. Major scale of E flat with *fa sol la* shapes.

la   mi   fa   sol   la   fa   sol   la

Ex. 5. Minor scale of f sharp with *fa sol la* shapes.

Among the nineteenth-century Southern compilers of singing school books using the *fa sol la* shapes were William Walker and his brother-in-law, Benjamin Franklin White, both from South Carolina. In 1835, Walker published his *Southern Harmony,* and, in 1844, White, who had moved to Georgia, published his *Sacred Harp.* "French Broad" from Walker's *Southern Harmony* illustrates the use of the four shape notes.

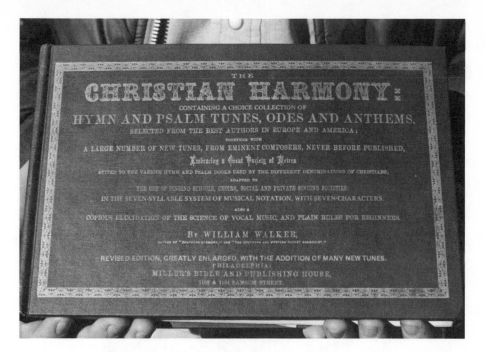

PLATE 71   William Walker's *Christian Harmony* book.

By this time, the content of the singing school books had changed somewhat. Still containing the "Rudiments of Music," they purported to include hymns, psalms, odes, and anthems, as had their New England forerunners. Some of these were in reality folk hymns, religious ballads, revival spirituals, and fuguing tunes, the latter having also appeared in New England collections.

Folk hymns are those "songs with old folk-tunes which everybody could sing with words that spoke from the heart of the devout in the language of the common man."[5] Religious ballads are the outgrowth of the folk hymn adhering to the literary format of the ballad; that is, they tell a complete story. Revival spirituals will be dealt with later, but the fuguing tunes were a vital part of these collections. They may be described as beginning with hymn-like harmony, but in the second section, each part enters successively utilizing some type of imitation, similar to a round. The parts then finish together.[6]

The highly ornamented style of singing, deplored by Cotton Mather and his fellow clergymen, but enjoyed by the common folk, had become traditional. These southern compilers wrote down from oral transmission the ornamentation that had become a part of the music. In doing so they provided an important service in preserving a musical heritage that might otherwise have been lost.

But even country folk like to keep up with "progress," and just before the middle of the nineteenth century, Jesse Aikin added three

FAITHFUL SOLDIER. 7s & 6s.

WM. WALKER.

1. Oh, when shall I see Je - sus, And reign with him a - bove?
And from the flow-ing foun-tain Drink ev - er - last - ing love? } When shall I be de-liv - er'd From this vain world of

2. But now I am a soldier, My Captain's gone be-fore;
He's giv-en me my or - ders, And bids me ne'er give o'er; } His prom - i - ses are faithful— A righteous crown he'll

sin?.............. And with my bless-ed Je - sus, Drink end - less pleasures in?

give,.............. And all his val - iant sol - diers E - ter - nal - ly shall live.

3 Through grace I am determined
    To conquer, though I die,
  And then away to Jesus,
    On wings of love I'll fly:
  Farewell to sin and sorrow,
    I bid them both adieu!
  And O, my friends! prove faithful,
    And on your way pursue.

4 Whene'er you meet with troubles
    And trials on your way,
  Then cast your care on Jesus,
    And don't forget to pray.
  Gird on the gospel armor
    Of faith, and hope, and love,
  And when the combat's ended,
    He'll carry you above.

PLATE 72

shapes to the *fa sol la* shapes to apply to the *do re mi* scale. His scale and syllable spelling taken from his *Christian Minstrel*, are as follows:

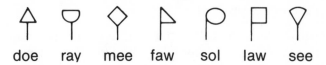

doe   ray   mee   faw   sol   law   see

Ex. 6. Aikin's shapes from his *Christian Minstrel*, 1848.

Most southern compilers, including Walker in his *Christian Harmony*, switched to the *do re mi* scale with its seven shapes. White continued to use the *fa sol la* scale as do the present-day *Sacred Harp* editions. Walker, along with others, invented his own shapes for the three additional notes, but Aikin's are the shapes that survived and are used today by gospel singers. "Faithful Soldier" from Walker's *Christian Harmony* illustrates his use of the seven shape notes.

These nineteenth-century southern singing school book compilers continued to write the three or four harmony parts in a style similar to the eighteenth-century New England writers; that is, each part moved independently of the others producing harmonies that were incidental to the melodic nature of each part. Today, with ears bombarded with harmony only in a supporting role, this music sounds archaic and "different." There is considerable use of the minor scale and that along with the unusual harmonies produces a music that is foreign to most listeners, and therefore more difficult to sing.

Those traditional singers of music from William Walker's *Christian Harmony*, like Quay Smathers and Richard Moss, perform the music slowly as directed in the "Rudiments" of the book. Although instructions in their "Rudiments" are very similar, *Sacred Harp* singers today sing much faster than do *Christian Harmony* singers. Also in the "Rudiments of Music," specific instructions are given to such things as volume, pronunciation, and ornamentation. In his *Southern Harmony* Walker has this to say concerning volume:

> . . . When singing in concert the bass should be sounded full, bold, and majestic, but not harsh; the tenor regular, firm, and distinct; the counter clear and plain; and the treble soft and mild, but not faint.

> . . . Yet how hard it is to make some believe soft singing is the more melodious, when at the same time loud singing is more like the hootings of the midnight bird than refined music.[7]

Concerning pronunciation, Walker said:

In singing, always keep sufficiency of breath to sound the notes full, round and smooth, and to pronounce the words distinct and plain; and never sing in pain, but sit erect on the seat and endeavour to sing with as much ease as you would talk in common conversation.[8]

All notes should be called plain by their proper names, and fairly articulated; and in applying the words great care should be taken that they be properly pronounced and not torn to pieces between the teeth, nor forced through the nose.[9]

On ornamentation, he said:

. . . a few observations on the ornamental part of singing, or what are generally termed graces. This is the name generally given to those occasional embellishments, which a performer or composer introduces to heighten the effect of a composition. It consists not only in giving due place to the apogiatura [sic], turn, shake, or trill, and other decorative additions, but in that easy, smooth, and natural expression of the passage which best conveys the native beauties and elegancies of the composition, and forms one of the first attributes of a cultivated and refined performer.[10]

Contemporary *Christian Harmony* singers usually ignore Walker's instructions on volume and sing with full voice, no vibrato, and no concept of blended voices. The part each sings is the important thing and they pride themselves on accuracy. With the moving parts, unusual harmonies, and added ornamentation, singing a part "by ear" is difficult.

In 1800, a "happening" occurred on the Kentucky frontier: The first camp meeting was held. This, and later such revivals, greatly influenced future religious affairs, especially religious music, for here was born the camp meeting song or spiritual. These camp meetings, attended largely by illiterate frontier settlers, were highly charged emotional gatherings. Both the events and the types of people attending these meetings necessitated a new kind of religious song. Traditional hymns, sung from memory, as well as folk hymns, were used. Many of these hymns underwent text simplification. Often a new song might spring to life spontaneously, including a combination of scriptural phrases and everyday language. Verses were shortened, refrains added and expressions and ejaculations interpolated. The tunes were lively with strongly marked rhythms.[11] This addition of a refrain was one of the most important contributions of the camp meeting to religious music. Often these songs were in the form of a dialogue, the call and response of folk song. The leader sang the first phrase, the congregation answered with a related phrase. This type of song was also related to the lining out technique of the old Psalm singers. An example of the transformation of a hymn to a revival-type spiritual is "Jesus My All to Heaven Has Gone," a poem by the English writer, John Cennick (1718–99). It was to become one of the most widely sung religious lyrics among the country folk of America during the more than two hundred years which have passed since it appeared.[12] It was the favorite song of *Christian Harmony* singer George Smathers of Canton, North Carolina, who died in 1979 at the age of 101. In the example given here from Walker's *Christian Harmony*, the response "and we'll all shout together in that morning," has been added as well as has the refrain.

Texts for these spirituals reflected the topics of the evangelistic sermons: conviction of sin, the joys of salvation, and the expectation of heaven. These topics had already been incorporated in some religious movements by the hymns of Isaac Watts and the writings of John and Charles Wesley.

Religious ballads, those narrating biblical happenings, were strong favorites. A not uncommon practice was the addition of one's own personal religious experience after a narrative from the Scriptures. The experiential or mourner's song began with the traditional "come all ye" and went on to explain how the subject was born in sin, experienced religion, was saved and became a Child of God. Such songs that stressed the short, temporal life and the imminence of the Judgment Day were effective in swaying the wavering sinner at the altar.[13] An even simpler form including much repetition was one in which new poetic lines were not added in subsequent stanzas but only one or two words were changed.[14]

In exhorting others to enjoy the advantages of the holy life, the campers often invoked a martial spirit. They viewed themselves as soldiers enlisted under the banner of Christ, pledged to wage unceasing warfare against sin.[15] (See previous illustration of "Faithful Soldier.")

Another important influence in the development of the gospel song was the Sunday school movement that began in this country in the latter part of the eighteenth century. By the mid-nineteenth century, numerous collections of Sunday school songs had been compiled. First designed solely for children, these songs were simple in character, popular in design, and intended for immediate appeal.[16] Almost all of them included a refrain.

The Y.M.C.A., organized in London in 1844, and shortly thereaf-

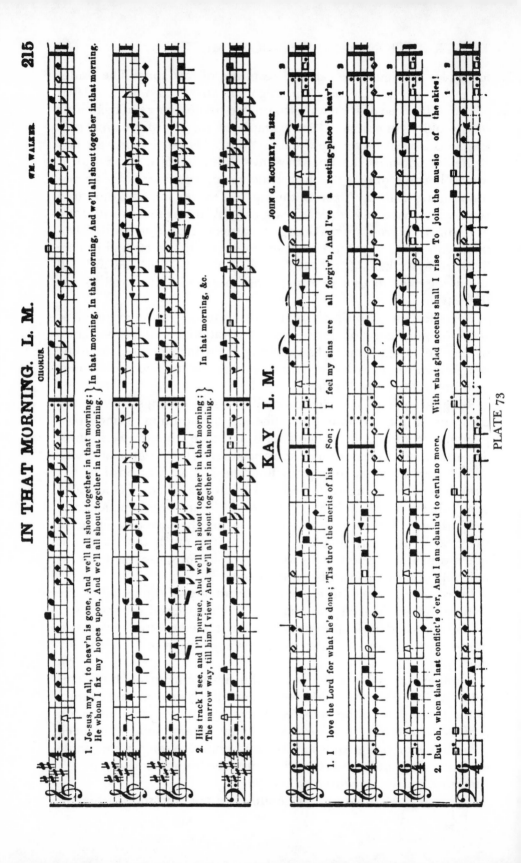

PLATE 73

ter in this country, featured the unison singing of familiar church hymns by male voices. These meetings, as well as union prayer meetings in large urban areas, developed spontaneity and brevity in the use of hymns.[17] It was through the Y.M.C.A. that Dwight L. Moody, the nineteenth-century evangelist, met Ira D. Sankey who was to bring all of these currents together in his *Gospel Hymns*. It was this title of Sankey's collection used in the evangelistic campaigns of Moody and Sankey that brought about the term, "gospel music" to identify popular religious hymnody. Neither the use of the term nor the style of the music was original with Moody and Sankey. These songs were the product of urban composers and lyricists, but they were intentionally designed to appeal to unpretentious tastes. The term, "gospel music," came also to be applied as an identification of southern religious hymnody.[18]

The singing schools of the South continued to operate throughout the nineteenth century. The compilers who lived in Virginia's Shenandoah Valley were both prolific and influential. Among the collections widely used was one by Joseph Funk, a Pennsylvanian, who, like William Walker, first utilized the four-shape note method, later switching to the seven shapes. Funk called his seven-shape note book *Harmonia Sacra* which the country folk quickly nicknamed "Hominy Soaker." Funk's grandson, Aldine S. Kieffer, established the Ruebush-Kieffer Music Publishing company in Virginia. A. J. Showalter, a descendant of the Funks in Pennsylvania and an associate of Kieffer, established a music publishing company in Georgia in 1887.[19] This company was the immediate forerunner of the popular gospel song publishers today.

It was Showalter who changed the format of the singing school books from four staves to two. The latter was much easier for instrumentalists to read, though harder for singers.[20] He also included more of the gospel songs than had his predecessors.

Contemporary gospel songs have many of the same subjects as their predecessors, being subjective, emotional, repetitive, and evangelistic in thought. Also they are not related to reason or doctrine. The music, though related to the earlier songs especially in the use of the seven-shape notes, is more modern. It is characterized by simple melodies, strong rhythmic design with some syncopation and limited harmonic changes. All of it is based on the major scale. Twentieth-century Christians, believing the old nineteenth-century romantic notion that minor music suggests sadness, rejected all minor music as having no place in a happy religion. The harmonies follow the melody, there being very limited melodic movement in the supporting parts.

A favorite contemporary song style is the statement-repetition style in which one voice carries the melody while the others sing a harmonic repetition of each phrase, either literally or in an altered form. In this style the melody may move from one voice to another. Frequently it is carried by the bass.[21]

Another related style that made its appearance in the 1920s utilizes the "afterbeat." This device, borrowed from band music popularized during and after World War I, has one voice that carries the melodic line while the other voices sing a word or a syllable on the second half of the beat. The effect is similar to the um-pah-pah heard in a brass band.[22]

A style that has not become as popular as the others is a contrapuntal style carried over from the earlier singing school fuguing tunes. In this style each part is a melodic line with its own text.[23]

There is a tendency to sing the songs rapidly and, with the syncopated beat inherent in much of the music, the tempo can become very lively.[24] This syncopated beat, with its displaced accent normally associated with ragtime and jazz, has been favored by contemporary songwriters. This rhythmic figure, probably more than any other, has given gospel music its dance-like character.[25]

With gospel singers, the piano has become a favorite accompanying instrument. Gospel song pianists have absorbed into their style of playing many of the popular music styles. The accompaniments today are a mixture of swing, jazz, full chords, octaves, and arpeggios.[26]

Because this music is fun to sing, it may have as many adherents outside of the church as inside, although many churches sing "gospel music." This recreational aspect of the singing has led to Friday night meetings in homes, the fifth Sunday sings at churches and other informal singing occasions.

The first singing convention came into being in the mid-nineteenth century, organized by *Sacred Harp* singers with their book author, B. F. White, as the first president.[27] These more or less loosely formed conventions, organized along geographical lines, survive today.

One institution that has helped to promote gospel music is the male quartet. First developed to assist in the sale and distribution of gospel songbooks, some of these groups have become highly commercial. However, to many others throughout the country, gospel singing means Christian fellowship, recreation and, most of all, participating with friends in a mutually satisfying musical experience.

SINGERS OF SHAPED-NOTE MUSIC

The remainder of this section on shaped-note singing is divided into two parts. First, Richard Moss and Quay Smathers talk about the old-time Christian Harmony singing. The second part investigates the more recent gospel-style shaped-note music still popular in this area today. In these interviews, our contacts describe Friday night singings, singing schools, and singing conventions and elaborate on the importance of music in their lives.

Both Richard Moss and Quay Smathers began singing Christian Harmony at a very early age. They have been associated with a number of singing schools, first as students and then as teachers at various workshops and colleges. Richard and Quay have sung gospel shaped-note music, but they prefer Christian Harmony. They are very concerned about the continuance of Christian Harmony as a tradition. Central figures in today's Christian Harmony activities in western North Carolina, they attend and support the few singings that still convene. They encourage young people to learn Christian Harmony and to keep the practice alive and Christian Harmony singing is attracting new participants. Here Richard and Quay discuss their lifelong involvement in this traditional musical style.

PAUL F. GILLESPIE

CHRISTIAN HARMONY: Richard Moss

I started singing Christian Harmony with my father when I was about fourteen or fifteen years old. He was a singer of that and I still have the old book he sang out of. I'd come home in the evening and he'd be sitting out on the porch with his book singing like the old people and keeping time. I would listen to him and hear him sing and then I'd sing it by memory, or as some people say "by heart." I later learned the rudiments of music. Then I could sing any of those songs I wanted to sing.

There is the old-time Christian Harmony singing that is not done too much anymore and there is this gospel-style of shaped-note singing. The Christian Harmony has a sad weeping tone and it also doesn't have any musical accompaniment. Back then, they didn't have any musical instruments whatsoever. People don't sing Christian Harmony as much anymore because it's so hard for them to learn the sound of it. A lot of people can sing the gospel music very well, but when they pick up that book of Christian Harmony songs, they just can't do it. It has that weeping tone and it's hard.

Christian Harmony used to be the only kind of music that was sung around here. People liked it because they were raised up with it. Most of the time they sung it at church but they did sing it some in their homes. In those days, you didn't have many places to go. Church was about the only place we had to go. People walked back then and boys took their dates to church with them. That's about the only place we got together.

When I started out [singing] I had to follow those adults. When they'd sound low, I'd sound with them. When they'd sound high, I'd sound with them too. I just sang along with them at the old church and I learned better that way too.

PLATE 74   Richard Moss.

My wife is a good Christian Harmony singer. And my wife's father, William Anderson, was excellent at that. He was a teacher in it and taught singing schools. They had singing schools for people to learn Christian Harmony. In fact, he was the first one that ever got me to lead a song. He'd always get up there and then say to me, "Come on, my singer." He called me his "singer." He'd want me to come on up and sing and I'd go up and sing with him. He was one of the best Christian Harmony singers that I believe they've ever had. He and I would sing right over here at the old church, a little log church. It was a Missionary Baptist Church.

I went to I don't know how many singing schools. Back then you'd pay fifty cents to go to singing school for ten days. That went for the teacher's salary. We'd go in the morning, take our lunch, and stay all day. The teacher would furnish the books and theories and such as that. They'd usually be from twenty to twenty-five [in classes], sometimes as many as thirty.

The [gospel] shaped-note singing that has musical instruments to go along with it began to come in later. I was living with my father and mother up here in the upper end of the field. I had two uncles who were starting out in this type of music. They both became teachers in it and they'd come up to the house and we'd sing it. That's how I came in contact with [that] style.

The [gospel] shaped-note singings of today are popular. When we get the paper, that's what everybody looks for first—to see where the singings are. I love it all right and there's nothing wrong with it. From time to time, I teach this type of singing school in this area. But, personally, I prefer the Christian Harmony over what is sung today. It has that special tone—sometimes it's called a sad weeping tone. I like it because it goes down in that tone. It puts something in your mind different from what the [gospel-style] music does.

There's been a great change in music and everything else since my childhood days. I was born in 1899 and lived in a log house. I don't feel like I'm that old and I still work for the Forest Service three days a week. It still doesn't bother me any.

INTERVIEW AND PHOTOGRAPH BY CAROL ROGERS

CHRISTIAN HARMONY: Quay Smathers

Christian Harmony singing is all that I do anymore. I was born in 1913 and I started out real young in it. I had an old friend by the name of Asbury Smathers. Just him and his wife lived together and when I was a young boy, I'd sit up there and sing with them. He was a great singer and he was a singing school teacher.

I went to my first singing school in 1919 out at the Morning Star Church, so I learned to sing the notes at an early age. I rode to Morning Star in a wagon. But my mother, I guess, was the main cause of me not forgetting all of this stuff—she was a Christian Harmony singer herself. She was brought up on it. That's probably the main reason I didn't drop it then and forget all I'd learned.

Christian Harmony books couldn't be bought—you'd have one over here and yonder through the community. One old gentleman told me, he said, "If you're going to sing Christian Harmony and if you'll sing out of it, I'll give you my book." So he gave me his book. Books were scarce and a few years later, he said, "I've got my brother's book and I'm going to give it to you, too. You can have it and if I ever call for it, you can give it back." He gave me that one. That was the second one I ever had. Before Asbury Smathers died, he gave me his. Before he died, he walked over to the mantel and got it. He could barely hobble over there. I collected up a bunch of them and had my own books.

A good singing school teacher would come into a community and in ten nights would teach you the principle. Teach you the shape notes and teach you hard. And if you learned anything about music and singing, you learned it through an old singing school teacher like that. He'd take a chalkboard or canvas and a little musical literature with him and if he was good, he'd take a group and you'd learn to sing in ten nights of singing school. That went on until they started out to teaching music in the schools. But they don't teach them shape notes in the school anymore.

I've been teaching school at Warren Wilson College now for the last four years. I've got workshops in Berea, Kentucky and some in Atlanta and all around. Just shape note workshops. There's no accompaniment with it of any kind—it's just that old time Christian Harmony. I went to Michigan last September and I did workshops out there in a pine thicket. Prettiest place you've ever seen and I've never heard such singing in all my life.

There's still a Christian Harmony convention twice a year up here at Etowah. We meet the first Sunday in September and the first Sunday in May. When I first went to Etowah they were singing in the Etowah church. Of course, it wasn't a very large church but they turned it over to us, the whole church, twice a year. We left there and went to the Etowah school and sang for a while in the auditorium. They made classrooms out of that and now we're down in the cafeteria. About all that comes to Etowah is singers; there aren't many spectators over there. I'll say it varies from thirty to fifty that do sing and not over ten or fifteen that don't sing. That's a pretty good group. The Etowah singings start on Sunday morning at ten o'clock and it goes all day till we get tired. You have to quit pretty early for Richard Moss to leave Etowah and drive back home. We usually quit about three-thirty.

We also meet at the Morning Star Church on the second Sunday in September. We have what is called the Old Folks Day. They've had Old Folks Day for about ninety years. They have morning Sunday school services and a guest speaker for the morning worship service. Then they have a dinner on the grounds and I mean *they have dinner.* And then just as quick as dinner is over, we have the Christian Harmony singing and we sing until we give out. There is no certain time to stop or anything like that. The only difference between Morning Star and Etowah, as far as the Christian Harmony singing goes, is that you start singing before dinner at Etowah and you start singing after the morning services and dinner on the grounds up here at Morning Star.

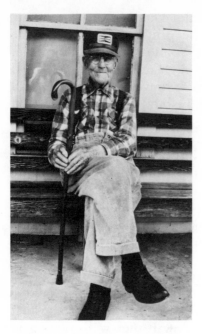

PLATE 76 George Smathers, Quay Smathers' father, was a well-known Christian Harmony singer. He died at the age of 101, in 1979.

There's as much difference as night and day between old-time Christian Harmony singing and the gospel shaped-note singing. Christian Harmony singing and gospel singing don't mix—they just don't go together. There isn't any use for a bunch of Christian Harmony singers going into a gospel singing and there isn't any use for gospel singers coming to Christian Harmony. They just don't go together. They both use shape note but they are sung differently. Mind you, I like good gospel shaped-note quartet singing. I've sung in a gospel quartet when I was a boy. I like them when they sing and take all this foolishness out of the background. Some of these groups have bass drums and snare drums and electric guitars, and I saw one group that had a fiddle in it. And some of them try to get it so fast that you can't understand them. That's the difference in music between now and the way it was back then.

There's not many Christian Harmony singers left. I studied a lot about it and it's a sight how many of the old Christian Harmony singers that I knew from around here have gone on. But I hope there is a new breed coming on with these workshops and the college music classes like Edith Card's that are doing it right. A lot of people enjoy it. But around here the older Christian Harmony singers are a dying breed. I don't care whether anybody sits and listens to me or not as long as I enjoy it.

INTERVIEW AND PHOTOGRAPHS BY CAROL ROGERS

PLATE 77   People gather to express their religion through the fellowship
of singing.

"I LOVE TO SING . . . "

Friday night singings, singing schools, and singing conventions
have long been a part of tradition in this area of northeast Georgia
and western North Carolina. For many years a group of people
here in Rabun County who enjoy the fellowship of group singing
have gathered on Friday evenings throughout the entire year to
sing together. They meet in homes, or sometimes at a church, to
sing religious songs. Their songbooks are ordered from various music book publishing houses, such as the Tennessee Publishing Company, the James D. Vaughn Publishing Company and Stamps-Baxter
Music of the Zondervan Corporation. There are many of these songbooks published, with book companies bringing out one or more
a year. Churches and singing groups, like the people who participate
in the Friday night singings, will order batches of books once or
twice a year so as to have a variety of new songs to choose from.
The president of the Friday night singing is responsible for ordering
the songbooks chosen for that period of time. The participants will
usually go through two or three different books a year, learning
almost all the songs in each one. These books are used at the annual
singing school and at the annual singing convention and then passed
on to a church or other singing group that can use them.

Each year in the early spring a singing school is conducted in
Rabun County. Members of the Friday night singings are present
and, although the majority of its participants are Baptists from the

PLATE 78

area's different churches, it is open to anyone interested in singing, and other denominations are represented. The school is held from 7 P.M. to 10 P.M., Monday through Friday for two weeks and the singing school class learns the rudiments of music—the shaped notes, timing, and signatures. For the past several years this school has been directed by Mr. Hyman Brown from Commerce, Georgia. As his "textbook," Mr. Brown uses *Vaughn's Up-to-Date Rudiments and Music Reader.* Most of the participants lead songs and frequently the young people are asked to come as a group to lead the rest of the congregation. Young piano players are called on to play the tune in the upper treble along with the pianist. Attendance is good. The class is not limited to new students; people young and old attend year after year. On the final Friday evening, singers crowd the church for a joyous finale.

In the past, singing schools were ordinarily held in the daytime when regular school for the children was not in session and when there was a lull in the farming, so that everyone in the community could attend if they wished. A person familiar with shaped-note music, and with a good singing voice, taught the class. Throughout our interviews, favorite singing teachers' names kept coming up— Mr. Johnny Cannon, Mr. Jim Raby, Mr. Tom King, and, today, Mr. Hyman Brown.

PLATE 79   Three people lead the congregation in song.

PLATE 80   The young people are often called on to lead songs as a group.

PLATE 81   A very young conductor with her group of leaders.

PLATE 82   Various gospel songbooks.

Counties are organized into singing conventions and each singing convention decides the way it wants to conduct its annual singings. The Rabun County Annual Singing Convention is held at a local church on the first Saturday evening and Sunday in October. A business meeting is held at that time; officers are elected and committees are appointed to carry on the business of the organization for the coming year. The officers decide where next year's convention will be held and what they may need to spend money on during the year. But more than business is attended to; the real business of the convention is to enjoy the fellowship of singing.

The convention begins on Saturday evening when everyone from Rabun County and the surrounding areas who is interested in singing gathers at the chosen church to sing for several hours. They reconvene Sunday morning at 10 A.M. and sing in lieu of a regular preaching service. A lunchtime they break and set out under the trees a wonderful variety of covered dishes of delicious food for a "dinner on the grounds." After an hour or two of food and fellowship outdoors in the fall sunshine, they go back inside the church and sing all afternoon.

The president of the convention calls on a "leader" to direct each song. This is a democratic gathering and everyone gets a chance to lead. The leader comes to the front of the church, calls out the title and number of the song, and everyone sings. Then another individual is called on to lead. This custom is also found in Christian Harmony singing, however in gospel-style singing, an entire class from a church will often come up and lead a song. But whether the music is led by one or by a dozen, almost always the entire gathering of people participate in the singing.

The list of people we could have talked to about singings and singing conventions is a very long one. Several people contributed valuable information that has helped us to understand our subject better even though we didn't record our conversations with them.

Mrs. Agnes Calloway's memories of her father, Jim Raby, helped us to understand the important role singing school teachers played in people's lives prior to radio, television, and easy travel. Mr. Henry Fountain, from Toccoa, Georgia, tells of the days when he was called a "one-man band." Aunt Addie Norton still sings whenever she can get to church or with a group of singers. Lonnie Smith and Horace Page were very helpful. These two men were responsible for starting the Friday night singings in Rabun County more than thirty years ago, and they have been instrumental in keeping the singing conventions going in Rabun County. Hyman Brown has made us aware that the art of shaped-note singing is still very much alive in our community. Esco Pitts directed the choir at the Head of Tennessee Baptist Church in Dillard, Georgia, for more than fifty years and we enjoyed his recollections of singings and singing conventions over such a long span of time. We had fun listening to Ernest Watts telling about experiences of his boyhood revolving around singings. And we talked with his cousin, Ferd Watts, who is also a very active member of the Friday night singings. Our last interview was with Wilbur Maney who is the current president of the Rabun County Singing Convention. Mr. Maney says that due to the influence of his father, Marlor, he has been singing shaped-note music "almost since I was born." Beginning with Lonnie Smith's interview, the final section of this article focuses on music in Rabun County.

INTERVIEW AND PHOTOGRAPHS BY CAROL ROGERS

GOSPEL SHAPED NOTE MUSIC: Jim Raby

We first heard about Jim Raby from his great-granddaughter, Lynn James, a student in the Foxfire class. He was born in 1883 in western North Carolina and became interested in shaped-note singing while still a boy. He died in 1971 at the age of 88, but Lynn remembers him well. She suggested that we ask her grandmother, Mrs. Leon (Agnes) Calloway, to tell us about him. Mr. Raby was Mrs. Calloway's father and she often went with him to singing schools and conventions as she was growing up.

Mr. Raby and his wife had seven children. Mrs. Calloway was born in 1918. She went to her first singing school when she was only eight years old. She said, "There were only two of the children who weren't interested in singing. We all sang at home and then we went to singings. We took part in all of them. We had a pedal organ in the church and Dad had one at home."

Mrs. Calloway met her husband when she was about eighteen years old. She had gone with her dad to teach a singing school in Highlands which Mr. Calloway attended. They've been married since 1936. While her children were small, Mrs. Calloway didn't attend singings as often as before. As the youngest children, Doyle and Gayle, got older, they became interested in music and singing the shaped-note songs.

Mrs. Calloway learned to play on a pedal organ and also used to play the piano. Her son, Doyle, plays several stringed instruments but Mrs. Calloway says they've all "sort of gotten out of attending the singings" like they used to.

In telling us about her father, she said, "Dad lived to be eighty-eight. He went to singings most of his life—since he was a teen-ager. They were even going on way back then."

Leon Calloway told us this story about visiting at the Rabys' house one time. He and Agnes' grandfather, who was in his nineties, were sitting on the front porch and the rest of the family were inside. Mr. Calloway told us, "I love hound dogs, and he did, too, and we were listening to the dogs run on the mountain. 'Bout that time her and her daddy and a bunch of 'em got the organ cranked up and they started singing. He said, 'A'hem. How the heck do they think we can even hear the dogs?' The Rabys always sang when they got together. They all took part."

FROM FOXFIRE MAGAZINE, VOL. 12, NO. 1

Dad was one of the oldest teachers around here of the old-fashioned shaped-note music. He taught schools in western North Carolina and northern Georgia [and at] nearly all the little churches in

PLATE 83 An old photograph from Mrs. Calloway's collection showing the members of a singing school taught by Jim Raby.

Macon County, North Carolina. He taught a school near Waynesville and one at East Sylva in Jackson County and one at Glenville.

I went with him to these schools for about ten or fifteen years, I guess, and helped him because I could play the organ a little bit. He liked to have me with him to help. I didn't really teach but he would get some people started with the letters and notes and then he would ask them to sound their notes and compare them with the organ. We had a pedal organ. We didn't have pianos in the churches back then. I'd play the notes on the organ and see if they were correct, or as near correct as they could get.

We just had a good time a lot of times. It was a lot of fun. We had our papers and pencils and wrote the lines and spaces and the times—like ¼ time. It had to be written—how to count your notes and the time and everything. This was a very full school because usually people couldn't pay for more than ten days. It was hard times then, you know, and a ten-day school was pretty long, though sometimes, they'd run over a little bit.

Dad told me that in earlier years, before they got the church organ, they had a tuning fork to sound the note with. In a lot of places, they didn't even have that. They just had to use their own judgment. They'd just sing the best they could and get on key. I've heard him talk about trying to start a tune at the church at Cowee years ago. They asked someone to "heist the tune" and this man got it so high they couldn't sing the song. They had to heist the tune a lot of times.

Dad taught one man how to read and to sing at the same time. Then that man went home and made a singing school teacher himself.

My father had decided, when he was about eighteen years old, that he wanted to learn to sing. He'd studied and had learned some from his father and from other people that sang around the community. Then he went to a school in Asheville. I've heard him laugh and tell about it. I think he walked or hitchhiked a ride to Sylva, and then went by train to Asheville. They had a music school there for ten days. He didn't have any money. He stayed with friends. He learned what he could and then came back and just helped everybody around to learn with him. Then he studied further and decided he would try teaching.

He said that he had never found but one person in his teaching that could not sing. I asked him what he meant by "could not sing." And he said, "He could not go up and down on the note scale. He *said* his *do, re, mi*'s. He was on the same tone. He never raised nor lowered his voice." He worked with him a long time and Dad said there wasn't any way to get him to sing.

You were always called on to get up and lead a song at a singing school. You could choose your song but you even had to beat your time instead of counting in your head. You might be the only one keeping the time. You could keep everybody together by their watching you.

When Dad was teaching a singing school, he made everybody beat that time. He'd show you first what he meant. You had to do it that way to keep the time in your mind. He had everybody standing up doing that. If it was hard for you to get the words with the notes, he would make you read the song, not sing it, but read it according to the time, just read the poetry and count the beat in your mind. In other words, just read the poem with the notes timed to it. And then put your words and notes together. If you would do that before you started to sing the notes, you could do a lot better. You'd get your words and everything correct.

My dad went to the state of Washington in 1938 and taught three singing schools. They paid his expenses on the train to go there and back, and gave a hundred dollars for each school. They asked him to come because he knew so many people that had gone there from here. Some of Mother's folks were there. He went about March, I guess, and stayed the biggest part of the summer and visited and taught singing schools.

Singing schools were provided to improve the music in the church. The congregation decided they needed one to help with their singing and their music, and they'd call a teacher. It was agreed the church would pay so much before the teacher was called. Then the church took up a collection. They had the money provided before they'd ask the teacher to come. And sometimes the members would mention at work or out in the community about the singing school, and somebody might say, "Well, I want to give some to that." They'd make a donation to help pay for the teacher coming. The whole community participated.

We usually bought our own songbooks. There might be somebody that was representing one of the companies that would have all these books and they'd come by and sell a bunch to people. Or you could order them from the company and send the money. We ordered books from Stamps-Baxter and the Winsett Company in Knoxville and the James D. Vaughn Music Company. Theodore Sisk and George Seaborn had music companies, too.

Almost all the songs in a newly printed songbook are brand new. We've never seen them before. You learn by singing them over and over. That's the way it's done. It's a challenge to you.

The weekly singings now are usually held at a church, although sometimes they're held in homes. My husband, Leon, and I used to go, but we've sort of gotten out of it lately.

The people sing mostly religious songs and of course carols at Christmastime. There used to be any number of people interested in this type of music, especially those in country churches.

Dad was a farmer. In early years he had a little country store that he and Mama ran. Later on he was in the sawmill business. And he was manager of the Farmers' Federation in Franklin. That's been years ago. They don't have a Farmers' Federation anymore. Teaching singing was kind of an extra sideline or hobby which he liked. He did that on weekends. Or if he had a singing school, he'd go and stay ten days. Actually, he taught more during hard times, during the Depression, when there wasn't much work to do. People would ask him to come and he didn't have that much work himself. So it was good that he could do that. But that wasn't his occupation.

Dad was president of the annual Macon County Singing Convention for about twenty-five or thirty years. Oscar Corbin was the first president that I remember and he died long ago. We usually had the convention in July or August. It used to be held for three days, Friday, Saturday, and Sunday, sometimes at the old Macon County courthouse in the courtroom and sometimes at one of the churches.

The host church would invite the convention to come. Then the members of that community would invite the singers to stay in their home. Sometimes we had more than a full house. You'd sleep on the floor or wherever you could, but it was all a lot of fun. Everybody got up and went to the singing and stayed all day and took a covered dish or a basket lunch and ate at the church. We enjoyed it very much. You think now it'd be an awful hardship to provide food for three days for a big crowd, but we enjoyed it then.

Everybody in the family usually came to the convention. Back then we didn't have much to do except go to church and singings. We couldn't afford to go to movies and things like that. We lived so far out, we couldn't do many things. We went to church and to all the community activities. It wasn't what you'd call a fancy dress-up, but we put on something nice like a Sunday dress, just like you were going to church. The singings were a very serious thing.

Everybody took part in the business meeting of the singing conventions. They didn't bar anybody that wanted to stay. They elected a president every year and a vice president and secretary. I don't remember hearing about a treasurer. They met their expenses as they came. They had an offering taken for extra expenses, but as a rule, the members of the host church bore the burden of it all. They didn't charge anything. The secretary of the convention sent out letters to all the churches of the county inviting them to the conventions and [announcing] when they'd be. Everybody was invited. They wanted them all to come.

They still have the annual singing convention, but it's only one day now. It got so big that they divided Macon County into two sections back when people began to get transportation. They now have a northern and a southern division and they're held the same day.

They still do have a homecoming at Yellow Mountain Baptist Church in Jackson County the first Sunday in October every year. And they have this type of singing all day for that. I haven't been to that singing in some time. We used to go to Valley Springs, which is near Asheville, for an all-day singing convention. It wouldn't seem like a long ways to go now, but when we went, it was a major trip to get there. We went all around in western North Carolina, where they were having a convention. We traveled to Swain County, North Carolina and went over to Hiawassee, Georgia, several times to conventions.

Before I was married, there were two quartets Dad and I sang in. We had ol' man Jess Keener that lived up toward Dillard and Olan Graham and Dad and me. Olan came in with the CC [Civil Conservation Corps] camps in Franklin and then married a local girl and stayed here. He's a real good singer and makes music, plays the piano and organ. That was one quartet. After I married, Dad and my two sisters, Mary and Dot, sang in a quartet with Olan Graham. We called Olan Graham "Pop." When we lived in Sylva, we had a quartet with Bob Higdon and McKinley Henley. Dad had another quartet, "The Hensons," Tom and Butch Henson and Dad and Pop Graham. We [always] went around to different churches and sang.

My daddy was the first person that ever invited a colored [Black] quartet near Franklin to come sing for the Fifth Sunday Singing. Some of the people [didn't like their coming but I think they] were terribly wrong feeling that way. I really enjoyed hearing them sing.

And [Dad] had several quartets that came over from the Cherokee Indian Reservation. In fact, he taught two or three singing schools at Cherokee. We went up to Smokemont, just above the Cherokee Reservation, and had a school for ten days in October before Leon and I were married. That was before the old Smokemont Church was torn down. That's all in the Smoky Mountain National Park now. We had several Indians come up there and sing with us. Hornbuckle and Owl and Chief Ross, chief of the Cherokee tribe, and Dad had a quartet.

Dad sang bass in his later years. He said it was easier for him. As he got older, he couldn't breathe as well. As a young man, he sang soprano and tenor all the time. As he got older, he could still read a lot of songs, but it was getting a bit hard for him. Then he fell and was in the hospital a long time. For six months he didn't know anything, but the last thing he ever did was to sit on the side of the hospital bed and sing to the nurses. His voice was just as clear. It didn't break. It didn't crack. And he was eighty-eight years old. He was quite a person.

I wish this interview could have been done when he was living. He could have written you a book on singing, because he did love his music—loved to teach and loved to help people sing.

PLATE 84 A family gathering of the Fountains in 1962. Henry Fountain is second from the right.

GOSPEL SHAPED NOTE MUSIC: Henry Fountain

Bit Carver talked to Mr. Henry Fountain of Toccoa, Georgia one summer afternoon in 1974. He told her some about his life as a banjo and harmonica player and how he and his wife and children performed together on a radio program and how he had been called a "one-man band." He attended many of the singing conventions nearby and occasionally went a long distance for one.

We sense that he didn't think he was an outstanding performer but others evidently did, because in subsequent interviews with others, his name kept being mentioned. They had wanted us to be sure and talk to him. He can't play his banjo anymore due to arthritis, but he still plays his harmonicas (he has at least one in every key) with a great deal of spirit and sings along with them.

Mr. Lonnie Smith told us: "He's a harp [harmonica] player. He hasn't been up here [to Rabun County] in a good while, but he used to go to conventions and singings pretty regularly. He's amazing. He's in his eighties and doesn't even have to wear glasses.

"I never got acquainted with him until about eight or ten years ago. I was down in Stephens or Banks County, somewhere down there. He thrilled me, because I had never seen him or heard him before. He got up to playing his french harp and singing a song. He'd sing all the parts of it; he'd come to one part and sing alto, then come to the bass part and sing that. I always liked to hear him. It was amazing how he could do it. I guess he's getting old now and can't sing as much as he used to."

We used to go everywhere for singings. I can't go much like I used to. I'm not able to drive anymore. But we used to go to one every Friday night and on Sunday, too, for a good while. I've been to about fourteen different counties for singings.

I've been going to singing conventions for about forty or fifty years. The biggest convention ever I was at was the Vaughan Memorial Singing. Old man J. P. Vaughan was a publisher of songbooks, and one of the best singers ever been in the world's history. He played his own songs and sang'em himself. Prettiest singing you ever heard in your life. Couldn't nobody beat him. They could be a church full of folks singing and if he was a'helping on that song you could tell his voice over all that crowd—so smooth, just as smooth and pretty.

I remember a big singing convention up here at Cornelia in 1931. It turned out right funny. I picked a banjo then and I carried my banjo with me to the convention. I didn't pick by myself. We had a piano and a B flat horn to play with us, and two or three violins.

There was this book publisher that lived at Lavonia and one of the song leaders, he got me to go with them to the convention. We got there and the chairman of the singing got up and announced, "We have got more leaders here than we can sing in two days to save our lives. So we're gonna sing everyone we can but we're gonna sing the best first."

So I figured that let me out. Then way up about the middle of the morning on Saturday, he says, "I'm gonna call on this old banjo picker here to lead us a lesson."

Well, I was surprised—you know, him a'singing all those big songs. I got up and led one and you never heard the like in your life! I was the only one that day that got an applause. They made the house ring. Then we went back on Sunday. Sometime during the day, the chairman said, "Now we want this old banjo picker to sing another one." I was surprised!

What was funny though—me and that book publisher and that other feller was coming on back home and he says, "I didn't much like it today. I carried my new songbook up there and they didn't give me much chance to sing."

I said, "Well, you heard what the man said yesterday, didn't you? 'We're gonna sing the best!'"

That tickled that feller to death that was with us. Of course, I just pulled it as a joke, you know. But it sure did turn out good.

I don't know round note music but I know the shaped notes. If it's in shaped notes, I can play it. Our family played on one of the first radio stations ever in Toccoa, Georgia. And then at one time

I was playing with another band outside my family. It was called the Battle Ax Bill Concert Family. I've got a harp holder and I used to play the banjo and harp together.

They used to have me sing "Rocking on the Waves" everywhere I went. They called me a one-man quartet. I'd play my harmonica and sing all the parts too. They had a tent meeting over there in South Carolina and I sang it one night for them. Then they made me sing it four nights in a stretch.

I've always liked to attend the Friday night singings at folks' homes. I can't go much now unless somebody takes me, though. You never saw such crowds! They really sing! You ought to listen at it! Then after the singings, the folks say, "Don't y'all leave now. We're gonna have something to eat." They go on in there and have a good supper—all kinds of good food, coffee, and soft drinks. We just have a wonderful time!

PLATE 85　Aunt Addie Norton.

GOSPEL SHAPED NOTE MUSIC:
Aunt Addie Norton

Mrs. Leon Calloway and several others who talked with us about shaped-note singing asked if we'd talked to Aunt Addie Norton about her singing. She had not made much mention of it in the interviews we'd taped for the personality article we'd done about her "Aunt Addie Norton," volume 10, number 3, Fall, 1976. It was from a statement by Aunt Addie that this section got its name. She finds happiness in singing, even when things aren't going well for her and she made the remark several times in our conversations, "I love to sing."

FROM FOXFIRE MAGAZINE, VOL. 12, NO. 1

Everybody came together at the annual singing convention for Macon County [North Carolina]. All the churches met together and they sang. Our choir would sing. If we had quartets in the choir, they would sing. People from Coweeta and all the other churches around here and people from Jackson County, North Carolina and everywhere, they'd come here to this singing convention. Mr. Jim Raby was the most wonderful man for singings that's ever been in Macon County. [He was the president of the singing convention for a long time.]

These conventions would be in different churches in the county. People would travel in wagons, buggies, and on horseback. There was always a committee appointed to take care of the singers that lived too far away to go home at night. They provided them a place to stay in different homes in the community. Their food and bed and also feed for the horses was furnished free. Now that was a time everybody had a good time and such wonderful singing and such beautiful Christian fellowship with everybody. There was lunch provided for everyone all three days of the convention. Sometimes the women of the host church would get very nervous wondering if they would have food enough to go around but there always seemed to be plenty.

We'd get up wagons, buggies, or whatever—fill'em full—and lots of folks would ride horseback. They'd tie up the horses somewhere away from the church—come for three days—and it was wonderful, honey! When the children were little, I took them if they wanted to go. But after they got bigger, they didn't care too much about it.

At our singings, we had quartets come from different communities and then the congregation would sing. In Georgia, they may have a few quartets to sing at the singing convention but usually they have people who lead the songs, who stand in front and start a song. Then another person is called on to lead one.

In North Carolina, we have leaders at the singing conventions, too as well as quartets. And sometimes the entire class from a church will come up front and sing. I've seen'em gathered up front maybe fifteen or twenty. They'd sing and everybody else would listen. Then another class would get up and sing. Usually they had one person as leader.

You know, I wanted my children to sing so badly and I've not got but one that's took after Mama—my baby, Neville. Oh, how he loves to sing! He doesn't know a thing about shaped notes but he loves to sing. And he loves to sing country music, too. He likes that very well. He used to pick a guitar all the time. He doesn't have much time to do that now and he's not got anybody to play with him. He used to have a little band of music—guitar and violin and all things like that. When he was about three or so, I took him to church and he always sat in my lap or down by me. I sang alto all the time and you know, honey, he'd sit there and listen to me singing it over one time and he'd take that tune with me next time just as good as I did and sing it just exactly right. I don't guess he was over three or four years old till he could sing alto just as good as I could.

Some people was kind of bashful when they got up front to lead a song. I never was. I've sung several solos and my knees would get kind of shaky the first time or two I went up there but I never was very nervous about things like that. A lot of people are but I'm not. If I make a mistake, it doesn't bother me anymore. Used to it did, because Mr. Holt [our singing leader] would get on to us if we made a mistake and I was afraid of him as I could be. [Aunt Addie laughs.] I told him one time, "Mr. Holt, do you know what? I used to be afraid of you."

He said, "What was you afraid of me for?"

I said, "I didn't know but what you was going to knock me down a few times for missing the notes."

He just laughed.

I can't remember when I started singing. I've sung all my life. My father was as good a bass singer as I think I've ever heard. If God gave me a talent, it was for singing. And I love it, honey. I have never been as near heaven of anything else in my life as I have at a singing. It's the most glorious, wonderful experience—anybody that loves to sing, anybody that has a talent to sing! It was special to me, and it is yet.

Singing has always been more sacred to me than anything in the world, honey. I don't know why. They's nothing in the world that bothers your mind if you love to sing. You're just as happy and as free as you can be if you're singing a good gospel song. I love it. I've taught the young'uns a lot—young people down here at Calvary Church and over here at Newman Chapel. We used to have singings over at Calvary every Friday night at the church. I used to belong over there, but now I belong to the Newman Chapel.

I can sing any song I want to, unless it's too complicated. And I can sing that, too, if I look over it long enough, even if it *is* complicated. I can sing all four parts, every part in the book. I love to sing tenor most. If the piano player only played by sound [couldn't read the music], I'd sing it over to them till they learned the song and then I'd teach the other parts to the other ones and I had the most wonderful little choirs you've ever seen over there in just a little while. When they'd first commence singing, they didn't know a thing in the world about it and they'd make *more* mistakes. They'd just keep making mistakes and I'd get it out of'em.

I can't sing any songs with the round notes. I know the shaped-notes' sound, time value and everything like that and I can't read the round notes at all. I didn't try to learn the lines or spaces much because that's for the piano, the musician. Sometimes I have to look over a new song two or three times before I can get the time right. I value the notes. If you don't know the valuation of these notes—the three-quarters and the whole notes and the half notes—you get mixed up. They teach all that in the singing schools. I can pick up a new songbook and look through it and run over the notes and learn the songs. I just love to. I can't keep my foot still to save my life when I'm a'listening *or* when I'm singing a song. I keep time with my foot.

I know a lot of people don't love music like I do but it's just so wonderful, just an inspiration. It's hard to believe, though, that they could not love it. I can't see why. I never heard but one or two people, though, say that they didn't love gospel music. How anybody could hate that beautiful spirit that's in the song, I can't understand. You know, I don't listen much to the tune of the song. It's the words that gets me.

We had an organ at home. I never seen a piano till I was a great big girl. I don't know how old I was. The churches always had an organ. You know, an organ goes way back. And it's beautiful yet. But I love a piano for singing better than I do an organ.

If John Holt had a dozen pianos and organs, too, he had his tuning fork and he'd listen to that first. Then he'd tell them what key it was if the piano player didn't know. A lot of times, the piano player plays by ear. Mr. Holt had that tuning fork in his pocket all the time. I've sung lots of times without any [piano or organ] music in people's houses where we'd go and sing.

Tom King, John Holt, and Jim Raby all stand out in my mind more than anyone else as singing school teachers. When I was fifteen or sixteen years old, we had a singing school in Persimmon community and Mr. King was our teacher. It lasted about two weeks and helped us young people a lot. We learned the shape and sound of the notes.

After I was married in 1910, I came to North Carolina and joined the church at Newman Chapel where Mr. Holt was our singing leader in church. Like Mr. King, he was a wonderful singer and a good teacher. We would go from church to church and sing. There would be all day singings where classes from different churches would gather and sing.

Mr. Raby was one of the most wonderful men I've ever seen in my life. He was a wonderful teacher! He taught over here at Newman Chapel one time. I had three children when I went to singing school over there to him. And I learned more, of course, because I was older. I put my mind to it and tried to learn. Of the schools that I went to when I was a girl, I done more courtin' than I did singing, you know. Mr. Raby did more for Macon County in singing than any one man that's ever been in this county. I know. I've been here and went with him. He started the fifth Sunday singing in Macon County. It's about faded out by now, I think, since he died. He kept it up as long as he lived. I've seen that courthouse [at Franklin] down there just as full as it'd hold. I never hear much about the fifth Sunday singings anymore. I don't know whether they still have them or not, but if they do, they only have a half day of it now—commences a little after twelve and people sing all Sunday afternoon.

I think we moved back here in 1926, and I knew Mr. Raby then. I knew him for years. He was one of the best singing instructors around and he held singing together. He kept up all the singings and everything. He arranged them. We certainly lost one of the best singers and best teachers that's ever been in Macon County when we lost Jim Raby. He was good to everybody. He treated people all just alike and if you could learn to sing, if you had singing in you, he'd learn you how. All of Mr. Raby's children are good singers. I never helped Mr. Raby with a singing school. I just went and tried to learn myself. I've went with him to a lot of singings. I've been with him and sung for him many a'time down at Franklin. Mr. Raby was one wonderful person. I thought a lot of him. He's been in my home many times.

Also, I had a quartet of my own. There was Margaret Holbrooks Sanders, Margaret Carpenter, Donna Ledford, and me. Then we got down to a trio. We sang over the radio every Sunday morning for a long time.

I do hope and pray that people will carry on good gospel singing until Jesus comes back to gather His children home. Won't it be wonderful to sing in heaven with all those good singers who have gone on before? I want to be in that number!

PLATE 86   Lonnie Smith.

GOSPEL SHAPED NOTE MUSIC: Lonnie Smith

I was born here in Rabun County. Then we moved to Anderson, South Carolina, and lived there about three years. Then we moved back here and I've been here ever since except for a period from about 1918 to 1926.

I attended singing schools and learned the shaped notes and the timing back when I was a boy. All my friends went, teenage boys. The school lasted ten days to two weeks—about the same as now.

I didn't go to any singing conventions then, but we had an all-day singing sometimes at the church and that was fun to me even though I didn't take any active part in it. All-day singing and dinner on the ground, but, lots of times, it was more like all-day dinner. I wouldn't sing; I'd just go. I had taken part in the singing school and learned my notes, but still I was stubborn about singing in church. I just sat in the audience. My mother was there but I usually sat with my friends. She insisted on me going to church whenever I was big enough for any activity, whatever was going on. And she saw to it that every Sunday morning, my little brother and I went to Sunday school. I can remember those little knee pants and waisties, and that's the way she dressed us. She saw that we went and that's the way I came up. I was raised up to go to church and I haven't forgot it.

[As I grew up,] I got away from singing. I never took up singing much publicly until I was grown and had several children. My children could sing and I reckon I was gifted to it, at least a little. My mother was a good singer and I suppose I inherited it some way or other.

My oldest daughter was big enough to play the organ before I took a real interest in singing. To tell the truth, I never really was a *Christian* until I was thirty years old. I was united with the church here at Chechero when I was about fourteen. I've always gone to church, but I didn't completely understand. When my first boy was born, that changed my life completely, because I had always heard it said, "Like father, like son," and I was doing things that I didn't want my boy to do.

And when [I began to understand the real meaning of being a Christian,] I became more interested in gospel singing. I was thirty years old then and I'm seventy-four now. That's been a long time!

What happened was Mr. John Cannon was teaching a singing school at our church. He was from Wolf Creek over near where Horace Page lives. At that time I was making crossties and I had split my foot open and I couldn't work. I didn't have anything else to do but go out there and listen to them.

I went and Mr. Cannon put me to work just as soon as I got there. He got to teaching me the notes and the time and one thing and another. I caught on pretty fast, so after the singing school was over, I was very much interested in singing. I went to Wolf Creek to an all-day singing and he called on me to get up and lead a song and I thought I'd fall down. I thought I'd tear my book up shaking, you know, but he insisted that I get up and lead a number and I did. From then on, why, I've been trying to sing. That's been nearly forty years ago.

I never could learn about line and space music. I know how it goes, but not fast enough to read it. The shaped notes aren't any problem. I could learn the different shape of the notes easier than I could learn the location. Once you learn to sing the scale, you can sound that note when you see it, no matter if it's halfway down in the scale.

It's amazing and I don't know how I can do it, but I can look at the notes, at the music, and at the words all at the same time. We learn it by practice. If you don't sing a song right, if you miss a note, it'll sure tell on you. The rhyme's right, the rhythm's right, and the time's right if you don't miss a note. It's not too awful difficult, but I'll say this, I don't know near as much about it as I'd like to know.

People come from all over Rabun County for the Friday night singing, and also from Stephens County, Habersham County, and Towns County, from Oconee County, South Carolina, and Macon County, North Carolina. The Friday night singings have been going on for more than thirty years that I know of. It started with a group

PLATE 87 Donna Henry and Doug Ivie co-lead a song at a Friday night singing at Bob Mean's home. Lonnie Smith and Horace Page were instrumental in starting the Friday night singings in Rabun County over thirty years ago.

PLATE 88

up around Clayton, Mr. Larry McClure and his wife—they were two good singers—and Walter Ramey and the Silborn Family. Then Horace Page and I participated. It just kept a'growing. One time we had the singing out here at our church (instead of someone's house) and we had a rule that whatever church the singing went to, the director of the singing in that church presided that night over the group. I was singing director and that night the church was full and we sang twenty-seven leaders.

PLATE 89   Future singers at the Friday night singing enjoy the fellowship, too.

Sometimes we have better turnouts and better singing than at other times. We have several piano players and at least one comes every time. My daughter plays sometimes. She's a good pianist. On occasion we've had a man from Towns County bring his guitar. Both he and his sister play. Sometimes he picks his guitar when class is singing, but usually we sing to piano.

I've been president of this Friday night singing for about four years, off and on, but my health's so bad here lately that I haven't always felt like going. I've got emphysema and my breath's too short a lot of times. I do sing some yet, but there are so many times that I can't go and feel good. Last Friday night I got the group to elect another man. We put it off on Wilbur Maney for a while.

The president decides on different song leaders for the meetings. Everybody decides where the meeting will be the next time. Someone calls for it in their home or at their church and we go there.

We've just received some new songbooks and we took them down to Doug Ivie's home in Habersham County and I'll declare, I've never been to a better singing in my life! None of us had ever seen those songs before. I didn't sing any at all, but sat back and listened to the rest of them and it was just like they'd had that book for a year.

We buy three different songbooks every year, one each from the Tennessee Publishing Company, the James D. Vaughn, and the Stamps-Baxter Book Company. We'll buy one hundred copies of one of the books and we'll sing out of that one all year; then we'll use those next year at the Rabun County Annual Singing Convention. About June we'll order fifty copies of another one of these books, and in December we'll get fifty copies of a book put out by the other company. This gives us a good variety of songs to sing. Song books are getting mighty expensive now. We take an offering every Friday night at our singings. We've been pretty fortunate in having enough money to pay for the books so far.

PLATE 90   Wolffork Baptist Church.

When the singings are held at home, everybody brings refreshments. We don't usually have food [if we meet] at the church, except on the Friday night at the close of a singing school. In a home, we have refreshments when we get through singing and chew the fat and visit around with each other. It's mighty good to get with people and associate with them. You're all friends and you [get a chance] to talk with them. It's worth something there.

1976 was the ninety-first year for the Rabun County Singing Convention. It was held at Wolffork Baptist Church in October. When the county convention was first organized, it consisted of three days—Friday, Saturday, and Sunday, or it may have been from Thursday through Saturday. But these last few years—the whole world's got to streamlining everything and cutting corners—it's got down to Saturday night and Sunday. People are living so fast now and they have so many different places that they go, they just don't seem to be as interested in the convention as they used to be. A lot of the old people have passed on and there are mighty few young people that are interested in it.

One of the duties of the convention president is to call the singing together. [The president of the Rabun County Singing Convention and the president of the Friday night singings are not necessarily or usually the same person.] As I've already said, they've got to streamlining this thing and they're leaving off a lot of stuff in these last few years. Now when I was president of the convention, it was a little more difficult than it is today.

PLATE 91　On Sunday morning, people gather at the church for an all-day singing and dinner on the grounds.

PLATE 92　The view from Wolffork Baptist Church.

There are about six delegates sent from each [participating] church—supposed to be both male and female—and they carry the letter from their church. The secretary of the convention has the responsibility of writing up the minutes of each convention and that person has the minutes printed up and sent out to each church.

The convention has a constitution and by-laws. We have a finance committee. Contributions are sent in from all the participating churches and the expenses of the convention are covered by this money. It's used for printing the minutes and then if there's a funeral [some member of the convention], we use some of it for buying flowers. Then we have a committee to decide on where the next year's convention will take place and a nominating committee to recommend the nominations for the next year's officers—president, vice president, chaplain, and secretary-treasurer.

The singing schools usually do pay for themselves [through the participants' contributions] but we have used some of the convention money to pay for them sometimes, if need be. Our church here will contribute to it even if they don't send anybody to the singing school that time. Hyman Brown taught our singing school this year at the Battle Branch Baptist Church and plans to hold one there next year. He has one up here in Rabun County each year.

The Rabun County Singing Convention is not limited to the Baptist church. We have a lot of other people that are interested in singing and they all support the convention and the singings and singing schools.

FROM FOXFIRE MAGAZINE, VOL. 12, NO. 1

GOSPEL SHAPED NOTE MUSIC:
Horace Page

I've been going to our Rabun County Friday night singings for about thirty-five years regular as I can. They are pretty organized. We have a set time to start, seven-thirty every Friday evening. We elect a president and a secretary. The president usually starts off the singings. We have an opening prayer and then go right into singing. The president leads the first song and then he calls on somebody else to lead the next one and he sits down. Why, even the youngest members get up and lead the songs. We have a nine year old granddaughter and she does it just like it was nothing. There are a lot of kids who go to our singings and they like it so much they keep coming. They usually go to singing school so they know every note and the time to the songs just as well as the adults.

The music we have is mostly religious. When we have a singing, we use a piano or sometimes an organ if it's available. When Mr. Henry Fountain from Toccoa comes over, he plays the harmonica for us to sing by. We always manage to have at least one piano player but sometimes a lot of the folks can play.

There's usually a pretty good number of people who attend our singings. It depends a lot on where it's being held. Sometimes we hold the meetings in someone's home and have refreshments afterwards. We have pretty good turnouts to this sort of singing.

It hasn't been too long since we had a singing here at our house. There were sixty people here that night. There was hardly a place to put them. They were hanging out the windows and doors. If you want to come to a singing, it's as much yours as it is ours. You are always welcome to come *anytime.* It helps for somebody who's interested to come. They may not learn all the notes but just them trying will give others the will power to come.

We have people coming all the way from Young Harris, Georgia, to our singings. One family with a grown son came and he met a girl who came regularly. They started dating and got married at a singing. The last night of our singing school that year, they pulled this preacher over to one side and whispered some things back and forth. Pretty soon they went outside down below the church and got married right there. In a few minutes they came back inside just like nothing had happened.

We buy our own songbooks with voluntary contributions. Then each week, the president brings them to wherever the singing is

PLATE 93   Bob Means leads a song.

PLATE 94   Ferd Watts leads.

being held. Every book we get has different songs than the last
one. People write the songs and send them to a publishing company
to be put into a book. We get two new books a year, one in January
and one in June. The old books that we no longer use are donated
to a church or some other group that wants them.

PLATE 95 Nina Folsom Cook talks with Ferd Watts.

I've gone to singing conventions as far away as Chipley and Winter Haven, Florida. We hear about singings and singing conventions from other people mostly and sometimes we get invitations in the mail. People get so enthused about coming because singings are so enjoyable. I guess I like'em too well.

FROM FOXFIRE MAGAZINE, VOL. 12, NO. 1

HYMAN BROWN SINGING SCHOOL

with
Hyman
Brown
Teacher

MARCH 20-31
BATTLE BRANCH BAPTIST CHURCH
WARWOMAN ROAD
CLAYTON, GA.

PLATE 96

GOSPEL SHAPED NOTE MUSIC:

Hyman Brown

The old music teacher we had [growing up] used to get up at the [singing] school and tell everybody that a man couldn't milk the cow at our farm if he didn't go to the barn singing. If he didn't sing, the cow would leave. I learned about singings when I was a child. I was the twelfth of thirteen children, eleven boys and two girls, and we all sang.

All my family sings. Both my sons write songs now. And one is teaching shaped notes. He really enjoys it. The family doesn't get to go to all the singings with me but they do if they can. My wife plays the piano. She was brought up in this kind of thing, too. As a matter of fact, we did most of our courting at singings. That's where a lot of kids used to go on their dates.

There's not as much interest in singings as there used to be. There are some singings that have spread out West but I think they are different than here. The interest in shaped-note singings is mainly concentrated in the South.

PLATE 97 Hyman Brown teaching the rudiments of music at a singing school.

I've taught singing schools since about 1961. I keep teaching most of the year. I take time off in November and December and some in the summer. In August, I sing at our home revival.

[Mr. Brown writes songs, too.] A song will come to you just like a thought. Most of the time, I just write the music.

I believe singers love one another better than anyone you've ever met.

FROM FOXFIRE MAGAZINE, VOL. 12, NO. 1

PLATE 98   Esco Pitts.

GOSPEL SHAPED NOTE MUSIC:
Esco Pitts

I've always liked music all my life and I like everybody that makes
it. My first recollection of music was my granddaddy. He was a
singer. He was always the first one in the church and he had a
certain seat up there next to the "amen corner." I never did see
anybody else sit in his seat. When he'd get in the church, he'd lay
his head back and close his eyes and go to singing. You could hear
him for about a half mile. He would sing until everyone would get
in the church and the preacher was in the pulpit. As the people
would come in, they'd join him in the song service. I never saw
him sing out of a book in my life. He knew all the songs by heart.
They were all religious songs like "Amazing Grace" and "What a
Friend We Have In Jesus" and that old song, "Over the River."
I can't *remember* all of them. Grandma would go to church with him,
but she'd sit back a pew or two.

He was a preacher—he wasn't ordained but he could really preach.
And he was a good Christian. He was just a happy man wherever
he went and he made people happy that he got with. I've seen
him get into the pulpit and take away the sermon from the preacher.
He'd go to preaching and he'd come down the aisle, shaking hands
with the people while he preached. He didn't stay in one place.
And pray! I've heard him pray in my sleep many a time.

He and another man, old Uncle Sam Taylor, a good Christian
man, would run revival meetings around all over the county. Uncle

Sam didn't know a letter in the book—he couldn't read or even write his name. Grandpa taught him the scripture by heart and he would get in the pulpit and quote the scripture to beat the band and preach and pray. And Grandpa would lead the singing.

They wouldn't take money for their preaching. One time they went over to Hale Ridge and ran a two week meeting over there. When they got through, the congregation made up thirty dollars and gave [it to] them. Grandpa said, "You just take this and give it to somebody that needs it." He said, "We've got a living at home." And he wouldn't have the money.

We lived about two and a half miles from our church and my mother carried us to church every Sunday from the time we were born. She'd carry a quilt and put it down on the floor and lay us down on the quilt when we were tiny kids. That was at Mountain Grove Baptist Church up in the Germany settlement. I was raised up there in the Blue Ridge.

My mother had an awful sweet voice and my daddy could sing. My oldest sister sang alto and my next sister sang soprano. I tell you, they could really sing!

We smaller children went to bed pretty early. There was no electricity then and the [grown folks] would sit around the fireplace and sing. I'd go to sleep listening to them sing. I don't know of anybody that could sing any sweeter. They'd sing old songs like "Ninety and Nine." I heard them sing that many a night.

We'd have visitors come and I remember an uncle who'd come. He was a good Christian man and he could pray a good, long prayer. They'd all sing and then have prayer.

As I got a little older, my sisters would let me go with them on weekend nights to singings in homes in our community. By the time I was about twelve years old, I was being called on to lead a song at the conventions. We made a whole day of it when we had a singing convention. I just sung by ear then—I didn't know the notes. Then when I was about thirteen, I was sitting at the breakfast table one morning and I told Mother I wanted her to teach me the notes. She got the songbook down and taught me the shaped notes right there at the breakfast table and from that day to this day I've known them. All we had were shaped notes then. We never saw round notes.

Then a little while after that we had a singing school there in Wolffork. A man from Clarkesville came up and taught it for ten days. He was James P. P. Franklin, a most lovable character. He knew his music! I went every day. My sisters and all the young folks in the community would go. Mr. Franklin had a big blackboard and he'd write the music scale down just like it was in the book—the staff and signatures and everything. I'd just sit there and drink it in. I loved it so much. He found out I could lead songs and he made me lead some of the songs and I've been leading ever since. From then on, I could sing the notes of any song that was written in shaped notes.

I've never conducted a singing school myself. I sort of wanted to, but I was busy at something else. I always had a job working at something.

[Getting together for a singing was our way of dating and socializing when I was a boy.] If anybody had a wagon and mules, we'd load up on that and go to someone's home in the settlement. If we didn't go in the wagon, we'd all get together and walk. We all had our sweethearts, and we'd each get with our girl and march down the road. We didn't have electric lights, so we sang by kerosene lamps. And most of the homes didn't have any musical instruments, so we sang without music. And lots of times we would have a candy drawing at the singing.

There wasn't much dancing where I was raised up because the old folks didn't believe in it. Now and then in certain places, they didn't care, but I never danced while I was young until I left home. I do remember two men who played [dance music]. One played the violin and the other picked a banjo. They could make awful good music and we would go and listen to them play. We wouldn't dance, just sat around and listened, but it was dancing music, not religious music.

When I was fourteen, I came to the Rabun Gap School. Dr. [Andrew] Ritchie, a native of Rabun County who'd graduated from Harvard University and taught at Baylor, came back here and started a school to get all the mountain children into high school. The children could come from the surrounding countryside and work their way through school. They didn't have money, you know. There wasn't any money in those days. I worked my way through that school, all the way from beginning to end. Then I was hired by the school after I graduated and worked for them for thirty years.

We always had opening exercises every morning at school—devotion, scripture reading and sang a couple of songs. Leora Grist played the organ and I would lead the singing. We would have a good song service every morning at the beginning of school.

When Sunday came, Dr. Ritchie would have all of us students to go wherever the church services were being held—one Sunday at the Methodist church and next Sunday at the Baptist. All of us

PLATE 99 Everyone is given the opportunity to lead a song at the 1976 Rabun County Singing Convention.

PLATE 100

PLATE 101

PLATE 102

boys and girls would walk in a body from the school right up the railroad [tracks] to the church.

I led the singing at church right from that time [when I was a young man]. They appointed me songleader at that [Head of Tennessee Baptist] church way back yonder in 1910 or 1911 and I led the songs there till about four years ago. Carrie Dillard Grist was the pianist and organist. She could play! Boy! I'm telling you, I've never seen anybody that could beat her in playing! She and I had charge of music for the church over there for right at fifty years. I'd go over to her house in the evenings and she would play and I would sing—we'd learn all the songs in any new songbooks as we got them. We'd sing for two or three hours a night.

I remember the annual Rabun County Singing Convention from way back before World War I. It's always held in the fall of the year. I hardly ever miss one unless I'm sick or something like that. They used to hold it at the courthouse some years, but most of the time it was held at a church. At the close of the singing convention each year, the president would give all the churches that were represented an opportunity to say they'd like the convention to be at their church the next year. A certain church was decided on and it was announced right then where the next year's convention would be. It went right on round and round to all the different churches different years.

I remember the first singing convention I went to. It was at a church at Powell Gap. The church is gone now and there are trees big enough for saw logs growing right where that church was. The convention was held on Saturday and Sunday. Everybody would take dinner both days—have dinner on the ground. We all went home on Saturday night, then came back on Sunday. People would go in their buggies and on their horses and those close enough would walk. There was generally a houseful. When the convention was held at the courthouse in Clayton, it would be just crammed— just standing room.

The old man that organized the first singing convention away back yonder was Mr. Tom King. He had three boys that could lead singing and he could lead himself. And every church in the county would send a song leader, or maybe two, to the convention.

One president of our singing convention was Martin Chastain. He was the school superintendent and he was a wonderful speaker. He loved music. Between songs he'd quote scripture and poetry. Do you remember "Song of the Chattahoochee"? He'd quote that or poetry by Longfellow. He was an emotional kind of fellow but

PLATE 103 At the convention, extra chairs are placed in the aisles and the doorway to accommodate the overflow crowd.

everybody loved him. Then Johnny Cannon was a president. He could sing and he was a good song leader. He had a daughter that could really play the piano.

Singing's been my life. [I consider it] a gift. If I couldn't sing, I don't know what I would have done. I love singing so much and I've loved everybody that made music.

FROM FOXFIRE MAGAZINE, VOL. 12, NO. 1

PLATE 104   Ernest Watts.

GOSPEL SHAPED NOTE MUSIC:

Ernest Watts

When I was about twelve to fourteen years old, I went to my first singing school at Liberty Church. We lived about a mile and a half out from Tiger, Georgia. Mr. Johnny Cannon taught that singing school. He'd ride a mule or come in a buggy. It was for a week or maybe two weeks and the singing school was held in the daytime. It was in the middle of the summer so we weren't having school then. The adults came, too. They didn't have too much work to do about then. It'd be in the middle of July, between corn laying-by and fodder cutting time. I'd been to singings all my life but that was my first singing school.

My daddy would order a dozen or two of those songbooks—everybody would chip in and buy, you know. This family would buy two or three, another family would buy two or three. Daddy would get four for us. He'd order them from some company through the mail. We used Vaughn's book and Stamps-Baxter quartet books and we used some *good* songs in them. We never did have organized quartets. We had a quartet of our own at home but we never were organized; we'd just sing. I sang bass and both my sisters sang alto and played the organ or piano. Back then we had a pump organ just like the one over at the church.

We had a good singing class at church. All the young people were interested about the time they got about fifteen or sixteen years old. We had a choir and we'd take those gospel songbooks and it wouldn't be but a couple of weeks before we'd know most of the songs in them to sing them.

PLATE 105   Dinner on the grounds.

I remember once going to a singing convention over at Boiling Springs. My father and I rode the mules from Liberty across Davis Gap and Timpson Creek. There were trails all through the mountains back then. There was a trail that went across the mountain there into where John Wilburn's store's at. Then we rode the roads from there to Boiling Springs.

When dinner came, why we had dinner on the *ground*, instead of putting the food on benches or tables. They always *said* "singing and dinner on the ground" but they generally put the dinner up on the table. That was the first and only time that I ever had dinner spread out on the ground like that.

For the dinner at all-day singings, people would generally bring chicken and ham and I have known people to bring barbecued goat or stewed goat. And nowadays, some bring steak. Back then you hardly ever had any steak because nobody ever killed any beef. They killed hogs and had pork chops and spare ribs.

And, of course, they had all kinds of cakes. I remember once they had a singing school down at Chechero. There was several of us boys, seventeen or eighteen years old then, who went the last day for the dinner. There was a Mr. Smith who took us in a truck down there. We carried a great big old black cake, chocolate cake. One of the boys cut a piece out of it and I got a piece. It was just as dark as it could be on the inside. I ate mine. I watched that other boy. He just held his piece. Directly, he throwed it out down the hill. I said, "What did you do with that cake?"

He said, "I was afraid that thing was poison. I was afraid to eat it." It was a rye cake, made with rye flour. It was good! I laughed at him for years about throwing that cake away. It didn't look right to him. People used to cook a lot with rye flour.

Once we boys and girls decided we'd have a singing up at Mr. Jeff Holcomb's. There were two places we could go for a singing. We'd have a good singing for about thirty minutes or an hour. And we'd always slip the old banjo with us and the guitar and after a little while we'd get around and ask the people of the house if we could dance a bit. They'd say, "Yeah-h-h, all right." So we'd get the fellows around and get the banjo and the guitar and start the music. Sometimes we'd have a fiddle. We'd dance an hour and a half or two hours and have a good time and go back home as if nothing had ever happened.

Then in about three or four weeks, we had another place we could go to—Doc Dickerson's. We had new books a lot of times and we'd learn the new songs in a week or two. We'd sing like everything for about an hour. Then we'd slip around and ask Doc if we could dance a little bit. He'd say, "Yes-s-s, I guess, if your daddy and mammy don't find out, it'll be all right." So we'd dance about an hour and a half. We always had to get in home before twelve o'clock.

We went to serenading one time. We never sang when we were serenading. I don't know how it got the name "serenading." They sing Christmas carols now but we didn't back then. We'd just holler and hoot. We never did play no dirty tricks on anybody. If they didn't treat us right, we just went on.

There was snow on the ground and it was pretty cold. We went up by Liberty [Church] and we serenaded Mr. and Mrs. Jim Callenback and it just tickled them to death. They were old and us young people went in and talked with them and they treated us [to refreshments]. We went on up the road to the Dave Crunkletons' and serenaded them; then we went on up to Lester Brown's. They always treated us. We all had firecrackers and we'd shoot'em. Lots of times I'd start to light one and if somebody'd already lit one, I'd throw mine anyhow. I didn't want it to go off in my fingers! Sometimes we'd ring a bell—we had an old cowbell. Just made a racket, a big racket! We hardly ever carried a shotgun because we were afraid somebody'd get shot. We'd just carry firecrackers.

We went on up to Mr. Isaac Brown's. He was about sixty-five or seventy years old. We asked him if he wanted to go with us and he said, "Yeah, I'll go with you." He was a spry old man. He could get about. We went on up to Mr. Jesse Carnes', then Mr. Mark Carnes', then on to old man Blyth Carnes'. Then we came on back to Liberty Church. This happened to be a New Year's Eve we were serenading on. We decided we'd ring the old year out and the new year in. We sat around till about midnight. Then come twelve o'clock and we rang the church bell for thirty minutes. Then we took off— went home!

The singing conventions used to be held in the old courthouse in Clayton. It's torn down now but they were held in the big courthouse upstairs the first Sunday in October and the Friday and Saturday before. They'd carry a piano in. Now it's still [held] the first Sunday in October, but just Saturday night and Sunday.

It changed because I guess people just have too much to do. They got to where they didn't come on Fridays. Then they'd do their business on Saturday and it got to where nobody came on Saturday and they'd have to have it just on Saturday night and Sunday. One time we had the convention down there in the gymnasium in Clayton but it wasn't good, 'cause it was too big. It echoed. You've got to have a building that's right for singings. They had it at the Tiger schoolhouse one time and once at the Persimmon schoolhouse. But most of the time now, they have 'em in the churches.

The first president of the Rabun County convention I remember was Mr. Martin Chastain. If someone got up to sing, why Mr. Chastain would have something to say. He'd tell about Ben Franklin or Abraham Lincoln or Thomas Edison or he'd quote some poem about something until the man would kind of get himself together, get over his stagefright. Then he'd tell the song and they would sing it. He was a soft-spoken fellow. Had a mustache. Everybody loved him. He was a good convention man.

Mr. Johnny Cannon was the president of the convention the year they held it in the Clayton gymnasium. People from all parts of the country would come—from Florida, South Carolina, Alabama, Tennessee, and North Carolina. They would come to ours and then people in Rabun County would return the visits to help them with their singings.

Hyman Brown of Banks County has some of the best singings I've ever been too. When you go to one of his singings, you act as if you were in church. If you start talking, he'll call you down and tell you to go on outside if you want to talk. [He'll say,] "We are singing to the glory of God. We're not singing just to show ourselves."

PLATE 106   Ferd Watts.

GOSPEL SHAPED NOTE MUSIC:

Ferd Watts

When Ferd Watts is called on to lead a song, he always gets up patting his foot and shaking his finger asking if we're ready to go. He's a very good bass singer and a long time member of the Rabun County Friday night singings. He has participated in singing schools and singing conventions in Rabun County most of his life.

FROM FOXFIRE MAGAZINE, VOL. 12, NO. 1

I was about ten years old when I went to my first singing school. That was up at Liberty Baptist Church and Johnny Cannon was the music director. It lasted for about two weeks. I went there the same time as [my cousin,] Ernest. The singing school was held along in July when we were out of school. I'm about the only one in my immediate family that's stayed with singing, but we could all sing.

I can remember the Rabun County Annual Singing Convention being held in the courthouse at Clayton. That's when I was about eight or nine years old. We went in a wagon. You didn't see any cars then. Everything closed up so that everyone could come to the singing. It was held on Friday, Saturday, and Sunday back then. At the Sunday service, there wasn't any preaching and anybody that wanted to could come. The courthouse was full and the Sunday service started at ten and went until about four in the afternoon. There wasn't any singing at night—just all day.

Just loving to sing encouraged us to get the Friday night singings started back in the thirties. I was president of that for about six years. I sing bass. I do lead some singing but not too much. Class singing is what we do mostly, but we have some specials. Class singing is when the whole group sings together with someone up

PLATE 107 The young songleaders love to have Mr. Watts sing with them.

PLATE 108 Ruth Maney, Paula Passmore, and Debbie Penland (left to right) lead a song and count out the "timing."

PLATE 109   A singing school graduation class.

front leading. Some people just like to sit back and listen but lots
of people think that they should lead a song if they come to a singing.

At the singings, we sing and we socialize together. I think that
everyone who comes to the singings have the same feelings—it's a
spiritual time. I hope the singings will continue.

You never quit learning music and I try to attend Hyman Brown's
singing schools now. He keeps bringing up stuff that he thought
we might know and might have forgotten. And there's usually something that I haven't learned before. Hyman says he learns something
new every day.

Singing is certainly a part of my religion. There's as much in
the Bible about this kind of singing as any other kind. When you
think of it, the Bible speaks of hymns as much as any other kind
of singing. In fact, the better the singing, the better the preaching
you will have. If you want a dull preaching, just have you a dull
singing.

PLATE 110   Wilbur Maney and his wife, Ouida.

GOSPEL SHAPED NOTE MUSIC:

Wilbur Maney

I'm fifty-three years old and my daddy, Marlor Maney, was teaching shaped notes to me when I was born! My dad is eighty-three years old and I'd say he's been singing them for nearly seventy years. The shaped notes that I sing haven't deviated; these are the same type that they were singing fifty years ago. My dad kept a few of those old songbooks put out by Henson, and one or two more of those publishers and this type of singing hasn't changed other than the new songbooks that come out.

Now I am not that good, but my dad can just hear these things in his head; he doesn't need a piano to pitch a song. He can just look at the key of it and he can hear it in his head. He still goes to shaped-note singings although he doesn't sing as much anymore. I never have written any songs either. I couldn't write one if I wanted to. That's a special need of people—and I believe in gospel singing or anything else—that the Lord just reveals it to you. I don't care whether it's a popular song or whatever; I just believe the Lord gives it to you.

I devote two hours to shaped-note singing at our Friday night singings every week and as much as six hours on a weekend this fall going to various singing conventions around. For example, we'll be in Banks County this Saturday and Sunday; we'll have our [Rabun County] convention at Liberty Baptist Church the first Saturday and Sunday in October; we'll be in White County the second Sunday

PLATE 111 Two of the Maneys' children, Ruth (left) and Debbie, have attended several singing schools and conventions in addition to being actively involved in Friday night singings. Both play instruments in the high school's concert and marching bands and both play the piano.

in October; we'll be in Banks County the third Sunday in October; and then maybe New Bridge in Gainesville the first Sunday in November; and then we'll come back to Tate's Creek the second Sunday in November. That will kindly play it out until we start over in the spring.

My wife, Ouida, and my daughters, Debbie and Ruth, sing shaped notes. My wife and two girls sing alto and I sing bass. We've taken them to singing schools. They're good! Even if they are my daughters, they're good. My daughter, Debbie, who is in the eleventh grade, sings alto just about as good as anybody in these mountains. She can stand up with anybody, I don't care who's leading or how hard the song is. She can sing. She's been to about five or six of these singing schools.

I've been president of the Rabun County singing convention for two years. This year we will have it down at Liberty Baptist Church and my job is to make sure the convention runs smoothly. A lot of singers is the key to a good singing convention, but nobody dominates it. This convention will convene [as most conventions do] on Saturday night at seven-thirty. I'll probably call on the officers [of the convention] to lead the first song. This is customary and it kicks it off. We then have a chaplain that will have a prayer and the minute he gets through, we have the first leader right on the floor to lead a song. And right before he announces his selection, we'll tell the next leader to be ready to follow. If you got a lot of leaders, you have to keep pushing them and telling them to keep their remarks short. Nobody came there to give a speech. They can hear a speech anywhere anytime. They came to sing. You may

PLATE 112   Mr. Maney, far left, conducts a well-attended singing school.

have to remind them a half a dozen times—there are people that just love to talk. But most of these people have been coming to these singings a long time and they understand these things. If we have thirty leaders, we sing thirty songs, so time is very important.

We start again at ten-thirty on the following Sunday morning. They don't have church, but we do ask their preacher to give a devotional. We sing awhile and have a big dinner there on the grounds for an hour. Then we go back and sing until we get through all the leaders that have come. Now the leaders that have led in the morning don't lead again in the afternoon—we don't double back in the afternoon.

Everybody that wants to gets to lead one song. Sometimes at these other county conventions, my two girls and I get up and lead together. They may call on each one of them, Debbie or Ruth, to lead one and they will call their own number. Let me say here that the leader should start [a song]. The piano should *not* start it. Now you can go to some of these churches around here and the piano will start out and the leader will then go in. You go to one of these shaped-note singings and those piano players will sit there all day if the leader doesn't go ahead and start the song. They've got to hit that note and get it pitched right. Then the minute the leader hits it, they go with it. But those piano players will sit there all day if the leader doesn't start it. They're not going to start it for you. They follow.

A leader better know a half a dozen songs or more that he can sing before he goes. If you're way on down [the list and don't get called upon until late in the afternoon] you better know a good number [of songs] in those books. If you go at ten o'clock and there's about forty leaders there, you don't know when you'll be called upon or how many songs will be sung. And we try never to sing the same song. If you get up and announce one they've already sung, they'll call you—they'll tell you. Most people can remember what's been sung.

Shaped-note singing is good fellowship. My girls know people from [singings] all over this side of the state. People do it for the fellowship; they get a real blessing out of it. They've been doing it all of their lives and it's a part of their lives and has real religious significance. I myself like it for the religious experience and the fellowship. We have a big time together.

INTERVIEW AND PHOTOGRAPHS BY CAROL ROGERS

BAPTISM

By Paul F. Gillespie

He that believeth and is baptized shall be saved;
but he that believeth not shall be damned.
—*Mark 16:16*

Baptism is the symbolic reenactment of Jesus' immersion in the River Jordan by John the Baptist. The southern Protestant denominations assign varying degrees of importance to baptism. To some, baptism is a visual testimony of conversion to the belief in Jesus Christ as savior; to others, such as members of the Church of Christ, it is a criteria for remission of sins, forgiveness, rebirth, and eventual admission into the heavenly kingdom.

Baptism may take the form of sprinkling, pouring, or total immersion. The ritual may be performed during the regular Sunday morning worship service or during a special service usually held on Sunday afternoon. A special baptism service may follow a week-long church school in which converts are instructed in the dogma of that denomination. Baptism service may also be held during or following a revival.

Today many of the denominations that practice baptism by immersion use a baptismal pool in the church. These pools resemble small, heated swimming pools, roughly five to six feet long, four to five feet wide, and three to four feet deep. However, many preachers and church members believe that the service should be performed in a creek or lake without regard to time of year or weather conditions. As preacher Joe Bishop says, "I baptized over here at Mountain Grove, on the pond there at old man Adams' mill. It froze and the water poured over there and there were icicles hanging down there as big as your leg. I'd baptize at twenty below just as quick—no difference to me. He called me to do the job; I'll do the job and leave the rest up to Him."

In the following photographs Reverend Waymond Lunsford baptizes Ervin Carpenter.

PLATE 113   The crowd gathers on the creek bank as Reverend Waymond Lunsford begins Ervin Carpenter's baptism.

PLATE 114   There is one body, and one Spirit, even as ye are called in one hope of your calling; One Lord, one faith, one baptism, One God and Father of all who is above all, and through all, and in you all.

—*Ephesians, 4:4–6*

PLATE 115

PLATE 116 John did baptize in the wilderness, and preach the baptism of repentance for the remission of sins.

—*Mark 1:4*

PLATE 117

PLATE 118 But when they believed Philip preaching the things concerning the kingdom of God, and the name of Jesus Christ, they were baptized, both men and women.

—*Acts 8:12*

PLATE 119 Then Peter said unto them, Repent, and be baptized every one of you in the name of Jesus Christ for the remission of sins, and ye shall receive the gift of the Holy Ghost.

—*Acts 2:38*

PLATE 120

PLATE 121 And Jesus, when he was baptized, went up straightway out of the water; and, lo, the heavens were opened unto him, and he saw the Spirit of God descending like a dove, and lighting upon him: . . .

PLATE 122 . . . And lo a voice from heaven, saying, This is my beloved Son, in whom I am well pleased.

—*Matthew 3:16–17*

FOOT WASHING

By Keith Head and Wendy Guyaux

During the course of our interviews with Reverend Ben Cook, we were extremely interested in his account of the foot washing that was regularly practiced within his church. Since Reverend Cook had been so cordial and receptive to us during those interviews, we carefully approached him asking permission to record such a service for our study of different aspects of mountain religion. Reverend Cook understood our sincerity in reporting these philosophies and practices and expressed the possibility of our bringing tape recorders and cameras into this special service. He offered to bring request before the new preacher and the Board of Deacons the next week. After an anxious week, he brought us word that we were more than welcome to document this service.

Right at six o'clock on the fifth and last Sunday in July, the bell at the little country church began to toll signaling the start of the evening church service which would include observance of the Lord's Supper and the foot washing. Members of the church found their places and the choir assembled at the front of the church. The service was begun with the singing of several old favorites including, "More, More About Jesus," "Rock of Ages, Hide Thou Me," and "I Heard My Savior Speak to Me." A member of the church then got up, made several announcements and welcomed everyone to the service. He then asked the ushers to come to the front of the church and gave the offertory prayer:

> Our heavenly Father, we thank Thee again for this privilege to call upon Thee, Father. We thank Thee, our Father, that You saved our souls one time, Father, that You've been with us, Lord, through this life, Father. Our Father, we thank Thee, Lord, for this little church and we thank Thee for the service that You are about to let us go into tonight, Father. Lead us and guide us and forgive us of our sins and bless the collection, Father. These favors we ask in Jesus' name. Amen.

PLATE 123   Children "try out" seats in the pulpit before the service begins.

PLATE 124   The New Hope Baptist Church choir leaders gather around the piano to lead the choir and the congregation in song.

After this prayer, the offering was taken while the choir sang another old Baptist favorite, "Power in the Blood." During the last chorus of the last verse, Reverend Paul Carden, Jr., made his way to the front of the church and upon the completion of the song, he started his introduction:

It's good to have each one of you with us tonight. We want to welcome these visitors [from Foxfire] and we pray tonight that each one has come, one mind and one heart and one accord. I feel this is one of the most sacred services we can have— our Lord's Supper and foot washing. I want us to remember the full purpose of why we are assembled at New Hope tonight; and most of all, let's keep Jesus at the center of all of it and realize He is still the Head of this church and all of our churches in our own association and all across the country. So let's remember tonight that we need to exalt Jesus above everything. We need to remember that He is the One who founded the church, He is the One we need to talk about and He is the One we need to do things for.

Following the opening remarks, a call was given by Reverend Carden to remember the sick. A prayer meeting, held in a sick member's home earlier that afternoon, was discussed and members commented upon the good spirit evident at that visit. Reverend Carden reiterated these comments:

A good number of us were there and we appreciate everyone that went. We received, I feel, a great blessing from it. He's been sick quite a while and when you see a man enjoying something like that, it's quite a blessing. He's not able to go to church and it's the church's duty to go to those who are not able to come out. Seeing him receive such a blessing made every minute worth it. We want to continue to remember him and others who are sick.

After these comments, everyone assembled around the altar at the front of the church for prayer. Reverend Ben Cook led the prayer and then each person simultaneously prayed his or her own prayer aloud for several minutes. After the prayer, a hymn, "Victory in Jesus," was sung and there was a time of fellowship as church members and visitors mingled around through the church, shaking hands and greeting each other.

Reverend Carden then called for personal testimonies. He invited anyone to stand up and say "a few words" concerning his or her religious experience or spiritual way of life. One person stood and

PLATE 125   The choir.

said simply, "I'd like to say I'm real happy to be a Christian." Another
followed and in front of the entire congregation, shared her feelings:

> I'd like to say I know the Lord and I'm not ashamed to stand
> up for Him because one day He's not going to be ashamed
> for me. And I'm so thankful for the many blessings I have,
> and I'm glad I was raised up in a place where I was taught
> about the Lord because there are so many people that don't
> know about the Lord. They've grown up not ever having known
> about Him. I'm just thankful for this and I want to do God's
> will.

After a period of quiet and a time of personal reflection that
followed these testimonies, the mood seemed perfect for the sermon
and Reverend Carden began to talk about the purpose and significance of the Lord's Supper and foot washing:

> We want to know tonight, before we partake of the things
> God would have us to partake of, what we're actually doing.
> We spoke this morning on Christianity and we want to continue
> tonight to keep in mind what a Christian is. One of the four
> things I mentioned this morning on what a Christian is was
> being Christlike or like Christ. So as we read in this passage
> of scripture tonight I want us to see some of the things Christ
> did. He set a supreme example for us to follow and there is
> nowhere in the scripture that it leads us astray or leads us off

on a detour from the highway that leads to heaven. We want to realize tonight that Jesus did set the example that we need to follow, did the things that we need to practice in our own day and time even though we are almost two thousand years later than when He was when He walked upon the face of the earth. But yet, even today, Jesus Christ still walks with us through the Holy Spirit and I feel things should be just as orderly today as they were two thousand years ago. So, follow along with me starting with the twenty-third verse of the eleventh chapter of I Corinthians. May the Lord add a blessing to the reading of His Word:

For I have received of the Lord that which also I delivered unto you, That the Lord Jesus the same night in which He was betrayed took bread; And when He had given thanks, He brake it, and said, Take, eat: this is My Body, which is broken for you: this do in remembrance of Me. After the same manner also He took the cup, when He had supped, saying, This cup is the new testament in My Blood: this do ye, as oft as ye drink it, in remembrance of Me. For as often as ye eat this bread, and drink this cup, ye do shew the Lord's death till He come. Wherefore whosoever shall eat this bread, and drink this cup of the Lord, unworthily, shall be guilty of the body and blood of the Lord. But let a man examine himself, and so let him eat of that bread, and drink of that cup. For he that eateth and drinketh unworthily, eateth and drinketh damnation to himself, not discerning the Lord's body.

[*I Corinthians 11:23–29*]

We want to speak for a few moments. We'll not speak too awful long tonight, but there is a few things in this passage of scripture that we need to look at and see what the Lord Jesus did for us. That night as He began to break bread and sup from that cup— and to see just exactly what we need to do tonight, to see just exactly what kind of example we're following and what kind of example Jesus laid down for us almost two thousand years ago.

Let's go back for a few moments. I've got about five things out of this passage that I want us to look at and take heed of what Jesus Christ is telling us and what He is trying to give us out of this passage of scripture. First of all, let's look back at verse twenty-three and we'll find Christ's incarnation. You know, Jesus came into this world just as human as we are today, but yet He came as being the supreme sacrifice for us and the supreme example—one particular way that we ourselves and the only way tonight that we can find our name written in the Lamb's Book of Life and the only way we can inherit the Kingdom of God tonight is through Jesus Christ.

We find in Romans 8:3 that He did come to this world in the *likeness* of sinful flesh. I never said sinful flesh. I said in the *likeness* of it. He had no sin. There was no sin about Jesus Christ. This is the reason that He could say as we partake of the bread and wine that we are partaking of His body—something that is not sinful. Something that is pure, something that man can let enter into his body as being a part of Jesus Christ. Something that is perfect.

We find in Philippians 2:7 that "He made Himself of no reputation when He took upon Himself the form of a servant." Let's look back a moment as Jesus Christ came into this world. You know, many of the Jews and others were looking for Him to come as a king, One to set upon a throne and One to have a crown setting upon His head. We find that He was born in a stable amongst the animals and we find He came merely as a servant. He came as a plain ordinary person and we would think of Him today as human form, but we know from the scripture He was indeed the King of Kings, the Lord of Lords and One that could set at the table that night as the disciples were gathered around Him and say, "Yes, this is My body" and "Yes, this is My blood of the New Testament which you are about to partake of." Now as we partake of the Lord's Supper I want us to stay in full remembrance of exactly what the bread stands for and exactly what the wine stands for and realize that even though we are not setting around the same table as those disciples did nearly two thousand years ago, and even though Jesus is not right here with us in the person and the flesh, it's still as sacred tonight as it was there in that upper room. We need to realize tonight as we gather here to partake of the Lord's Supper that we need to be in full reverence of the Lord Jesus Christ. There may be some here tonight that will deny Jesus. There may be some here tonight that will be in the same shape Judas was in: They'll come into God's house and they'll partake of the things God would have them to do, even as Judas did that night, but yet they'll depart and they'll begin to betray our Lord Jesus Christ. But Jesus came to this earth not to make a reputation for Himself, not to set upon a throne, not to make everyone bow down, but He came as the poorest of the poor where people would take Him upon faith, where people would follow Him by the leadership of God.

Then we go on down in these verses and we see Jesus' devotion. Christ was a devoted man. If He hadn't been He'd a never hung up on the cross for us. It says, "The Lord Jesus the same night in which he was betrayed took bread," and it goes on in the twenty-fourth verse, "and when He had given thanks He broke it." When *He* had given thanks. Jesus Himself. He never looked over and said, "Judas, would you bless this for us? Judas, would you pray over this meal for us?" The scripture said, Jesus Christ Himself gave thanks that night. What was He giving thanks for? What did the symbol of breaking bread mean? It was the meaning of the breaking of His own body. He gave thanks to the Father because His own physical body was going to have to be broken—because it was going to have to hang upon the cross and those precious drops of blood were going to have to flow out of Him for the redemption of myself and you and all the people as long as time lasts here upon earth. And if you don't believe that, rather than take of the Lord's Supper, you ought to bow in this altar and ask forgiveness from God. Begin to ask God to show you the way, the way you ought to lead your life. Jesus, through His devotion, said, "not My will be done, but Thy will be done." The Father's will be done in this. Jesus did not want any glory from it all even though He was God in the flesh and He would receive the glory such as we glorify Him tonight. He was to do the Father's will and be about His Father's business.

And as we're gathered here tonight, we need to be about the Father's business in our Lord's Supper and our foot washing. We need to realize that these are things Jesus did and if Jesus was here tonight, I wonder how many people would be here in New Hope Baptist Church. I would venture to say we'd have to roll the windows on out and they'd be out here in the yard. They'd be out in the parking lot in chairs. But brothers and sisters, He's just as much here tonight as if He was here in the flesh. He's just as much here in the spirit tonight as He was that day in the flesh. People don't realize that it is the same Jesus that's with us tonight that walked on the earth two thousand years ago. Brothers, we need to realize that that Jesus is the One that died for us, standing at the Right Hand of God making intercession for our sins. And every one of us has sinned against God. I don't care who you are or how close you walk to Him, you're going to sin against Him and Jesus stands at the Right Hand of God making intercession for us. He's still devoted. Still devoted.

You know, when we have the Lord's Supper, our churches ought to be running over. When we gather together to worship the Lord Jesus Christ, our churches ought to be running over. But people don't realize today the pain and the agony and the suffering Jesus went through where we can live in a nation like we live in today.

PLATE 126   Reverend Carden.

Where we can gather together in fellowship, where we can come together and partake of this Lord's Supper freely and be able to do it without our government taking over and saying we can do this and we can't do that. We ought to fall down on our knees and thank God tonight that He put us in a place where we have the freedom to stand to proclaim the Word of God, to stand and do the things Jesus Christ did.

Another thing we need to look at is the invitation that Jesus Christ gives. Always giving man an invitation. Always offering man something. He said, "take and eat." He said, "Here it is. It's yours if you want it." But then, it gives a few qualifications for those that eat and those that don't eat. He goes on down in the scripture and says, "But let a man examine himself and so let him eat of that bread and drink of that cup." Now you've heard me speak on self-examination I know and Jesus wants every one of us to examine our own lives and find out if we're worthy to take of this bread and this cup. He said if you drink of it unworthily then you're drinking damnation in your own life. You are making a mockery of God. He said to let a man examine his own self—personal examination. I cannot stand behind this pulpit and say this one and that one and the other one is all that's allowed to come up here tonight. All that I can say for tonight is for myself. The only person I can examine tonight is me. It's between you and Jesus and you know whether you're worthy or not. It says, "For he that eateth and drinketh unworthily, eateth and drinketh damnation to himself."

I want us to look for a moment before we go any further into this service and see if we're worthy to partake of the Lord's Supper. You know, this is a serious moment. This is a serious time in our lives. If you've never been saved, if you've never accepted Christ as your own personal Savior, then you don't need to partake of the Lord's Supper. If you do, you are eating and drinking damnation upon yourself. But if you're here tonight and you've accepted Jesus Christ as your own personal Savior, it is your obligation to the Father to partake of the Son's body and do it in remembrance of Him. Not to do it for ourselves or anybody else but in remembrance of Jesus Christ Himself. I want us to make sure we stand worthy before God tonight.

One other thing I want to say tonight. I want us to turn our minds to the thirteenth chapter of John. The Bible says, "And after supper, Jesus girded a towel about Him, took water in a basin and began to wash the disciples' feet." Now I don't know how many here tonight believes in foot washing. That doesn't bother me. My convictions are between me and the Lord Jesus Christ. But let me tell you something. The Bible says a Christian is Christlike—being like Jesus Christ. The Bible says, "after supper He girded a towel about Him and took a basin of water and began to wash the disciples' feet." Now you can participate in the foot washing tonight if you want to or you don't have to and I'll not say one word because that's between you and God. I'm no judge. But I tell you right now the greatest time I've ever had in my life was when I put my bare feet in that pan of water. The only time I've ever shouted to victory in my life is when I sat down on this pew and I got my feet wet and the Spirit filled me so much I couldn't stand it. And if you've never had this experience, you shed those shoes and socks and you put your feet in the water and do it to praise the Kingdom of God—not to tell people you participated in a foot washing but because you want to and God tells you you need to. You are going to get one of the greatest blessings out of it that you've ever had in your life! I got a blessing seeing this young lady saved here this morning. I got a blessing out of the revival that run that length of time. But I also get a great blessing by putting my feet in that pan of water and knowing that I was doing it because Jesus Christ Himself had humbled Himself enough to get down upon His knees and take a towel and gird it about Him and take those disciples' feet and bow down before them, put them in that water and wash them. And, brother, I'm no better than Jesus Christ is and you're no better than Jesus Christ is and I'm going to bow down on my knees tonight and I'm going to wash people's feet. Jesus did it and I'm no better

PLATE 127

PLATE 128 Following the sermon, Reverend Ben Cook, former pastor of New Hope Church, says a few words about the Lord's Supper and foot washing.

PLATE 129   Reverend Cook presides over the Lord's Supper.

PLATE 130   Two of the deacons administer the Lord's Supper to the congregation.

PLATE 131

and I'm going to do it too. I'm sinning when I don't do it and
I'm wrong against God.

And you say, "Well, you've not done it all your life." No, I haven't.
This is the only church I've ever been in that had foot washing. I
didn't know what it was! I dreaded it! I was scared to death the
first night we had foot washing. We came to church and I said,
"What are we going to do?"

They said, "Do the same thing everybody else does." I got wound
up a little bit better than everyone else did one night and I'm not
ashamed of it either. I'd like to see the windows fall out here tonight,
people shouting and stomping the floors. Praising the name of Jesus!
Let us pray:

> Our Father and Lord, we thank Thee for the service tonight.
> Father, as we go further in this service, as we begin to partake
> of the Lord's Supper, God, we want to do it in remembrance
> of the Lord Jesus Christ. We want to show the world that yes
> we are still a Christian people, that yes we are still Christlike,
> yes we're still Christlike, yes we're still willing to follow the
> example that our Lord sat down for us two thousand years
> ago. Lord, bless each one here tonight, God, and God, may
> each one go by their own convictions. It's in Thy name we
> ask it. Amen.

PLATE 132 The congrega-
tion members begin the foot
washing service by laying out
towels and pouring water into
pans that have been set in
front of the pews.

PLATE 133 For this ceremony, the men and women are segregated, men
washing men's feet . . .

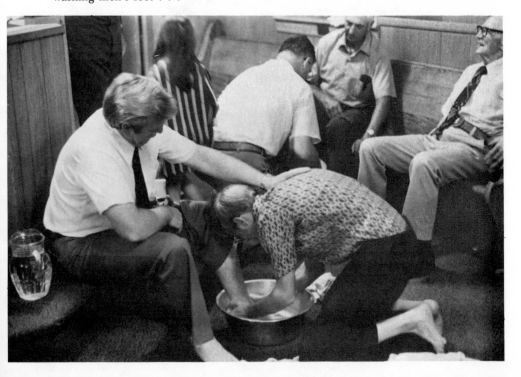

PLATE 134 . . . women administering to women.

PLATE 135

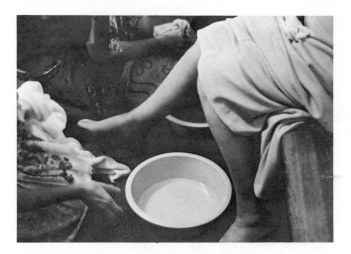

PLATE 136

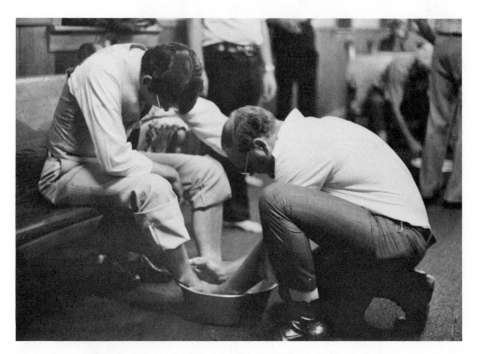

PLATE 137　A brother washes Reverend Carden's feet.

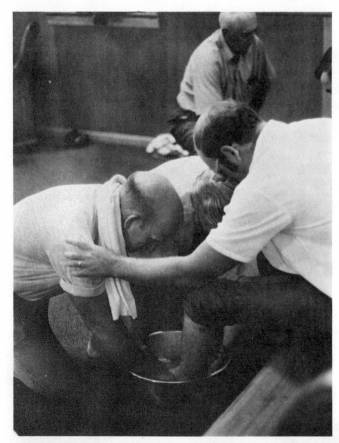

PLATE 138

PLATE 139

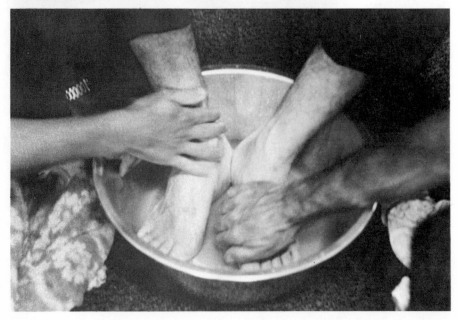

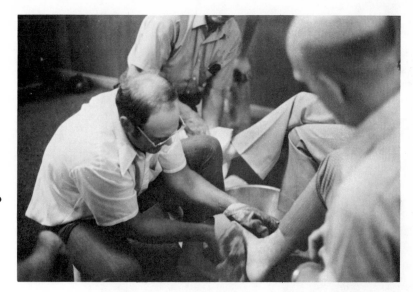

PLATE 140

PLATE 141 Reverend Ben Cook washes feet . . .

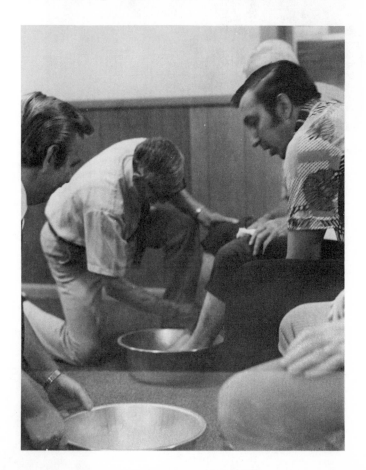

PLATE 142 . . . and receives the service.

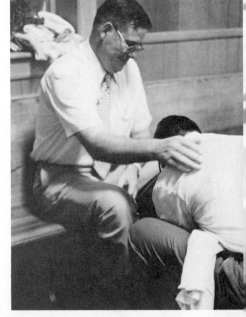

PLATE 143 The congregation members become collectively emotional and outreaching to one another.

PLATE 144

PLATE 145

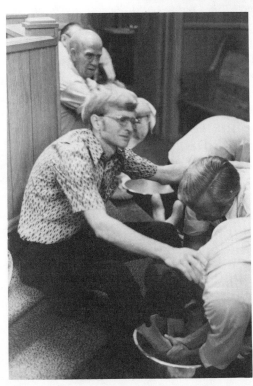

PLATE 146

THE PEOPLE WHO TAKE UP SERPENTS

By Elliot Wigginton

"Now the serpent was more subtle than any beast of the field which the Lord God had made. And he said to the woman, Yea, hath God said, ye shall not eat of every tree of the garden."
—*Genesis 3:1*

This chapter began with an invitation to witness and record a series of religious services that few journalists have been allowed to see—much less record. We thought it was important that we accept, not only because of the unique nature of such churches, but also because of the amount of rumor and myth and misunderstanding surrounding them. We had been led to believe, for example, that the serpents used were either rubber dummies or had had their fangs pulled. We can now lay both of those rumors to rest. Rubber rattlesnakes don't sing and strike at the tops of their cage and the preachers that have been bitten and have died weren't gummed to death.

From the beginning, we were asked not to reveal the location of this mountain church and, as is our policy, we have adhered to that. We were not restricted in any way from our recording, however; Karen Cox, David Wilson, and Gary Warfield, the students who covered three homecoming services in August, were given totally free rein to work inside the church with cameras and videotape and tape recorders. It was a display of generosity on the part of the congregation that dumfounded me. And the students worked more intensely and more closely as a team than I had ever seen them do before. David was so intent on getting photographs from the very center of the activity that at one point, eye glued to the viewfinder, he swung his camera around right into the side of a giant rattler. A photograph we missed: the expression on Karen's face when she was offered a copperhead.

Our involvement with the church spanned several visits over a nine-month period—the time it took us to get what we felt was a fair portrayal. During the first visit, we attended three separate services and interviewed a number of people outside the context of the meetings. On the last visit, I took Ernest Flanagan, Tom Carlton, and Randall Hardy solely to interview the preacher and members of the congregation. We wanted it all to be as accurate as possible and, on the last visit, we even carried every photograph that we had planned to use with us to have them checked and approved for publication.

But always the feeling of all of us was that it was going to be impossible to get this one down on paper. For even if we could rig it so that when you opened this section, you were flooded with the noise and the songs, and at the same time rig it so that the photographs all swirled simultaneously around you as their subjects did around us, there would still be the immensely complicated intricacy of a style of worship that varied with each service and took place not only from the pulpit, but from every corner of a three-dimensional room. It's lost on the flat pages of this silent book. What remains is an echo.

So how do we proceed? To include the entire texts of five-hour services would be nearly impossible. On Saturday night, for example, the following took place in this order: four sermons in a row, the last from a man in the congregation; a request for prayer for a hospitalized woman; singing, combined with people coming to the altar; loud music and serpent handling; another sermon; three women and then three men giving testimony in random order; a girl singing a solo and then testifying; a woman and then two more men testifying; a man asking prayers for his sick wife; a woman testifying; more singing; requests for prayer for a boy, a woman going into surgery, and another boy; and then dismissal late that night. And that was just Saturday.

So what we've done is try to combine the two major services, group the types of events, and give you a sampling of each type from pieces of sermon and testimony from various people, through photographs of serpent handling and healing and speaking in tongues; and give them to you in some sort of order, knowing full well that most of the services lack that tidy order.

So remember that the events flow naturally into, and combine with, each other without the fragmentation we have imposed. Beyond this flaw, we've tried to tell it straight to the best of our ability. None of us was in a position to accurately judge what was happening. All of us are human beings trying to find our own place in the maze of religious beliefs and strike our own balance. We will not judge this church except to say that despite the fact we will probably never handle serpents, each of us found this a church of incredible strengths, of tremendous energy and honesty and of total commitment to God and to the congregation. It is not a church of talk, but of action so dynamic that beside it, more conventional forms of worship seem stale and lifeless.

It was an experience none of us will forget.

B. ELIOT WIGGINTON

PLATE 147

A CHURCH OF GOD

Afterward He appeared unto the eleven as they sat at meat and upbraided them with their unbelief and hardness of heart, because they believed not them which had seen Him after He was risen. And He said unto them, Go ye into all the world, and preach the gospel to every creature. He that believeth and is baptized shall be saved, but he that believeth not shall be damned. And these signs shall follow them that believe; In My name shall they cast out devils; they shall speak with new tongues; they shall take up serpents; and if they drink any deadly thing, it shall not hurt them; they shall lay hands on the sick, and they shall recover. So then after the Lord had spoken unto them, He was received up into heaven, and sat on the right hand of God. And they went forth and preached everywhere, the Lord working with them, and confirming the Word with signs following. Amen.

—Mark 16:14–20

PLATE 148 "Believin' is part of th'faith. If you don't believe, you can't do this. See, it says, 'These signs shall follow them that believe.' It's to th'man that believes.

"I can't understand why th'people can't see it. Right there it is in th'Bible. You boys ought'a read that and study that so's you can teach that and say, 'now people, that's th'Lord's sayin'. That's not my sayin'. That's Jesus'.' Ain't it? It gets looked over all th'time. Other churches won't have it at all. Just own't have it. Won't let'cha come in with it. They just won't allow it at all."
—*Reverend Browning*

In 1909, the preceding verses from St. Mark so struck George Went Hensley that, so the story goes, he chased down a rattler, held a meeting of his neighbors, and handled it and passed it among them. No one was bitten and the movement was launched. Hensley himself, after supposedly being bitten 446 times, finally died of the 447th at the age of 75 during a meeting in an abandoned blacksmith shop outside Altha, Florida. Refusing to allow anyone to call a doctor, he died belching blood and writhing on the floor according to the eyewitness report of Don Kimsey, an Atlanta *Journal* correspondent [Atlanta *Journal,* January 8, 1973: p. 9D].

Since that time, numerous others have died of either the same causes, or of drinking poison; despite that, and despite the fact that the practice is outlawed in most states, the movement that Hensley founded—though largely underground—is still very much alive.

The church we visited—the location of which, at the request of

PLATE 149

the preacher, must remain nameless—was founded in 1931. Two years after its founding, the members began to handle serpents. As the preacher, Reverend Browning, tells it: "I was thirty-four years old. Th'Lord called me t'preach this. He began t'reveal th'faith t'me. It was through th'revelation of Him.

"It was revealed t'me in this Bible when it said t'take'em up; and I was preachin' one day and I didn't know that verse was to us. I thought it was to th'Apostles. And th'Lord revealed it t'me, and then I got t'preachin' it. And they brought one one time and said, 'Can we bring it in?'

"And somebody said, 'Yeah, bring it in.'

"And they said, 'Th'preacher'll have t'tell us.' And I went out to'em and hollered to'em t'bring it in."

They've been bringing it in ever since.

Though their church is a Church of God, it is only one of a number of wings of that denomination, a denomination that takes its name from Acts 20:28 [Take heed therefore unto yourselves, and to all the flock, over which the Holy Ghost hath made you overseers, to feed the church of God, which he hath purchased with his own blood]. The name is also mentioned in I Corinthians 1:2, II Corinthians 1:1 and 10:32, Galatians 1:13, I Thessalonians 2:14, and II Thessalonians 1:4. Browning's particular sect, subtitled the "Apostle Doctrine," differs in some respects from the other Churches of God—to Browning's dismay. Of the Church of Christ, for example, he says, "If you're the father and he's the son, what's yours is his and what's his is yours; and if it's a Church of God, it's a Church of Christ. Church of Christ, it's a Church of God. But the Church of Christ don't teach the Holy Ghost like I teach it—that you speak in tongues. They won't have that. They teach all you have to do to be saved is be baptized and that gets you to heaven."

For Browning and his followers, there is only one church, and only one set of doctrines to follow. The foundation for that faith is found in what they consider the most important books of the Bible: Matthew, Mark, Luke, John, and Acts. Of these, the most important is Acts. As Browning says, "That's the beginning of the new plan. This is like a door into a church. This is a door book. You can read all of th'old Bible [Old Testament] and it don't tell you how to get in th'church. This is th'book that tells you how t'get in th'church. This is th'last words He said t'them, 'And, when He had spoken these things, while they beheld it, He was taken up and a cloud received Him out of their sight.' They weren't but eleven of them there, but they choose another'n in this chapter. And he was numbered with th'eleven apostles.

"Acts is th'most important of all. That's when He built th'church. In th'sixteenth chapter of Matthew, He said, 'Upon this rock will I build my church, but He never built it till He died. He had t'give His life for th'church. This twentieth chapter here in Acts said that He purchased it with His own blood. There ain't nary another book like this."

And of the guidelines laid down in those five books, the keystone—and the belief that sets this sect apart from the others—is the rigid adherence to the idea of the spiritual "gift." From baptism and

PLATE 150

anointing, the faithful must proceed to prove their faith by having
"victory" over snakes, fire, poison, or all of these. Then, in a moment
of supreme ecstasy, they receive a "blessing" from the Holy Ghost,
Himself, and subsequent gifts, which are proof that they have been
blessed and rewarded for their untarnished devotion. These gifts,
elaborated upon later, are such things as spiritual knowledge, the
ability to prophesy, the gift of discerning spirits, and the speaking
in tongues. Until the member of the congregation has reached this
plateau, he is still damned.

It is on this point that Browning is often challenged; but his de-
fense is that though it does not say specifically in the Bible that
one must speak in tongues, it does say that when the apostles received the Holy Ghost, *they* did; and when the twelve received the
Holy Ghost, *they* did, and on and on through example after example.
And that's good enough for him.

One of the touchstones concerning gifts is found in I Corinthians.
Though it implies that not all the members of the church must
speak in tongues ["for no matter what their gifts, they are all of
the same body and all vital parts of each other"], it is still a touch-

stone, and a verse he points to often when outlining the gifts with
which the faithful are rewarded:

> Now concerning spiritual gifts, brethren, I would not have you
> ignorant. Ye know that ye were Gentiles, carried away unto
> these dumb idols, even as ye were led. Wherefore I give you
> to understand that no man speaking by the Spirit of God calleth
> Jesus accursed: and that no man can say that Jesus is the Lord,
> but by the Holy Ghost. Now there are diversities of gifts, but
> the same Spirit. And there are differences of administrations,
> but the same Lord. And there are diversities of operations, but
> it is the same God which worketh all in all. But the manifestation
> of the Spirit is given to every man to profit withal. For to one
> is given by the Spirit the word of wisdom; to another the word
> of knowledge by the same Spirit; to another faith by the same
> Spirit; to another the gifts of healing by the same Spirit; to
> another the working of miracles; to another prophecy; to an-
> other discerning of spirits; to another divers kinds of tongues;
> to another the interpretation of tongues: but all these worketh
> that one and the selfsame Spirit, dividing to every man severally
> as he will. For as the body is one, and hath many members,
> and all the members of that one body, being many, are one
> body: so also is Christ.
>
> —*I Corinthians 12:1–12*

> Now ye are the body of Christ and members in particular. And
> God hath set some in the church, first apostles, secondarily
> prophets, thirdly teachers, after that miracles, then gifts of heal-
> ings, helps, governments, diversities of tongues.
>
> —*I Corinthians 12:27,28*

Just as important in the minds of Browning and his flock as the
striving for a blessing is the solidarity and indivisibility of the group.
Enough Bible verses warn that outside elements will try to tear them
apart to demand that they give this full attention:

> Take heed therefore unto yourselves, and to all the flock, over
> the which the Holy Ghost hath made you overseers, to feed
> the church of God, which he hath purchased with his own blood.
> For I know this, that after my departing shall grievous wolves
> enter in among you, not sparing the flock. Also of your own
> selves shall men arise, speaking perverse things, to draw away
> disciples after them.
>
> —*Acts 20:28–30*

I marvel that ye are so soon removed from him that called
you into the grace of Christ unto another gospel: Which is not
another; but there be some that trouble you, and would pervert
the gospel of Christ. But though we, or an angel from heaven,
preach any other gospel unto you than that which we have
preached unto you, let him be accursed. As we said before,
so say I now again, If any man preach any other gospel unto
you than that ye have received, let him be accursed.

—*Galatians 1:6–9*

There is only one church, and it must be safeguarded. The result
of this belief is a closing of the ranks. If a member strays, everything
possible must be done to bring him back to the fold. And if he
steadfastly refuses to return, he must be damned and avoided.
Browning repeats this, citing scripture:

"[If we've received the Word and not accepted it] then we've
turned it down. Now this is what you *must* preach—what He give
these men. And you go to th'last of these four books. They don't
mean you can't talk on these others, but the doctrine they preached
must be preached. Now listen at this man talk after he come in—
have you read the ninth chapter of Acts where this man, Saul, was
a'persecutin' th'church? The Lord spoke to him, said, Saul, Saul,
why persecutist thou me? Now he'uz a strong Pharisee. And had
that kinda religion, but he was tryin' t'put this down. And he said,
Who art thou, Lord?

"And he said, I am Jesus whom thou persecutist. It is hard for
thee to kick against the priest. This is so sharp, if you kick again'
it, it'll take you down.

"Now here in the twentieth chapter [Acts 20:28] says, Take heed
therefore unto yourselves and all the flock over which the Holy
Ghost has made you overseers, to *feed the church of God.* Now th'people
won't let it go by th'name of th'Church of God. They'll change it
to whatever they want t'call it, don't they? But there's just one church,
Which he hath purchased with his own blood. See. He suffered
for this church. For I know this, [Acts 20:29] I was preachin' on
this last night, that after my departing shall grievous wolves enter
in among you, not sparing the flock.

"Now He's a'callin' everybody a wolf that starts preachin' different.
Also of your own selves [Acts 20:30] shall men arise, speaking per-
verse things to draw away disciples after them.

"Then He wrote a letter over here. [Galatians 1:6–8] 'I marvel that ye are so soon removed from him that called you into the grace of Christ unto another gospel.' Said he's a'preachin' th'right one and I start preachin' another'n and some a'his members is a'listenin' at me and they're comin' out from hearin' him. 'Which is not another; but there be some that trouble you, and would pervert the gospel of Christ. But though we, or an angel from heaven, preach any other gospel unto you than that which we have preached unto you, let him be accursed.'

"Now he's gonna' say it again: 'As we said before, so say I now again. If any man preach any other gospel unto you than that ye have received, let him be accursed.' Now if you preach, you better preach this. If there's a curse on ever'body that don't preach this, we better preach this. He picked these men and sent them to the people.

"Now we can read another verse right here. Said, 'Now, I beseech you, brethren. [Romans 16:17–18] Mark them which cause divisions and offenses contrary to the doctrine which ye have learned; and avoid them.' And listen what he says now: 'For they that are such serve not our Lord Jesus Christ, but their own belly; and by good words and fair speeches deceive the hearts of the simple.'

"And mark'em, He said, so you can see who they are and you won't get in with'em. It's awful *close,* this is! Yes, it's *close.* That's close. They say th'government's strict, but now this, *this* is strict.

"Some people never pay much attention t'this chapter here [Luke 16:22–31]. 'And it came to pass, that the beggar died, and was carried by the angels into Abraham's bosom: the rich man also died, and was buried; and in hell he lift up his eyes, being in torments, and seeth Abraham afar off, and Lazarus in his bosom. And he cried and said, Father Abraham, have mercy on me, and send Lazarus, that he may dip the tip of his finger in water, and cool my tongue; for I am tormented in this flame.' Abraham's gonna talk back to him. 'But Abraham said, Son, remember that thou in thy lifetime receivedst thy good things, and likewise Lazarus evil things: but now he is comforted, and thou art tormented. And beside all this, between us and you there is a great gulf fixed: so that they which would pass from hence to you cannot; neither can they pass to us, that would come from thence. Then he said, I pray thee therefore, father, that thou wouldest send him to my father's house: for I have five brethren; that he may testify unto them, lest they also come into this place of torment.' Gon' talk back to him. 'Abraham saith unto him, They have Moses and the prophets; let them hear them.

And he said, Nay, Father Abraham: but if one went unto them from the dead, they will repent.' Now he's gonna talk back. 'And he said unto him, If they hear not Moses and the prophets, neither will they be persuaded, though one rose from the dead.' Now God just had Moses and th'prophets there. He's not gonna change it t'suit that man. Now He sent His Son here and made Him suffer and die and He's not gonna change it for me and you. God's too big t'do that. He won't change it for *nobody*. Now if we don't teach this, we'll come t'th'judgment and we'll sure go down.

"And it says, 'Withdraw yourself from every brother that walkest disorderly.' They's so many people that don't believe this, and I try t'prove this by chapter and verse to'em, and you can't do a thing with some. They'll preach right on just like they been preachin' and you tell'em. Now let me read a verse'r'two here. [Matthew 18:15–17] 'Moreover if thy brother shall trespass against thee, go and tell him his fault between thee and him alone: if he shall hear thee, thou has gained thy brother. But if he will not hear thee, then take with thee one or two more, that in the mouth of two or three witnesses every word may be established. And if he shall neglect to hear them, tell it unto the church: but if he neglect to hear the church, let him be unto thee as an heathen man and a publican.' Now that'll put th'thing on y'! God's got a purpose for everything in here—and it cost Him th'best He had [to establish His church]. Let's read one more, and then this boy [one of the *Foxfire* editors] will make a preacher. [Matthew 16:13–19] 'When Jesus came into the coasts of Caesarea Philippi, he asked his disciples, saying, Whom do men say that I the Son of man am? And they said, Some say that thou art John the Baptist: some Elias; and others, Jeremias, or one of the prophets. He saith unto them, But whom say ye that I am? And Simon Peter answered and said, Thou art the Christ, the Son of the living God. And Jesus answered and said unto him, Blessed art thou, Simon Barjona: for flesh and blood hath not revealed it unto thee, but my Father which is in heaven. And I say also unto thee, That thou art Peter, and upon this rock I will build my church; and the gates of hell shall not prevail against it. And I will give unto thee the keys of the kingdom of heaven: and whatsoever thou shalt bind on earth shall be bound in heaven: and whatsoever thou shalt loose on earth shall be loosed in heaven.' Now what if he goes out preachin' one church and me another and you'll say, 'Well, which one did He build? The one he's a'preachin' or the one I'm preachin'?' He just built one church. Now say we've three or four preachers here, and one of us gets offended and he

PLATE 151

don't want a fellowship with us no more and he goes out and starts him up a thing he calls a church and he's gonna name it somethin'r'-nother, well, that'll divide somebody up, and that's th'way they get started. These men was of one accord when they got started. This is where it started. The church He built, that's where all these churches started from.

"Now that's th'only thing I love about this [article]. It's not to show me up that I'm somethin'r'nother, but t'show that this is God's way. I wouldn't want a bit of a slur, 'ner nothin'. I want this sincere."

"For Where Two or Three are Gathered Together in My Name, There Am I in the Midst of Them."

Sunday. It is 9:30 in the morning. People begin arriving early for an annual homecoming service that promises to be a big one with family members coming in from as far away as Ohio and Indiana and Florida. In no time at all, the church is packed.

The center of interest before the service is Dexter Callahan who arrives bearing two flat boxes. On the end of one, in white paint, are the words, "In Jesus' Name." Inside the boxes are live rattlesnakes and copperheads. As he reaches the building, people crowd around and the rattlers inside buzz furiously. Then he pushes through the crowd, carries the boxes up to the front of the church, and slides them under a low bench behind the pulpit.

The service starts with hymns. "Pull Off Your Shoes, Moses," "On the Resurrection Morning," "Running Up the King's Highway," and "Amazing Grace" are old favorites. From there on, however, it happens as the spirit dictates: a series of different preachers stand and talk whenever the spirit moves them to do so; people in the congregation do likewise, either testifying or asking the prayers of the group for themselves or an ailing relative; and periodically through the meeting, the music starts, serpents are brought out, and there are periods of intense activity.

PLATE 152 Dexter arrives with the serpents for the service.

PLATE 153

I KNOW THE BIBLE'S RIGHT—SOMEBODY'S WRONG

Well, I know a lot of preachers who had druther be dead
Than to preach to their people what the Bible said.
I know the Bible's right, somebody's wrong,
I know the Bible's right, somebody's wrong.

Well, I told you once, and I'll tell you twice,
You can't go to Heaven with the other man's life.

I know the Bible's right, somebody's wrong,
I know the Bible's right, somebody's wrong.

Well, I told you once, and you'll live to regret,
You can't go to Heaven smokin' cigarettes.
I know the Bible's right, somebody's wrong,
I know the Bible's right, somebody's wrong.

Well, I told you once, and I'll tell you again,
You can't go to Heaven with that ambure* on your chin.
I know the Bible's right, somebody's wrong,
I know the Bible's right, somebody's wrong.

*amber (tobacco juice)

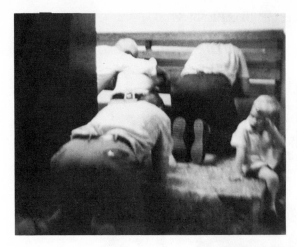

PLATE 154 As decreed by
I Timothy, the actual services
begin with prayer; everyone
on their knees or feet, praying
individual prayers aloud.

PLATE 155 I exhort there-
fore, that, first of all, supplica-
tions, prayers, intercessions,
and giving of thanks, be made
for all men.

—*I Timothy 2:1*

PLATE 156 I will, therefore, that men pray every where, lifting up holy
hands, without wrath and doubting.

—*I Timothy 2:8*

Music is provided by guitars—some of them electric. There are no hymn books; the congregation knows the hymns by heart. Children with tambourines provide rhythm and a staccato punctuation to the verses.

"Praise th'Lord! He that believeth and be baptized *SHALL* be saved! Praise th'Lord! He that believeth and be baptized *SHALL* be saved! A man has got to *believe* th'Word of God! Praise th'Lord! If he hears th'Word of God and don't do it, it won't be no good. If people go down t'th'river and are baptized an' don't believe God's Word, you're baptized in vain! Hallelujah! Praise God! It's not th'hearer that's justified but th'doer! Hallelujah! And He says, 'And these signs shall follow them that believe.' I'm *glad* God put that in m'heart! I'm *GLAD* He put that in m'heart! 'An' these signs shall follow them that believe,' He said, 'in my name.' There's th'name a'Jesus again. You can't get around th'name a'Jesus. Hallelujah! 'In my name shall they cast out devils.' Hallelujah to God, they *SHALL* speak with new tongues! Praise th'Lord! They *SHALL* take up serpents. Hallelujah t'God, they *SHALL* take up serpents! And if they drink of any deadly thing, it *SHALL* not hurt them! They *SHALL* handle th'sick an' they *SHALL* recover. Hallelujah t'God! Why is it we pray for the sick an' they don't recover? Because we don't believe God's Word! We don't believe it! If we did, they'd be healed! Hallelujah t'God! An' He said, 'These signs shall follow them that believe in my name.' Hallelujah t'God! He said, 'They *SHALL* handle th'sick and they *SHALL* recover.' If they's one of us sick, an' I lay my hand on her in th'name a'Jesus, she'd be made whole! Because God's Word said that it would be, I believe that it's so! Praise the Lord! As th'Bible says—I believe James said—'If there's any buried, let'em sing songs!' Hallelujah t'God, if there's any afflicted, let him pray. If there's any sick among ye, hallelujah t'God, let them pray over him in th'name of th'Lord! There's that name again [much clapping]. You can't get around it, boys. You can't get around th'name a'Him. Anoint'em in oil in th'name of th'Lord. God is real! I'm glad tonight He's in my life. I'm glad He's in my soul.

"I love Him tonight. Hadn't a'been fer Him, me and you'd a'still been lost tonight. Praise God, praise God! I'd love t'say this. Scripture says, and He said in that fourth verse, 'I have manifested thy name.' Not *my* name, but *thy* name. 'I have manifested thy name to th'men to which thou gavest me out of th'world. An' thou gavest them to me. An' they have kept th'Word.' Didn't He say that? They kept th'Word! 'For I have given unto them Thy words which Thou gavest unto me, an' they have received them.' Didn't they say that?

PLATE 157

PLATE 158

He said, 'I pray for them. I pray not for the world but for those which Thou hast given me, for they're Thine, and all mine are thine, and I am glorified in this.' Didn't he say that?" [The congregation answers, "Yes, He said that!"]

"But these are in th'world, keep to thy own name holy, those that thou hast given me, that they may be one, as we are. If me an' you aren't one tonight in Jesus Christ, someone's a hypocrite [shouting]!" [Answer from congregation, "Amen! That's right!"]

"He says, 'I am no more in the world but these are in the world. Keep to Thy holy name, those who thou hast given me, that they may be one, as we are. And when I was with them in th'world, I kept them in Thy name, those thou gavest me I have helped, and none of them is lost, but that th'scripture might be fulfilled.' Amen. Praise God! 'These things I speak in th'world, that they might have my joy fulfilled in themselves. I have given unto them th'Word Thou hast given as I'm not of th'world. I pray not that Thou shouldest take them out of the world, but Thou should keepest them from th'evil.' Amen! You know what that next verse said? 'Sanctify him through Thy truth!' Seventeenth verse of John 17. 'Sanctify him through Thy truth.' What did He say was truth? The *Word* is truth! Hallelujah! Didn't he say that [shouting]? The Word is truth! Save your time, pull out th'truth. The Word is truth!

" 'Thou hast sent me into th'world, even so I am also a'sendin' them into th'world, an'for their sake, I sanctify myself that they might also be sanctified through th'truth.' Listen t'what this next verse says, 'Neither pray I for these alone, but for *all-l-l* that believe on me through their works.' Is that what He said? Somebody said we won't have an apostle doctrine. But if we don't, we won't have th'Word of God. Amen!

"I believe in God's signs! I believe in th'Word of God. I believe in God. I believe in takin' up serpents with all my heart. I believe in drinkin' strychnine'n'deadly poison. I believe in whatever God puts on me t'do, that's what I wanta do! I believe in God. If we're led by th'Spirit of God, hallelujah to God, and feel with th'Spirit a'God that it won't be no harm come t'us.

"Praise God! His great big eye's watchin' ever' one of us. Hallelujah to God! I'm glad tonight that I'm sheltered in the arms of th'Lord. [Softer and almost tearfully.] I'm glad th'Lord's savin' souls tonight. Hallelujah to God if you've ever seen a man sincere t'God's Word. I believe in God's Word with all my heart. Hallelujah t'God! I said, 'Lord, I don't want t'die a natural death. I don't want t'die a natural death. I want t'die in th'name a'Jesus.' Hallelujah to God, I wanta be born jus' like th'apostles was [still soft and tearful]. I wanta be like Paul was. I wanta carry my cross. Hallelujah to God! I wanta serve God in th'truth jus' like He said t'do. Th'Bible says praise th'Lord. Hallelujah t'God! There's no fear in love, there's no fear in love. Hallelujah t'God! Perfect love casteth out fear. Hallelujah to God! If a man's got perfect love, he's got no fear in his heart. Hallelujah t'God. [Shouting] I've got perfect love in m'heart! Glory t'God, in th'name a'Jesus, I believe with all my heart. Last Sunday, I believe if there'd been a den o'lions here, if it had been God's will, I believe I coulda opened th'door an' walked right in there!

Because they's no fear in my heart. It may be someday they might throw me in a den a'lions er somethin'another. God oughta know. But th'thing I wanta do is to be in shape, that I know I can go forward an' God will back me up. Praise th'Lord."

[Congregation] "Yes, He will!"

ZACCHAEUS TOO HIGH IN A SYCAMORE TREE

Lord Jesus came a walkin' along one day
With a crowd all gathered around.
He cast his eyes in a sycamore tree,
And what d'you think He found?
He found a man a lookin' for him
Way up in a sycamore tree.
He said, "Zacchaeus, you come down,
Today I must abide with thee."

Chorus:

Well, all you people with your little proud hearts,
This is what you are to me.
You're just another Zacchaeus
When th'Lord come to bless you,
Too high in the sycamore tree,
Too high in the sycamore tree.

Well, some of our sisters, they go to church
With their hair cut off and gone.
Their little eyebrows that God gave them,
Just won't leave them alone.
With a little paint here and a little paint there,
Just can't hardly tell;
Instead a wantin' to look like Jesus Christ,
They look like a Jezebel. (Chorus)

Well, some of our sisters, they love this world;
They won't give it up at all.
When they go out to buy their clothes,
They get'em wa-a-y too small.
Well, what is th'Lord gonna do,
What is He gonna say?
When He finds that th'sisters wear their clothes so tight,
That they can't kneel down to pray. (Chorus)

PLATE 159

PLATE 160

Well, some of our brothers, they go to church
With a stiff collar and a little bow tie.
They like a pat upon the back,
And they set in their seats so high.
Their eyes is on their brother's lap;
Their heart's so full of doubt.
If th'Lord was to come to bless their soul,
They'd be too proud to shout. (Chorus)

Well, brother, you can watch my life,
Ain't got a thing to hide.
Since God came down and saved my soul,
Had to give up my pride.
Now, if you're walkin' this narrow road
Leadin' to th'gates of pearl;
When you meet your neighbors out on the street,
Then you won't look like th'world. (Chorus)

AMEN, AMEN, THERE'S A HIGHER POWER

Well, some come crippled and some come sick;
There's a higher power.
Till the healin's done, we ought not quit;
There's a higher power.

Chorus:

Amen, amen, there's a higher power;
Amen, amen, there's a higher power.

Well, when you get over in the book of Acts,
There's a higher power.
Plenty of people want to have that;
There's a higher power. (Chorus)

Well, Jesus said, "You shall be damned;"
There's a higher power.
You'd better let signs follow you around;
There's a higher power. (Chorus)

Well, some folks says a serpent is a man;
There's a higher power.
Those kind of people don't understand;
There's a higher power. (Chorus)

PLATE 161

Well, once Sister Browning gets on the floor:
There's a higher power.
You oughta' watch people hit the doors:
There's a higher power. (Chorus)

Following, as recorded during the service, are pieces of sermons and testimony extracted from the whole in an attempt to give some feeling for the spirit evident in these two aspects of a long and complicated service.

"I'm s'hoarse I can't hardly talk. How thankful I am that that Savior died for me. Brother! He's been good t'me! I've been in th'hospital an' th'doctor gave me up t'die. They sent me home—there was no hope. But th'Lord wasn't finished with me. No, He wasn't finished with me. He spared my life. I wanta' serve Him more than anything else in th'world. Y'know, th'Lord moved on me t'go up there an'take up that fire. Y'know, I used t'get up an' just hold it in my hands, an' I felt it not. Praise be t'God!"

"As I watched those brothers with th'serpents, it come t'me an' I thought, 'Lord, those things are deadly!' This song was on my mind and I said, 'Lord, these things are just as deadly t'us, the things of th'flesh are just as deadly to us as these serpents are to our flesh. It's death t'us th'same way if we let th'fruits of th'flesh

PLATE 162

ruin our lives. We're not of God, we're dead! We're dead as sin.'
I thought, 'Lord, that same spirit that's able to conquer that serpent,
yeah, that same spirit can save us from ruining our lives.' Glory
t'God!''

"You know, this seems more like old-time salvation than anything
I've seen or heared of. But still, I got t'work out m'own salvation.
I've got t'testify what th'Lord's done f'me, an' He has done a'plenty
for me. He's been *so* good t'me an' merciful t'me. I just pray tonight
for th'plan a'salvation that He has left here f'us. Tonight is th'way
built from earth t'heaven. I declare He wrote that f'us t'go by.
Y'know, when y'start out on a long trip, I've noticed, my children,
that y'have t'have a map t'go by. Y'know, children, they don't go
by th'map, they don't know where they a'going! Y'know, tonight,
that Bible's just like that. Hallelujah! Praise His Name! Oh, hallelujah, that it came t'me each day!

"We know, Brother Browning, we've heard enough good preachin'
here tonight, t'save th'whole world. If they'd just bow down and
accept th'Lord. Just let Him into our heart an' serve Him in the
beauty of holiness. Anything shorter than th'Word of God, you're
not a'gonna' make it. I'm gonna' climb higher an' higher an' higher.
Tonight, children, we're gonna' have t'look up, for th'perfect gift
comes from above. Hallelujah! We need some of them good gifts
tonight, don't we?

"You know, I see them signs upon our believers tonight. Oh, children, where else can He go t'see them signs? The full gospel preached, praise th'Lord! You know, people won't talk about th'signs that follow'em, children. I mean the serpents that's a dangerous sign. They don't care a bit t'go over there an' pray fer th'sick now because they know I'll tell them that sick person ain't a'gonna hurt-'em. But, boy, let a Baptist get a'hold of a big ol' snake an' they'll shore back off. I believe that with all m'heart. You know, tonight I wanta hold t'th'good Word of God. I don't believe we've got much longer to'hold *HIM* up—I believe He's a'comin' back. Everyone of ye pray for me."

"I'll tell ye what. Before I ever come up here, I always talk t'th'Lord about it. Then I ain't afraid t'come, if everything's all right, it's all right. 'At's a rule to go by. I don't pay no 'tention t'what my sister said, but I *have* to obey th'Lord. I've *GOT* to do what th'Lord says. I'm s'glad tonight that I'm livin' an' know Jesus. I'm glad tonight of th'name a'Jesus.

"I got t'thinkin' this, that th'Lord has been s'good t'us! But you know what? I'm more than glad, can't hardly wait f'th'time t'get started up. I'm not afraid when th'Lord tells me so.

"I done got paid tonight f'this trip a'ready. If I don't get t'stay f'tomorrow's service, I done got paid tonight. I believe in th'Holy Ghost tonight, an' I believe tonight that I really got it! An' second business, I *know* I got it! It won't let me go around a'talkin' 'bout my brothers an' sisters. An' it won't *let* me go down t'th'church an' just set an' look an' see what I can see an' see if I can see somethin' t'talk about. I'll tell ye tonight, I *LOVE* th'Lord!

"I believe in serpent handlin' a hun'erd percent. My wife never did believe in it. She always told me wasn't nothin' to it. Said it'uz th'devil's work. An' I got bit over here. 'At's been a long time ago. I've been a'handlin' 'em ever since. I ain't never quit. I won't *NEVER* quit! Until th'Lord tells me. Pray fer me."

The sermon stops, guitar chords blending in behind the final shouts and exhortations and hallelujahs. And suddenly the tiny frame building is filled with music. It is so loud it jams every crack, fills every crevice; and the congregation is on its feet, singing, clapping, swaying, filled with a joy and an urgency and an intensity that brings even those in the back crowding to the front. It is deafening. But it is not chaotic clamor. The hymn is still there, clear and strong and true, soaring above the noise and the shouts.

PLATE 163

Over the music and the rhythmic clapping of a hundred pairs of
hands, people begin to speak in tongues, to jerk involuntarily, to
raise their arms high and cry out the name of Jesus. And if the
spirit is true—if all the necessary conditions blend perfectly—suddenly a long flat box slides out from under a pew and serpents
are everywhere.

". . . they shall take up serpents . . ."

The following sections picture members of the congregation in
the act of receiving four of the gifts previously outlined (handling
serpents, holding fire, talking in tongues, and healing). We have
divided the gifts into sections for convenience as there are Bible
verses, pieces of interviews and so on that belong especially to each
gift. In an actual service, however, all of these things take place
simultaneously. The drinking of deadly poisons is not illustrated
here as that was not done in the services we attended. It had been
done in the past, however—once, we were told, even being verified

PLATE 164 "Th'Lord told us what we could do and that's exactly what we're doin'."

—Dexter

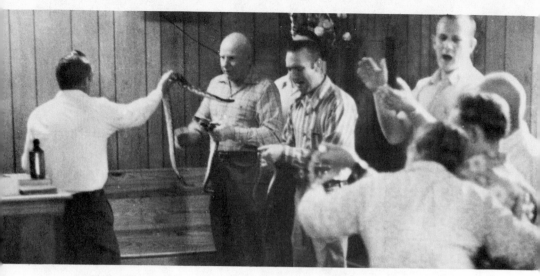

PLATE 165 As the music thunders, Dexter, who says, "I think th'most [serpents] I've held at one time is nine," pulls them from their boxes and passes them out to reaching hands. And as the intensity swells, some members of the congregation become so involved they find themselves dancing and waving their arms, despite the fact that poisonous serpents dangle from their hands.

PLATE 166 "If you believe that it ain't gonna bite you, then you got power. That gives you faith. And then th'Holy Ghost just has t'be there. You must have that. [When I hold a serpent] I just get down and hold it right out there. Sometimes I pray, but if I get afraid, or lose my faith, I get shed of it as quick as I can. If y'don't, it's dangerous. Say you got one and you lose faith, you better get shed of it or it'll bite you.

"Now they was a drunk man down here at a little church and he said, 'That thing won't bite.' And th'old man that had it said, 'That'll bite'cha directly.' And he raised th'lid hisself and he said, 'Now, that'll bite'cha.'

"And th'man said, 'It won't bite. It's got its teeth pulled.' And he had a handkerchief goin' around over it and it struck him on th'finger there. And he just dropped ever'thing and split that with a knife and began t'suck that. But he had t'go t'th'doctor with it. That'll rot your finger off. If th'Lord don't kill it, you better."

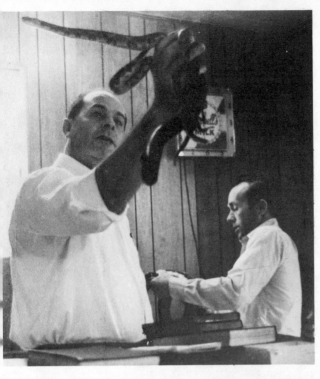

PLATE 167 "Preacher that I know got up and preached something and then he said, 'My brother's a preacher, too.'

"And I said, 'Let him come on.' He got up a'preachin', and when he got to preachin', he went and got three rattlesnakes that they brought out of that box, and he handled them a little bit and laid them up on th'Bible stand. And his brother was sittin' over right in th'corner and he was a'lookin' right this way like he was taking every word of it in.

"And he took these three over there and laid them right down right in his hand and they began to crawl. And one of them crawled up and bit him.

"This man was a'speakin' at that time and said, 'There's someone back here that believes their teeth's pulled.' And there was his brother bit. And he said, 'It ain't a'gonna hurt him.'

"My wife said—I don't know whether she said it out loud or not—said, 'It's a'gonna' kill that man.'

"Well, he got sick in a little bit and they took him out. And they prayed about an hour out in th'car lot. And somebody took him to Tennessee and his folks, after they'd see'd him, they took him to th'hospital. But by that time it was too late. He died in twenty-six hours."

PLATE 168 "One of th'members died in '40. That was a day, now, that I told 'em not t'bring-'em in. I told'em not t'bring'em in because these brothers in th'church had a little disagreement and weren't a'feelin' good towards each other. And I said, 'Don't bring'em in. Don't need it today.' And this man just brought one in over me and he took it in and took it out and this other boy got it and had it and just lookin' back over th'crowd and it bit him. That was on Sunday and he lived till Friday. Doctor come and he wouldn't let him doctor him. That's th'only one we ever had."

PLATE 169 "Th'way I feel about this, now—I been asked t'get out here and handle serpents and let'em take my picture. I don't believe in nothin' like that. If somebody catches me in th'spirit handlin' serpents, that's all right. But I don't get out here for a show. Th'only time that I handle anything is when th'Lord moves upon me—th'spirit of th'Lord.

—*Dexter*

PLATE 170 "Serpents is Dexter's work. He likes to do that and th'Lord just blesses him. Now that's his work. He gets blessed and he enjoys that just like some preachers do somebody that's lost and getting them converted. Now that's my work. [Not everybody wants to hold serpents at first.] In one church, they had a copperhead there and they held it and th'man set it on one of th'Bible stands and let loose of it. And it jumped way out into th'middle of th'floor. You should have seen th'people gettin' up from there and gettin' on top of their seats. But they caught it."

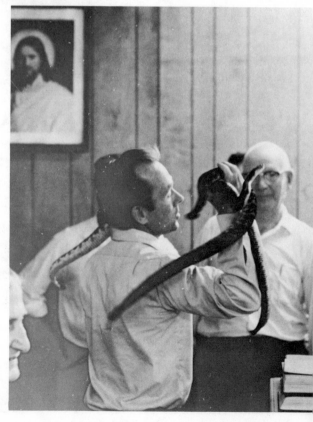

PLATE 171 "Everything done here is done by th'spirit of th'Lord. See, before th'Lord saved me, I could be out a'squirrel huntin' or somethin' like that and I would find one a'these [snakes] and it'd scare me s'bad I'd track my sign back—or maybe shoot th'thing and kill it and track my sign back, I'uz so afraid of it. And then th'Lord saved me and I never did think no more about it. This is th'job th'Lord give me t'do."

—*Dexter*

by a scientist from Clemson University. On that occasion, a man drank strychnine, supplied in a sealed vial by the scientist.

Of all the above ways of having "victory," perhaps the most visually dramatic is the holding of rattlesnakes and copperheads. The congregation member most actively involved with serpents is Dexter Callahan. He has been involved with them since that day he was saved and came to Christ ten years ago. Believing that God blessed him and gave him that job, he is the man who keeps most of the snakes used in the services. He believes it is his calling. A newspaper clipping he carries in his wallet tells of his recent arrest and fine by a local sheriff for carrying serpents to a public gathering—a custom outlawed by the state. And a recent piece written about him by a couple of journalists infuriated him because it hinted that he was simply unusually proficient at handling snakes, and gave not a word to his complete conviction that his ability to handle them is not a personal skill, but is totally a gift of the Holy Ghost.

Dexter is far from casual about his attitude toward serpents as his wife's brother-in-law was bitten and died, and he himself has been bitten twelve times—three of those in one night. He admits that he was "laid up" as a result of two of those bites, but claims that he wasn't affected at all by the other ten. Several times he was "in the spirit" when he first took them up, but the spirit left him while he was holding them. At other times, there were bad feelings in the room that ruined the effect of the blessing, and caused the serpents to strike. He remembers that when he was bitten by a copperhead, it felt like he had put his whole hand in fire.

So he approaches them with a respect bred of experience. He can sometimes pick them up in the woods, but only when he has his mind on the Lord. If he has what he calls a "carnal mind" (his thoughts on worldly things rather than God), he leaves them alone. But, during the service, when the spirit is upon him, he is a center of activity.

PLATE 172 "Everybody's got a certain amount of faith. If your intentions are goin' back home, you've got faith that you're goin' t'make it.
"Take my little boy. When he was about three years old, he didn't really understand what he was doin'. He said, 'Daddy, I want t'handle a big one [serpent].' I gave him a big one. I just gave him a *big* one. And he held his hand out and took it and I started telling him, I said, 'Son, if you do this, you gotta live with it.'"

—*Brother Huff*

PLATE 173 "I've seen people put snakes around their necks—in their bosoms. There was a woman once that had pretty long hair and a copperhead crawled right up in her hair. Th'copperheads ain't as dangerous as th'rattlers. Copperheads will bite you quicker, but th'rattle snakes'll kill you. They bust a man's heart. I heard a man say th'doctor said one man's heart was busted. He was killed."

PLATE 174 "I tell'em not t'keep th'snakes through th'wintertime, but they do sometimes. It's out a'season. It's a cold air thing that needs to be in th'ground when it comes their time. Then when it comes warm, they come out theirself. Dexter's got about eighty serpents, I think. He's got them at his house. Now I teach that two of them is enough, but they've had three boxes of them. Sometimes we can get our minds more on this than getting someone saved. The soul of th'man is worth more than this. Maybe you think you can do something that nobody else can do and then you get shook up and don't want to do that. Now that's a dangerous spot t'be in."

PLATE 175 "I been bit one time. It just stung for a few minutes and I never felt it n'more. Just a little sting. I might not a'been anointed. I just went t'stick m'hand out t'take it and it bit me right in th'palm of my hand. It never did bite me before and it never did bite me since." The speaker's wife believes that the bite might have been designed to be a sign to the congregation that even though he got bitten, he didn't get sick because he had the proper faith in God. "When I hold serpents, there's no feelin's. Nothin' but that there ain't no fear about you."

PLATE 176

PLATE 177 "Faith will kill the power of fire. Fire's got power, you know. It will burn you. It will burn up whole woods. It will burn up a house or whatever it gets to.

"Now I've seen this little bottle of propane gas been handled and that's hot. And there was another man one time that said he could handle that fire and he got his hands burnt to two big crispers."
—*Brother Huff*

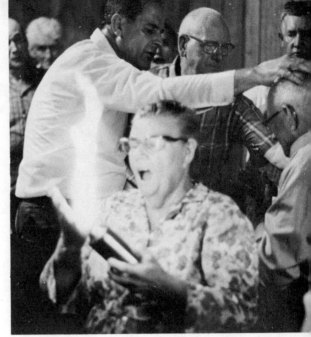

". . . nor was a hair of their head singed."

"See, they was goin' t'put these three Hebrew boys in th'fiery furnace if they didn't bow and worship what th'King had set up fer'em t'worship. And they refused. And th'strongest men they had bound these boys. And as they dropped'em in, it consumed these strong men, but it didn't hurt them three nary a bit. They got in there loose and walked about. Saw four then. That fourth one was like unto th'Son of God.

"We started with fire before we had serpents. Before we had any electricity, we had these little kerosene lamps that has a glass chimney that sits down on them. You know what I'm talking about? And they was hot, and we had them in th'church. It was the only kind of light we had. And [my wife] would shout up and dance up to that globe and take that off, and if it wasn't for the good Lord, it would blister you as soon as it touched you. It gets hot enough to blister you. My hands would be tougher than a woman's hands, but it would blister my hands. If I picked it up and lifted it off, it would leave a blister on each hand. But she would, and just shout right around and just feel fine.

"And she'd raise her hair up that way and run it through a carbide light [and it wouldn't singe]. You ever seen a carbide light? Them that's got a red streak that sticks out farther than that? My nephew said, 'That old fire won't burn.' He got that carbide light and stuck

PLATE 178 "My father, one time, was laying on th'floor sick and they come in and prayed for him. They had carbide lights back then. Money was hard t'get a'hold of. And so when they prayed for him, they said he come up a'jumpin', and he took one of them carbide lights right by th'face. And th'blaze should have burnt his hands off. But one of them fellows checked his hands for burns. No burns there.

"When I hold fire, it feels cool just like there's no fire there. One time I thought in myself I had a little faith and I wanted to handle it in such a way that people couldn't doubt that fire. You know, y'see people that kindly waver. I wanted them t'know there was no doubt about it. Well, I had a little faith and I pulled my shoe off and stuck [the flame] to my sock and left it there plenty long enough t'cut my sock apart. And about that time it come apart. It had been there long enough t'catch it on fire."
—*Brother Huff*

PLATE 179

it right to his hand there and it burnt a place. It burnt right through that tough part of his hand. He said, 'It *will* burn, won't it?' "

Several containers rested on the pulpit. Two of them were filled with kerosene and had large wicks in their necks. One was a Pepsi bottle, the other, a metal canister. Despite the activity swirling all around us, it was hard not to notice when one of these was lit, for the flames often rose a foot or more into the air.

We saw men at a pitch of intensity strip off their shoes and socks and hold the flames for minutes at a time under their bare feet. A woman thrust the fire right into her hair and held it there, and not a hair was singed.

". . . they shall lay hands on the sick, and they shall recover."

Throughout the church, oblivious for the moment to the serpents and fire around them, are tiny clusters of people, their attention riveted on a man or woman or child in the center. Usually that person is ill and has asked (or his parents have asked) that he be prayed for. Hands reach out, sometimes touching the afflicted part and sometimes not, and those outside the little circle often touch those who are touching the afflicted as if to make a human chain of energy.

PLATE 180

PLATE 181 [When there are five or six working over one person,] "maybe she will be anointed and th'rest of'em will be praying. Say you're sick. I don't know whether I'll be [able to anoint] till I come to you and pray. And then if th'anointin' gets in my hands, then I know it. You can feel it. Like electricity."

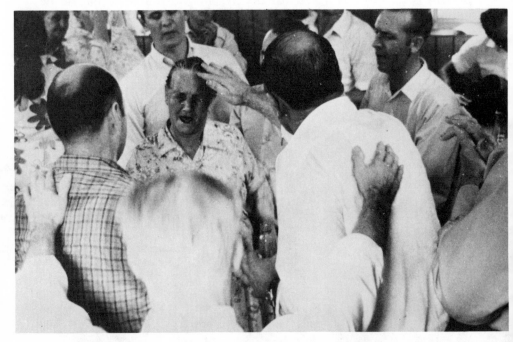

PLATE 182 A woman is being prayed for and anointed (note bottle of olive oil in the left hand of the man touching her forehead). Browning said, "And she gets healed. She got so she couldn't walk and they prayed for her, and she got up and danced all over th'place."

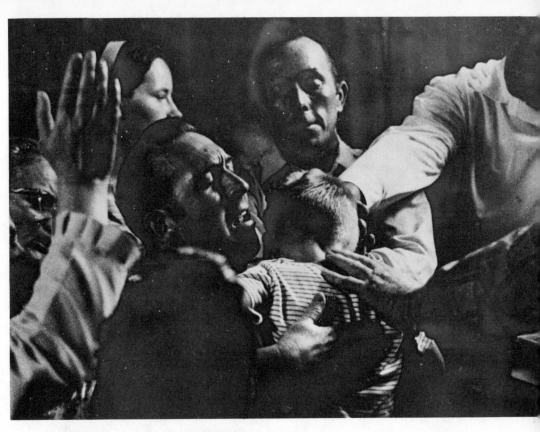

PLATE 183 "They brought a child to one of these here all day meetin's—and she was three or four year old—that couldn't walk. They'd set her down and her feet'ud just go all around. She couldn't stand on her feet. They brought her up there and prayed for her and then they brought her back and she'd walk. About four year old. It was just like th'man at th'beautiful gate that hadn't never walked."

PLATE 184 A diabetic is prayed for.

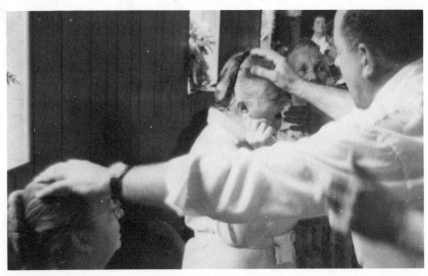

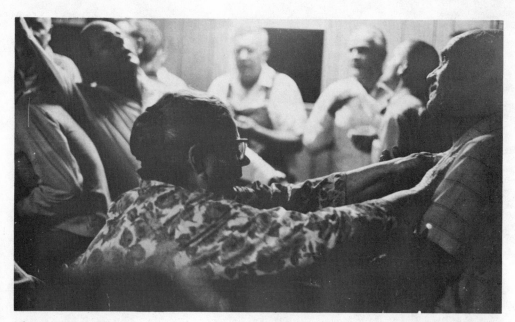

PLATE 185 Mrs. Browning prays for a man who has "an affliction in his chest."

PLATE 186 "This boy of mine had a cancer on his chin. We took him out t'th'doctor and he said, 'I don't know what it is but I'll cut this off and see what it is.' When he got th'report on it, it was cancer. And before I got t'th'doctor with him, I showed [my wife] at home that it was cancer. And she laid hands on him and healed him."

PLATE 187 "My wife can get in th'spirit and pick out a man that's sick and know he's sick and she don't know his name ner never seen him before. She can find he's sick. That spirit in her will let her know. Don't nobody have t'tell her."

PLATE 188 "I didn't learn from school or books. I learned from th'Lord. Before th'Lord saved me, I couldn't even read. I couldn't read at all. After th'Lord saved me, I got started in th'readin'. Now I've been servin' th'Lord ten year and ain't took as much as a cough drop. Before th'Lord saved me, it was a sight at th'medicine I took. Pockets full."

—Dexter

PLATE 189

"In my name shall they cast out devils, they shall speak with new tongues . . ."

The peak of intensity. The pinnacle of the service during which time those who are the luckiest, the most faithful, the most deserving receive the ultimate gift on earth: the gift of the Holy Ghost. Everything leads up to this. Holding serpents and handling fire are but the preliminaries. This is the climax. It is visible proof that you have received the Spirit of God; for when you have the true Spirit, you receive the Holy Ghost, and when you receive the Holy Ghost, you speak in tongues. And until you speak in tongues (which is the Spirit talking through you), you haven't carried your faith far enough; you haven't believed strongly enough. Only a few will make it which is, Browning and his followers believe, as it must be for "Jesus said only a few would find Him." Thus the intensity of the requests. "You've got to *ask* for the Holy Ghost to come!"

People crowd to the altar. They are anointed with olive oil, prayed over, demons are driven out, and those cleansed sometimes fall to their knees in an effort to reach the peak.

And when the Holy Ghost has come and gone, the fortunate are left with a gift to use to prove their faith: that of speaking in tongues, of being able to prophesy, of discerning spirits, or of knowledge.

> And when the day Pentecost was fully come, they were all with one accord in one place. And suddenly there came a sound from heaven as of a rushing mighty wind, and it filled all the house where they were sitting. And there appeared unto them cloven tongues like as of fire, and it sat upon each of them. And they were all filled with the Holy Ghost, and began to speak with other tongues, as the Spirit gave them utterance. And there were dwelling at Jerusalem Jews, devout men, out of every nation under heaven. Now when this was noised abroad, the multitude came together, and were confounded, because that every man heard them speak in his own language.
>
> —*Acts 2:1–6*

> And it shall come to pass in the last days, saith God, I will pour out of my Spirit upon all flesh: and your sons and your daughters shall prophesy, and your young men shall see visions, and your old men shall dream dreams; And on my servants and on my handmaidens I will pour out in those days of my Spirit; and they shall prophesy.
>
> —*Acts 2:17–18*

Then Peter said unto them, Repent, and be baptized every one
of you in the name of Jesus Christ for the remission of sins,
and ye shall receive the gift of the Holy Ghost.

—*Acts 2:38*

"Now that gift of the Holy Ghost, when you get that gift, you
can get a spiritual gift. So you come to this church here, and you
get a spiritual gift. You may get the gift of prophecy, or the gift
of praying. Or you may get the gift of discerning spirits, or the
gift of knowledge. If you get the gift of knowledge through that
spirit, then you'll have the knowledge of this Bible and you can
teach everyone of this knowledge."

"You've got to *ask* for th'Holy Ghost to come. [If it doesn't come]
you just ask for it more. Just keep asking. When it comes, it just
moves on you. It just operates. It's a feeling in th'flesh. You feel
good and you feel clear and you feel there's not any sin about you.
It'll come on you at times. We sit here, and you see th'wind blow
and we hear th'sound and we hear th'roar of the wind, but we can't
tell when it's coming and we can't tell where it's going. It goes
on. 'So is everyone born of th'Spirit', said th'Spirit. There's a sound
goes with it. Say you get th'Holy Ghost and you speak in tongues,
I can hear th'sound but I can't tell what you're sayin'. Let you be
a sound. Well, your tongue is gonna' speak when He comes—the
Holy Ghost. 'When He comes, He shall testify of me.' We read
that here in John 15:26."

"First time I got th'Holy Ghost, I spoke in tongues, and then I
didn't speak in it no more for a long time. I lost a day's work. I
was boss of th'railroad up here. Th'man was holdin' a Bible. And
I prayed and asked for [a blessing] over and over and over. And
other people were gettin' th'Holy Ghost—that was on a revival—
and I felt like I wanted it the worst I ever did in my life. And I
told my wife, I said, 'Don't fix me anything nice. I'm going to let
my men work today without me.' I was th'boss.

"And she said, 'Why?'

"And I said, 'I'm gonna pray.' I was gonna pray ten hours before
I went t'church. I was gonna pray till time t'go to church. And
she went off and let me. And I got on th'altar and got down to
pray. I was just layin' there and prayed. I prayed from six o'clock
to nine o'clock, and I know what I was saying. I was saying, 'Lord,
take my life and give me the Holy Ghost.'

"And then th'Holy Ghost came in and I was speakin'. I didn't

PLATE 190

PLATE 191   But ye shall receive power, after that the Holy Ghost is come upon you: and ye shall be witnesses unto me both in Jerusalem, and in all Judea, and in Samaria, and unto the uttermost part of the earth.

—*Acts 1:8*

know what. I knowed my tongue was movin' but I didn't know what
I was sayin' till that moved on.

"I guess it lasted fifteen minutes—or maybe not that long. Then
I came to myself and I could talk back. That's a mystery, ain't it?
That's a mystery."

Follow after charity, and desire spiritual gifts, but rather that
ye may prophesy. For he that speaketh in an unknown tongue
speaketh not unto men, but unto God: for no man understand-
eth him; howbeit in the spirit he speaketh mysteries. But he
that prophesieth edifieth the church. I would that ye all spake
with tongues, but rather that ye prophesied: for greater is he
that prophesieth than he that speaketh with tongues, except
he interpret, that the church may receive edifying.
                                                        —*I Corinthians 14:1–5*

Wherefore let him that speaketh in an unknown tongue pray
that he may interpret. For if I pray in an unknown tongue,
my spirit prayeth, but my understanding is unfruitful.
                                                        —*I Corinthians 14:13–14*

I thank my God, I speak with tongues more than ye all: yet in
the church I had rather speak five words with my understanding,
that by my voice I might teach others also, than ten thousand
words in an unknown tongue.
                                                        —*I Corinthians 14:18–19*

How is it then, brethren? when ye come together, every one
of you hath a psalm, hath a doctrine, hath a tongue, hath a
revelation, hath an interpretation. Let all things be done unto
edifying. If any man speak in an unknown tongue, let it be by
two, or at the most by three, and that by course; and let one
interpret. But if there be no interpreter, let him keep silence
in the church; and let him speak to himself, and to God.
                                                        —*I Corinthians 14:26–28*

Wherefore, brethren, covet to prophesy, and forbid not to speak
with tongues. Let all things be done decently and in order.
                                                        —*I Corinthians 14:39–40*

Browning says that when his followers are challenged, it is often
on the basis of the above passages of scripture. But he points out
that it is only better to prophesy *if* there is no interpreter available;
and it does say, ". . . forbid *not* to speak with tongues. . . ."

"When you speak in tongues, it just takes, and you don't know.

PLATE 192 But a certain man named Ananias, with Sapphira his wife, sold a possession, and kept back part of the price, his wife also being privy to it, and brought a certain part, and laid it at the apostles' feet. But Peter said, Ananias, why hath Satan filled thine heart to lie to the Holy Ghost, and to keep back part of the price of the land?

—*Acts 5:1–3*

Maybe you're praying, and it just comes down and you quit speaking in unknown tongues. It's a good feeling, a good feeling.

"If you're speaking in tongues and interpreting, we're getting what you're saying. See, you'll stop speaking to God and you'll go to speaking to us telling what the Holy Ghost is saying through you. Then it edifies us. But if you can't interpret it, you're still speaking to God.

"If you can speak in tongues and then interpret, you're just as great as Him speaking every word we can understand. You can speak in tongues and then tell us what it said, [but if you can't interpret], it still edifies you. And you're getting the knowledge of God about something or other that you can tell us later on when you get to speaking back naturally again."

"My wife has two gifts. She has the gifts of discerning and prophecy. Discerning means she can tell whether it's a'workin'. She can be a'talkin' to you and tell whether you believe it or not. You ain't a'speakin' it, but she can tell. If you're thinkin' somethin' about th'Bible, she can tell what you're thinkin' about it.

"It's like in Acts 5:1–3. He knew he'd left some of it back. He [was discerning]. Like I say, 'Me and her sold this and we're bringin' you all the money.' But we put some back—laid some away. And we just say we sold it for [the amount] we brought you. If you have the gift of discerning, then you know all that. That's th'way it works. Now it may not work all th'time, but it's got to work when that Spirit is at work. When that Spirit works that way, you can tell if anyone's lyin' to you.

"Now I'll tell you one thing that she prophesied about. She prophesied there was going to be a casket brought in the church house and it's not going to be open. She didn't know who the person was. But she gave that prophecy out and said there was going to be one. Well, this man I was telling you about got bit by that rattlesnake and died. And the undertakers came and got him and brought him over and said, 'We can't open it. That poison's gone through his system.' And they never did open that casket up.

"Well, then later she prophesied again. She said, 'There's going to be another casket brought in and it's not going to be opened.' We still didn't know who that was. And it was an eleven-year-old boy. There was a man over there holding a revival and in the meeting was a boy that had some feed for somebody that he was going to take after the meeting. He had one of these big long trucks with dual wheels, two wheels, you know, them big wheels. And the meeting broke and he got this truck and started up the road and this little boy jumped on the back of the truck—on the flat bed, you know. And he went up the road just a little and he must have jerked him off. Some thought there might be one that shoved the boy off, but we never did know. He went up and unloaded the feed and came back and saw the boy in the road and he blowed at him and he never moved. And he blowed again; he never moved. And he got out and his head was just smashed flat and they brought him to the undertakers and said, 'You can't open the casket.' But she knowed about it.

"There was another man. This man was a man that would maybe pray for a little while and then quit. Seemed like if you called him out and offered him a dram of whiskey and, well, he couldn't resist that. Or he'd want to play pool or somethin'r'nother. She was sitting by her sister-in-law and she said, 'I see somebody's light go out tonight.' She said that meant the Spirit.

"We was sitting in the church house, and her sister-in-law later said, 'You know who?'

"She said, 'No.' Then in a few minutes I think she said, 'Yes, I do now.' She said, 'It's that man sitting right there.' Well, he went

PLATE 193   Then Philip went down to the city of Samaria, and preached Christ unto them. And the people with one accord gave heed unto those things which Philip spake, hearing and seeing the miracles which he did. For unclean spirits, crying with loud voice, came out of many that were possessed with them: and many taken with palsies, and that were lame, were healed. And there was great joy in that city. But there was a certain man, called Simon, which beforetime in the same city used sorcery, and bewitched the people of Samaria, giving out that himself was some great one: To whom they all gave heed, from the least to the greatest, saying, This man is the great power of God: And to him they had regard because that of long time he had bewitched them with sorceries. But when they believed Philip preaching the things concerning the kingdom of God, and the name of Jesus Christ, they were baptized, both men and women. Then Simon himself believed also: And when he was baptized, he continued with Philip, and wondered, beholding the miracles and signs which were done. Now when the apostles which were at Jerusalem heard that Samaria had received the Word of God, they sent unto them Peter and John: who, when they were come down, prayed for them, that they might receive the Holy Ghost: (For as yet he was fallen upon none of them: only they were baptized in the name of the Lord Jesus.) Then laid they their hands on them, and they received the Holy Ghost.

—*Acts 8:5–17*

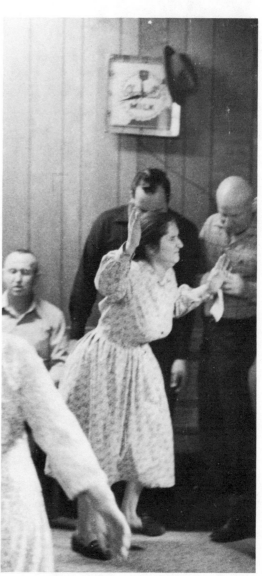

PLATE 194 And he commanded us to preach unto the people, and to testify that it is he which was ordained of God to be the Judge of the quick and dead. To him give all the prophets witness, that through his name whosoever believeth in him shall receive remission of sins. While Peter yet spake these words, the Holy Ghost fell on all them which heard the Word. And they of the circumcision which believed were astonished, as many as came with Peter, because that on the Gentiles also was poured out the gift of the Holy Ghost. For they heard them speak with tongues, and magnify God. Then answered Peter, can any man forbid water, that these should not be baptized which have received the Holy Ghost as well as we? And he commanded them to be baptized in the name of the Lord. Then prayed them him to tarry certain days.

—Acts 10:42–48

PLATE 195

PLATE 196 "My wife'll go t'speakin' in tongues, and we'll not nary a'one know what she's sayin'. She'll speak in tongues maybe for an hour and then interpret it herself—tell us what she's sayin'."

PLATE 197 "If they speak in tongues, nobody understands'em but God. But God can anoint you t'interpret and then you can tell what I'm a'sayin' if I'm speakin' in tongues. If th'same Spirit I'm speakin' with, you get it, then you can tell till we can all understand. But it's got t'come from th'same Spirit."

PLATE 198

out of the church house and never did come back in no more till later. I was having a prayer meeting just across the road. I was having a prayer meeting there on Thursday night and he come in. I believe he had a gun. You know what a pistol is, don't you? I believe he had a gun on him. And he came in and I went to him and he was sitting in a chair, and I was trying to get him to come back and pray for the Lord. Finally, he said, 'Kenneth, I won't tonight but I will later,' and that was on Thursday night. That Sunday him and his son-in-law got some whiskey and they got to drinking. They lived up in the holler above the church. They went on down, him and his son-in-law, about three miles down below the valley. They got in a fight and his son-in-law beat him up and throwed him out. He was by the side of the road and they brought him to the new hospital. I went to see him and they had him up and he never did speak. He just hollered. And they moved him to Louisville, and I believe he lived fifty-one days and died. She said that the man's lights were out. That was in the Spirit. She saw this.

PLATE 199

DINNER ON THE GROUNDS

It is four-thirty in the afternoon. The Sunday service has lasted nearly six hours without pause. Everyone is drained. They walk out of the church and across the street where, set out on long tables, are covered dishes the women in the congregation brought with them that morning. It comes near to being more food than we have

PLATE 200

PLATE 201

ever seen before. We are so tired from the exertion of running videotape equipment, three cameras, and three tape recorders that we simply stretch out on the grass under trees and eat, hardly speaking to each other, barely able to find the energy to take even a few photographs of the picnic itself. And, later in the day, we go back to the building, pack our equipment, and drive across the mountain to set up again in the little frame church where Reverend Browning will hold yet another service before time for sleep.

PLATE 202

SUNDAY NIGHT

Sunday night a handful of weary people turn up in the little church. The pace of the last few days shows in Browning's face. And rather than a full sermon, he simply talks, quietly and with tremendous sincerity. At times his voice is almost inaudible. But the people feel his warmth—know he cares and they respond. In many ways, it is the most personal, most moving service of all.

"In th'last days, th'Bible tells us, a prayerless time'll come, when men will be lovers of their own selves, proud and blasphemous, disobedient of th'parents, truce-breakers, false security, without natural affection. Oh, it's terrible. It ain't just one talkin', it's everybody you see right here, just talkin' 'bout just how the time is changin', how the time is changin'; it certainly is.

"I'm thinkin', while I'm settin' there an' singin' that song, th'young people, if they don't know nothin' 'bout th'Lord, they ain't got nothin' t'build th'future on, have they? [Congregation: "Right. True."]

"Y'know there's s'many people that don't know what's gonna happen, an' they don't know of th'here-after, an' they're just a'goin', and they don't understand just what is gonna happen. They don't understand where they goin' to, if death was t'come along. Do they? [Congregation: "No-o-o."]

"Now I'uz thinkin' about down at—, a man had a girl, an' her boyfriend, they were started back to a college, an' on their way, they got killed in a car wreck. Both of them got killed. Y'know, we might start out tonight in a car from here t'—. And th' people, they don't understand th'danger an' you can hear s'many people gettin' in wrecks. Y'just heard th'news that somebody's going out [getting killed] every time y'hear it nearly. Like my daughter and I was coming from—an' I don't know if Brother Clifford or Brother David was with me a'drivin', and I said, 'Aren't you afraid?' She said, 'No, I'm not afraid,' I said, 'Aren't you afraid of this seventy mile an hour, something to happen to th'car, or a blow-out or something?' She said, 'No, I ain't afraid.' Y'know, seems like it's th'hardest thing t'git into th'people's minds that they's something out here that we got t'build up and while we're alive, or we go down into a lake of fire. Go down into a lake of fire. Y'know, people ain't taught that, they ain't taught that an' they seem like they don't understand about it. Y'can't hardly git nobody t'pay any attention now, can ye? [Congregation: "No."]

"I remember what Brother Turner said. That man went down on to the city Samaria an' changed that city down there. Yeah. The city of Samaria. An' went an' preached Christ to'em. An' they gave heed t'that. Y'know, preachin' would be a good job if people would just give heed. [Congregation: Yeah.]

"Yeah, just give heed. Now y'know when my parents raised me, an' I was up growin', an' I didn't know—I just thought that'd be all they was to it [life]. I just thought that'd be all they was to it. I'uz never taught heaven or a new earth t'go to, or a people who'd never have n'more sorrow nor pain nor death, nor the part we'd go to if we died in our sins. I didn't know about that. Just come in a little bit of killin' a man a time or two, and just thought— well, I didn't think about no penitentiary, I didn't think about no man locking me up if I did bad, and maybe for years an' years that I'd not be able t'get out. And I ain't been taught about that. Y'know this Bible will teach us peace, peace with all men, and never harm nobody. To have our minds set on heavenly things. That they's a spiritual kingdom that we got to get into while we're here. It said they was first preached that they'd not get in because of un- believin'. Here we got t'believe just th'right way t'get in. We can't just think if somebody's been teachin' us, we can't believe if they're not teachin' us right, if they won't let us in. We've got t'have this plan. I seen in th'paper the other day—had a boy's picture—that he started preachin' when he was four years old. I don't know what kind of a preacher. But I do know when I hear somebody preachin', I do know when they're preachin' these things that Jesus set down. I do know that. An' if we're not taught that kind of a doctrine, we're not gonna make it. I don't know why. I can't understand why that they's s'many different ways in a Bible, and they teach it one way, and the Bible teaches more than one faith, and how many different sects of religion they are in our world. One man told me they was twenty-three hundred different churches in the United States. And you heard me read today that Jesus sent out Peter—'upon this rock I'll build my church'—now, that's the only one we ever know anything about. That's the only one you can ever find out about in this Book. You can't read about those other churches in this—the one He built is the only one you can read about. But you can't hardly get nobody to believe it. [Congregation: That's right.]

"Back when I was a boy, the first Bible I ever saw was in such fine print, and it had no concordance and no reference, and you just had to turn through it till you found something about it. Now they got it where you can just git a subject up, an' seems like it's

PLATE 203

s'much easier. In my day, when I was a boy, they ain't nobody who'd ever seen nobody hardly, readin' [the Bible]. When I was gettin' up about growed, I saw my uncle on Sunday sittin' out under th'shade of a tree in a warm meader a'readin' th'Bible. He was the only man. When we got married, we didn't know nary a thing about th'law. We didn't know nothin'. We'd heard somebody in the old time preachin' that God so loved th'world that He gave His only begotten Son. Said, whoever believes in you shall not perish, but have Everlasting Life. Now then, tell us how we could get Eternal Life. You might read every bit of this till you find out what to do— it won't help *me* none. I've got t'know how t'do this. [Congregation: That's right.]

"So it seems t'me that men and women today has gotta have somebody that knows about this God t'tell'em. God is tellin' ya'what t'do. I just thought, 'Well, I'm kinda tired, we've had meetin' for a few nights standin'—five or six nights—and a lengthy meetin' to-day' and I thought, 'Well, they'll not be many out and I'm not much interested.' But seems like I got here and I got so interested in this. And you know I've got interested in this tonight—far more than when the house was full. Sometimes we say, 'Well, there won't be many out, but there's some soul out there that needs help.' You know, if the Man hadn't taken a lot of pains fer me, I never would have made it. I never would have got into this if He hadn't taken a lot of pains to straighten me out. And tried and tried. You know, He told th'preacher, He said, 'Preach th'Word.' And He told him t'be incessant. Sometimes you get up here and you think there's no ceasing with this. You've got to get up here and make an effort. But if He said, 'Just sit down,' you wouldn't do nothin'. Getting up—that's what He's talking about, ain't it? To be incessant. Now it's good when you're incessant, and it's a tribute to you.

"You know I'm s'pleased with Bobby [directing his attention to a boy in the congregation] tonight, that I could read [that] Jesus went through death, and give His life, and suffered for th'church, that He called these men [apostles] and give'em His command t'go and teach'em. All nations, and that fits us into it, too. That it's Russia; that it's ever' nation under heaven, to hear the apostles teach. Now different sects, there's a difference in Bible teaching. That's a little bit different, well, that's what we'll do. Some of'em's teachin' one way and some another—and they're getting mixed up.

"I know this Book—when I got started out in this, when I was a deacon in th'church, and they taught just like it is in the King James Version. But now this don't suit ever'body. My brother-in-law dreamed a dream about me and said I had this here King James Version; I'm a'preachin' an' somebody come up behind me with a gun, and said, 'Now, you can't preach that. You can't preach out of that King James Version no more.' Try and stop me from it.

"You know, we don't know what we gettin' into. We don't know if th'world's gonna stand for fifty years or twenty-five years, and it might be the shortest time. [Congregation: Yeah, it might.]

"People don't know. He said when they say peace and safety—then some destruction come upon mankind, and they shall not escape. You know, there's nations might think they're gettin' together, and all this time they're gettin' prepared t'take men's lives. And we just might be destroyed at any time. I don't believe God will let any man, any nation, destroy the world. I believe He'll do it Hisself when He gits ready. I believe He's gonna burn it up. I believe He's gonna burn it up with th'fire and brimstone that He's got in store. He's gonna do. Yeah. They may be a third part of th' people killed or just an awful lot of them, but when God gets ready, He's gonna destroy every man on earth. [Congregation: Yes, He is.]

"I wish I'd known this when I was a boy, I'll tell ya. I would of done a lot better. Don't you think so? I shore do. I didn't know what t'do. Instead of lookin' on somebody don't know a thing about this—we ought to be sorry for'em. They don't know. Ain't that right? Any of you read about that man that they called Solomon in the Old Testament? And think about th'things, the harmful things that he done, and he said he done it, too. Didn't he? He didn't know what to do. He didn't know what to do. He thought he was doin' th'will of God. Didn't he? I just thought about that scripture, and I'll read it now. Th'last chapter of th'Old Bible. [He reads the scripture.] We hear about earthquakes—said they'd be in diverse places—

several places. And you know we could be right here in th'church house and there'd come an earthquake and we'd never know what happened. They come in different places, and we just don't know when this is comin'. They've got s'much wisdom in th'world, and they've been makin' s'many new inventions. The world of wisdom knew not God. Well, it's comin' from some other source then. It's coming from the wicked man. He's invented all evil things. He's th'inventor of that. And it's just gettin' worse and worse and worse. I told m'granddaughter that went down to college—I told her to take her a Bible along, and I told her I wanted her to read the Acts of the Apostles. I said that's th'book that we need to know about. All these children ain't never heard nobody preach out of Acts of the Apostles. I didn't know they was any such a thing as th'gift of th'Holy Ghost. I didn't know He said to repent. I didn't know He said these things. The Bible says, 'God hath revealeth unto us by His Spirit.' By His Spirit. God said unto me—He's not going to reveal unto me what I want to look for, but He's revealing t'people an' givin' them th'revelation of things what *He* wants them t'know about. An' He has t'do that by th'Spirit of God. That's right. [Congregation: Amen.]

"I think it would be good for us to pray. Y'know they's s'many things, an' y'know these people that they call th'Holiness people, when ever'thing fails, they want them to pray. I'm s'glad I started praying when I was not sick. Not down sick. And they'll say, 'Lord, I'm sick and I want you to heal me.' I started out in this when I wasn't sick. An' I've never been sick in m'life. I've never lost a day's work of being sick in my life. Praise th'name of Jesus. And I say it's th'Lord that gives us strength. It's th'Lord that keeps diseases off us. That's right. I believe that. [Congregation: That's right. I know it is.]

"If this young man started out in this and held th'Lord, well, he's got wonderful promises, ain't he? 'Honor the Creator,' and He said, 'Honor thy father and mother, and thy days shall be long upon the earth.' Didn't He? Hallelujah!

[Whole congregation prays out loud, each his own prayer.]

"If we live right, we won't have a bit of trouble. Not a bit of trouble. If we live the way it's on the paper here. What about that? And the Spirit'll let us know. Here's this sister right here that's never been able t'go t'school t'read, but th'Spirit of God will let her know things. Hallelujah! Jesus never went to school. Nobody's talked about Him. How does He know letters? His parents never sent Him to school—He had the wisdom of God. How does He know such wisdom as He's got? Hallelujah! It come from the Wise

Man, the Man that gives us our wisdom. Praise the name of Jesus, praise His wonderful name. I wish I could get ever'one of you tonight—that you'd say, 'Jesus, I need You more than anything.' Hallelujah, praise the name of Jesus. They ain't but one way that we can know. We can't see God, we can't see th'Holy Ghost, we can't see Jesus. They're all up yonder, but the Holy Ghost is here, but He's something that you can't see here on earth. One man was all that was ever able to see that [Holy Ghost]. That's John the Baptist. God said unto him, 'You see the Holy Ghost.' Glory to God! I can see you moving, but I can't see in you. It's something that gets inside. He's in th'Father, he's in Jesus. He'll be in you. Jesus had Him in Him when He was baptized. He saw It come to Him in the bodily shape of a dove. Ain't that so? If God made man in the image of the Holy Ghost, you couldn't see man. He never made him in the image of the Holy Ghost because the Holy Ghost is different from God. God is a person. But you can't see Him. I believe that's the reason so many people don't believe in Him.

"The young people in school comin' up now is in a different shape. Lot of them don't believe in God. They just don't know just what kind of shape they are in. We ought t'be so sorry for these young people—we ought to do our greatest to try to help them. Ain't that right? It certainly is right.

"Praise the name of Jesus! On the Word of God we find out who God is. We certainly do. It's good to have education. I'm not saying nothing about that. It's good t'have the education to read this Bible.

"Everything went so good today—everything went s'good. Yes, praise the name of Jesus! Bobby, pray, and when you feel like it, that you want to go to th'water and be brave in His name, don't be a bit ashamed to say, 'Preacher, I want to be baptized.' They's something promised for people who repent and are baptized. There's something promised, Dorothy [directing his attention to a girl in the group], when we repent, when you get ready to be baptized, they's something that the Lord has promised to you, that nobody can't take from you. They can't nobody take from you that, can they? [Congregation: No. Praise th'Lord!]

"Still, there's s'many people that want us t'pray for'em. They's s'many people that's in trouble. When you give in a request the Lord knows just what you need. He said just let your request be made known. I'm going to invite ever'body that will to get on their knees and pray for Bobby tonight. God bless this young man."

[Everybody prays out loud. Then they sing several songs together and the service ends.]

APPENDIX

By Bill Leonard

BAPTISTS

The Baptists are perhaps the most diverse denomination in America. At last count there were at least fifty-three groups in the United States claiming the name Baptist in one form or another. The Baptists spread across Appalachia in such structured denominations as the Southern Baptist Convention, in loosely knit groups of Primitive Baptists, and in fiercely independent local congregations. Beyond the name, and a few common practices, the people called Baptists could not always agree on where they came from nor what they believed about the gospel and the church.

Baptist Beliefs:
Agreement and Disagreement

There are, however, some common beliefs shared by most Baptist denominations. First, Baptists magnify the importance of the scripture as the primary source of authority for the church. They are among those Christian bodies which advocate "no creed but the Bible" in matters of faith and doctrine. Historically, Baptists tend to avoid the use of creeds as binding upon the conscience of the individual.

The concern for freedom of conscience, or "soul liberty," has been a second characteristic of most Baptist groups. The individual is ultimately responsible for personal decisions regarding Christian faith and God alone is the ultimate judge of human conscience. This concern for soul competency was a major factor in the long-time Baptist support for freedom of religion and opposition to any state interference in matters of religion.

Third, most Baptists place great emphasis on the autonomy of the local church in determining policies and procedures without the coersion of external ecclesiastical structure. Local autonomy, as much as any factor, has led to the proliferation of a variety of

Baptist denominations, individual churches, and doctrinal differences, as well as a hesitancy to cooperate with other Christian groups. In most Baptist denominations, each congregation functions independently of any other. Baptists have defended this belief as strenuously as any which they possess. The stress on local autonomy has led most Baptists to be hesitant to speak of the "Baptist Church" but rather of "Baptist churches," each one responsible for its own policies.

Fourth, Baptists often define the church as a local congregation, composed of believers who have professed personal faith in Christ and have received baptism by immersion. The church, therefore, is to be made up only of those who testify to an evangelical, pietistic experience of heart religion. Faith is highly personal and often comes to the individual through a dramatic, life-changing conversion experience.

Fifth, baptism is viewed as that symbolic expression of inward grace through which the believer identifies with Christ's burial and resurrection. It is symbolic in the sense that it carries no inherent grace and points to an internalized experience of conversion. Baptism is to be administered only to believers by means of the immersion or dipping of the entire body in water. In this method, the new Christian reenacts Christ's baptism and is received into membership of the local congregation. In the earliest Baptist churches of the seventeenth and eighteenth centuries, baptism was usually administered to adults upon profession of faith in Christ. By the nineteenth and twentieth centuries, however, many Baptist groups were baptizing children and adolescents in increasing numbers, sometimes as early as five or six years of age.[1]

Beyond these common characteristics, Baptists are divided over numerous matters of theology and practice. Questions regarding who may be saved, the process of salvation, the possibility of falling from grace, the role of the clergy, and the place of missions receive varied response from Baptist groups. Perhaps no greater differences have occurred among Baptists than in the theories regarding origins.

Baptist Origins: Whence and Whither?

The most familiar and popular explanation for Baptist beginnings, particularly prominent among the churches of Appalachia, is the view that Baptists can be traced along a "trail of blood" back to John "the Baptist" the New Testament Church. In this theory Baptists stand in a line of churches directly descended from the church of the New Testament era and are, therefore, older than Catholic or Protestant expressions of the church.

This view was particularly important on the American frontier as Baptists sought to establish the credibility of their biblical interpretation and their origins. When debating Methodists or Presbyterians, Baptists could point beyond Wesley or Calvin to a church founded at the time the New Testament was being written. In debating Campbellites who claimed to have restored the New Testament church, Baptists could insist that their churches had always existed in some form throughout Christian history and therefore needed no restoration.

This nineteenth-century movement was known as Landmarkism. Its advocates sought to distinguish the "landmark" principles which constituted the true church on earth. They cited Proverbs 22:28: "Remove not the ancient landmark which thy fathers have set."

In Landmarkism, the church was founded on Jesus Christ, who had conferred his authority, not on a succession of apostles, but on a succession of local congregations made up of duly baptized believers who professed personal faith in Christ. For the Landmarkist there were seven marks of the true church:

1. The church composes the Kingdom of God.
2. The church is a visible institution.
3. The church's locality is on earth (no universal church).
4. The church is a local organization, a single congregation.
5. Church membership is limited to those who have experienced personal faith and regeneration.
6. Baptism is a symbol, administered only to believers (by immersion).
7. The Lord's Supper is an ordinance, a memorial given only to members of the local congregation.

Throughout Christian history God had preserved churches of this nature and, thus, the true church had survived. Religious groups which did not conform to these New Testament doctrines were not churches but "societies," lacking proper ordination, baptism, and biblical doctrines.

Landmark concepts of the church indirectly influenced Baptist policies on baptism and church membership. Even today, many Baptist churches or denominations refuse to accept the baptism of those who have been baptized by other methods (sprinkling or pouring) or by other non-Baptist churches. Some require re-baptism of all who have not received immersion, while others require the re-immer-

sion of all who have not received baptism in a Baptist church. Landmark views were also applied to the phrase "close communion,"
which restricted the Lord's Supper only to those who were members
of the local congregation in which the Supper is observed. Landmarkism is more prominent in the South and Southwest, having
begun in the 1850s in Tennessee and Kentucky. The principles of
a succession of "Baptist" churches existing from the New Testament
times to the present, appears in various forms among Baptists in
America and in Europe.[2]

A second theory of origins is that modern Baptists were indirectly
related to the radical Anabaptists of the sixteenth-century Protestant
Reformation. These Swiss and German dissenters refused to baptize
infants, favoring a baptism of believers, usually administered by
pouring water on the convert's head. The first Anabaptists appear
in 1525 in Zurich, and are best represented today in the Mennonite
and Hutterite communions. Their concern for a believer's church,
adult baptism, congregational church polity, and freedom of religion
are compatible with Baptist views. However, their practice of passive
resistance to war and their refusal to take oaths in civil matters
distinguish them from early Baptists. Their influence is at best indi-
rect, though many historians are divided over the matter of Anabap-
tist impact on early Baptists.[3]

A third theory proposes that modern Baptists grew out of English
Separatist Puritanism of the early 1600s. The Separatists were convinced that the Anglican Church was a false church and desired to
separate themselves from it. They founded a church of believers,
made up only of those who could profess personal faith in Christ.
Members constituted the church on the basis of a covenant with
God and one another.

Under the leadership of John Smyth a group of Separate Baptists
fled to Holland in 1608. There they became convinced that baptism
was to be given only after persons experienced personal faith in
Christ (the Separatist Puritans continued the baptism of infants).
Around 1609, Smyth baptized himself and the other members of
his small congregation, and the first recognizable Baptist church
was born. By 1612, a group of them had returned to England and
churches soon spread throughout Great Britain. Many scholars support this theory as the clearest explanation of Baptist origins.[4]

Baptist Beliefs:
Doctrinal Positions

These early English believers were later known as General Baptists, because of their belief that Christ died for all persons (general atonement). They subscribed to the views of Jacob Arminius, the Dutch theologian, who proposed an alternative to the hyper-Calvinism and predestinarian views prevalent in many Protestant churches in the seventeenth century.

The General Baptists believed that God would save all who came to Him by repentance and faith. This salvation was available to those who responded to God's grace by an act of their free will. Men and women were, therefore, free to choose, reject, or ignore the grace of God. If the human will could actively choose Christ, it was also free to reject Him later on. Thus, General Baptists believed that it was possible to "fall from grace" and reject the salvation which one had once possessed. General and Free Will Baptists continue to hold this doctrine.

The Calvinist perspective was represented by the Particular Baptists, who suggested that Christ's death applied only to an elect minority. All persons were totally depraved and could be saved only by the grace of God. If and when grace was given, the individual could not resist it. God was sovereign, and salvation came only from Him. The atonement of Christ applied only to those who were elected by God to salvation. Primitive and Two-Seed-in-the-Spirit-Predestinarian Baptists represent this view.

The Particular Baptists are credited by many scholars with establishing immersion as the basic method of baptism in Baptist churches. This probably began around 1641 in England, and took the form of dipping the whole body in water as a sign of burial and resurrection with Christ. Prior to that time, the method of baptism was by afflusion, the pouring of water on the head of the new convert.

Baptists in America:
Persecution and Growth

Baptists generally trace their American roots to that perennial religious radical, Roger Williams, who came to Massachusetts in 1631 as a Separatist Puritan preacher. His abrasive personality, his criticisms of Puritan intolerance, and their exploitation of the Indians led to his exile from that colony in 1636. Given sanctuary by the Narragansett Indians, Williams purchased land from them, founding

Rhode Island as a haven for other dissenters. Williams was also instrumental in the establishing of the First Baptist Church in America at Providence, probably in 1639. While soon rejecting Baptist views to become a "Seeker," awaiting some new revelation, Williams was an important influence on early American Baptists. Others came to Rhode Island and by 1641 a congregation was founded at Newport. These churches were Calvinistic in theology. Indeed, Calvinism was a major influence upon colonial Baptists. Persecution of Baptists continued in Massachusetts and Connecticut, while Baptist churches spread to the middle colonies, particularly Pennsylvania.

Baptists headed south in the 1690s and founded what is now the First Baptist Church of Charleston, South Carolina. The congregation was made up of immigrants from England and Maine, some of whom shared both General and Particular Baptist views. The first pastor, William Screven, who arrived in 1696, was a Particular Baptist who shaped the Calvinistic direction of the church and succeeding churches which spread into certain parts of the South. These "old" Baptist churches, with their Calvinistic theology, educated clergy and ordered worship later characterized by Baptists in the more urban, aristocratic arenas of southern life.

Another source of Baptist influence in the South came from the Separate Baptists of the first Great Awakening. The awakening, which reached its height in the 1740s, was a period of religious enthusiasm characterized by emotional worship services, dramatic conversions, and exuberant preaching. Presbyterians, Congregationalists, Baptists, and other religious groups were affected by these revivals.

Many Baptists were divided over the emotionalism and methods of the awakening. The Regular Baptists looked with suspicion upon revival techniques, favoring the more traditional ways of preaching and conversion. The Separate Baptists were those who supported the actions of revivalists and advocated a more aggressive style of evangelism.

In 1755, a group of Separate Baptists came from New England to Sandy Creek, North Carolina. Led by two preachers, Shubal Stearns and Daniel Marshall, these Separates formed the Sandy Creek Baptist Church. Within the next twenty years it became the mother church of some forty-two churches.

The Separate Baptists brought their revivalistic preaching and conversionalistic theology into the South. The churches of Appalachia have been greatly affected by this strong emphasis on personal evangelism.

Separate Baptist churches spread rapidly in Virginia, where the preachers frequently came in contact with the long arm of the law over their refusal to adhere to laws regulating the relationship of church and state. In Virginia, where the Anglican Church was the official religion, non-Anglican preachers had to secure licenses from the state. All citizens, Anglican or not, were taxed for support of the Anglican establishment. When Baptists and others refused to secure the proper licenses or attacked the established church, they were harassed and often imprisoned by the authorities. Increasingly Baptists supported separation of church and state in Virginia and throughout the colonies.

The Baptist Ministry in the Mountains: The Farmer-Preacher

As Baptist churches were established in the southern highlands and other frontier areas, they turned for leadership to the farmer-preacher, an individual who reflected the practical situation and met the spiritual needs of the mountain churches. These early pastors were men who settled in the mountains, worked their land during the week, exercising their ministerial calling alongside their physical labor. They were often laymen, converted in revivals and "called" to preach. With the autonomy of Baptist congregations they could found churches wherever they could gather a group. The church acknowledged their leadership and often that was ordination enough. Sometimes they were licensed to preach, sometimes formally ordained in the presence of other ordained church leaders, and sometimes they had no formal ordination beyond recognition of the local church.

Most of these men had little formal education; some could not read at all. But they could preach, visit, offer hope to the sick and the dying and for those not necessarily educated or sophisticated, those were the primary pastorly gifts. In fact, Appalachian Baptists have long been suspicious of education for the clergy lest it interfere with the simple preaching of heart religion. While this view is changing in many Baptist churches, some still warn that college and seminary "ruined many a good preacher." Others hope that head learning will enhance, not destroy, genuine piety.

The other officer of a Baptist church is the deacon, elected by the congregation on the basis of such biblical criteria as I Timothy 3:8–13. Deacons are laypersons who assist the pastor in worship services, particularly in the distribution of the Lord's Supper and in care for the physical and spiritual needs of the church members. Deacons help to guide the church, see to its financial condition, and watch after the poor and the sick. The interaction between deacons and pastors has sometimes been a source of tension, which can lead divisons in Baptist churches.

Baptist Denominations: Their Name Is Legion

Though Baptist churches in the southern mountains and elsewhere shared many common qualities of practice and church order, there were also many differences. Baptists disagreed over such issues as denominational alignment versus independence; falling from grace versus eternal security; general versus particular theories of Christ's atonement; and missions versus anti-mission emphasis. The following is a brief sketch of different types of Baptists found in Appalachia.

The Southern Baptist Convention

Churches associated with the Southern Baptist Convention are perhaps the most numerous Baptist churches in Appalachia and in the South. Beginning in 1845, in the slavery controversy and the developing sectionalism of the pre-Civil War era, Southern Baptists are today the largest Protestant denomination in America, numbering some thirteen million persons.

The split with the Northern Baptists (now American Baptist Churches, USA) culminated a lengthy debate over the role of mission boards in dictating policies affecting local congregations. The central issue was in the decision of the Baptist mission boards, home and foreign, not to appoint slaveholders to the mission field. Southerners, already angry at the force of northern abolitionist sentiment, insisted that this was an extraneous issue and that no outside body could dictate policy to autonomous congregations.

Aggressively evangelistic and deeply concerned to spread the gospel around the world, Southern Baptists grew rapidly across the South and Southwest following the Civil War. As already noted, they became the dominant Protestant force in southern culture. They have maintained, not without struggle, the autonomy of local churches, while developing a powerful centralized organization for missionary and other endeavors.

Authority in the SBC is said to originate "from the bottom up," rather than at the top of a hierarchy. Denominational gatherings, on local, state, or national levels, are made up of "messengers" elected by local churches.

The association, a gathering of churches in a given region for fellowship, cooperation, and mission action, is the most basic form of Baptist unity. State conventions are formed by local churches in a particular state. Messengers from individual congregations provide representation to the yearly meeting of the Southern Baptist Convention itself. So basic is local autonomy that individual churches may be removed from membership in one group—association, state, or national convention—without automatically losing membership in another.

The strong concern for local autonomy has meant that there is tremendous diversity in the SBC itself. Churches in close proximity may have very different approaches to worship, ethics, ministry, and evangelism.

The basis of this unity in diversity among Southern Baptists is, first and foremost, missions. By means of a "Cooperative Program," local congregations contribute funds which are used in associations and state and national conventions to underwrite a wide variety of mission endeavors. On the convention-wide level these financial resources provide for the work of the home and foreign mission boards, a Sunday school board which produces masses of literature for use in churches, six seminaries coast to coast for the training of ministers, and a multitude of other commissions and agencies. No church is compelled to give a prescribed amount to the Cooperative Program, though giving for mission work is greatly encouraged throughout the convention. Southern Baptist churches in Appalachia reflect the diversity of churches convention-wide. All these churches, however, will likely be concerned for personal evangelism, missions, and the unique Baptist witness in the community and the world. Because of their concern for missions, southern Baptists in Appalachia are frequently known as "Missionary Baptists."

Southern Baptist Beliefs

Historically, Southern Baptists are pietistic evangelicals, concerned for the personal regeneration of every person through faith in Jesus Christ. Regeneration occurs at conversion, a dramatic event when the individual exercises faith in Christ as personal savior and experiences the gift of God's saving grace.

Conversion is formally registered by "public profession of faith," usually by "walking the aisle" during a revival or regular service of worship. Baptism by immersion follows as a symbol of the believer's inward transformation. Each new Christian is urged, and often instructed, to share the faith with others, and personal witness is a vital concern of most Southern Baptist congregations.

Theologically, Southern Baptists frequently refer to themselves as "modified Calvinists." By this they mean that salvation is by God's grace, but requires the cooperation of individual free will. The true convert is eternally secure and cannot lose salvation or "fall from grace." The idea of the eternal security of the believer is frequently popularized in the phrase "once saved, always saved." This belief has been a frequent topic of debate among Baptists and other denominations.

Doctrinally, Southern Baptists are conservative but not necessarily fundamentalist. Traditionally they have permitted some latitude in matters of dogma as long as cooperating individuals and churches could affirm the reality of a personal faith and a commitment to Baptist efforts of world evangelism.

While hesitant to develop creeds which might threaten the authority of scripture, Southern Baptists have preferred to express doctrinal sentiments in confessions of faith. These documents normally serve as guidelines for churches, but are not binding on the conscience of the individual.

The official confession of faith now used by Southern Baptists is the Baptist Faith and Message statement approved in 1963 at Kansas City. Its articles deal with issues as scripture, religious liberty, and the final judgment. In recent years, this document has been used by some groups in the SBC as a formal statement of dogma to be rigidly interpreted. One of the major issues confronting Southern Baptists is whether or not they can maintain both diversity and unity in the midst of controversies over doctrine, creeds, and fundamentalist debates.

Independent Baptists

Fundamentalism represents the primary doctrinal position of another type of Baptist in Appalachia, the independent. Independent churches maintain no official denominational affiliations beyond the individual congregation. Given Baptist obsession with autonomy and the rugged individualism of the mountains, as well as the tendency toward competition and doctrinal debate, it is no surprise that independent churches flourish in Appalachia. Many of these congregations are formed around a charismatic, often autocratic, pastor; some grow out of splits with other churches; others are constituted from churches once in the SBC or other denominations.

A major influence on the development of independent Baptist churches was the debate over mission boards. Some Baptists opposed such boards as a threat to local autonomy, fearing that outside agencies could dictate mission policies to local churches. Independent Baptists generally believe in missions but favor the direct support of individual missionaries sent out or funded by the local church alone. Elaborate administrative structures for regulating mission activities are rejected as wasteful and harmful to the authority of the local church.

Independent churches are usually quite strong in their Landmark emphasis. They are vocal in their opposition to ecumenical endeavors, seeking to retain baptismal and communal purity. They normally practice "close communion," and require re-immersion of those whose earlier baptism does not conform closely with their own.

While they are rabidly evangelistic and aggressive in personal witnessing, independents also tend toward a strong doctrinal rigidity. Fundamentalist dogmas regarding biblical inerrancy, personal devil, virgin birth, bodily resurrection, and a premillennial theory of Christ's second coming are prominent doctrines among independent Baptist congregations. Although they respond to the physical needs of individuals in church and community, most independent Baptists would fiercely attack the "social gospel" as obscuring the church's primary task: the salvation of "lost" men and women. Worship in independent churches tends to be informal, folksy, and unrehearsed. Sermons are loud and long, with a major emphasis on the need for immediate conversion. Threats of hell, promises of heaven, invitations to receive Christ before it is too late, promises of heaven, invitations to receive Christ before it is too late, attacks on worldliness and personal immorality characterize most sermons. Independent Baptists tend to be intense about their faith and in their sense of right and wrong. They often disagree among themselves and with other Christians, but they tend to grow large and enthusiastic churches.

Primitive Baptists

The Primitive or "Hardshell" Baptists represent the Calvinistic or even hyper-Calvinistic wing of Baptist denominations. They came to the mountains relatively early. Disagreements over missions, Bible societies, and seminaries led to the beginning of the Primitive Baptist movement in North Carolina in 1827. The initial division was followed by numerous splits over the nature of predestination, new birth, music, offerings, and other issues. Their church life is characterized by local autonomy with some loose-knit associational and national organization. It reflects little of the elaborate structure of Southern Baptist denominationalism. Like other Baptists they stress the authority of scripture, the importance of baptismal immersion, and congregational polity. Beyond these basic similarities the Primitives part company with most other evangelical Baptists. For Primitive Baptists, God is sovereign and his ways "past finding out."

Salvation, therefore, is completely the work of God's grace. Sinful human beings can do nothing to facilitate their salvation. Men and women by nature are unconcerned about redemption and incapable of discovering God for themselves. For Primitive Baptists the doctrine of election means that God has chosen some individuals for salvation, while others have not received grace or have received election to damnation. How and when predestination of the elect occurred is a matter of debate among Baptists and other Calvinist groups.

Some supralapserian Primitive Baptists believe that even before the fall of Adam, God had elected some persons to salvation and others to damnation. Thus, He caused the fall in order that He might save the elect. Others, who might be called infralapserian Primitive Baptists believe that God elected individuals only after the fall.

Whatever the terms of the process, neither the elect nor the damned have any reason to boast or complain, as salvation lies solely with God. The elect are saved only by grace, unconditionally, and not on the basis of any good they do or gifts they exhibit. The damned are totally depraved and, thus, deserve nothing but damnation. God's Sovereignty, His decision to save some and damn others, is beyond human comprehension. Christ's death, therefore, was efficacious only for the elect, not for the entire race. This hyper-Calvinism is a far cry from the doctrines of the sixteenth reformer of Geneva, John Calvin, but it has greatly influenced the life and practice of Primitive Baptist churches.

Unlike most other Baptist groups, Primitive Baptists are not aggressively evangelistic. They preach the gospel of election and redemption in their churches, but believe that God in His good time will awaken all the elect to salvation. They hesitate to preach revivals or evangelistic meetings calling for conversion, and prefer to allow the sovereign God to save whom He will.

Primitives believe the church to be the fellowship of the elect, the community of faith. They usually practice foot washing, along with baptism and the Supper, as ordinances of the church.

Primitive Baptists keep ecclesiastical organization to a minimum. They seldom take offerings and have few paid clergy. Preachers work at secular vocations and serve congregations on Sunday. Many churches have no Sunday school or other services beyond preaching and worship. The use of organs, pianos, or other musical instruments is frowned upon in many of the churches.

Free Will Baptists

The Free Will Baptists occupy the other end of the spectrum from the Primitives. They began in North Carolina around 1727 under the leadership of Paul Palmer. Palmer preached a doctrine of free grace, free will, and free salvation. Another Free Will group was begun in New Hampshire by Benjamin Randall in 1780. These movements experienced continued division, particularly during the Civil War, but were united in 1935 into the National Association of Free Will Baptists.[5]

This national organization supports limited work in both foreign and home missions, with denominational offices in Nashville, Tennessee. Most Free Will Baptist churches practice three ordinances: immersion baptism, Lord's Supper, and foot washing. They stress local autonomy and congregational church government. Theologically, they represent the strongest commitment to Arminianism evident among Baptist groups. The grace of God is for all persons who respond to the gospel demands for repentance and faith. Thus all are potentially in the elect. Although tainted with sin, all human beings have the free will to move toward God and respond to His grace. Since the human will is free to choose Christ, it also remains free to reject Him at some future time. Free Will Baptists thus maintain the possibility of "falling from grace" or willfully repudiating one's salvation.

The Free Will Baptists are evangelistic in their preaching and active in efforts at personal witnessing. Their services are warm and folksy, ordered but not formal. Their views on falling from grace have led to frequent debates with those other Baptist groups which preach doctrines of eternal security and perseverance of the saints.

Baptists are truly a unique lot! Critics of the Free Will Baptists could sing:

> Baptist, Baptist, Baptist,
> Baptist once for all,
> I'll always be a Baptist
> Unless, of course, I fall.

The Black Baptist Tradition

There are many Baptist groups in America made up primarily of Blacks. These denominations began in the post-slavery era as Blacks separated from the white churches, where they had previously been members, and established their own organizations outside the domination of whites. Baptist church autonomy and congregational government was conducive to the establishment of independent Black churches in both the North and the South. These congregations were usually served by itinerant Black farmer-preachers, normally unpaid and lacking formal education.

The first national organization of Black Baptists was formed in 1880 as the Foreign Mission Baptist Convention in Montgomery, Alabama. The American National Baptist Convention followed, established at St. Louis in 1886, and the Baptist National Education Convention was founded at Washington, D.C. in 1893. These three groups were united in the formation of the National Baptist Convention in 1895.[1]

Divisions have plagued the Black Baptist churches, beginning as early as 1915, over the use of a charter and the formation of a publishing house. This division led to the formation of the National Baptist Convention of America and the National Baptist Convention of the USA, Incorporated. The latter body maintains a publishing house. In 1961, the National Baptist Convention Incorporated was again divided and the Progressive Baptist Convention founded.

The Black Baptist churches are firm in their commitment to the autonomy of the local church and, quite often, the position of the pastor as the authoritative "shepherd of the flock." Like their white counterparts, the Black Baptists of Appalachia are experiencing change and controversy as their ministers increasingly receive education in colleges and seminaries.

Worship in these churches is exuberant and spontaneous, with a strong emphasis on the centrality of preaching. Worship is an "event" which is not limited by the boundaries of time or schedule. Black churches continue to retain the tradition of the "answering congregation," in which the people respond freely and audibly to the proclamation of the minister. Shouting, singing, tears, and other physical responses are not uncommon within the worship services.

In many areas of the country, including Appalachia, the church continues to be a place where Blacks can exercise leadership gifts in ways not always available in the white-dominated society as a whole. At the same time, however, Appalachian Baptists, Black and white, share many common characteristics and practices. Some Black Baptist congregations are beginning to accept "dual affiliation" with American or Southern Baptist denominations.

Baptists are diverse. No doubt this brief chapter has omitted something which readers see as crucial to an understanding of Baptists. Baptists often make up in fervor what they lack in consistency.

ROMAN CATHOLICS

Roman Catholicism began slowly in America. Although some of the earliest explorers of the sixteenth century brought their Catholicism with them and founded churches in the Southwest and the North, Catholics were a minority among the English-speaking colonists. Maryland was an early center of Catholic influence in America, chartered by the Calvert family, who extended religious tolerance to non-Catholics in order to attract colonists. A member of another distinguished Maryland family, John Carroll, was consecrated archbishop of Baltimore in 1808, the first Catholic bishop in America. Nonetheless, the church was slow to grow in the midst of the Protestant establishment. It was not until the mid-nineteenth century that the church began to experience phenomenal growth as multitudes of immigrants—many of them European Catholics—descended upon America, introducing a new and powerful force into American religion. Their numbers, their non-Anglo traditions and their "foreign" religion were seen by many "100 percent Americans" as a threat to the American and Protestant way of life.

This anti-Catholic sentiment, or nativism, was particularly strong in many northern industrial areas where the immigrants congregated, providing cheap labor and a "papist" faith. It was also true in the Protestant South, not because there were large numbers of Catholics, but because Catholicism was characterized as the ultimate enemy of "Bible-believing," born-again Christians. Many southern preachers denounced the evils of creeping Catholicism bent on turning Christians from faith in Christ to subservience to a Roman pope. Many still reveal a strong bias toward Catholic doctrines and practices. The Ku Klux Klan sometimes targeted Catholics as well as Blacks for harassment with cross-burning and other fear tactics. Many evangelical groups consider Catholics to be "lost," outside Christian salvation, who need to be won to Christianity and away from Catholic influence. Many Appalachian preachers label the pope as antichrist and warn of plots to impose Catholic views on the society and the churches in America. This argument was particularly strong during the presidential campaigns of Catholics Al Smith in 1928 and John Kennedy in 1960. Protestant pulpits and periodicals thundered with warnings of papal control of the presidency, destruction of religious liberty, and the loss of separation of church and state.

During those years the Catholics, themselves, sometimes seemed their own worst enemies. Papal decrees condemned public education, democracy, and freedom of religion. Protestant missionaries in predominately Catholic countries were harassed and the church made highly publicized claims for papal infallibility and Roman superiority as the true church. The people of the South and the highlands were particularly susceptible to the negative aspects of Catholicism, as there were few Catholics around and the popular stereotypes helped make an obvious enemy for preachers to attack. Indeed in 1973, when the American Catholic Church reported some 48,465,438 members, the two geographical areas which showed the smallest percentage of Catholics were the Baptist South and the Methodist "southern North."[1] Baptists might disagree over Baptist doctrine or moral issues or Baptist politics, but they could all agree that Catholics were wrong and far off from the truth.

The situation began to change in 1960 when John Kennedy was elected President of the United States and the capital was not moved to Rome. Kennedy's commitment to American freedoms dispelled, for some at least, fears of direct papal influence in American politics. (Catholics themselves were a formidable political force nonetheless.)

A second major influence on the changing attitude of and toward Catholics was due to the Second Vatican Council, called in 1961 by the beloved Pope John XXIII. The changes in worship, biblical studies, parish life, and church order profoundly affected Catholics and the Protestant view of the Roman church. Vernacular mass, a revival interest in preaching, lay participation, scripture study, and communion given to the people in both elements, along with some new appreciation for ecumenical endeavors led many to label the reform as more Protestant in emphasis. Others responded that it merely made the church more "Catholic," calling it to move beyond the encrustations of the Middle Ages and the modern siege mentality to the practices of the earliest Christian communities.

Third, the growing pluralism and mobility of Americans meant that Catholics now moved into the South, intermarried more easily with Protestants and participated in more cooperative endeavors.

Thus, the church struggles to succeed in the mountains fighting critics on both sides. Some have left because it has ceased to be "church" without Latin mass, surefire doctrines, and the security of unchanging faith. Others continue to warn of the danger of compromise with the forces of the papacy—continuing anti-Catholic campaigns.

Interestingly enough, some have seen parallels between southern religion (particularly Southern Baptists) and the religious traditions of Roman Catholicism. Sam Hill notes at least four such similarities: 1. Both are committed to the spread of "their own institutional brand of Christianity"; 2. both stress the need "to conserve dogma, particularly old forms of old dogma"; 3. both tend to be "ingrown" separated from "the broader Christian community"; and 4. both have dominated their cultural setting with little tendency to become "self-critical and reformist."[2]

Nonetheless, Catholic beliefs are in many respects quite unique from Protestants', particularly Appalachians'. No effort can be made to describe all the intricate facets of American Catholicism since space is limited. Basic doctrines are described here as an introduction to what Catholics really believe. A summary might be developed around the following areas: authority, salvation, worship, and transition.

Authority is a primary issue among Roman Catholics. The church itself—apostolic and universal—is the agent of God's grace in the world. The church possesses true doctrine and is the guardian of that doctrine in the world. It continues the work of Jesus Christ on earth. As such, the Holy Spirit guides the church by two equally important sources: scripture (Old and New Testaments) and tradition (the authoritative pronouncements of church councils, popes, and ecclesiastical laws). Scripture is primary, but scripture as interpreted and enlightened by the tradition and continuing heritage of the church.

For Catholics, the government of the church has also been formed by God through ancient traditions and practices. The church is governed by a *hierarchy,* a "chain of command," which interprets doctrine, administers church affairs, and provides the authority for the church's activity of grace in the world. The hierarchy begins with the pope who is the vicar (the chief representative) of Christ on earth. He is the successor of St. Peter and, thus, represents the truth of church dogma as passed on from the first-century Christian community to the present. Through Peter and his successors was given the authority of Jesus Christ. Christ said to Peter:

Upon this rock I will build My church and the gates of hell shall not prevail against it and I will give to you the keys of the kingdom of heaven and whatsoever you bind on earth will be bound in heaven; whosoever you loose on earth will be loosed in heaven.

(Matthew 16:18–19)

Peter and his successors possess the "power of the keys" to govern the church spiritually and temporally.

The pope is considered infallible only when he speaks "ex cathedra" from his office as Christ's representative and only on matters of "faith and morals." Contrary to some popular caricatures, the pope is not considered "perfect" nor infallible in every pronouncement. Few papal statements have been made "ex cathedra" since the doctrine was officially approved at Vatican Council I in 1870.

The pope is the bishop of Rome and is chief bishop among all other bishops. The office of bishop, however, is the church's chief spiritual and administrative office. The bishop stands in a line directly from the apostles Catholics believe. It is by his authority that the church administers its sacraments and cares for the faithful. Bishops oversee Catholic work in regional areas throughout the world. Increasingly since the 1960s they have played a larger role in the overall governing of the church through their role as advisors to the pope.

Priests or presbyters form the most basic ministerial position in the hierarchy. They carry out the ministry of the church on the local or parish level. To them, through the authority of the bishop, is given the power to bring the sacramental grace of the church to the people of God. Priests serve as pastors of local Catholic churches and provide other basic administrative and ministerial services.

From the hierarchy the "community of faith" receives the teachings, doctrines, and sacraments of the church. Lay persons participate in various local and regional affairs of the church but their role is distinct and separate from the role of those persons (clergy) duly ordained to carry out spiritual functions in the church. Since Vatican II, however, lay persons have taken a broader role in the ministry and administration of the church.

A second realm of distinct Catholic doctrine concerns salvation and the living out of the Christian life. In Catholic thought, salvation is a process which begins at baptism (usually administered to infants) and continues until death. Throughout this process the church makes available various "signs" of God's grace which nurture the Christian in the faith. These "signs" are best known as sacraments: "visible and outward signs of a spiritual and inward grace." Through the grace of the sacraments, the faith of the individual and the resulting good works, human beings secure salvation and new life in Christ.

This idea of process and the cooperation of faith *and works* for salvation is probably the most difficult aspect for Protestants, particularly in the South, to understand. There is no one experience which brings immediate salvation. Though such experiences may occur, the process of salvation is life long, not once and for all.

The sacraments of the church are seven in number. They are "mysteries," whereby the grace of God comes to sinful human beings as mediated by the priest. They include:

1. BAPTISM: Entrance into the church; the gift of "new birth"; old life put off and new life put on. Administered to infants and adult converts.

2. CONFIRMATION: The faith pledged at baptism is internalized by the individual. At infant baptism, faith is pledged by adults, at confirmation, the baptized individual makes faith his or her own.

3. COMMUNION (the mass): The continuing experience of grace. Catholics take Jesus' words, "This is my body," very literally, believing that by the mystery of consecration, the bread and wine of communion become the very body and blood of Christ. Believers, thus, literally feed on Christ and receive his life into themselves. This is known as transubstantiation.

4. MARRIAGE: The grace of God in marriage, sanctifying this unique human relationship around which the family is formed.

5. HOLY ORDERS (ordination): A special grace is given to those who minister and mediate the grace of God to the church.

6. PENANCE: The forgiveness of sins committed after baptism is provided for those who confess, repent, and do acts of restitution. Again, the priest is the vehicle of grace who speaks in Christ's name the words, "Go on your way, your sins are forgiven."

7. EXTREME UNCTION (last rites): The dying are anointed with oil and prayers are said to prepare the individual for death.

Salvation then is process. The church through the sacraments nurtures persons by the grace of God throughout the journey of life. Christ's death and resurrection are celebrated, recalled, and made tangible for the church in every age.

A third quality of Roman Catholic life is worship. The liturgy of the mass, the prayers of the faithful, the Divine office are central aspects of the Catholic community. The mass is the daily and weekly worship celebration. It follows a basic order with prayers, scripture, sermon (usually brief), confession, absolution, consecration of the elements, communion, and benediction. For centuries, the mass was said in Latin in every Catholic church throughout the world. Since the 1960s, it has been changed to the vernacular, the language of the people. This has led to increased participation of the laity in worship. Lay readers read scripture lessons, lead in prayers, and offer homilies (sermons). Congregational singing has increased and some laity may even help distribute communion under special circumstances. Catholic worship is highly structured and the priest continues to play the central role, but there is variety, particularly in response to ethnic and social customs, music, and dress. In many churches communion is given to the faithful in both bread and wine (a departure from the past), and received in the hand not on the tongue.

Thus the Catholic church is in a significant period of transition. Changes since Vatican II have been significant. There is a renewal of interest in Bible study, lay involvement, and spiritual life. In fact, a strong charismatic or neo-pentecostal movement has flourished among many faithful, contemporary Catholics. Changes in the church have produced controversy and some conservative reaction as groups seek to return to the more traditional and truly "Catholic" practices. Where these changes and reactions will take the church is difficult to foretell. It may be, however, that the transitions within the church have made it more acceptable in certain areas such as the South and Appalachia. At the same time, mobility and pluralism may help to make the mountains a more open area to diverse religious groups than ever before.

Catholicism, a changing Catholicism, is present in the southern highlands. What its impact will be and how other Christian groups, many still strongly anti-Catholic, will respond to it remains to be seen.

CHURCHES OF CHRIST

The Churches of Christ represent one segment of the "Disciples" or "Christian" movement, one of the earliest indigenous denominations in American religious history. While developing out of the frontier revivals of the nineteenth century, they insist on a "restoration" approach to the church. In their view, the true Church of

Christ was obscured for centuries by the multiple sects and denomination. These false churches departed from the biblical teachings of Christ and the first Christians, giving way to apostasy.[1] The teachings were restored and the church recovered in the work of a new generation of disciples.

Barton W. Stone and The "Christians"

Barton W. Stone was one of those early disciples. A Presbyterian pastor of the church at Cane Ridge, Kentucky, Stone called the infamous camp meeting held there in August 1801. Out of the ferment of his religious awakening, Stone rejected the creedal and predestinarian positions of the Presbyterians in an effort to reconstitute a church based only on the Bible. In 1804, Stone and others wrote the "Last Will and Testament of the Springfield Presbytery," in which they affirmed certain "Christian" principles including the Bible as their only guide, no ordination for ministers, congregational church government, and an Arminian theology.[2] The movement was highly evangelistic and spread rapidly across the frontier.

Alexander Campbell and the "Disciples"

Another faction involved in the frontier revivals was represented by Thomas and Alexander Campbell and a group which took the name, "Disciples of Christ." Like Stone, Thomas Campbell was a Presbyterian preacher who became disillusioned with the theology and practice of that denomination. In 1809, he organized a non-denominational group, which accepted this basic principle of biblical interpretation: "Where the Scriptures speak we speak; where the Scriptures are silent we are silent."[3]

The elder Campbell sought to develop Christian unity around the Bible and a set of simple doctrines, but his argumentative son, Alexander, expressed these beliefs in a more divisive manner. Alexander Campbell was an able debater who did not hesitate to point out the errors of the churches of Christendom. For a time the younger Campbell was affiliated with the Redstone Baptist Association in Pennsylvania but broke with them in 1827. Through the publication of such periodicals as *The Christian Baptist* and *The Millennial Harbinger,* Campbell's views were circulated and found sympathetic response from many who were dissatisfied with the traditionalism of existing denominations. The "Disciples of Christ," while initially seeking to abolish denominationalism, succeeded in becoming a new denomination in themselves.

Campbell and his followers sought to restore the true teaching of the New Testament church. They insisted on baptism by immersion, based on the controversial phrase "for the remission of sins." They observed the Lord's Supper each Sunday, affirmed congregational polity and looked to the New Testament alone as the primary guide for the church.[4]

Basic Beliefs

The churches of the Disciples tradition hold many common beliefs with other mainline Protestants. They favor a regenerate church membership, baptismal immersion, memorial view of the Lord's Supper, local autonomy, and religious liberty.

Some identify their distinctiveness by the following statements:

No book but the Bible

No name but the divine

No plea but the gospel

No aim but to save

In Christ—unity

In opinions—liberty

In all things—charity[5]

Their basic principles include:

1.   No creed but the Bible, with particular emphasis on New Testament revelation.

2.   Conversion based on a rational assent to the tenets of the gospel.

3.   Baptism as necessary for conversion through the "remission of sins." It is an act of obedience by which salvation is completed.

4.   Little or no formal distinction between clergy and laity. Many reject formal ordination, calls, or special titles for clergy.

5.   The Lord's Supper to be celebrated every Sunday as administered by any duly authorized member.[6]

Unity and Division

Although not agreeing on every doctrine, Stone, Campbell, and their followers agreed, in 1832, to cooperate together without establishing a formal organization. Each group retained the name it preferred. Thus such terms as "Christian Church," "Disciples of Christ," or "Churches of Christ" were used by various churches identifying with the basic beliefs of Stone, Campbell, and other anti-denominationalists. They repudiated the titles, "Stonites" or "Campbellites" which their critics (who were many) placed upon them.

In time, however, several distinct denominations were formed from this loosely knit movement. They included: The Christian Church, The Christian Church (Disciples of Christ), and the Churches of Christ.

The Christian Church

The Christian Church, prevalent in Indiana, Kentucky, and Tennessee, holds a middle position between the more conservative Church of Christ and the more liberal Disciples. The Christian Church was formed in 1924, due to disagreements with the Disciples over more ecumenical endeavors and baptismal policies. The Christian Churches are more cautious in their ecumenical involvements and less likely to accept members who have not been baptized by immersion.

The Disciples of Christ

The Christian Churches (Disciples of Christ) International Convention took its present name in 1957. Prior to that the church had grown out of the Stonite/Campbellite movement, with first official national convention and mission organization held in 1849.

They seek to restore the practices of the New Testament church, insist on no creed but the Bible, and maintain a denominationalism bound by local autonomy. In recent years, Disciples have participated in ecumenical efforts and even joined in conferences on union with other denominations. They have tended to become more liturgically oriented in their larger congregations, placed more emphasis on educated ministry and have been accused of more "liberal" theology.

Churches of Christ

The Churches of Christ separated from the Disciples movement around 1906. They were particularly opposed to the development of missionary societies, favoring instead the support of missionaries directly through local congregations. They also rejected the use of musical instruments in services of worship. Such instruments were not explicitly permitted by the New Testament. Churches of Christ tend to be very concerned about Bible study and use the Bible extensively as proof for their doctrines and practices. They observe the Lord's Supper each Sunday and their ministers serve with formal recognition of the congregation, but without ordination. Local autonomy is very strong and duly elected elders control much of the affairs of the church.

Members of this community are often noble controversialists who debate other groups over biblical doctrines. This has led many to an unbending dogmatism which declares the dogmas of the Churches of Christ to be the only true doctrines of the church. They often demonstrate little patience with those whose doctrines differ from their own. As pluralism of education and region expands within the churches, doctrines also are expanded. Churches of Christ now face many questions regarding their approach to traditional dogmas, ecumenism, social action, and progressive ideas.

EPISCOPALIANS

The spontaneity of Pentecostal and Baptist worship services seems a far cry from the stately ritual of the Episcopal Church and its *Book of Common Prayer*. For many mountain evangelicals the nurturing and confirmation process of Episcopal evangelism seems foreign to conversionistic, "born-again" religion. The written prayers, the robed clergy, and the prescribed scriptures, are signs of institutionalization, which many mountain preachers vehemently denounce. The Episcopal *via media* or middle way between Catholic liturgy and Protestant theology appears to many mountain fundamentalists as a compromise in doctrine and an accommodation with the world. After all, Episcopalians *do* use real wine in the Lord's Supper and have been known to use alcohol on less religious occasions as well! Furthermore, the Episcopal communion has often been identified with the wealthy and powerful, not the small farmers, sharecroppers, and disenfranchised people of the mountains. In earlier days, at least, it was considered the religion of the gentry and that was reason enough for the less affluent to shun it.

Nonetheless, Episcopal religion appeared in the southern highlands. The church was brought there by a determined young priest who grew old seeking to minister to mountain folk in ways consistent with Episcopal tradition but responsive to the needs and distinctives of the region. In what may be one of the most valuable accounts in this volume, the story of Episcopal work in Appalachia, as recalled by one of its pioneers, is retold.

American Anglicanism began in the South. When the first permanent English settlement was formed at Jamestown in 1607, its religion was Anglican. During the colonial period the Anglican church was the official religion of numerous colonies including Virginia, Georgia, and the Carolinas. Anglican missionaries were sent to America by the Society for the Propagation of the Gospel in Foreign Parts. In addition to their work with the settlers, these clergymen also made some of the earliest efforts at converting the Indians and later at bringing Christianity to the Black African slaves. The work was difficult since clergy were few, farms and plantations were widespread, and there was no resident bishop to direct church affairs.

The religion which these early Anglicans brought was that of a church established in 1536 through the struggles of King Henry VIII to provide the stability of a male heir for the English throne and the upstart Tudor dynasty. But the genius behind both Tudor and Anglican stability in England was not Henry's sole male heir, Edward VI, who died before reaching adulthood. It was his daughter, the politically astute and religiously expedient Elizabeth I whose policies kept England Protestant and Anglican. Elizabeth, who ruled 1558–1603, sought to steer a moderate course between pro-papal Catholicism and extreme Protestantism. During her reign, the thirty-nine articles were approved as the official confession of faith of the church. Theologically, the articles reflect Lutheran and Calvinistic views but with broad enough terms to permit a wide range of doctrinal interpretation. The liturgy of the church seems to be more Catholic in nature with a tendency toward elaborate ritual and carefully structured worship. But the church is also diverse enough to allow "high church" Anglicans to stress the more ornate style of worship and "evangelical" Anglicans to utilize the same Prayer Book with less formal interpretations.

As the church developed in America it was almost completely identified with the British and, therefore, with the Tory cause in the American Revolution. Following the American victory, colonial Anglicanism was in disarray, associated with the defeated enemy, its clergy in exile or hiding, its organization splintered and revenues gone. After a period of frustration, division, and debate, the church was finally constituted into the Protestant Episcopal Church in 1784 and following a complicated procedure, secured ordination of its first bishops from Anglicans in Great Britain. Under the leadership of two early bishops, Samuel Seabury and William White, the church sought to regroup and establish an American identity. Its government centers around a bicameral legislative body found in a house of bishops and a house of delegates made up of clergy and lay representatives. Its confession of faith is closely parallel to that of the thirty-nine articles.

The Episcopal church has retained its image as the church of the wealthy and has often numbered the more affluent Americans among its members. In recent years, an effort to relate Episcopal ministry more closely to the poor and disenfranchized has met with both enthusiasm and opposition from members, creating debate and controversy within the church. American Episcopalians have sometimes been described as representative of one of three ecclesiastical types: high church, broad church, and evangelical. The high church emphasis is on the beauty, dignity, and sacramentalism of the Anglican liturgy and worship. Evangelicals stress preaching, personal spirituality, and conversion, while broad church Anglicans seek to incorporate both elements with particular concern for ministry to the social needs. These forces often overlap and are not clearly defined in many segments of the church. They do illustrate the church's ability to adapt various situations and circumstances, however.[1]

Episcopal Beliefs

The Episcopal church places great emphasis on the nurture of individuals in faith through the teaching, worship, and sacraments of the church. Conversion is less likely to be a dramatic, once-for-all experience than a process whereby the individual grows in the "nurture and admonition" of God. The sacraments are, thus, very important as vehicles of God's grace to the church. Through the sacraments, particularly baptism and the Lord's Supper, persons are nurtured in faith and Christian living.

Through baptism, normally given to infants, the individual becomes a part of the church, the Body of Christ. That faith is pledged for infants by parents or godparents and confirmed by the individual in late childhood or early adolescence. The role of the church as parent, aiding the development of faith in every member, is particularly important to Episcopalians.

The Lord's Supper is another significant nurturing event in the Episcopal church. As the church gathers at the table, sins are confessed, faith reaffirmed, and spiritual strength provided. The Supper is a memorial but it is more than that. For Episcopal communicants, Christ is mysteriously present in the sharing of communion in ways he is not experienced elsewhere in the life of the church. The bread and wine are not changed into Christ's body and blood, but there is a new and unique experience of his presence as the elements are shared. Confirmation, penance, ordination, marriage, and last rites all have sacramental qualities in the life of the church.

These sacraments are "outward and visible signs of an inward and visible grace." They are to be administered only by those duly ordained priests of the church. The priest receives ordination in succession from the apostles as transferred through the bishop. The bishop's office (episcopacy) is the chief spiritual and administrative office of the church. Priests and deacons serve as the other orders of Episcopal ministers.

The Episcopal church encourages "loyalty to the doctrine, discipline, and worship of the one holy Catholic Apostolic Church in all the essentials, but allows great liberty in nonessentials."[2] While maintaining elaborate hierarchy, and ecclesiastical tradition, it has also made room for a wide variety of doctrinal viewpoints. The Protestant Episcopal Church, USA, was the one denomination strong in both North and South which did not officially divide over the Civil War. Some organizational changes were made but no formal division occurred, a fact which aided the church in its own reconstruction after the war. More recently, however, questions over social action, the ordination of women, revision of the Prayer Book, and other liberalizing trends have led to increased debate and controversy among American Episcopalians. As the ecumenical movement progressed, Episcopalians have frequently appealed to their broad church tradition as a model for dialogues on Christian unity. Their claim to incorporate the best of many traditions would serve as a *via media* by which many groups might be united.

Episcopal Churches in Appalachia

The Episcopal church has had an important role in southern religion. Its influence was particularly strong in the colonial period and prior to the Civil War. While it led in the early efforts at Christianizing slaves and has long been concerned with programs among the southern poor, the church has been identified with the upper economic and social classes. Its work in the southern highlands was slow, tedious, and rather late in developing. Through the work of the Reverend Rufus Morgan the growth of Episcopal churches in Appalachia is described and preserved. In this interview he tells his own story concerning the Episcopal presence in the southern highlands.

Jehovah's Witnesses

Perhaps there is no more controversial religious group in the southern highlands than those who call themselves Jehovah's Witnesses. They arrived in the mountains in the thirties and forties with a theology very different than that of the "mainline" Protestant denominations prominent in Appalachia. Their evangelism, their beliefs, and the extensive circulation of their literature has helped to make "JW's" one of the fastest-growing religious bodies in the nation.

The interview published here offers a basic summary of their beliefs as explained by one of Jehovah's Witnesses. This introduction represents an effort to provide a historical overview of the group as evidenced in its leaders and its most significant doctrines.

While tracing their roots back to the Biblical period, Jehovah's Witnesses acknowledge that the modern expression of their views began with the work of "Pastor" Charles Taze Russell (1852–1916) and a group of his followers known as International Bible Students. Russell was influenced by the Adventist movement of the late nineteenth century but through systematic Bible study soon disagreed with their views that Christ would come in the flesh in 1874. He recognized that Jesus would return as a spirit, and so be present though invisible. (1 Pet. 3:18) This led Russell to the writing of a pamphlet entitled *The Object and Manner of the Lord's Return,* of which some 50,000 copies were published.

Russell briefly joined forces with another former Adventist, N. H. Barbour, and the two produced a book in 1877 called *Three Worlds or Plan of Redemption.* Nothing like it had ever been published before. It combined for the first time the explanations of time prophecies with the work of Restitution. At this early date they recognized that the end of Satan's period of uninterrupted rule of the earth, called "Gentile Times" would come in 1914.

By 1879, Russell had broken with Barbour to begin his own period-ical, *Zion's Watch Tower and Herald of Christ's Presence*, now called *The Watchtower*. The first issue of *Zion's Watch Tower* consisted of only about 6,000 copies. Today its circulation exceeds an average of 8,750,000 copies per issue in over 106 languages.

Marking 1881 was the formation of the "Watch Tower Tract Soci-ety," which was incorporated under Pennsylvania law in 1884 as "Zion's Watch Tower Tract Society" (now called "Watchtower Bible and Tract Society of Pennsylvania"). Its charter states: The purpose for which the Corporation is formed is, the dissemination of Bible truths in various languages by means of the publication of tracts, pamphlets, papers and other religious documents, and by the use of all other lawful means which its Board of Directors, duly constituted, shall deem expedient for the furtherance of the purpose stated. This and other corporations of similar purpose are merely legal instruments used by Jehovah's Witnesses.

By 1880, Russell was the recognized leader of small congregations in the North and Northeast United States, particularly concentrated around Pittsburgh. Members were urged to give personal witness to their faith at every opportunity. In the early 1900s, the Bible Students organized an international newspaper syndicate. At one time about 3,000 newspapers in the United States, Canada, and Europe were publishing C. T. Russell's sermons.

In 1912, Russell determined to give a great witness through a new medium. Although motion pictures were still in their infancy he wrote and produced the *Photo-Drama of Creation*, an eight-hour-long slide, motion picture, and sound production outlining the di-vine purpose for the earth and mankind from creation down to the end of Jesus Christ's thousand-year reign. (Rev. 20:6) Shown in four parts, the Photo-Drama combined phonograph recordings with slides and motion pictures. It was seen by millions.

Charles Taze Russell died in October 1916 while on a preaching tour in Texas. Russell was succeeded by "Judge" Joseph F. Ruther-ford (1869–1942) who established the Witnesses in much of the doctrine by which they are known today. A lawyer by trade, Ruther-ford was known as Judge although he never officially held such an office. He read Russell's literature, accepted the doctrines, and was baptized in 1906.

During World War I, soon after he succeeded Russell as leader, Rutherford and seven others prominently associated with the society were arrested, later tried, and convicted on charges of violating the Espionage Act because of their belief of neutrality toward mili-tary service. After months in the federal penitentiary at Atlanta,

Georgia, they were freed on bail. By May 14, 1919, their erroneous convictions were reversed, and on May 5, 1920, they were completely exonerated.

After his release, Rutherford set out to solidify the organization through restatement of dogma and person to person evangelism. Among other things they received a new instrument for use in their preaching work. It was *The Golden Age,* a journal drawing attention to the hope and comfort found in the scriptures. Today it has the same purpose under a new name, *Awake!*

In 1922, the Bible Students assembled at Cedar Point, Ohio. J. F. Rutherford's discourse on the subject "The Kingdom" was especially significant to them. He concluded with the words: "Behold, the King reigns! You are his publicity agents. Therefore advertise, advertise, advertise the King and his Kingdom." That Kingdom has been advertised by Jehovah's Witnesses ever since.

During the 1930s and 1940s there were many arrests of Witnesses for doing this work, and court cases were fought in the interest of preserving freedom of speech, press, assembly, and worship. In the United States, appeals from lower courts resulted in the Witnesses' winning 43 cases before the Supreme Court of the United States. Similarly, favorable judgments have been obtained from high courts in other lands. Concerning these court victories, Professor C. S. Braden, in his book *These Also Believe,* said of the Witnesses: "They have performed a signal service to democracy by their fight to preserve their civil rights, for in their struggle they have done much to secure those rights for every minority group in America."

At another convention at Columbus, Ohio, in 1931, the Bible Students by resolution embraced the name "Jehovah's Witnesses." (Isa. 43:10–12) This also signaled the emphasis they put on Jehovah as the name of the one indivisible God.

It had been known and taught by the Bible Students from the beginning of Pastor Russell's ministry that, in addition to those who would inherit heavenly life as joint heirs with Christ, mankind in general would be restored to perfect life on earth. Rutherford gave new insight to this at a convention in Washington, D.C., in 1935. Scriptural evidence was produced to prove that the great multitude of Revelation 7:9 was identical with the sheep class of Matthew 25:31–46.

Rutherford also led in establishing the Watchtower Bible and Tract Society of New York, Incorporated which became the major publishing house of the Witnesses. Watchtower publications are used extensively in the door to door work of Jehovah's Witnesses.

Judge Rutherford died in 1942. Five days later N. H. Knorr (1905–77) was unanimously elected president of the Watchtower Society. He and his associates promptly embarked upon an extensive educational work. February 1, 1943, marked the dedication and inauguration of the Watchtower Bible School of Gilead. Through the years this institution has equipped thousands of ministers for foreign missionary work.

In 1943, a new school was also started in the individual congregations of Jehovah's Witnesses. It was the Theocratic Ministry School, originally open for male enrollment. Enrollees are taught to gather, develop, and present Biblical information.

Of no little significance have been their large gatherings. Among these was an International Assembly held in 1958, when 253,922 Witnesses packed out New York City's Yankee Stadium and Polo Grounds. N. H. Knorr delivered the talk on the subject "God's Kingdom Rules—Is the World's End Near?"

By 1961, the New World Translation of the Holy Scriptures was completed and published in one volume, and this Bible, which was offered on a contribution of only one dollar a copy, has had a phenomenal distribution. Since 1950 Jehovah's Witnesses had been distributing the Greek Scriptures of the New World Translation and individual volumes of the Hebrew Scriptures as they had been completed. But even before that Jehovah's Witnesses were urging people to read the King James Version, the American Standard Version, or any other translation of the Bible, because they say God's words of truth are contained in any Bible.

N. H. Knorr died in 1977, after many months of illness, and Frederick W. Franz was elected president. Franz had worked in close association with N. H. Knorr at the world headquarters of Jehovah's Witnesses in Brooklyn, New York, and his reputation as an eminent Bible scholar is well known.

Jehovah's Witnesses continue to stress that the world is in the last days spoken of in Matthew 24, Mark 13, and Luke 21 and a warning must be given before it is too late. The Witnesses believe that the end of this system will occur with the battle of Armageddon. (Rev. 16:14,16) They do not predict when it will take place but believe it will be soon. In this battle, Jehovah and his son, Jesus, will fight and prevail against Satan and his legions. After the great destruction of Armageddon the earth will be restored to paradise conditions and the great majority of the survivors will dwell on the new earth. (Psalms 37:10,11) These are the "other sheep," whose number is limitless. (John 10:16; Rev. 7:9) They were faithful to

Jehovah in this life or chose him after the resurrection. Only a select 144,000 will actually enjoy the reality of heavenly life with Jesus. These will serve as kings and priests with him. (Rev. 20:6) Those who refuse to follow Jehovah even after the resurrection judgment will be annihilated and forgotten.

Jehovah's Witnesses are a highly motivated people dedicated to the proliferation of their views. Once baptized, by immersion, each Witness is considered a minister and takes no pay for services. They meet together in Kingdom Halls, where they study scripture and offer mutual encouragement. Witnesses also favor the use of Assemblies and Conventions.

As these interviews indicate Jehovah's Witnesses came to Appalachia during the 1940s and have grown extensively since that time. Their theology, sectarian practices, their criticism of organized religion, and their evangelism have often brought them into conflict with mainline Protestants. They again illustrate the pluralism of American religion and its impact even on the once isolated religious environment of Appalachia.

METHODISTS

The Methodist Church seemed made for America. With its gospel of free grace and free will, its system of church organization, and its heart-warming gospel, Methodism seemed providentially prepared for the democratic, free-wheeling environment of the American frontier. It began not in the coarse exuberance of the camp meeting but in the staid cathedrals of Anglicanism. John and Charles Wesley were "high church" sons of the Anglican communion, raised in an Anglican rectory and educated at Oxford in the rich liturgical traditions of Anglican worship. While at Oxford in the early 1700s, the Wesleys helped to found the Holy Club, an organization of devout students concerned for personal devotion, strict ethics, and methodical Bible study. In these small groups the early stages of Methodism took shape.

In 1736, John made his first and only trip to America, traveling to the new colony of Georgia to serve as pastor to the settlers and missionary to the Indians. He wrote that his chief motive for going was to save his own soul. Wesley apparently believed that one might be saved better in Georgia, than in England!

Georgia was a disaster for Wesley. His rigorous pastoral demands alienated him from almost everyone. The Indians, he soon realized, were not waiting with open arms for the white man's gospel. And he fell in love, only to reject and publicly humiliate the woman to whom he originally pledged his devotion. Her family threatened a lawsuit, and Wesley decided that the Lord was leading him back to England.

In Georgia, however, Wesley made two important discoveries. First, as a pastor he developed many of the small group practices which later came to characterize Methodism. Second, Wesley encountered the Moravians, German pietists whose personal faith, assurance of salvation, and sense of divine direction made a profound impression upon him.

On returning to England, Wesley met other Moravians and in one of their gatherings at Aldersgate, on May 24, 1738, he experienced a new sense of the Divine Presence on the direction of his life. Wesley describes it as that moment "when I felt my heart strangely warmed, and I felt I did trust Christ, Christ alone for salvation; and an assurance was given me that he had taken away my sins, even mine and saved me from the law of sin and death."[2]

Wesley then went forth, preaching the necessity the "new birth," known by faith in Christ. Soon small Methodist societies were formed within the Church of England, made up of those who expressed sorrow for their sin and a desire "to flee from the wrath to come." These groups worshipped in Anglican churches but met in small groups for prayer, Bible study, and mutual exhortation. The gatherings were led by lay persons who preached, taught, and ministered to the spiritual welfare of the members. With time, the societies were organized into two distinct bodies, with separate functions. The Band was composed of five to six members of the same sex for mutual confession and consolation. The Class included some 12 members of both sexes for Bible study, prayer, and fellowship. This became the basic structure of Methodist organization.

As opposition developed toward Wesley's methods, many Anglican pulpits were closed to him. Thus, in 1739, he began another innovative practice of early Methodism—field preaching—proclaiming the gospel outdoors in "the highways and byways" of England. The Methodist preachers used these outdoor services to reach that segment of society often neglected by more formal religion. With these enthusiastic and unorthodox procedures, the Methodist societies soon spread throughout England and were on their way to America. Throughout these years, the Wesleys remained clergymen within the Church of England.

Methodism in America

The earliest Methodist society in America was organized in New York by Philip Embury. By 1768, the John Street Chapel was founded in New York City as the first Methodist Chapel in the new world. A year later Wesley sent Richard Boardman and Joseph Pilmoor as itinerant preachers for America and by 1771, Francis Asbury had arrived. Asbury, the "American Wesley," shaped the life of early American Methodism as no other individual.

With the coming of the American Revolution, the Methodists, like the Anglicans, were often associated with the Tory cause. Many preachers fled the country and Wesley, himself, condemned the American revolt.

After the war the scene was set for a break with the Church of England and the establishment of the Methodist Church. Wesley had become convinced that the New Testament taught that presbyters (pastors) could ordain new clergy without the presence of a bishop. Thus, in 1784, he and Dr. Thomas Coke ordained Richard Whatcoat and Henry Vasey as Methodist clergymen for America. Wesley then appointed Coke and Francis Asbury as superintendents to direct the societies in America. With this act, though Wesley himself never officially left the Anglican Church, the Methodist Church was born. In December 1784, at the now famous Christmas Conference in Baltimore, the Methodist Episcopal Church was formally constituted.

In the early days after organization Methodists continued to be a minority among America denominations. But the theology, the system, and the preachers were ready and the frontier was waiting. On the American frontier the Methodists thrived and by the mid-nineteenth century they had become the largest Protestant denomination in America. Methodist preachers were present at most of the camp meetings of the early 1800s and their work soon led to the establishment of new southern churches in the Carolinas, Kentucky, and Georgia as well as in the "West," Ohio, Indiana, and Illinois. With time, the camp meeting became almost the exclusive domain of Methodist revivalists.

The revivals shaped the style of Methodist worship incorporating Wesley's concern for the sacraments of baptism and the Lord's Supper into the spontaneity, exuberance, and enthusiasm of frontier religious experience. Methodist meetings were characterized by loud preaching, enthusiastic singing, shouting, and exuberant congregational response. Methodist theology, organization, and ministry provided the impetus for growth in America.

First, Methodist theology made Arminianism respectable. Methodist preachers stressed the possibility of conversion for every person. All were "elect" who chose to come to God by repentance and faith.

Once the new birth was secured, the believer could know assurance of salvation through the witness of the Holy Spirit. One did not merely hope that redemption would take place but experienced it as a divine gift. This involved a "witness in the heart," the power to live as Christ lived and the spirit of love for others.[3]

Closely linked with the doctrine of assurance was the idea of Christian perfection, another important and controversial Methodist emphasis. Perfection or sanctification, is that process of going on in grace, growing more Christlike, and maturing daily in Christian faith. Temptations might come but sin could be avoided. Article XI of the United Methodist confession of faith defines sanctification as

> The work of God's grace through the Word and the Spirit, by which those who have been born again are cleansed from sin in their thoughts, words, and acts, and are enabled to live in accordance with God's will, and to strive for holiness without which no one will see the Lord.[4]

Perfectionism is related to another controversial Methodist doctrine, falling from grace. Individuals who were free to choose Christ were also free to reject him, consciously turning away from salvation. The Methodists denied the claims of some Baptists regarding faith as "once saved, always saved." Since salvation depended on faithfulness, sanctification was essential.

The concern for human freedom, for the reality of human choice in the process of eternal salvation, seemed almost made to order for the rugged individualism and democratic idealism of the American frontier. The Methodists grew rapidly on the frontier and the success of their doctrines influenced other groups to modify a once strict Calvinism in more Arminian directions.

A second factor in Methodist success was the system around which the church was organized. The "connectional system" united local churches in regional and national organizations. The primary legislative body is the General Conference which meets every four years and is the national governing body of the church. Delegates, clergy and laity, are chosen by local congregations. The present church is also divided into five geographic jurisdictions: North Central, Northeastern, Southeastern, South Central, and Western. These sectional conferences also meet every four years to elect bishops and appoint members to boards and committees of the church.[5]

The yearly Annual Conference is the primary organizational unit of Methodism. It is a gathering of clergy and laity from a particular region. Here ministers are ordained and appointed, discipline carried out and procedures governing local churches established.

The Methodist Church has three basic ministerial offices: deacon, elder, and bishop. The deacon in Methodism is not usually given to the laity but is the first step in the clerical office. Deacons function in all ministerial capacities with one exception. The deacon may not "administer the sacrament of Holy Communion outside the bounds of his/her own charge" (parish).[6] Elders hold the basic ministerial officers of Methodist churches. They are officially called "preachers in charge," carrying out pastoral tasks in the local congregation. Bishops, the chief administrative officers, are elders who have been elected at the Jurisdictional Conference and received consecration to their office. They ordain and appoint preachers to local churches, and administer the affairs of the conference.

Within this system all individual churches are related to the one church. Autonomy is possible but within the bounds of discipline, administration, and procedures set by the various conferences and under direction of the bishops.

A third factor in Methodist growth was the itinerant system, represented on the frontier by the circuit rider. The small, isolated Methodist congregations, unable to secure permanent ministerial leadership, were held together by the circuit riders who traveled throughout a given area, baptizing, burying, preaching, and establishing churches. In the mountain regions preachers traveled great distances and were often on the circuit for months at a time. In their absence, lay leaders conducted Bible studies and prayer meetings, monitoring the day to day spiritual needs of the congregation.

The itineracy meant that many churches over a wide region could receive pastoral care from a relatively small number of preachers. As the itinerant system developed, bishops appointed clergy to local parishes. Churches have no direct say in who will be their pastor, nor are pastors allowed to choose their own charges. Appointments are made yearly at the Annual Conference. This system enables the church to provide a place of service for every minister, to fill every pulpit without extended vacancies or "interims." This method does place considerable pressure on the bishops whose choices and motives do not always go unquestioned by ministers or churches. Nonetheless, the Methodist system has proved to be a unique and basically efficient practice for administering churches.

Methodism in the Mountains

The Methodists thrived in the southern highlands. Circuit riders were invaluable in providing ministry for remote mountain churches. The connectional system linked the churches, providing a sense of unity beyond local congregations. Methodist theology appealed to the individualism of the early settlers.

Two other factors, worship and ecumenicity, illustrate the way in which Methodism adapted to the religious context of the mountains. The Methodist *Book of Worship* served as a guide for the churches, particularly in the administration of the sacraments of baptism and Lord's Supper. It gave uniformity and dignity to those significant events in the life of the church and the individual.

The Methodist *Hymnal* was likewise an important source of theological instruction. John wrote many hymns, but Charles Wesley was the real genius, composing over 4,000 pieces. The Wesleys realized that more theology can be taught in one hymn than in a multitude of sermons. In one brief couplet, for example, Wesley taught the doctrine of free grace:

> For me, for me the Savior died;
> Surely thy grace for all is free.
> I feel it now by faith applied,
> Who died for all hath died for me.

Wesley's ritual, hymnody, and heart-warming religion combined with the revivalism of the frontier and the folkways of the mountains to produce a particular style of mountain Methodism. As the individuals interviewed in this volume recall, Methodists were known for their revivalism, shouting, and singing. Dramatic conversions, camp meetings, and "brush arbor" revivals were common in Methodist gatherings. As these interviews indicate, recent efforts to change the style of worship and preaching have not met with enthusiastic response from some "old-time" Appalachian Methodists.

Methodist ecumenism is also evident in the mountains. Wesley long emphasized the relationship of all Christians who shared common faith in Christ. He wrote: "Dost thou love and fear God? It is enough! I give thee the right hand of fellowship."[7] Although Methodists did compete with other frontier denominations, debating their unique doctrines with Baptists, Presbyterians, or Campbellites, they were also known for their cooperation. As the Methodists in these interviews testify, Methodists and other denominations frequently held revivals and other services together. Where resources and ministers were in limited supply, Methodists joined with Baptists and others in common worship and ministry.

At times, Methodist ecumenicity led pastors to provide alternative modes of baptism beyond the normal practice of sprinkling. In fact, many Appalachian Methodist churches administered baptism by immersion as frequently as they did by sprinkling.

Divisions Among the Methodists

Although the Methodists did not divide as frequently as the Baptists, they naturally experienced schisms over social and theological issues. The original organization, The Methodist Episcopal Church, has experienced numerous divisions and reunifications. Divided in 1845 over slavery and abolition, the Methodist Episcopal Churches, North and South, were reunited in 1939, along with the Methodist Protestant Church, another antislavery denomination. In 1968, the Methodist Episcopal Church was joined with the Evangelical United Brethren to form the United Methodist Church. It remains the largest Methodist body in the United States.

The Congregational Methodist Church was formed in 1852 in a separation from the Methodist Episcopal Church, South, due to differences over the Methodist system of bishops and itinerant ministers. In these churches, pastors are called by local congregations, not appointed by bishops. They stress local autonomy and associational fellowship instead of episcopal administration.

The Wesleyan Methodist Church of America began in 1843 in a dispute over episcopacy and slavery. This body places stress on holiness and offers strong opposition to alcohol, tobacco, and personal immorality.

The Free Methodist Church of North America, founded in 1860, represents a highly conservative branch of Methodism. Members claim to represent true Methodist original Methodist teaching, stressing personal conversion, conservative theology, and the experience of sanctification for all believers. Free Methodists have strong roots in Appalachia, particularly through Asbury Theological Seminary, in Wilmore, Kentucky.

There are many other Methodist groups less relevant to this particular study. Significant among these other denominations are the

Black Methodist bodies such as the African Methodist Episcopal Church and the African Methodist Episcopal Church, Zion.

Methodism made a unique contribution to American, and Appalachian religion. Its concern for hearty religion and evangelism, its stress on education and organization were united in a response to the free spirit of American democracy. The Methodists made a significant impact on American religious life.

PENTECOSTALS

Perhaps no other group of Appalachian Christians has been more misunderstood, caricatured, and maligned than the people of the Holiness/Pentecostal tradition. For many they are the "holy rollers" whose religion is equated with superstition, ignorance, and rabid emotionalism. They are sometimes confused with snake handlers, their leaders labeled as charlatans, and their worship services the object of ridicule. They are much misunderstood and sometimes abused for their faith.

Perhaps the Pentecostals represent the ultimate expression of the Reformation concept of the priesthood of the believer. In their view, the individual can become a vehicle of divine inspiration and the mouthpiece of the divine word. Through the medium of the believer the Holy Spirit speaks anew in tongues known and unknown. Theirs is sometimes an extreme subjectivism in which the individual alone stands before God and speaks to him in a language which only God can know. They are a people confident that the Word of God is true because they have spoken it for themselves. Pentecostals offer themselves as living proof that Jesus Christ is alive and well and living in their hearts. They provide an important response to the questing of where one goes following Christian conversion.

The Holiness Movement:
Sanctification and Perfection

In the Holiness movement of the nineteenth century, Christians sought to answer the questions of what to do after Jesus comes into your heart. The Methodists had made this an important doctrine in their early days, but by the late 1800s many had become disenchanted with what they felt to be a decline in Methodist zeal for holiness. Many of these persons had been converted in camp meetings or urban revival campaigns and were frustrated with the spiritual infirmity they often experienced after the initial enthusiasm of conversion had passed. Advocates of Holiness ideology suggested that just as a person was justified by faith in a critical encounter with God, so the new believer must be sanctified, baptized with the Holy Spirit, in a second dramatic event. This experience empowered the convert to live the Christian life, to combat temptation and enjoy the fruits of the Spirit.

Holiness groups appeared in many American denominations, particularly among the Methodists, in the late nineteenth century. These societies did not immediately separate from the parent bodies, but met outside organized services for mutual encouragement and discussion of holiness. In time, however, as mainline denominations reacted negatively toward Holiness doctrines and as members themselves disagreed over such questions as when sanctification occurred and what were its signs, new Holiness denominations were founded. Perhaps the best known such group was the Church of the Nazarene founded by Phineas Brezee in 1908. They held to the following doctrines:

1. Personal morality
2. Conservative theologically and politically
3. Local church autonomy
4. Concern for personal conversion and evangelism
5. Holiness and Spirit baptism emphasized but the process less clearly defined or formalized[1]

The Holiness churches, therefore, believed that sanctification was an experience which occurred after conversion, empowering the Christian in holiness of life and service for Christ in the world. The terms of this experience varied from believer to believer and group to group. Pentecostalism represents the development of a definite process whereby the "second baptism" was known and secured.

Pentecostalism:
The Early Stages

Pentecostals trace their modern beginnings to the life and work of Charles Fox Parham in 1901. Parham, long interested in Divine healing and prayer for the sick, founded the "College of Bethel" in Topeka, Kansas, in 1900, for the purpose of teaching the Bible with particular attention to the Holy Ghost and healing. To this small "school" came Agnes N. Ozman, an impressionable person in delicate health. It was Ozman who, in December 1900, under Parham's guidance, experienced the gift of the Spirit as evidenced by speaking in tongues. Parham and Miss Ozman insisted that she spoke for days in the Chinese language.

Pentecostals believe that this was the reenactment of the day of Pentecost as described in the book of Acts. It represents the beginning of the "latter rain" of the Holy Spirit upon the church preparatory to the second coming of Jesus Christ.

Parham and his followers traveled throughout Kansas and the Midwest, spreading the word of these experiences. The faith of the apostles had been rediscovered and the Apostolic Faith Movement was on its way. It was left only for a disciple of Parham, W. J. Seymour, to bring the movement to Los Angeles and the Azusa Street Mission, a name which became synonymous with Pentecostal origins. In this mission church in an impoverished neighborhood, a revival broke out with an emphasis on Spirit baptism, healing, and spiritual gifts. Hundreds of people came through the mission and helped spread the enthusiasm throughout the country. Periodicals telling of miraculous occurrences were published and small Pentecostal congregations were organized.[2]

Pentecostal ideas also spread through the work of a number of revivalists who traveled from coast to coast preaching in tents, outdoor rallies, and store front churches. They were the charismatic personalities, healers, radio preachers, and celebrities of the fledgling movement. With the exception of Oral Roberts and Kathryn Kuhlman, perhaps the most famous of the Pentecostal preachers, these evangelists were almost unknown outside the Pentecostal subculture. Within that community, however, they were the apostolic spokespersons of the latter days. Their crusades were attended by multitudes and were for Pentecostals, the scene of miraculous healings, dramatic conversions, and enthusiastic response. These preachers often had little formal education or seminary training. They were sometimes self-ordained following a momentous conversion, Spirit baptism, and "call" to preach. They were controversial and sometimes abrasive, condemned by the secular press and mainline churches as charlatans and outright crooks. Their methods were sensational and they frequently would tolerate no opposition to their divinely ordained task.

Their names are today a roll call of early Pentecostal "saints."

William Branham (1909–65) one of the earliest and most famous of the faith healers.

Oral Roberts, whose Pentecostalism and media exposure made him the best known Pentecostal of all times. (He is now a Methodist and College President.)

Jack Coe (1918–57) whose strong appeal to the common people made him extremely popular particularly in the South.

Kathryn Kuhlman (1910–76) whose recent death brought an end to one of the most famous women Pentecostal leaders.

These are but a few of the more prominent figures of the movement. Pentecostalism, as perhaps no other American denomination, has known a multitude of local and regional evangelists who traveled their own circuits of small towns and mountain churches often offering the same fare as Roberts or Kuhlman to the people in the backwater places of America. But big time or small time Pentecostalism flourished in what some have called "the healing and charismatic revivals" of the twentieth century.[3]

Pentecostal Beliefs: Orthodox, Controversy, and Schism

It is difficult to generalize about the beliefs of the Pentecostals. Small sects and large denominations with Pentecostal emphasis vary in specific doctrines and minute definitions of dogma. In a recent history of the movement, Robert M. Anderson identifies the beliefs generally held by most Pentecostal bodies. They are summarized here with some additions. Generalizations of otherwise intricate doctrines are inevitable.

First, it is important to note that on most traditional dogmas of the church—trinity, creation, virgin birth, atonement, resurrection—Pentecostals are for the most part in agreement with other Protestant denominations. There are exceptions, but most could affirm a certain evangelical orthodoxy similar to that of certain fundamentalist or conservative churches. Their orthodoxy often becomes questionable to non-Pentecostals due to some of their methods of worship and ministry as well as their perspective on the two characteristically Pentecostal doctrines, healing and speaking in tongues.

Second, students of Pentecostalism have underestimated the significance of another controversial Christian doctrine, eschatology, on the theology of the Pentecostals. Eschatology (the doctrine of last things) is a foundation for other doctrines in the church. The world, most Pentecostals believe, is living in the "last days." Although these ideas are not limited to Pentecostal churches, they have played an important part of the Holiness/Pentecostal movements and are a popular topic of the preachers.

Although there are numerous theories regarding the second coming, Pentecostals tend to favor what is known as a premillennial view of the second coming. Premillennialists insist that Jesus will return to earth to rescue (rapture) his church prior to the "great tribulation" of the world and the establishment of Christ's kingdom for a thousand years (millennium). Before the millennium, Christ will return, raise the dead in Christ and those who are alive will "meet Christ in the air." After this a time of tribulation occurs in the world from which the saints are spared. Christ then returns to earth and the millennial kingdom of peace and joy is founded.[4]

Many Pentecostals also hold to a dispensational premillennialism. This view which was popularized in England by J. N. Darby in 1903, and America by Cyrus Scofield in 1909, was an important doctrine for explaining the gifts of healing as experienced by Pentecostals. It suggests that time is divided into seven dispensations, whereby the terms for salvation (different in each dispensation) are made known. The world is on the edge of the seventh and final millenniumists culminating in Christ's return.

The outpourings of healing and tongues were evidence of that "latter rain" which God's people would experience prior to Christ's return. They were predicted by the prophet Joel who wrote: "And it shall come to pass afterward, that I will pour out my spirit upon all flesh; and your sons and your daughters shall prophesy, your old men shall dream dreams, your young men shall see visions." (Joel 2:28)

Tongues and healings then are not merely exercises of spiritual life for the enjoyment of the faithful. They are signposts along the way to the end of the age and the beginning of the true spiritual kingdom.

A third distinctive in Pentecostal thought is the gift of tongues, or glossolalia. It is the "ecstatic utterance" discussed by Paul in I Corinthians 12:10,28. The experience of tongues, Pentecostals believe, is the evidence of the baptism of the Holy Spirit. It is a spiritual gift to the church and a sign that God is preparing to reenact Pentecost before the second coming.

The gift of tongues may be for the edification of the individual believer or as a word from God to the church. In the latter case another person present will usually serve as interpreter.

The experience of tongues—as other languages or as ecstatic utterances—is mentioned in the New Testament, Acts 2:1–13 and in certain writings of St. Paul. It has occurred in earlier periods of Christian history among various sectarian groups. Only since 1900 has it produced such a major impact on so many segments of the Christian community. Whether or not it is required of all Christians is a matter of debate among Pentecostals and non-Pentecostals alike.

Even more controversial than the question of glossolalia is that of healing. It has been the source of severe criticism for Pentecostals, the message of both the sincere and the charlatan "faith healers," and the cause of great speculation among the faithful across many denominations.

In the recovery of Pentecost, many believe that the apostolic gifts of healing were also restored to the church. Scripture was filled with promises regarding healing and accounts of miracles performed by both Jesus and the disciples. With the renewal of Pentecostal power could not those deeds be repeated with good measure?

In some Pentecostal churches the prayer of the faithful was offered in behalf of the community by the elders of the church. In keeping with James 5:14–15 they anointed the sick with oil and prayed for healing. Others claimed to have received unique gifts of healing to be shared with the church. These were the faith healers, some functioning in local congregations, others traveling across the country holding sensational meetings where the masses could receive the touch and the prayer of healing.

For many the gift of healing came through special signs and experiences. William Branham and Oral Roberts both claimed to have received a warm sensation in one hand which served as the contact point between human suffering and Divine healing. Others, like Kathryn Kuhlman were able to sense, rather than touch, those who were to receive healing. Still others made promises to persons on the edge of hopelessness.

As noted in these accounts, the reports of miracles continue along with accompanying debates. Nonetheless, Pentecostal theology stresses possibility, indeed, the reality of healing as part of the latter-rain of the Spirit.

A fifth aspect of Pentecostal belief is found in their view of worship. Here the unique quality of Pentecostal life, particularly in the mountains, becomes evident. There is diversity, from "ordered spontaneity," where even the experience of tongues has its proper place, to the absolute abandon of simultaneous dancing, preaching, healing, and singing.

Pentecostals brought drums, electric guitars, and other "worldly" instruments into their churches long before the 1960s made such instruments vogue in more sophisticated churches. Their music is frequently loud and its words almost inaudible to those not familiar with it. In some mountain churches, music provides a background for the frenzied sermons, the shouts, and the glossolalia which may occur at any time. The Spirit is to have complete control so the services often go where Spirit seems to go and end when Spirit seems to have completed its work. Preachers pace the platform calling for congregational response, stopping while others speak in tongues, or leading persons to be "slain in the Spirit," knocked to the ground as a sign of the power of God.

Worship is personal and highly subjective among Pentecostals. Few participants would feel that worship occurs unless the individual is dramatically touched by the Spirit of God. Personal experience of the divine Spirit is of great importance. Believers claim to have experienced visions, voices, and other manifestations of the miraculous. They seek to cast out demons, stress the need for personal conversion, and desire that every Christian receive Spirit baptism. While they observe baptism (usually by immersion) and the Lord's Supper (a memorial), they appear to be less concerned for these outer forms of spiritual expression than for the inner reality of spiritual experience.

Finally, by way of summary, Pentecostals have traditionally maintained a strict personal morality, conducting crusades against worldliness and immorality. They generally oppose dancing, tobacco, liquor, cards, gambling, and other personal practices which they deem unbecoming to the Christian. Many Pentecostals have affirmed their moral uniqueness by dressing in accordance with certain biblical admonitions. Women are particularly obvious. They often wear no makeup, refuse to cut their hair, and wear dresses with a specified length and style.

Pentecostals seek to recreate the primitive Christian community by exercising their gifts, preaching the "old-time" gospel and living separate from the world. Their doctrines are guides whereby the emotionalism and subjective religious experience of Pentecostal religion may be cultivated.

Pentecostal Groups

Like the Baptists, congregational autonomy means that many Pentecostal churches are completely independent of any denominational affiliation. Many take denominational names but have little or nominal connection with the parent body. These local churches abound in the mountains. Others have some relationship to some of the mainline Pentecostal denominations in America. The churches described here are primarily those mentioned in the interviews.

The *Assemblies of God, General Council* is the largest Pentecostal denomination, founded in 1914 from a union of several small Pentecostal groups. While they maintain a strong local autonomy, each of the forty-six districts have presbyteries (gatherings of ministers) which oversee ordination of pastors. The General Conference, made up of clerical and lay representatives, determines doctrines and missionary policies.

The Fire-Baptized Holiness Association was formally organized in Anderson, South Carolina, in 1898, following a series of revival services where tongues and other enthusiastic outbursts took place. These Pentecostals emphasized Wesleyan sanctification and proposed a third experience of grace beyond conversion and baptism of the Spirit. This was a "Baptism of Fire," which empowered the believer with the life of the Spirit.[5] The churches are organized around a Methodist system of episcopal government. They are evangelistic and their services emotional, accented by ecstatic experiences.

Some two hundred different bodies claim the title, Church of God. Some are Pentecostal; others are not.

One of the more prominent is the *Church of God (Cleveland, Tennessee)*, which was organized in 1886, but accepted its Pentecostal views in 1908. The church has experienced numerous divisions and names. Doctrines stress justification by faith, baptism by the Holy Ghost, healing, and Arminian theology. Churches maintain a strong moral code, repudiating the use of tobacco, alcohol, and jewelry. They practice baptism by immersion, the Lord's Supper, and foot washing.[6]

The original *Church of God, Inc.*, split from the other Cleveland group in 1917, insisting that it represents the true teaching of the Church of God as formed in 1886. They reject creeds as unbiblical, preach faith, sanctification, and tongues and their churches emphasize local autonomy.

The Pentecostal Holiness Church is a union of a group of the Fire-Baptized Holiness Church and the Pentecostal Holiness Church, formed in 1911. They maintain a Methodist polity with bishops and yearly conferences. Theologically, the church preaches justification and sanctification as distinct works of grace along with a third experience, Spirit baptism, evidenced in speaking in tongues.

PRESBYTERIANS

With the Presbyterians most of the caricatures of mountain religion fall apart. They do not speak in tongues, nor handle snakes; their worship is ordered, their preachers are usually well educated, and their churches well organized. Yet the Presbyterians brought revivalism to the American frontier and were among the first to plant the Christian faith in Appalachia. They remain in the mountains today, not as loud as some groups or as influential as others. Perhaps they are, as one writer describes them, "God's minority."[1]

John Calvin:
Father and Theologian

It is to John Calvin, the reformer of Geneva, that Presbyterians trace their beginnings. Although modified in other times and circumstances, Calvin's thought has shaped the directions of Presbyterian theology up to the present day.

Born in 1509 in France, Calvin intended to become a lawyer until conversion turned him to the embattled Protestantism of the sixteenth century. By the age of twenty-seven Calvin had written the first edition of *The Institutes of the Christian Religion,* a work which became one of the most important and formative documents in Christian history. Its systematic approach to Christian doctrine, and its insights into the nature of the church has made it the primary theological text book of Reformation ideas.

Calvin's views as set forth in the *Institutes* were applied to the church in Geneva where he began work in 1536. After struggles with himself and with the city fathers and after an angry exile of some three years, Calvin succeeded in establishing the city as the model of Reformed theology and piety. "The most perfect school of Christ" since the time of the apostles, said the obviously biased Scottish Presbyterian, John Knox. Nonetheless, the principles of early Presbyterian church life were set forth and exemplified in Geneva.

With Geneva as a base, Calvinism spread throughout Europe and soon became the most influential of the Reformation movements. In France, the Huguenots (French Calvinists) flourished, challenging the Catholic establishment for domination of the French court. The infamous St. Bartholomew's Day Massacre, August 24, 1572, saw thousands of French Protestants die at the hands of French troops. Although toleration was finally established in 1598 by the once Protestant king, Henry of Navarre, the Huguenots never regained strength in France.

In Scotland, the work and personality of John Knox made Calvinism a major religious force in a Catholic land. After centuries of debates and battles against Catholics and Episcopalians, the Presbyterian Church was secured in Scotland. By 1929, the major Presbyterian bodies had united into the Church of Scotland, the largest Presbyterian communion in Britain.[2]

Presbyterianism in England has exhibited a colorful and stormy history. In England the Calvinist position was represented in those "Puritans" who sought to reform the Anglican Church in more Protestant directions. Although they were divided over the type of church government—Episcopal, Congregational, Presbyterian—and whether or not Anglicanism could indeed be "purified," the Puritans were the theological heirs of John Calvin in England. After years of confrontation with the English crown, the Anglican establishment and a resulting civil war, the British Presbyterians gained a momentary victory of the Westminster Assembly of 1643. There they produced the Westminster Confession and related documents which became the guiding doctrinal statements for Presbyterians to this day. Although they did not succeed in maintaining Presbyterianism as the official religion of England, the Westminster divines provided a system of doctrine which was carried throughout the world, most significantly perhaps to America.

Presbyterians in America

The persecution of Calvinists and other dissenters in England, Scotland, and Ireland under the Stuart monarchs and their Anglican allies brought many Presbyterians to the new world. They were a minority in New England where Puritan congregationalism was the official religion. Presbyterians also settled in Virginia and Maryland by the mid-1600s and found their earliest substantial strength in the South "in the 'back country' of the Piedmont and in the Valley of Virginia."[3]

These scattered Presbyterian churches discovered their first organizational leader in Francis Makemie who in 1706 founded the first American Presbytery, in Maryland. Thus, the official structures of the Presbyterian system were established and other Presbyterian organizations soon followed throughout the colonies.

It was in the revivals of the first Great Awakening that Presbyterians began to increase their numbers and extend their influence in American religious life. Revivalistic Presbyterian preachers brought enthusiasm to the pulpits, converts to the altar, and schism to the church. Such revivalists as William Tennent and his son Gilbert drew sharp distinctions between the preachers of evangelical conversion and the ministers who continued to cling to the more traditional methods of nurture and creedal formulas. As the Great Awakening swept the colonies, Presbyterians and others divided over revivalistic methods and results. In 1741, the traditionalists broke with the revivalists, dividing Presbyterians, into New Side (pro-revival) and Old Side (anti-revival) forces. They were reunited in 1758 in a compromise move.

With the American Revolution and independence, Presbyterians were a leading force in the religious life of the new nation. They were prepared to take the gospel to the wilds, to bring civilization and Christianity to the developing frontier. Presbyterian preachers were among the first to invade the frontier areas of the Carolinas and Kentucky, helping to produce a new wave of Awakenings which sent Presbyterians deeper into the South and West.

By 1800, Presbyterian preachers, like James McCready and Barton W. Stone, aided the growth of camp meeting revivals which spread throughout the backwoods. From their base in Kentucky they organized meetings in which thousands were converted and from which new churches and denominations were founded.

Stone called the now famous Cane Ridge meeting in August 1801, the largest such meeting of the period with attendance of ten to twenty thousand people. Soon division had again occurred over revival methods, the ordaining of untrained clergy, and the doctrine of predestination. As a result of these controversies, the Cumberland Presbyterian Church was founded in 1810.

Although the Presbyterians spread throughout the South and the rest of the nation, divisions over polity, revivals, education, slavery, and the Civil War, split the church into several different bodies. They are listed and described here by way of summary:

OLD SCHOOL: Traditional, concerned over a Congregationalist; encroachments; seeking to preserve Calvinism without revivalistic innovations.

NEW SCHOOL: Cooperating closely with Congregationalists; revivalistic in practice and theology.

These divisions occurred in 1837, with both sides retaining the same name, the Presbyterian Church in the United States of America. With the Civil War, there was further division, North and South, in 1861.

Old School, North
Old School, South
New School, North
New School, South

By 1864 the southern churches had united to form the Presbyterian Church of the Confederate States of America. Following the war this Southern Presbyterian Church became the Presbyterian Church in the United States. It exists today and exercises the greatest influence among Presbyterians in the Appalachians. Its northern counterpart, the Presbyterian Church in the United States of America, represents the other major Presbyterian denomination in contemporary America. That church has also sent pastors, missionaries, and teachers into Appalachia.[4]

Presbyterians in Appalachia

The Presbyterians in the mountains defy many of the stereotypes often associated with Appalachian religion. Their services are more orderly, their ministers more educated, their church life more uniform and perhaps less independent than that of other mountain religious groups. Much of the Presbyterian influence has come less from the revivals they have held (though they do hold revivals) than by the educational institutions they have founded. Indeed, the Presbyterians were among the earliest educators to establish schools in the mountains. These schools were founded to provide basic education and spiritual instruction, as well as practical, vocational training. Efforts were made to found schools where both men and women could receive balanced education. Schools for boys and for girls were organized in West Virginia, Kentucky, North Carolina, and Tennessee.[5]

The founders of these schools were not as concerned to turn students toward Presbyterian theology as toward basic educational and moral values. That approach, along with the more structured, less aggressively evangelistic methods of Presbyterian churches, has meant that they are a minority denomination in the mountains.

Presbyterian Belief and Practice

The interviews in this section, particularly those of the Reverends Clyde Hicks and L. B. Gibbs, provide excellent descriptions of Presbyterian faith and practice as developed in Appalachia. Their comments need only to be placed within a broader historical context.

They illustrate the way in which Presbyterian churches have retained a unique historical identity while being shaped by the social and religious setting of the mountains.

First, Presbyterians maintain a strong sense of worship and church order. In Calvin's view the church is found where the Word of God is preached, the sacraments (baptism and Lord's Supper) observed, and discipline maintained. The sense of order began with the sovereignty of God and its place in human events.

The idea of Providence, a benevolent spirit guiding the affairs of human beings and the directions of the universe, was the foundation of Calvinistic thought. For Calvin, the world is not governed by a purposeless caprice or fate. The divine will is ultimately supreme.

Presbyterian worship is as simple as it is dignified, ordered, and stately. Early Presbyterians, for example, refused to sing "manmade" hymns, favoring only the words of the Psalms set to music. The sermon was the central event of worship and the Word of God informed the entire worship experience.

Order characterized ecclesiastical organization as Presbyterians put Calvin's concepts of church government into practice. In early Presbyterianism leadership was vested in four officers.

PASTORS preached the word of God and saw to the spiritual needs of the congregation.

TEACHERS instructed the church in scripture and doctrine attending to the instruction of the young in the faith.

DEACONS cared for the physical needs of the church, the needy. They were responsible for providing food, clothing, and other material goods to the poor, the sick, and the needy.

ELDERS were the only non-ordained officers. They were responsible for the administration of church affairs.

The sense of order also influenced Presbyterian concern for an educated, well-trained ministry. Presbyterians historically have placed great emphasis on the fulfillment of strenuous educational requirements prior to the granting of ordination. These requirements often led to divisions within the church as revivalism brought new and untrained converts who sensed an immediate call to preach.

In the Presbyterian system individual congregations are closely related. Sessions represent the governing board of the local church and are made up of clergy and elected laity. Presbyteries are gatherings of clergy and laity from various churches to decide in matters of church government, programs, and cooperation.

With their sense of order, their concern for ministerial training, and their more structured connectionalism, Presbyterians often lacked the spontaneity, autonomy, and individualism so characteristic of mountain religion. Nonetheless, as these materials indicate, Presbyterian churches in the mountains were greatly influenced by their setting. Many Presbyterian churches were strongly concerned for revivalism and evangelical conversion. As already noted, Presbyterians helped to bring revivalistic Christianity onto the American frontier. Unlike such hyper-Calvinist groups as the Primitive Baptists, who rejected evangelistic preaching, Presbyterians preached the necessity for personal repentance and conversion, believing by the "foolishness of preaching" God has chosen to awaken the elect. Thus, Presbyterians have produced generations of outstanding evangelical preachers.

On the other hand, Presbyterian concern for nurture and growth in grace influence many members toward a more gradual process of conversion. These "once-born" Christians reflect the Presbyterian view of baptism and Christian nurture. Infants are baptized under the covenant of grace and then instructed through the church until the once promised faith is internalized. This personal faith may develop gradually or dramatically, but its source is God discovered through the witness of the nurturing community, the church.

These studies also reveal that mountain Presbyterians have been influenced by the Pentecostal/Charismatic tradition in the use of tongues and the anointing with oil. Among some Appalachian Presbyterians, there is also a tendency toward more spontaneity and informality in worship.

Controversy has plagued the two major Presbyterian bodies in America during the last two decades. Efforts to respond to the civil rights upheavals and the Vietnam war of the 1960s produced strong divisions within the bodies. Revisions in the Confession of Faith approved in 1967 provoked debates between conservatives, moderates, and liberals. Like other of the "mainline" American denominations during this period, Presbyterians have experienced some decline in membership and a new quest for identity. The churches of Appalachia, somewhat insulated from these changes, have nonetheless been affected by modern trends, divisions, and controversies.

SNAKE HANDLERS

"Snake Handler." . . . Perhaps no other term so colors the popular image of Appalachian religion. For many outsiders, the primary religious expression of the southern highlands is found in the people who "take up serpents."

Truth is that snake handlers represent a small minority in the mountains though they are more prevalent there than anywhere else. Their bizarre practices, their legal battles, and the extensive attention they have received from the media, contribute to the mythology surrounding their beliefs and accompanying observances. The snake handlers represent a sectarian expression of the Pentecostal/Holiness tradition. Theologically they affirm a basic fundamentalism particularly evident in the biblical literalism of their snake-handling, fire-holding, poison-drinking observances. They insist on a dramatic conversion experience for each individual followed by the baptism of the Holy Spirit with the accompanying signs of tongues and healing.

Members are urged to observe a strict moral code which condemns gambling, alcohol, tobacco, illicit sex, movies, dancing, and other worldly amusements. Jewelry, "bobbed hair," and expensive clothes are forbidden to women.

In many respects their services are little different from those of the mountain Pentecostals with shouting, tongues speaking, prayers for healing, loud preaching, frenzied movement, and emotional enthusiasm, all carried out to the beat of drums and the rhythm of electric guitars.

But the distinctiveness of the snake handlers is a real one. They take up serpents—poisonous rattlers, copperheads, and water moccasins—and therein is their biblical literalism most evident. The snake handlers read the verses located in the final portion of the Gospel of Mark and insist that those words must be taken literally. Indeed they declare that if those prophecies are not true, none of the Bible is true. If they cannot be taken literally and fulfilled, then no other doctrines, particularly those related to salvation, can be trustworthy. The verses state:

> and these signs shall follow them that believe: In my name shall they cast out devils; they shall speak with new tongues; They shall take up serpents; and if they drink any deadly thing, it shall not hurt them; they shall lay hands on the sick, and they shall recover.
>
> —*Mark 16:17–18, KJV*

Most people called snake handlers do it all—take up serpents, put fire to their bodies, drink doses of poison. "We must do it," they declare "or else Jesus is a liar." "If we don't do it, God will raise up a people who will do it."[1]

Modern biblical scholars point out that this ending does not exist in the earliest manuscripts of the New Testament; that it was apparently an addendum placed there by later scribes as a testimony to the power of the apostolic church. But that is of little consequence to the people who take up serpents. Their King James Version of the Bible contains the passage and it is the very Word of God. The fact that some "liberals" would question its validity is further evidence of its truth and the apostasy of the modern day church.

The people who take up serpents are sincere and fervent in their conviction that they must do "their thing" if the scripture is to be proved true. Failure is to violate God's Word and deny his power.

It began in 1909, when a Tennessean, George W. Hensley, came preaching the need to follow the practices of Mark 16. Hensley traveled to several Pentecostal churches preaching his doctrines and handling snakes. Small groups accepted his views and gathered to worship, speaking in tongues, praying for healing, and taking up serpents. After some ten years, Hensley moved near Harlan, Kentucky, where his beliefs were accepted by members of a local Church of God. By the thirties and forties the movement had spread throughout the Appalachian region. Some participants had died from snake bites or from drinking poison. Court cases against the group became common and, in their minds, a general period of persecution resulted.[2] For the most part the churches are small, rural congregations, many in remote or semi-remote places. More recent devotees have sought remote areas to escape the long arm of the law and the fascinated gaze of the curious. The churches are composed largely of persons who see themselves as followers of the simple but demanding way of Christ which requires them to place ultimate trust in God. Most repudiate the idea that they act out of sensationalism or from their own abilities. They argue that no one is to take up serpents who does not receive the "gift" to do so, an overpowering urge to respond to the urgings of the Spirit. The handling of snakes, like speaking in tongues, is a manifestation of Spirit possession. Most testify to a fear of the snakes until the unction to touch them is given by God.

They do not perform such acts during a specific time in the service but when other activities—singing, shouting, shaking, or speaking in tongues are occurring. Believers may grab snakes by head, middle, or tail, drape multiple snakes across their bodies or hold several in each hand at once.

Others simultaneously may hold hands and faces over torches or drink doses of poison. All insist that such religious experiences are dynamic and inexplicable. They insist that snakes are not "milked," fangs removed or poison diluted. The sight of a crowd of people gyrating, shouting, singing, with tongues blaring and snakes everywhere is a strange and terrifying experience. But the participants are assured that it is a powerful demonstration of the Spirit.

The people who take up serpents are decent, loving people who take care of their own. Both men and women "greet one another with a holy kiss" (Romans 16:16), and the uniqueness of their worship, the threat of persecution, and the victory over the serpent bind them together in a strong fellowship. In conquering the serpent they show their contempt for the forces of evil which it has long represented. The "gift" to take up serpents is but one of many signs of divine power available to the true believer.

Multiple explanations—psychological, sociological, religious, and economic—are frequently suggested. Some see it as a tangible way of proving God and verifying faith. Others see it as a social phenomenon or propose a mass hypnotism for snake and handler alike.

Suffice it to say that the snake handlers are good, hardworking folks who expect more from religion than many mainline Protestants. They have a worship format in which all may choose to participate, holding snakes, speaking in tongues, praying, shouting, and which is freewheeling and spontaneous. Snakes are not held in every service, and not in every season.

The relative isolation of the mountains as well as the educational deficiencies have had a decided effect on the growth of snake handling in Appalachia. Their legal battles raise serious questions about the states' ability to define religion and the growth of American pluralism. Court cases are usually ended in rulings against the church but the martyr complex impells them on, even when breaking laws.

Snake handlers are not a popular group in the mountains. The Pentecostals seek to escape identification with them; the mainline Protestants look down upon them and the courts seek to inhibit their free exercise of religion. They are a strange phenomenon of the religion of Appalachia, a religion fast becoming an expression of the ultimate in literalism and fundamentalist dogma.

NOTES

HISTORICAL OVERVIEW

1. This scene is taken from a film entitled, *In the Old-Fashioned Way,* produced by Appleshop.
2. Eleanor Dickinson and Barbara Benziger, *Revival!* (New York: Harper and Row, 1974), p. 127.
3. Ibid., pp. 127–28.
4. William G. McLoughlin, *Revivals, Awakenings and Reform* (Chicago: University of Chicago Press, 1978), p. xiii.
5. William Warren Sweet, *Religion in the Development of American Culture* (New York: Charles Scribner's Sons, 1952), pp. 157–58.
6. Sidney Mead, *The Lively Experiment* (New York: Harper and Row, 1963), pp. 108–9.
7. Ibid., p. 123.

THE TRADITION OF SHAPED-NOTE SINGING

1. Perry Miller and Thomas N. Johnson, *The Puritans,* Vol. II, rev. ed. (New York: Harper and Row, Publishers, 1963), pp. 450–53.
2. Henry Wilder Foote, *Three Centuries of American Hymnody* (Hamden, Conn.: The Shoe String Press, 1961), pp. 102–3.
3. Allen P. Britten, "Theoretical Introductions in American Tune-Books to 1800," unpublished Ph.D. dissertation, University of Michigan, 1949, pp. 32–34.
4. Gilbert Chase, *America's Music from the Pilgrims to the Present,* rev. 2nd. ed. (New York: McGraw-Hill Book Co., 1966), p. 187.
5. George Pullen Jackson, *Spiritual Folk-Songs of Early America* (New York: J. J. Augustin, 1937; reprint ed., New York: Dover Publications, Inc., 1964), p. 6.
6. Irving Lowens, *Music and Musicians in Early America* (New York: W. W. Norton and Co., Inc., 1964), pp. 40–41.
7. William Walker, *Southern Harmony* (Philadelphia: Thomas, Cowperthwait and Co., 1845), pp. xxvii–xxix.
8. William Walker, *Southern and Western Pocket Harmonist* (Philadelphia: Thomas, Cowperthwait and Co., 1846), p. 10.
9. Walker, *Southern Harmony,* p. xxviii.
10. Ibid., p. xxvii.

11. Charles A. Johnson, *The Frontier Camp Meeting* (Dallas: Southern Methodist University Press, 1955), p. 201.

12. George Pullen Jackson, *White and Negro Spirituals* (New York: J. J. Augustin Publisher, 1943), p. 20.

13. Johnson, *The Frontier Camp Meeting*, p. 197.

14. Ibid., p. 201.

15. Ibid., p. 189.

16. William J. Reynolds, *Companion to Baptist Hymnal* (Nashville: Broadman Press, 1976), p. 19.

17. Louis F. Benson, *The English Hymn* (Richmond: John Knox Press, 1962), p. 483.

18. Stanley H. Brobston, "A Brief History of White Southern Gospel Music and a Study of Selected Amateur Family Gospel Music Singing in Rural Georgia," unpublished Ph.D. dissertation, New York University, 1977, p. 329.

19. William J. Reynolds, *A Survey of Christian Hymnody* (New York: Holt, Rinehart and Winston, Inc., 1963), p. 114.

20. George Pullen Jackson, *White Spirituals in the Southern Uplands*, (Chapel Hill: University of North Carolina Press, 1933; reprint ed., New York: Dover Publication, Inc., 1965), p. 364.

21. Shirley Lorraine Beary, "The Stamps-Baxter Music and Printing Co.: A Continuing American Tradition," unpublished DMA dissertation, Southwestern Baptist Theological Seminary, Forth Worth, 1977, p. 282.

22. Ibid., p. 284.

23. Ibid., p. 285.

24. Ibid., p. 274.

25. Ibid., p. 275.

26. Ibid., pp. 251–52.

27. Jackson, *White Spirituals in the Southern Uplands*, p. 100.

APPENDIX

THE BAPTISTS

1. Robert G. Torbet, *A History of the Baptists,* revised ed. (Philadelphia: The Judson Press, 1950), pp. 15–34.

2. Robert G. Torbet, *A History of the Baptists,* 3rd ed. (Valley Forge: Judson Press, 1963), pp. 18–19, 281–82.

3. Ibid., pp. 19–20.

4. Ibid., pp. 20–21.

5. D. C. Dodd, "Free Will Baptists, National Convention of," Encyclopedia of Southern Baptists, Volume I, ed. Norman W. Cox (Nashville: Broadman Press, 1958), pp. 506–7.

THE BLACK BAPTISTS

1. Frank S. Mead, *Handbook of Denominations in the United States,* 4th ed. (Nashville: Abingdon, 1965), p. 34.

THE CATHOLICS

1. Jackson W. Carroll, Douglas W. Johnson, and Martin E. Marty, *Religion in America, 1950 to the Present* (New York: Harper and Row, 1979), p. 72.
2. Samuel S. Hill, Jr., *Southern Churches in Crisis* (Boston: Beacon Press, 1967), pp. 227–28.

THE CHURCHES OF CHRIST

1. Robert S. Paul, *The Church in Search of Its Self* (Grand Rapids: Wm. B. Eerdmans Publishing Co., 1972), pp. 108–9.
2. Sydney Ahlstrom, *A Religious History of the American People* (New Haven: Yale University Press, 1972), pp. 445–46.
3. Ibid., p. 447.
4. Ibid., p. 448.
5. Milton V. Backman, *Christian Churches in America* (Provo, Utah: Brigham Young Press, 1976), p. 146.
6. Ahlstrom, *A Religious History of the American People,* pp. 450–51.

THE EPISCOPALIANS

1. Milton V. Backman, *Christian Churches of America* (Provo, Utah: Brigham Young University Press, 1976), pp. 95–96.
2. Frank S. Mead, *Handbook of Denominations in the U.S.* (New York: Abingdon Press, 1965), p. 187.

THE METHODISTS

1. Percy Livingstone Parker, ed., *The Journal of John Wesley* (Chicago: Moody Press, n.d.), p. 64.
2. Nolan B. Harmon, *Understanding the United Methodist Church* (Nashville: Abingdon, 1977), pp. 64–66.
3. Ibid., pp. 70–71.
4. Ibid., pp. 98–100.
5. Ibid., p. 114.
6. Winthrop S. Hudson, "Denominationalism as a Basis for Ecumenicity: A Seventeenth Century Concept," in *Denominationalism,* edited by Russell Richey, (Nashville: Abingdon, 1977), p. 21.

THE PENTECOSTALS

1. Robert M. Anderson, *Vision of the Disinherited: The Making of American Pentecostalism* (New York: Oxford University Press, 1979), pp. 28–46.
2. Ibid., pp. 47–61.
3. David E. Harrell, Jr., *All Things Are Possible: The Healing and Charismatic Revivals in America* (Bloomington, Ind.: Indiana University Press, 1975), pp. 53–83.
4. Timothy P. Weber, *Living in the Light of the Second Coming: American Premillennialism, 1875–1925* (New York: Oxford University Press, 1979), pp. 8–12.
5. Anderson, *Vision of the Disinherited*, p. 289.
6. Frank S. Mead, *Handbook of Denominations in the U.S.* (New York: Abingdon Press, 1965), pp. 74–75.

THE PRESBYTERIANS

1. W. D. Weatherford, ed., *Religion in the Appalachian Mountains* (Berea, Kentucky: Berea College, 1955), p. 36.
2. Lefferts A. Loetscher, *A Brief History of the Presbyterians*, 3rd edition (Philadelphia: The Westminster Press, 1978), p. 42.
3. Ibid., p. 4.
4. Weatherford, pp. 45–48.
5. Ibid., p. 42.

SNAKE HANDLERS

1. Eleanor Dickinson and Barbara Benziger, *Revival!* (New York: Harper and Row, 1974), pp. 127–28.
2. Weston La Barre, *They Shall Take up Serpents* (Minneapolis: University of Minnesota Press, 1962), pp. 11–23.

GLOSSARY

Altar Call: A public invitation to Christian conversion usually made at the end of a worship service. Sinners are invited to the altar or the front of the church for prayer, counseling and public profession of Christian faith.

Amillennialist: An interpretation of Christian eschatology which views the millennium as symbolic, having only spiritual, not literal, fulfillment. See Rev. 20:1–7.

Anointing with Oil: An observance associated with healing, practiced by many Protestant churches, particularly in the Episcopal and Pentecostal traditions. See James 5:14–15.

Baptism of the Holy Ghost (Spirit):   A special outpouring of the Holy Spirit after initial conversion experience. Some groups view it as accompanying conversion; others believe it is a separate, sanctifying experience which empowers the Christian for service and holiness of life.

Born Again: Term used to describe the experience of Christian conversion and accompanying new life in Christ. See John 3:1–8.

Broadman Hymnal: One of the earliest Southern Baptist hymnbooks to be published by a convention agency, published 1940.

Brush Arbors: Open-sided structures built from rough hewn poles and covered with brush to provide shade for worshippers.

BYPU: Baptist Young People's Union organized in 1890 as a service and study organization for young people in Baptist churches. Taught scripture, doctrine, morality, and community responsibility to Baptist youth. Formally disbanded in 1941.

Call to Preach: Term which describes a sense of divine guidance leading toward a vocation as a preacher and minister.

"Churching":   A term used to describe disciplinary practices in which church members are expelled for behavior unbecoming to a Christian.

"Close Communion":   A practice for determining those who may or may not receive the Lord's Supper. In its most common form close communion permits only members of a local congregation to receive communion in that congregation.

Cottage Prayer Meeting: Gatherings of Christians in homes for prayer, Bible study, and mutual exhortation.

Falling from Grace: The turning from salvation by one who earlier claimed Christian conversion; rejecting the grace of God which has earlier been received.

Foot Washing: Observed in many Baptist and Pentecostal churches as a symbol of community and humility. See John 13:1–16.

Laying on of Hands: Usually observed at the ordination of ministers or deacons, symbolizing their being set aside for service in the church; some administer it to all candidates following baptism; others lay hands on the sick along with prayers for healing.

Missionary Baptists: Describes those Baptists who favor the support of missionaries, home and foreign, as opposed to anti-mission Baptists who repudiate the need to send out missionaries. Missionary Baptists may be represented by those churches which support individual missionaries directly, rather than contributing to a central mission agency.

Missionary Circle: Gatherings of women for study and support of mission activities, home and foreign. Serves as a basic source of mission education in local churches.

Mourner's Bench: Special section in many revivalistic churches where sinners could go to mourn their sinful ways, receive words of encouragement and prayers of the faithful.

Postmillennialist: A view of the millennium which suggests that Christ will return following the church's establishment of the kindgom on earth. The church helps to bring in a "golden age" of religious and moral enthusiasm.

Premillennial: A particular view of the second coming of Christ which stresses his return prior to the thousand year reign of peace on earth. Christ returns, "raptures" (takes up) his church to heaven, chaos strikes the earth, Christ brings his church back to earth, and reigns a thousand years. See Revelation 20:1–7.

Protracted Meeting: A series of revival services extended over a period of days or weeks, sometimes ending only when religious enthusiasm wanes.

Revival: A series of church services held for the purpose of renewing the zeal of church members and converting non-Christians to the faith; may also refer to a dramatic resurgence of spiritual fervor in the church.

Sanctification: The process of growing in grace; living the Christian life in holiness and manifesting the "fruits of the Spirit" after conversion. In some churches sanctification occurs in a decisive experience following justification (conversion).

Saved: Term used to describe the experience of Christian conversion, i.e. "saved" from hell, "saved" to new life in Christ.

Singing Schools: Song fests where the "shaped-note" singing was taught to enable those with little musical background to read music; occasions of religious enthusiasm and community life.

Sunbeams: An organization for children in Baptist churches. It stresses music, missions, and Christian virtues for preschool and elementary age children.

Supply Preacher: A visiting minister who preaches in the absence of the regular pastor.

Tent Maker: Name for a bi-vocational minister, who receives little or no salary from a church and is supported by employment outside the church. See Acts 18:3.

Testimony Meeting: Services in which believers testify publicly as to their personal encounters with God, and relate various types of religious experiences.

Wednesday Night Prayer Meeting: A weekly gathering of church members for Bible study and prayer. A particularly strong tradition in Baptist churches.

EDITORIAL CONTRIBUTORS

SENIOR STUDENT EDITORS:
Wendy Guyaux, Keith Head, Carol Rogers

CONTRIBUTING STUDENT EDITORS:

GOSPEL SINGING:
Scott Bradley, Judy Pierce Burch, Bit Carver,
Nina Folsom Cook, Debbie Penland,
Julie Radke, Susan Woodall

OLD LYSTRA PRIMITIVE BAPTIST CHURCH:
Mike Drake

SNAKE HANDLING:
Laurie Brunson, Tom Carlton, Karen Cox,
Ernest Flanagan, Randall Hardy, Joyce Moore,
Annette Reems, Annette Sutherland, Gary Warfield,
David Wilson, Barbara Taylor Woodall

ASSISTANT ADULT EDITOR:
Susan Davis

ADULT CONTRIBUTORS:
Dr. Edith Card, Dr. Bill J. Leonard

Other *Foxfire* books available from Anchor Press/Doubleday:

FOXFIRE 1
FOXFIRE 2
FOXFIRE 3
FOXFIRE 4
FOXFIRE 5
FOXFIRE 6

Foxfire Records Now Available

Foxfire is proud to announce the publication of two LP recordings, designed to accompany the material presented here in FOXFIRE 7. For five years now the Foxfire students have been making field recordings of the Rabun County Gospel Singing Convention in Georgia, and the Christian Harmony Singings in Dutch Cove and Etowah, North Carolina. Both of these recordings are enjoyable and informative pieces of documentary research, recorded on location at actual singings and accompanied by extensive interview material and historical research. They represent two distinct but concurrent "shape-note" singing traditions that survive today in the Southern Mountains.

In addition to these recordings Foxfire Records has produced a fascinating documentary recording of instrument makers Stanley Hicks, Tedra Harmon, and Leonard and Clifford Glenn, all of whom were featured in FOXFIRE 3. The album, entitled *It Still Lives*, includes banjo and dulcimer instrumentals, traditional narratives, and riddles. A twenty page insert provides interviews, transcriptions of recorded dialogue, and extensive research notes.

Along with traditional musicians Foxfire Records features songwriters emanating from the region. The first in this series of records is *North Georgia Mountains*, by Joyce Brookshire, an urban-appalachian composer of country songs who grew up in the cotton mill village in Atlanta, Georgia.

For further information, write to Foxfire Records, Rabun Gap, Georgia, 30568.

INDEX

Abolitionism, 436, 466
Abortion, 170, 184, 186
Adams, E. L., 170, 171–74
Adventist movement, 456
Africa, 102–3
African Methodist Episcopal Church, 467
African Methodist Episcopal Church, Zion, 467
Aikin, Jesse, 285–87
Alcohol
    Baptists and, 13
    crusades against, 20
    Jehovah's Witnesses and, 152–53
    Methodists and, 184, 466
    Pentecostals and, 473, 481
    Presbyterians and, 249
Allison, Ocie, 272–73
Altar calls, 25
    by Baptists, 13, 84
    at camp meetings, 13
    by Presbyterians, 253
    at revivals, 18
American Baptist Churches, USA, 436
American Indians, see Indians, American
American National Baptist Convention, 442
American Revolution, 283, 453, 477
    Anglicans and, 462
    Methodists and, 462
Anabaptists, 17
    Baptists and, 432
Anderson, Robert M., 470
Anglicans, 120, 435, 453–54
    American Indians and, 460–61
    American Revolution and, 462
    in Great Britain, 432, 453, 454, 460, 461, 476
    Methodists and, 460–61
    missions and, 460–61
    the thirty-nine articles of, 453, 454
Apostolic Faith Movement, 469
Appalachia, 13–27
    the culture of, 19–24
    folk ways in, 25
    individualism in, 24, 25
    influences on the religion of, 15, 17, 19–24
    isolation in, 24
    lifestyle in, 25–26
    pluralism in, 16, 17, 19, 24–27

stereotypes of, 15, 26
uniformity in, 16, 17, 18–19
Arminianism, 463, 474
Arminius, Jacob, 433
Asbury, Francis, 462
Asbury Theological Seminary, 466
Assemblies of God, General Council, 474
Atheism, 151
Authority
    of the Bible, 17, 21–22, 429, 439, 440
    Churches of Christ and, 112
    of God, 108, 236
    of Jesus Christ, 445
    Roman Catholics and, 445–46
Awake!, 144, 164, 458

Ballads, 285, 289
Baptism, 26, 347–50
    by Baptists, 16, 21, 33, 36, 46–50, 55, 63–64, 78–79, 94, 173–74, 430–33, 437, 439, 440, 441
    by Churches of Christ, 21, 114, 347
    conversion and, 23
    diversity in methods of, 16
    by Episcopalians, 120, 122, 454
    faith and, 432
    God and, 33, 226–27, 350
    by immersion, 16, 21, 114, 150, 173, 254, 347, 430–33, 437, 439, 440, 441
    by Jehovah's Witnesses, 140, 148, 150, 460
    Jesus Christ and, 168, 226, 254, 347, 349, 350, 430
    by Methodists, 16, 173, 175, 176, 184, 185, 462, 465
    by Pentecostals, 200, 213, 214, 220, 225–27, 469, 473, 474
    by pouring, 347
    by Presbyterians, 16, 254–55, 479, 480
    by Roman Catholics, 446, 447
    salvation and, 63–64, 78–79
    sanctification and, 23
    second, 23, 176, 255, 431–32, 439
    sin and, 347
    speaking in tongues and, 23
    by sprinkling, 16, 254, 255, 347
Baptist Faith and Message statement (1963), 438
Baptist National Education Convention, 442

Baptists, 24, 28–103, 135, 140, 143, 247, 429–43, 452
  alcohol and, 13
  altar calls by, 13, 84
  Anabaptists and, 432
  the answering congregation, 442
  baptism by, 16, 21, 33, 36, 46–50, 55, 63–64, 78–79, 94, 173–74, 430–33, 437, 439, 440, 441
  beliefs of, 429–30
    doctrinal positions, 433
  the Bible and, 14, 34, 43–44, 64, 79, 429, 431, 435, 439, 440
    disbelieving in, 13
  Black, 28, 100–3, 442–43
  born again, 63, 80–81, 439
  the call to preach, 31–32, 45, 55, 56, 62, 64, 79–80, 435
  camp meetings of, 13–15, 265
  the church and, 41, 63, 67, 80–81, 98, 103, 430, 431, 440
  churching by, 65–66, 184, 196, 201
  circuit riders, 28–41, 48–52, 85–86
  Communion and, 14, 66, 78, 184, 197, 431, 432, 435, 440, 441
  competition by, 16, 18
  congregational government of, 25, 78, 430
  conversion and, 101–2, 430, 435, 437, 439
  on creeds, 429
  dancing and, 13, 14, 97, 98
  deacons, 435–36
  disagreement among, 28, 433, 434, 436, 438, 439
  diversity of sects of, 19–20, 28, 429, 430, 436–43
  Divine healing and, 40, 50–51, 58–59, 67, 83–85, 95
  dual affiliation of, 443
  education and, 49, 57, 79–80, 101, 435, 437, 439, 442
  on the end of the world, 69–70, 98
  evangelism of, 434, 436, 438–41
  faith and, 186, 429–31, 433, 437, 438
  first church in America, 434
  foot washing and, 14, 29, 39–40, 66, 74, 82, 96–97, 196, 440, 441
  freedom of religion and, 429
  Free Will, 28, 62, 77–87, 441
  on free will, 79, 433, 438, 441
  fundamentalism of, 438–39
  General, 433, 434
  God and, 13, 14, 33, 34, 37–44, 51, 53–60, 62–63, 69–70, 88, 93–94, 431, 433, 437, 440, 441
    as the ultimate judge, 429
  grace and, 32, 430, 433, 436, 437, 440, 441
  Great Awakening and, 434
  in Great Britain, 432, 433, 434
  growth of, 433–35
  harassment of, 433–35
  heart religion and, 430, 435

  on heaven, 90, 439
  on hell, 53, 439
  Holy Spirit and, 44, 45, 58, 204
    rejecting of, 13
  Independent, 19–20, 21, 28, 53–60, 82, 438–39
  infralapserian, 440
  interviews with, 28–103
  Jehovah's Witnesses and, 140, 143, 163
  Jesus Christ and, 13, 14, 38–41, 44, 51, 55, 65, 69, 90, 93–94, 430–33, 437, 439
  Landmarkism of, 431–32, 439
  local autonomy of, 25, 28, 53–60, 78, 429–30, 435–42
  messengers of, 436–37
  Methodists and, 16, 18, 170–73, 178–84, 187, 193, 194, 463, 466
  Missionary, 19–20, 62, 78, 82, 437
  missions and, 57, 82, 102–3, 430, 436, 437, 439
  motion pictures and, 13, 82–83
  music and, 51–52, 61, 64–65, 88, 439, 441
  New Testament Church and, 430–32
  Northern, 436
  number of, 436
  on offerings, 67, 439, 440
  origins of, 430–32, 433, 434
  Particular, 433, 434
  Pentecostals and, 205–6
  praying by, 30, 32, 35, 37, 46, 48, 58, 80, 83, 90–91
  preaching by, 13–15, 53, 64, 434–35, 439, 442
    farmer-preachers, 435–36, 442
  on predestination, 19–20, 61–63, 256, 433, 439, 440
  Presbyterians and, 16, 242, 253, 259
  Primitive (Hardshell), 28, 61–76, 256, 429, 433, 439–41, 480
  publishing house of, 442
  Regular, 19–20, 434
  revivals of, 17, 33–35, 46, 49, 65, 81–82, 86–87, 93, 103, 434
  Roman Catholics and, 106, 444, 445
  salvation and, 30–31, 37–38, 44–49, 54, 78–79, 90–91, 204, 430, 433, 438, 440, 441, 463
    doubt of, 64, 78
  sanctification and, 204
  Separate, 19–20, 434–35
  on sexuality, 13
  sexual segregation by, 14, 40, 66, 74, 82
  shouting by, 30, 34, 37–39, 46, 50, 58, 92, 442
  sin and, 13, 39, 63, 440
  singing by, 34–35, 86–87, 195, 442
  on skipping church, 13, 95
  slavery and, 73–74, 100, 436
  snake handling and, 38, 51, 68, 83, 97
  the soul and, 47, 52, 429

Southern (Southern Baptist Convention),
    19–20, 28–41, 56–58, 82, 429, 436–38
speaking in tongues and, 52, 67, 81–82
splits, 28, 57, 62, 78, 80–81, 82, 436, 438,
    439, 442
sports and, 82–83
supralapserian, 440
Two-Seed-in-the-Spirit-Predestinarian,
    19–20, 433
visions and, 52
witnessing by, 55, 437, 439
Barbour, N. H., 456
Bay Psalm Book, 282
Bethel, College of, 468–69
Bible, the, 104, 139, 347, 370, 449–50, 460
    authority of, 17, 21–22, 429, 439, 440
    Baptists and, 14, 34, 43–44, 64, 79, 429,
        431, 435, 439, 440
    disbelieving in, 13
    Calvinism and, 236
    Churches of Christ and, 111–17, 449, 452
    Episcopalians and, 121
    errors in, 108, 160–62
    fundamentalism and, 21–22, 23
    inerrancy of, 21–22, 439
    internalizing of the Gospels, 24
    Jehovah's Witnesses and, 140–43, 146–69,
        456–59
        new version published, 459
    King James Version, 22, 43, 56–57, 108,
        160–62, 165, 185, 186, 188, 459, 482
    Methodists and, 177, 183–88, 192, 461,
        462
    modern versions of, 22, 56, 459
    Pentecostals and, 14, 198–200, 207, 219,
        223–28, 232, 468, 471
    Presbyterians and, 234–39, 243, 247, 251–
        58, 263
    Revised Standard Version, 56
    Roman Catholics and, 108, 109, 444, 445,
        448
    snake handling and, 14, 481, 482, 483
Bible Belt, 14, 19–24
Bishop, Joe, 42, 48–52, 347
Bishop, Pearl, 48
Blacks
    Baptists, 28, 100–3, 442–43
    education of, 442
    Episcopalians, 120, 121, 123, 130, 131,
        453, 455–56
    harassment of, 443
    Methodists, 170, 178–86, 467
    segregation of, 184, 186
    slavery and, 73–74, 100, 180, 436, 456,
        466, 477
Blasphemous syllables, 282–83
Boardman, Richard, 462
Book of Common Prayer, 452, 455
Book of Worship, 465
Braden, C. S., 458
Branham, William, 469, 472

Brezee, Phineas, 468
Brown, Hyman, 328–29
Brush arbors, 181, 190, 465

Calloway, Leon, 304
Calloway, Mrs. Leon, 304, 305, 313
Call to preach, *see* Preaching; the call to
    preach
Calvert family, 443
Calvin, John, 17, 113, 236, 431, 440, 475–
    76, 479
Calvinism, 433, 434, 438–40, 453, 475–76
    the Bible and, 236
    Methodists and, 463
    Presbyterians and, 236–37, 256, 257, 475–
        79
Campbell, Thomas and Alexander, 113, 449–
    50, 451
Campbellites, 431, 451, 466
Camp meetings, 13–15, 17, 265–79
    altar calls at, 13
    answering congregation at, 13
    of Baptists, 13–15, 265
    interviews, 267–79
    of Methodists, 170, 176, 181, 190, 265–71,
        460, 462, 465
    music at, 13, 266
    of Pentecostals, 227
    preaching at, 13–15, 266, 270
    of Presbyterians, 243, 265
    shouting at, 13
    singing at, 13, 266, 277
        revival spirituals, 288–89
    as a social event, 265, 266
Cane Ridge meeting (1801), 477
Cardeira, Joseph, 159
Carden, Paul, Jr., 353–62, 365
Card playing, 177, 473
Carpenter, Ervin, 347–50
Carroll, John, 443
Cartwright, Peter, 265
Catholics, *see* Roman Catholics
Cennick, John, 289
Charismatic Movement, 255, 259, 262, 263,
    480
Cheating, 13
Christian Baptist, The, 449
Christian Church, The, 451
Christian Harmony (Walker), 285, 287, 288,
    289
Christian Harmony singing, 293–303
Christian Hymns, 110
Christian Minstrel (Aikin), 287
Christian Scientists, 135
Christmas celebrations, 139, 150, 241
Church, the
    Baptists and, 41, 63, 67, 80–81, 98, 103,
        430, 431, 440
    Churches of Christ and, 113, 115
    Episcopalians and, 454–55
    Methodists and, 171, 185–88, 196

Pentecostals and, 199
Presbyterians and, 237, 254–55, 479
Roman Catholics and, 106, 445–46
Churches of Christ, 110–17, 448–52
  authority and, 112
  baptism by, 21, 114, 347
  the Bible and, 111–17, 449, 452
  the church and, 113, 115
  Communion and, 112, 117, 452
  denominationalism and, 110, 111, 449
  Divine healing and, 116
  education and, 452
  evangelism of, 115
  faith and, 115, 116
  God and, 110–17
  on heaven, 115
  Holy Spirit and, 114
  interview, 110–17
  Jesus Christ and, 110–15, 117, 449
  laying on of hands and, 116
  miracles and, 116
  missions and, 116, 452
  music and, 116, 452
  New Testament Church and, 110, 113, 114
  pluralism and, 452
  praying by, 112
  preaching by, 110, 113–17
  salvation and, 112
  sin and, 111–12, 114
  snake handling and, 115–16
  speaking in tongues and, 116
Churching
  by Baptists, 65–66, 184, 196, 201
  by Jehovah's Witnesses, 151–52
  by Methodists, 184, 196
  by Pentecostals, 199, 229–30
Church of England, see Anglicans
Church of God, 81, 198, 199, 200, 201, 203,
    205, 206, 207, 209–23, 247, 372–402,
    474
  See also Pentecostals
Church of God (Cleveland, Tennessee), 474
Church of God, Inc., 474
Church of Scotland, 476
Church of the Nazarene, 468
Circuit riders
  Baptists, 28–41, 48–52, 85–86
  Methodists, 20, 171, 248, 265, 464, 465
  Presbyterians, 236, 248, 250
Civil rights movement, 480
Civil War, 272, 436, 441
  Episcopalians and, 455
  Methodists and, 172
  Presbyterians and, 477, 478
Clark, Cindy and Amy, 139, 142
Clark, Ernest, 136–69
Clark, Mrs. Ernest, 139, 142
Clendennon, B. H., 276, 278, 279
Coe, Jack, 470
Coke, Dr. Thomas, 462

Communion
  Baptists and, 14, 66, 78, 184, 197, 431, 432,
    435, 440, 441
  Churches of Christ and, 112, 117, 452
  closed, 184, 197
  Episcopalians and, 124, 452, 454, 455
  Jehovah's Witnesses and, 150
  Methodists and, 184, 185, 462, 465
  open, 184, 185, 197
  Pentecostals and, 473, 474
  Presbyterians and, 242, 243, 479
  Roman Catholics and, 107, 109, 444, 447
Congregationalism, 476, 477
  Great Awakening and, 434
Congregational Methodist Church, 171, 466
Conversion, 17, 101–2
  baptism and, 23
  Baptists and, 101–2, 430, 435, 437, 439
  Episcopalians and, 454
  faith and, 14
  fundamentalism and, 22–23
  God and, 19, 22–23
  grace and, 23
  heaven and, 18, 22–23
  hell and, 18, 22–23
  imperative for, 22–23
  Jehovah's Witnesses and, 149–50
  Jesus Christ and, 19, 22, 91, 347, 430
  lifestyle and, 20
  Methodists and, 174, 463, 465, 466
  Pentecostals and, 231, 232, 469, 473, 474
  as a personal experience, 19, 26
  Presbyterians and, 234, 249, 262, 477, 480
  at revivals, 18
  sanctification and, 23
  symbols of, 25
Cook, Ben, 7, 28–41, 42, 48, 351, 353, 360,
    361, 367
Cook, Mrs. Ben, 29
Cook, Floyd, 29
Cosmetics, 20
Cullasaja Assembly of God Campmeeting and
    Campground, 274–79
Cumberland Presbyterian Church, 477

Dancing, 20
  Baptists and, 13, 14, 97, 98
  Pentecostals and, 14, 473, 481
Darby, J. N., 471
Davis, John, 104
Davis, Lina, 104–9
Dead Sea Scrolls, 161
Democracy
  Methodists and, 460, 463, 467
  Roman Catholics and, 444
Denominationalism, 110, 111, 449, 451
Dickinson, Eleanor, 14
Disciples of Christ, The, 20, 448–51
  basic beliefs of, 450
  New Testament Church and, 450, 451
Disney, Walt, 105

Divine healing, 405–10
  Baptists and, 40, 50–51, 58–59, 67, 83–85, 95
  Churches of Christ and, 116
  God and, 50, 67, 83–85, 155, 192, 228–29, 245
  Jehovah's Witnesses and, 155, 160
  Jesus Christ and, 40, 155, 472
  Methodists and, 184, 192, 257
  Pentecostals and, 20, 198, 201, 207–8, 215, 223, 228–29, 468–72
  praying and, 83–85
  Presbyterians and, 245, 256–58, 263–64
Dreams, 24
Drinking, see Alcohol
Drinking of poison, 97, 159, 162, 244–45
Dryman, Ray, 7, 198–203

Easter celebrations, 150, 241
Education, 26, 57
  Baptists and, 49, 57, 79–80, 101, 435, 437, 439, 442
  of Blacks, 442
  Churches of Christ and, 452
  Episcopalians and, 118, 122–27
  Jehovah's Witnesses and, 148–49, 153–55, 168, 459
  Methodists and, 466, 467
  Pentecostals and, 469
  Presbyterians and, 233, 238, 254, 475, 477–80
    schools established by, 478
  Roman Catholics and, 106, 108, 444
  singing schools and, 280–82, 283
Edward VI, King, 453
Elizabeth I, Queen, 453
Embury, Philip, 462
End of the world, see World, end of
Episcopalians, 20, 118–38, 452–56
  American Indians and, 121, 123, 124, 132, 453
  baptism by, 120, 122, 454
  beliefs of, 454–55
  the Bible and, 121
  Black, 120, 121, 123, 130, 131, 453, 455–56
  the church and, 454–55
  Civil War and, 455
  Communion and, 124, 453, 454, 455
  conversion and, 454
  education and, 118, 122–27
  evangelism of, 452, 453
  faith and, 118, 454–55
  God and, 119, 122, 136, 138, 454
  grace and, 454, 455
  growth of, 118, 456
  harassment of, 106
  institutionalization of, 452
  interview, 118–38
  Jesus Christ and, 119, 136, 454, 455
  lay readers of, 120, 454
  missions and, 121, 453
  music and, 120, 121
  on offerings, 134
  ordination of women by, 455
  praying by, 121, 122, 452
  preaching by, 118–38, 454
  Presbyterians and, 476
  slavery and, 456
  stately ritual of, 452, 453, 454
  tradition and, 452, 454, 455
Espionage Act, 457
Evangelical United Brethren, 466
Evangelism, 18–19, 20, 23, 25, 33
  of Baptists, 434, 436, 438–41
  of Churches of Christ, 115
  of Episcopalians, 452, 453
  international, 20
  of Jehovah's Witnesses, 456, 460
    door-to-door, 139, 145, 458
  personal, 20, 434
  of Presbyterians, 241, 477, 480
  radio, 20, 26
Evolution, theory of, 21
Excommunications, see Churching

Faith, 20, 26
  baptism and, 432
  Baptists and, 186, 429–31, 433, 437, 438
  Churches of Christ and, 115, 116
  conversion and, 14
  Episcopalians and, 118, 454–55
  fundamentalism and, 21, 22
  God and, 433
  gospel singing and, 280
  Jehovah's Witnesses and, 459–60
  Jesus Christ and, 20, 430, 432, 437
  justification by, 17
  Methodists and, 186, 187, 193, 197, 463, 465
  Pentecostals and, 219, 467, 471, 472
  Presbyterians and, 249, 254–56, 475, 479
  Roman Catholics and, 443–48
  salvation and, 16
  snake handling and, 244–45, 256
Farmer-preachers, 435–36, 442
Fire-Baptized Holiness Association, The, 474
Fire-Baptized Holiness Church, 198, 224–32, 474
  See also Pentecostals
Fire handling, 202, 206–7, 403–5
First Baptist Church (Charleston, SC), 434
First Baptist Church (Providence, RI), 434
Folk hymns, 285, 288
Foot washing, 15
  Baptists and, 14, 29, 39–40, 66, 74, 82, 96–97, 196, 440, 441
    first-hand account of, 351–69
  Jehovah's Witnesses and, 157–58
  Jesus Christ and, 39, 66, 82, 157–58, 243, 353, 359
  Methodists and, 191–92, 196

Pentecostals and, 202, 223, 228, 474
Presbyterians and, 233, 243–44
Foreign Mission Baptist Convention, 442
Fountain, Henry, 310–12
France, Huguenots in, 475–76
Francis of Assisi, Saint, 138
Franz, Frederick W., 459
Freedom of conscience, 429
Freedom of religion, 16
  Baptists and, 429
  Roman Catholics and, 104, 444
Free Methodist Church of North America,
  466
Free will
  Baptists on, 79, 433, 438, 441
  Methodists and, 460
Free Will Baptists, 28, 62, 77–87, 441
Free Will Baptist State Association, 78
Friebus, Carl, 154, 159
Fuging tunes, 285, 292
Fundamentalism, 21–23, 452
  of Baptists, 438–39
  the Bible and, 21–22, 23
  conversion and, 22–23
  faith and, 21, 22
Funk, Joseph, 291

Gambling, 473, 481
  crusades against, 20
General Baptists, 433, 434
Genevan Psalter, 282
Gibbs, L. B., 233, 234–47, 478–79
Glossary, 488–90
Glossolalia, see Speaking in tongues
Glover, Porter, 267–71
God, 17
  authority of, 108, 236
  baptism and, 33, 226–27, 350
  Baptists and, 13, 14, 33, 34, 37–44, 51, 53–
    60, 62–63, 69–70, 88, 93–94, 431, 433,
    437, 440, 441
  as the ultimate judge, 429
  Churches of Christ and, 110–17
  conversion and, 19, 22–23
  Divine healing and, 50, 67, 83–85, 155,
    192, 228–29, 245
  Episcopalians and, 119, 122, 136, 138, 454
  faith and, 433
  free will and, 79
  fundamentalism and, 21, 22
  grace of, 433, 437, 438, 440, 441, 446–47,
    454, 463
  Jehovah's Witnesses and, 147, 149, 155–
    57, 162–69, 458–60
  Methodists and, 171, 177, 181, 185, 186,
    189, 192, 463
  music and, 51
  Pentecostals and, 200, 202, 207–12, 215–
    21, 225–27, 231, 232, 467, 471, 473
  predestination and, 62–63

Presbyterians and, 236, 244–47, 250, 253–
  57, 260–64, 479, 480
Roman Catholics and, 107–9, 446–47
salvation and, 16, 23, 37, 38, 90–91, 108,
  162, 433, 440
shouting and, 39, 50
sin and, 53, 63
snake handling and, 38, 51, 83, 244–45,
  482
the soul and, 52
speaking in tongues and, 52
visions and, 52, 216–18
Golden Age, The, 458
Gospel Hymns (Sankey), 291
Gospel singing, 280, 289–92, 339–42
  faith and, 280
  interviews, 304–46
  as a social event, 280
Grace
  Baptists and, 32, 430, 433, 436, 437, 440,
    441
  conversion and, 23
  Episcopalians and, 454, 455
  fall from, 433, 438, 441, 463
  free, 441
  of God, 433, 437, 438, 440, 441, 446–47,
    454, 463
  Methodists and, 460, 463
  Pentecostals and, 226, 228, 474
  Presbyterians and, 480
  Roman Catholics and, 446–47
Great Awakenings, 17
  Baptists and, 434
  Congregationalists and, 434
  Presbyterians and, 434, 476–77
Great Britain, 22
  Anglicans in, 432, 453, 454, 460, 461, 476
  Baptists in, 432, 433, 434
  Calvinists in, 476
  Pentecostals in, 471
  Presbyterians in, 236, 476
Guitar music, 25, 472–73
Gun control, 184

Harassment
  of Baptists, 433–35
  of Blacks, 443
  of Episcopalians, 106
  of Jehovah's Witnesses, 16, 460
  of Pentecostals, 201, 231, 247, 467
  of practitioners of snake handling, 16, 481,
    482
  of Presbyterians, 234, 251
  of Roman Catholics, 106, 443–44
Hardshell (Primitive) Baptists, 28, 61–76,
  256, 429, 433, 439–41, 480
Harmonia Sacra (Funk), 291
Heart religion, 14, 430, 435
Heaven
  Baptists on, 90, 439
  Churches of Christ on, 115

conversion and, 18, 22–23
    Jehovah's Witnesses on, 150, 163
    revival spirituals and, 289
    Roman Catholics on, 107
Hell
    Baptists on, 53, 439
    conversion and, 18, 22–23
    Jehovah's Witnesses on, 139, 143, 163–66
Henry, Conley, 170, 178–86
Henry, Donna, 320
Henry, Mrs. Conley, 179, 181, 183, 184
Henry VIII, King, 453
Henry of Navarre, 476
Hensley, George W., 482
Hicks, Clyde, 233, 248–58, 478–79
Hicks, Dolly, 248
Hill, Sam, 445
Holiness movement, 14–15, 17, 23, 25, 26,
    81–82, 96, 103, 158, 198, 200–1, 205,
    212, 214–15, 222, 225, 247, 467–68
    See also Pentecostals
Holy Club, 460
Holy Spirit
    Baptists and, 44, 45, 58, 204
        rejecting of, 13
    Churches of Christ and, 114
    Methodists and, 177, 185, 188, 463
    Pentecostals and, 198–203, 213, 220–27,
        467–69, 473, 474
    Presbyterians and, 245–46, 255, 259, 262–
        63
    Roman Catholics and, 108, 445
Homosexuality, 185–86
Huguenots, 475–76
Hutterites, 432
Hyman Brown Singing School, 328–29
Hymnal, 465
Hymns, 18, 34, 110, 289, 290
    folk, 285, 288
    of Methodists, 170, 191, 195, 465

Independent Baptists, 19–20, 21, 28, 53–60,
    82, 438–39
Indian Reservation of the Eastern Band of
    the Cherokees, 123
Indians, American, 62, 433
    Anglicans and, 460–61
    Episcopalians and, 121, 123, 124, 132, 453
    Methodists and, 460–61
Infralapserian Baptists, 440
Institutes of the Christian Religion, The (Calvin),
    475
International Bible Students, 456, 458
Isolation, 24
Italians, 104–9
Ivie, Doug, 320

James, Lynn, 304
James D. Vaughn Music Company, 299, 307,
    311, 321
Jazz, 292

Jehovah, use of the name, 162–63, 458
Jehovah's Witnesses, 139–69, 456–60
    alcohol and, 152–53
    baptism by, 140, 148, 150, 460
    Baptists and, 140, 143, 163
    the Bible and, 140–43, 146–69, 456–59
        new version published, 459
    on blood transfusions, 139, 155–57
    on Christmas celebrations, 139, 150
    churchings by, 151–52
    Communion and, 150
    conversion and, 149–50
    Divine healing and, 155, 160
    drinking of poison and, 159, 162
    on Easter celebrations, 150
    education and, 148–49, 153–55, 168, 459
    elders of, 147–48, 151, 152, 159
    on the end of the world, 166–69, 456, 459–
        60
    evangelism of, 456, 460
        door-to-door, 139, 145, 458
    faith and, 459–60
    financing by, 143–47
    foot washing and, 157–58
    God and, 147, 149, 155–57, 162–69, 458–
        60
    growth of, 143, 456, 460
    harassment of, 16, 460
    on heaven, 150, 163
    on hell, 139, 143, 163–66
    International Assembly (1958), 459
    interviews, 139–69
    Jesus Christ and, 147, 149, 150, 154–57,
        162, 163, 166–68, 456–60
    laying on of hands and, 160
    missions and, 141–45, 154, 460
    motion picture produced by, 143, 457
    newspaper syndicate of, 457
    on offerings, 145
    pluralism and, 460
    praying by, 158
    repentance by, 151
    salvation and, 162
    on sexuality, 151
    sin and, 151–52, 153
    snake handling and, 159–62
    the soul and, 163–66
    speaking in tongues and, 158–59
    special pioneers of, 141, 154
    tobacco and, 152–53
    U.S. Supreme Court and, 458
    witnessing by, 457
    world headquarters of, 143–44, 459
    World War I and, 457–58
Jehovah's Witnesses in the 20th Century, 143
Jesus Christ
    authority of, 445
    baptism and, 168, 226, 254, 347, 349, 350,
        430
    Baptists and, 13, 14, 38–41, 44, 51, 55, 65,
        69, 90, 93–94, 430–33, 437, 439

Churches of Christ and, 110–15, 117, 449
conversion and, 19, 22, 91, 347, 430
death of, 433, 440, 447
Divine healing and, 40, 155, 472
Episcopalians and, 119, 136, 454, 455
faith and, 20, 430, 432, 437
foot washing and, 39, 66, 82, 157–58, 243, 353, 359
free will and, 79
fundamentalism and, 22
Jehovah's Witnesses and, 147, 149, 150, 154–57, 162, 163, 166–68, 456–60
Methodists and, 183, 185–88, 461, 463, 465
miracles of, 22, 40, 472
Pentecostals and, 14–15, 211, 223, 226, 227, 232, 467, 469, 471
Presbyterians and, 234, 237, 241, 243, 247, 249, 253–55, 258, 263
resurrection of, 22, 92, 109, 241, 430, 433, 439, 447
Roman Catholics and, 107, 109, 445–47
salvation and, 16, 20, 23
second coming of, 22, 69, 90, 99, 166–69, 187, 188, 439, 469, 471
shouting and, 38–39
sin and, 63
snake handling and, 14–15, 51, 244–45, 482
tracing origins to, 17
virgin birth of, 22, 57, 185, 439
"Jesus My All to Heaven Has Gone" (Cennick), 289
Jewelry, 20, 481
Jews, 17, 106
converted to Christianity, 113
John Street Chapel, 462
John the Baptist, Saint, 17, 108, 226, 347, 430
John XXIII, Pope, 109, 444
Jones, Reppie, 139–41

Kennedy, John F., 444
Kieffer, Aldine S., 291
King James Version of the Bible, 22, 43, 56–57, 108, 160–62, 165, 185, 186, 188, 459, 482
Knorr, N. H., 459
Knox, John, 475, 476
Kuhlman, Kathryn, 263–64, 469, 470
Ku Klux Klan, 443

Landmarkism, 431–32, 439
Laney, Ted, 77–82, 84–85
Laying on of hands, 116, 160
Lee, Brenda, 224
Lee, Charles, 224–32
Lifestyle, 40
in Appalachia, 25–26
conversion and, 20
Lily Foundation, 251

Lining out, 282
Little, William, 284
Living Bible, 22
Lord's Supper, *see* Communion
Loudsville United Methodist Campground, 267–71
Loudsville United Methodist Church, 273
Lunsford, Waymond, 347–50
Luther, Martin, 17, 108, 113
Lutherans, 113, 453
Lystra Primitive Baptist Church, 64, 65, 67, 68, 71–76

McCarty, Sid, 233, 259–64
McClure, Julie, 170, 171, 175–77
McGready, James, 265, 477
McRae, Barbara, 175
Makemie, Francis, 476
Male quartets, 292
Maney, Debbie, 344
Maney, Ouida, 343
Maney, Ruth, 341, 344
Maney, Wilbur, 343–46
Marriage
open, 170, 184, 186
Roman Catholics and, 106–7, 447
Marshall, Daniel, 434
Mary, Saint, 107, 185
Mather, Cotton, 282, 285
Means, Bob, 320, 326
Mennonites, 432
Methodist Episcopal Church, 462, 466
Methodist Protestant Church, 466
Methodists, 19, 20, 24, 102, 113, 170–97, 200, 201, 206, 460–67, 474
on abortion, 170, 184, 186
alcohol and, 184, 466
American Indians and, 460–61
American Revolution and, 462
Anglicans and, 460–61
the answering congregation, 187, 462–63
Arminianism and, 463
baptism by, 16, 173, 175, 176, 184, 185, 462, 465
Baptists and, 16, 18, 170–73, 178–84, 187, 193, 194, 463, 466
the Bible and, 177, 183–88, 192, 461, 462
Black, 170, 178–86, 467
born again, 188, 190, 461
brush arbors of, 181, 190, 465
Calvinism and, 463
camp meetings, 170, 176, 181, 190, 265–71, 460, 462, 465
on card playing, 177
the church and, 171, 185–88, 196
churching by, 184, 196
circuit riders, 20, 171, 248, 265, 464, 465
Civil War and, 172
combining of the two churches, 171, 172, 184–86, 466
Communion and, 184, 185, 462, 465

competition by, 16, 18, 465–66
Congregational, 171, 466
conversion and, 175, 463, 465, 466
democracy and, 460, 463, 467
Divine healing and, 184, 192, 257
divisions among, 466–67
ecumenism of, 465–66
education and, 466, 467
on the end of the world, 177, 187
faith and, 186, 187, 193, 197, 463, 465
foot washing and, 191–92, 196
free will and, 460
in frontier areas, 462, 464
geographic jurisdictions of, 464
God and, 171, 177, 181, 185, 186, 189, 192, 463
grace and, 460, 463
growth of, 462, 463
Holy Spirit and, 177, 185, 188, 463
hymns of, 170, 191, 195, 465
individualism of, 460, 463
interviews, 170–97
Jesus Christ and, 183, 185–88, 461, 463, 465
ministerial offices of, 464–65
missions and, 171, 460–61
motion pictures and, 193
music and, 196
Northern, 171, 173, 184, 466
on open marriage, 170, 184, 186
ordination of women by, 170, 186
praying by, 171–73, 177, 189, 461
preaching by, 176, 185, 186, 188, 195, 462, 463
Presbyterians and, 16, 242, 253, 259, 466
protracted meetings of, 175, 176, 181, 249
revivals of, 17, 173, 176, 180–81, 187, 190, 194, 462–66
salvation and, 188, 189, 199, 461, 463
sanctification and, 463, 466, 467, 468
on sexuality, 170, 184
    homosexuality, 185–86
shouting by, 180, 187, 196–97, 203, 253, 462, 465
sin and, 170, 177, 184–86, 190, 461, 466
singing by, 170, 172–73, 183, 191, 195–96, 462, 465
slavery and, 180, 466
snake handling and, 184
the soul and, 460
Southern, 171, 172, 184, 185, 466
speaking in tongues and, 184
sports and, 193–94
tobacco and, 466
tradition and, 175
on the younger generation, 170–71
Millennial Harbinger, The, 449
Millenniumists, 471
Miracles
    Churches of Christ and, 116

of Jesus Christ, 22, 40, 472
    Roman Catholics and, 109
Missionary Baptists, 19–20, 62, 78, 82, 437
Missions, 20
    Anglicans and, 460–61
    Baptists and, 57, 82, 102–3, 430, 436, 437, 439
    Churches of Christ and, 110, 114, 452
    Episcopalians and, 121, 453
    Jehovah's Witnesses and, 141–45, 154, 460
    Methodists and, 171, 460–61
    Presbyterians and, 478
    Roman Catholics and, 105
Moody, Dwight L., 291
Moravians, 461
Morgan, Rufus, 118–38, 456
Mormons, 108
Mosely, Selma, 88–99
Moss, Richard, 287, 293–95
Mossy Creek Campground, 269
Motion pictures, 20
    Baptists and, 13, 82–83
    Jehovah's Witnesses and, 143, 457
    Methodists and, 193
    Pentecostals and, 230, 481
Music, 18, 20, 25
    Baptists and, 51–52, 61, 64–65, 88, 439, 441
    at camp meetings, 13, 266
    Churches of Christ and, 116, 452
    Episcopalians and, 120, 121
    God and, 51
    Methodists and, 196
    Pentecostals and, 14, 472–73
    Presbyterians and, 242–43
    See also Singing; types of music

National Association of Free Will Baptists, 441
National Baptist Convention, 442
National Baptist Convention of America, 442
National Baptist Convention of the USA, Inc., 442
Nations, Clyde, Jr., 77–87
Nations, Clyde, Sr., 77, 79–86
Netherlands, the, 432
New Testament Church, 17, 19, 430–31
    Baptists and, 430–32
    Churches of Christ and, 110, 113, 114
    Disciples of Christ and, 450, 451
New World Translation of the Holy Scriptures, 164, 459
Night watch, 227, 241
Norton, Aunt Addie, 313–17

Object and Manner of the Lord's Return, The (Russell), 456
Oral history, 15, 26
Organ music, 13, 14, 25, 120, 196
Owens, Bly, 42–47, 48
Ozman, Agnes N., 469

Page, Horace, 320, 325–27
Palmer, Paul, 441
Parham, Charles Fox, 468–69
Parham, Howard, 61–76
Particular Baptists, 433, 434
Passmore, Paula, 341
Pentecostal Holiness Church, 474
Pentecostals, 20, 26, 198–232, 253, 452
  alcohol and, 473, 481
  Arminianism and, 474
  baptism by, 200, 213, 214, 220, 225–27,
    469, 473, 474
  Baptists and, 205–6
  beliefs of, 470–73
  the Bible and, 14, 198–200, 207, 219, 223–
    28, 232, 468, 471
  born again, 211, 232
  camp meetings of, 227
  on card playing, 473
  the church and, 199
  churching by, 199, 229–30
  clothing worn by, 199–200, 230–31, 473
  Communion and, 473, 474
  conversion and, 231, 232, 469, 473, 474
  dancing and, 14, 473, 481
  Divine healing and, 20, 198, 201, 207–8,
    215, 223, 228–29, 468–72
  education and, 469
  on the end of the world, 470–71
  faith and, 219, 467, 471, 472
  fire handling and, 202, 206–7
  foot washing and, 202, 223, 228, 474
  gambling and, 473, 481
  God and, 200, 202, 207–12, 215–21, 225–
    27, 231, 232, 467, 471, 473
  grace and, 226, 228, 474
  in Great Britain, 471
  growth of, 468–69
  harassment of, 201, 231, 247, 467
  Holy Spirit and, 198–203, 213, 220–27,
    467–69, 473, 474
  independence of, 473–74
  interviews, 198–232
  Jesus Christ and, 14–15, 211, 223, 226,
    227, 232, 467, 469, 471
  jewelry and, 481
  motion pictures and, 230, 481
  music and, 14, 472–73
  night watch of, 227
  praying by, 208, 209, 210, 215–16, 218
  preaching by, 14, 200, 219–21, 225–27,
    469, 473
  prophecy and, 198
  revivals of, 206, 219, 227
  salvation and, 199, 211, 225, 471
  sanctification and, 23, 200, 203, 225, 232,
    467–68, 474
  on sexuality, 481
  shouting and, 14, 203, 206–7, 214
  sin and, 199–200, 209–11, 226, 229–32,
    473, 481

  singing by, 14, 227–28
  snake handling and, 14–15, 200, 202, 207,
    223, 467, 481, 483
  speaking in tongues and, 14, 20–23, 198,
    201, 206–7, 227, 469–74
  sports and, 200, 230
  television and, 229–30
  tobacco and, 473, 481
  visions and, 216–18, 473
Perfectionism, see Sanctification
Perry, Beulah, 100–3
Perseverance of the saints, 16
Peter, Saint, 108, 445–46
Photo-Drama of Creation (motion picture), 143,
  457
Pilmoor, Joseph, 462
Pitts, Esco, 330–35
Pluralism, 16–19, 24–27, 444, 448, 452, 460
Poison, drinking of, 97, 159, 162, 244–45
Poverty, 25, 108–9
Praying
  by Baptists, 30, 32, 35, 37, 46, 48, 58, 80,
    83, 90–91
  by Churches of Christ, 112
  Divine healing and, 83–85
  by Episcopalians, 121, 122, 452
  by Jehovah's Witnesses, 158
  by Methodists, 171–73, 177, 189, 461
  by Pentecostals, 208–10, 215–16, 218
  by Presbyterians, 249–50, 261, 263
  by Roman Catholics, 107, 108, 448
  salvation and, 30, 37, 46, 48, 88, 90–91
Preaching, 13, 18, 25, 26
  by Baptists, 13–15, 53, 64, 434–35, 439,
    442
    farmer-preachers, 435–36, 442
    the call to preach, 23–24, 31–32, 45, 56,
      62, 64, 79–80, 220, 225, 235, 249, 435,
      469, 479
    visions and, 24
  at camp meetings, 13–15, 266, 270
  by Churches of Christ, 110, 113–17
  by Episcopalians, 118–38, 454
  loud, 17, 439, 462
  by Methodists, 176, 185, 186, 188, 195,
    462, 463
  by Pentecostals, 14, 200, 219–21, 225–27,
    469, 473
  by Presbyterians, 234, 242, 248, 249, 476–
    79
  at revivals, 17–18, 19
  by Roman Catholics, 444
Preast, Elzie, 14–15
Predestination, 433
  Baptists on, 19–20, 61–63, 256, 433, 439,
    440
  God and, 62–63
  Presbyterians on, 62, 256, 449
Premillennialists, 471
Presbyterian Church in the United States, 478

Presbyterian Church in the United States of America, 477, 478
Presbyterian Church of the Confederate States of America, 478
Presbyterians, 20, 113, 137, 233–64, 475–80
  alcohol and, 249
  altar calls by, 253
  baptism by, 16, 254–55, 479, 480
  Baptists and, 16, 242, 253, 259
  beliefs of, 478–80
  the Bible and, 234–39, 243, 247, 251–58, 263
  born again, 234, 480
  Calvinism and, 236–37, 256, 257, 475–79
  camp meetings of, 243, 265
  Charismatic Movement of, 255, 259, 262, 263, 480
  the church and, 237, 254–55, 479
  circuit riders, 236, 248, 250
  Civil War and, 477, 478
  Communion and, 242, 243, 479
  competition by, 16, 240
  conversion and, 234, 249, 262, 477, 480
  Divine healing and, 245, 256–58, 263–64
  drinking of poison and, 244–45
  education and, 233, 238, 254, 475, 477–80
    schools established by, 478
  elders of, 250–51, 479
  Episcopalians and, 476
  evangelism of, 241, 477, 480
  faith and, 249, 254–56, 475, 479
  foot washing and, 233, 243–44
  God and, 236, 244–47, 250, 253–57, 260–64, 479, 480
  grace and, 480
  Great Awakening and, 434, 476–77
  in Great Britain, 236, 476
  harassment of, 234, 251
  Holy Spirit and, 245–46, 255, 259, 262–63
  homecomings of, 241–42, 252–53
  independence of, 251–52, 478
  interviews, 233–64
  Jesus Christ and, 234, 237, 241, 243, 247, 249, 253–55, 258, 263
  Methodists and, 16, 242, 253, 259, 466
  missions and, 478
  music and, 242–43
  New Side, 477–78
  night watch of, 241
  on offerings, 240
  Old Side, 477–78
  ordination of women by, 239
  origins in Switzerland, 475–76
  poison taking and, 244–45
  praying by, 249–50, 261, 263
  preaching by, 234, 242, 248, 249, 476–79
  on predestination, 62, 256, 449
  revivals of, 17, 233, 238, 241, 253, 259–60, 475–80

Roman Catholics and, 476
  salvation and, 253, 260
  self-help program of, 251–52
  on sexuality, 249
  shouting by, 246
  sin and, 249
  singing by, 252, 253, 479
  slavery and, 477
  snake handling and, 233, 244–45, 256, 475
  speaking in tongues and, 245–46, 255–56, 259, 262–63, 475, 480
  tobacco and, 249
  tradition and, 480
  Vietnam War and, 480
  visions and, 250
  Westminster Confession of Faith, 236–37, 247, 476, 480
  witnessing by, 480
Presley, E. C., 170, 193–97
Primitive (Hardshell) Baptists, 28, 61–76, 256, 429, 433, 439–41, 480
Progressive Baptist Convention, 442
Prophecy, 198
Prostitution, crusades against, 20
Protestant establishment, 17, 19–20, 443
Protestant Reformation, 17, 236, 475–76
Purgatory, Roman Catholics on, 107–8
Puritans, 432, 433, 476

Quakers, 45, 254
Quilliams, Jake, 219–23

Raby, Jim, 304–9
Radio evangelism, 20, 26
Ragtime, 292
Randall, Benjamin, 441
Rawlings, Mrs. Wayne, 110, 111
Rawlings, Wayne, 110–17
Redstone Baptist Association, 449
Reed, Granny, 209–18
Regular Baptists, 19–20, 434
Religion in the Development of American Culture (Sweet), 170 n
Repentance, 13, 16, 23, 151, 463
Revivalism, definition of, 17
Revivalism (Dickinson), 14
Revivals, 17–19, 26
  of Baptists, 17, 33–35, 46, 49, 65, 81–82, 86–87, 93, 103, 434
  of Methodists, 17, 173, 176, 180–81, 187, 190, 194, 462–66
  of Pentecostals, 206, 219, 227
  preaching at, 17–18, 19
  of Presbyterians, 17, 233, 238, 241, 253, 259–60, 475–80
Revival spirituals, 285, 288–89
Roberts, Oral, 469, 470, 472
Roman Catholics, 17, 20, 61, 104–9, 113, 135, 143, 174, 247, 431, 443–48, 452, 453
  authority and, 445–46
  baptism by, 446, 447

Baptists and, 106, 444, 445
the Bible and, 108, 109, 444, 445, 448
the church and, 106, 445–46
Communion and, 107, 109, 444, 447
democracy and, 444
dispensation for, 107
education and, 106, 108, 444
faith and, 443–48
freedom of religion and, 104, 444
God and, 107–9, 446–47
grace and, 446–47
growth of, 104, 443
harassment of, 106, 443–44
on heaven, 107
Holy Spirit and, 108, 445
interview, 104–9
Jesus Christ and, 107, 109, 445–47
marriage and, 106–7, 447
the mass of, 105, 444, 445, 448
miracles and, 109
missions and, 105
number of, 444
pluralism and, 444, 448
the pope and, 109, 443–44, 445
  infallibility question, 446
praying by, 107, 108, 448
preaching by, 444
Presbyterians and, 476
on purgatory, 107–8
sacraments of, 107, 109, 444–47
salvation and, 108, 445–47
sin and, 108, 109
tradition and, 445
transitions of, 445, 448
Ruebush-Kieffer Music Publishing Company, 291
Russell, Charles Taze, 142–43, 456–57
Rutherford, Joseph F., 457–59

Sacred Harp (White), 284, 287, 292
St. Bartholomew's Day Massacre (1572), 475
St. John's Donor Foundation, 134
Saints, perseverance of, 16
Salvation, 17, 19, 23
baptism and, 63–64, 78–79
Baptists and, 30–31, 37–38, 44–49, 54, 78–
  79, 90–91, 204, 430, 433, 438, 440,
  441, 463
  doubt of, 64, 78
Churches of Christ and, 112
diversity in process of, 16, 23
faith and, 16
God and, 16, 23, 37, 38, 90–91, 108, 162,
  433, 440
Jehovah's Witnesses and, 162
Jesus Christ and, 16, 20, 23
Methodists and, 188, 189, 199, 461, 463
Pentecostals and, 199, 211, 225, 471
praying and, 30, 37, 46, 48, 88, 90–91
Presbyterians and, 253, 260
revival spirituals and, 289

Roman Catholics and, 108, 445–47
sin and, 16, 23, 91
Sanctification
baptism and, 23
Baptists and, 204
conversion and, 23
Methodists and, 463, 466, 467, 468
Pentecostals and, 23, 200, 203, 225, 232,
  467–68, 474
Sandy Creek Baptist Church, 434
Sankey, Ira D., 291
Santa Claus, belief in, 150–51
Saturnalia, Day of, 150
Sawmill Hill Free Will Baptist Church, 77–
  87
Schott, Jerome, 159
Scofield, Cyrus, 471
Scopes' Monkey Trial, 21
Scotland, 113, 476
Screven, William, 434
Seabury, Samuel, 454
Segregation
of Blacks, 184, 186
of women, 14, 40, 66, 74, 82, 363, 364
Separate Baptists, 19–20, 434–35
Sexuality
Baptists on, 13
Jehovah's Witnesses on, 151
Methodists on, 170, 184, 185–86
  homosexuality, 185–86
Pentecostals on, 481
Presbyterians on, 249
Seymour, W. J., 469
Shakers, 265
Shaped note music, 280–346
history of development of, 280–92
interviews, 293–346
See also types of music
Shouting
by Baptists, 30, 34, 37–39, 46, 50, 58, 92,
  442
at camp meetings, 13
God and, 39, 50
Jesus Christ and, 38–39
by Methodists, 180, 187, 196–97, 203, 253,
  462, 465
by Pentecostals, 14, 203, 206–7, 214
by Presbyterians, 246
Showalter, A. J., 291
Sin
baptism and, 347
Baptists and, 13, 39, 63, 440
Churches of Christ and, 111–12, 114
God and, 53, 63
Jehovah's Witnesses and, 151–52, 153
Jesus Christ and, 63
Methodists and, 170, 177, 184–86, 190,
  461, 466
Pentecostals and, 199–200, 209–11, 226,
  229–32, 473, 481
Presbyterians and, 249

repentance of, 13, 16
Roman Catholics and, 108, 109
salvation and, 16, 23, 91
Singing
  by Baptists, 34–35, 86–87, 195, 442
  at camp meetings, 13, 266, 277
    revival spirituals, 288–89
  Christian Harmony, 293–303
  by Methodists, 170, 172–73, 183, 191, 195–
    96, 462, 465
  by Pentecostals, 14, 227–28
  by Presbyterians, 252, 253, 479
  See also Music; types of singing
Singing conventions, 86–87, 280, 292
  interviews, 293–346
Singing schools, 280–88, 391, 392
  blasphemous syllables and, 282–83
  books of, 284–88, 291
  education and, 280–82, 283
Slavery, 73–74, 100, 180, 436, 456, 466, 477
Smathers, George, 289, 298
Smathers, Quay, 287, 293, 296–98
Smith, Al, 444
Smith, Joseph, 108
Smith, Lonnie, 310, 318–24
Smith, William, 284
Smoking, see Tobacco
Smyth, John, 432
Snake handling, 16, 22, 26, 481–83
  Baptists and, 38, 51, 68, 83, 97
  the Bible and, 14, 481, 482, 483
  Churches of Christ and, 115–16
  faith and, 244–45, 256
  first-hand account of, 370–402
  God and, 38, 51, 83, 244–45, 482
  harassment of practitioners of, 16, 481, 482
  Jehovah's Witnesses and, 159–62
  Jesus Christ and, 14–15, 51, 244–45, 482
  Methodists and, 184
  Pentecostals and, 14–15, 200, 202, 207,
    223, 467, 481, 483
  Presbyterians and, 233, 244–45, 256, 475
Society for the Propagation of the Gospel in
  Foreign Parts, 453
Soul liberty, 429
Southards, Howard, 53–60
Southern culture, 19–24
Southern Harmony (Walker), 284, 287
Southworth, Henry, 159
Speaking in tongues, 15, 18, 22, 25, 411–20
  baptism and, 23
  Baptists and, 52, 67, 81–82
  Churches of Christ and, 116
  God and, 52
  Jehovah's Witnesses and, 158–59
  Methodists and, 184
  Pentecostals and, 14, 20–23, 198, 201, 206–
    7, 227, 469–74
  Presbyterians and, 245–46, 255–56, 259,
    262–63, 475, 480

Spirituals, revival, 285, 288–89
Sports
  Baptists and, 82–83
  Methodists and, 193–94
  Pentecostals and, 200, 230
Stamps-Baxter Music Company, 299, 307,
  321
Stearns, Shubal, 434
Stockton, Ruth, 139–69
Stone, Barton W., 265, 449, 451, 477
Stonites, 451
String music, 64–65
Sunday, Billy, 23
Supralapserian Baptists, 440
Sweet, William Warren, 170 n
Switzerland, 432, 475–76
Syllables, blasphemous, 282–83
Symbols, 25, 26

Television, 20, 194, 229–30
Tennent, Gilbert and William, 477
Tennessee Publishing Company, 299, 321
Theocratic Ministry School, 459
These Also Believe (Braden), 458
Three Worlds or Plan of Redemption (Russell and
  Barbour), 456
Tobacco, 20, 152–53, 249, 466, 473, 481
Two-Seed-in-the-Spirit-Predestinarian
  Baptists, 19–20, 433

United Methodist Church, 171, 172, 184,
  185–86, 466
U.S. Constitution, First Amendment to, 16
U.S. Supreme Court, Jehovah's Witnesses
  and, 458

Vasey, Henry, 462
Vatican Council I, 446
Vatican Council II, 444, 446, 448
Vaughn's Up-to-Date Rudiments and Music
  Reader, 300
Vietnam War, 480
Vinson, Ruby, 204, 208
Vinson, Toliver, 204–8
Visions, 24, 52, 216–18, 250, 473
Vissage, Leonard, 170–71, 187–92
Voices, hearing of, 24

Walker, William, 284, 285, 287–88, 289, 291
Watchtower, The, 143, 144, 153, 158, 163,
  457
Watchtower Bible and Tract Society, 143,
  144, 146, 148, 457, 458
Watchtower Bible School of Gilead, 459
Watchtower Society, The, 143, 144
Watch Tower Tract Society, 457
Watts, Ernest, 336–39
Watts, Ferd, 326, 327, 340–42
Watts, Isaac, 289
Wesley, Charles, 289, 460, 461, 465

Wesley, John, 113, 289, 431, 460–61, 462, 465
Wesleyan Methodist Church of America, 466
Westminster Confession of Faith, 236–37, 247, 476, 480
Whatcoat, Richard, 462
White, Benjamin Franklin, 284, 287, 292
White, William, 454
Williams, Roger, 433–34
Wilson, Benjamin, 160–61
Winsett Company, 307
Witnessing, 20, 55, 437, 439, 457, 480
Wolffork Baptist Church, 322, 323
Women, 20, 24, 481
    ordination of, 170, 186, 239, 455
    segregation of, 14, 40, 66, 74, 82, 363, 364

World, end of
    Baptists on, 69–70, 98
    Jehovah's Witnesses on, 166–69, 456, 459–60
    Methodists on, 177, 187
    Pentecostals on, 470–71
World War I, 292, 457–58
World War II, 179, 184

Young Men's Christian Association (YMCA), 289–91

Zion's Watch Tower and Herald of Christ's Presence, 457
Zion's Watchtower Society, 143
Zion's Watch Tower Tract Society, 457